Party Systems and Voter Alignments Revisited

This timely book updates, and takes stock of, Lipset and Rokkan's classic work *Party Systems and Voter Alignments: Cross-National Perspectives* which has been influential since 1967. With an introduction by the original author, Seymour Martin Lipset, it examines the significance of the original volume for the history of political sociology, and assesses its theoretical and empirical relevance for the study of elections, voters and parties now, at the beginning of the twenty-first century. Most importantly, this edition extends the scope of the original work to new areas such as consociational democracies, small island states, and newly democratising Eastern and Central European and Third World countries.

Party Systems and Voter Alignments Revisited covers theoretical and methodological issues such as the notion of 'the freezing of party systems', and the effects of the data technological revolution on the study of parties and voters. The editors genuinely revisit the empirical areas in the original volume from 1967, with several of the original researchers. The book includes comparative studies of the English-speaking democracies and of Western Europe, and national case studies of Japan, Finland and Spain. Alongside this, there are important studies of consociational democracies, of the party systems developing in Eastern and Central Europe after the fall of communism, in the new democracies of the Third World, and in the small island states of the world.

The studies in this book highlight the continued relevance of the Lipset/Rokkan approach, as well as the problems related to structural change in the West and conditions particular to cases outside the West. This book will be of great importance to all those working in politics or international relations, and anyone interested in the conditions of parties and electoral politics in the contemporary world.

Lauri Karvonen is Professor of Political Science and Chairman of the Department of Political Science at Åbo Akademi, Finland. He has written extensively on comparative politics, including most recently *Fragmentation and Consensus: Political Organisation and the Interwar Crisis in Europe*. **Stein Kuhnle** is Professor of Comparative Politics at the University of Bergen, Norway. He has edited a number of books, including *Survival of the Welfare State, Government and Voluntary Organizations*, and *Small States Compared: Politics of Norway and Slovenia*.

Routledge Advances in International Relations and Politics

Party Systems and Voter Alignments Revisited

Edited by
Lauri Karvonen and Stein Kuhnle

With an Introduction by
Seymour Martin Lipset

London and New York

First published 2001
by Routledge
11 New Fetter Lane, London EC4P 4EE

Simultaneously published in the USA and Canada
by Routledge
29 West 35th Street, New York, NY 10001

Reprinted 2002

Routledge is an imprint of the Taylor & Francis Group

Typeset in Baskerville by
Exe Valley Dataset Ltd, Exeter
Printed and bound in Great Britain by
TJI Digital, Padstow, Cornwall

British Library Cataloguing in Publication Data
A catalogue record for this book is available
from the British Library

Library of Congress Cataloguing in Publication Data
Party systems and voter alignments revisited/edited by Lauri Karvonen
    and Stein Kuhnle.
        p.   cm.—(Routledge advances in international relations and politics)
    Includes bibliographical references and index.
    1. Political parties.   2. Voting.   3. Comparative government.
    I. Karvonen, Lauri.   II. Kuhnle, Stein.   III. Series.

    JF2051.P296 2000
    324.9–dc21   00–029115

ISBN 0–415–23720–3

Contents

Figures

Tables

Contributors

Erik Allardt is Emeritus Professor of Sociology at the University of Helsinki, Finland

Dag Anckar is Professor of Political Science at Åbo Akademi, Finland

Kris Deschouwer is Professor of Political Science at Vrije Universiteit Brussel, Belgium

Mattei Dogan is Research Director at the Centre National de la Recherche Scientifique, Paris, France

Lauri Karvonen is Professor of Political Science at Åbo Akademi, Finland

Richard S. Katz is Professor of Political Science at Johns Hopkins University, Baltimore, Maryland, USA

Stein Kuhnle is Professor of Comparative Politics at the University of Bergen, Norway

Ulf Lindström is Professor of Comparative Politics at the University of Bergen, Norway

Juan J. Linz is Sterling Professor of Political and Social Science, Yale University, USA

Seymour Martin Lipset is Hazel Professor of Public Policy at George Mason University, Fairfax, Virginia, USA

Peter Mair is Professor of Political Science at Rijksuniversiteit Leiden, Netherlands

José Ramón Montero is Professor at Instituto Juan March, Madrid, Spain

Pertti Pesonen is former Professor of Political Science at the University of Helsinki, Finland

Vicky Randall is Lecturer at the Department of Government, University of Essex, UK

Jostein Ryssevik is Senior Adviser at the Norwegian Social Science Data Services (NSD), Bergen, Norway

Joji Watanuki is Professor of Political Science at Soka University, Tokyo, Japan

Preface

This book is the result of an international conference called "Party Systems and Voter Alignments: Thirty Years After" which was held in Bergen, Norway, on 24–27 April 1997. The aim of the conference was to mark the thirtieth anniversary of the publication of the landmark volume *Party Systems and Voter Alignments: Cross-National Perspectives* edited by Seymour Martin Lipset and Stein Rokkan and published in 1967 by the Free Press.

More than three decades after its publication, *Party Systems and Voter Alignments* is still immensely influential in the study of political parties and elections. It continues to be one of the major sources of inspiration to scholars in this field. Its thirtieth anniversary created a natural opportunity to assess its contribution to this central area of political research as well as to look ahead towards new empirical research tasks and methodological avenues.

As suggested by the title of this volume, the conference as well as the present book had a double aim. On the one hand, we wished to examine the significance of the original volume and to place some of its central themes in a thirty-year perspective. In order to achieve this aim, several contributors to the original volume were invited to participate in the conference as well as in this book. Moreover, there was a special focus on a number of topics and issues raised in the 1967 book. What was the general significance of *Party Systems and Voter Alignments* in the history of political sociology and the study of parties and voters? How relevant are its central theoretical tenets to the study of parties, elections and voters? What empirical patterns can be detected in some of the empirical contexts examined in the original volume? How do these relate to the findings and conclusions presented in 1967?

On the other hand, the world in which the ideas presented in *Party Systems and Voter Alignments* seem applicable has of course changed and expanded considerably since the late 1960s. New generations of expertise on parties and voters have entered the stage. How relevant and accurate are the generalizations and findings presented in 1967 for newly democratized regions and countries outside the stable democracies of the West?

How do these ideas relate to some more recent theoretical contributions pertinent to this field of study? In short, it seemed necessary to invite outstanding younger experts as contributors and expand the empirical scope of the book considerably.

The structure of this volume largely reflects these aims. In his Introduction to the book, Seymour Martin Lipset reflects on the role of parties in relation to both old and new cleavages relevant to the structuring of political life. Part I focuses on theoretical and methodological issues in particular. Erik Allardt – one of the contributors to the original volume – discusses *Party Systems and Voter Alignments* as part of the general tradition of political sociology. The perhaps best known theoretical concept originating from the 1967 volume, the notion of the Freezing of Party Systems is highlighted in the second chapter, whereas the third contribution to this section analyses the effects of the technological revolution on the study of parties and voters. Part II revisits several of the empirical areas included in *Party Systems and Voter Alignments*. The English-speaking countries and Western Europe are studied in a comparative fashion; in addition, three single-country studies are included. Of these, Finland has had a competitive party system since 1906, whereas Japan is a democracy which emerged from the settlement after World War II. Spain, finally, represents a more recent transition to democracy. The chapter on Spain in fact includes two important contributions in one: besides the nationwide party system, the peculiar party systems at the level of the Spanish regions are analyzed here. All three countries were portrayed in the 1967 book as well.

The third and final part of the volume extends the scope of research to new areas, theoretical as well as empirical. The chapter on the consociational democracies marries Lipset and Rokkan's ideas with the notion of consociationalism which gained currency as a political science theory from the 1970s on. Eastern and Central Europe, Third World countries and small island states all represent challenges to the ideas presented in 1967. Each of these themes is represented by a chapter in the present book.

Save for the Introduction and the chapter on Eastern Europe, all contributions to this book were presented in a draft form at the 1997 conference. The final versions reflect ideas and impulses gained from the conference, which is why it is our pleasant duty to thank all participants in the Bergen meeting. Our special thanks are due to Richard Braungart, David Farrell, Kay Lawson, Birgitta Nedelmann and Henry Valen.

The success of the Bergen conference was a crucial precondition of this volume. The work done in preparing and arranging the conference was therefore entirely necessary for the publication of this volume as well. The Organizing Committee of the Conference was based on three institutions closely associated with the editors of the 1967 volume: the Committee on Political Sociology (CPS, the joint research committee of the International Political Science Association and the International Sociological Association), the Department of Comparative Politics, University of Bergen, and the Norwegian Social Science Data Services (NSD). As members of the Organizing Committee, Björn Henrichsen (NSD) and Gerd Pettersen (Department of Comparative Politics) did an outstanding job to make the project possible. We extend our heartfelt thanks to these friends and colleagues.

Our thanks are also due to Marina Hamberg of the Department of Political Science, Åbo Akademi. She played a central role in the editorial work on this book.

Several institutions helped finance the 1997 conference. It gives us great pleasure to extend our thanks to the Norwegian Research Council, the Norwegian Social Science Data Services, Scandinavian Airlines Systems (SAS), the Department of Comparative Politics, University of Bergen and the Faculty for Social Sciences, University of Bergen. The Bergen Faculty generously continued its support during the editorial work on the volume.

Finally, we would like to express our special gratitude to the authors of the various chapters in this book. It has been an exquisite pleasure to cooperate with such an outstanding group of scholars. Thank you for your excellent contributions to the conference and to this book, your numerous ideas and suggestions in the course of the editorial work, as well as for your understanding and patience.

Lauri Karvonen
and Stein Kuhnle
Åbo and Canberra
November 1999

Introduction

1 Cleavages, parties and democracy

Seymour Martin Lipset

In evaluating the conditions for democracy, I have long stressed the need for the institutionalization of cleavages, that is the creation of stable political parties. Democracy means the rule of the people, the demos, a system in which a majority can select those at the summit of the polity, the office-holders, one in which voters can influence, determine, the policies pursued by their leaders. In small polities, where the electorate may have direct knowledge of the traits and opinions of contenders for office, a democratic system can function like a town meeting. Citizens or members can judge among potential office-holders, and comment, debate, and listen to different points of view. Such office-holders will remain close to, responsive to the citizenry or membership as a whole. Inequalities in social background, in status, wealth, personal traits, intelligence, may be associated with varying degrees of influence, but essentially in small democratic polities the people can affect political outcomes.

Mechanisms to facilitate democratic governance have existed in tribal societies and small polities such as Swiss cantons, New England town meetings open to all, and in the local bodies of assorted voluntary associations such as trade unions, and professional or other occupational associations that have elected leaders. Ancient Athens had a unique system, in which members of the community council were chosen by lot, so that every male had an equal chance to represent or be represented.

Efforts have been made in larger communities and organizations to continue democratic representation through the election of delegates to councils or conventions. The American and Russian revolutions gave rise to personal, though indirect, systems of choosing leaders. The American case was intended to select members of an Electoral College, essentially leading trustworthy citizens of each state, known to all, who would meet to choose a President and Vice-President. The Russian Revolution of 1905 produced a Soviet (Council) form of government, while the second upheaval (1917) designed a formal structure with lower-level councils that would both govern their area or community and choose representatives to serve on a higher level, regional, Soviet. The process would eventually result in a Supreme Soviet and presidium for the entire state. Many private organizations, such as professional associations, lodges, ethnic groups and trade unions, essentially follow this model.

The ability of members or citizens to control governance as polities enlarge and a full-time (professional) executive emerges, is, of course, questionable. Robert Michels, a German protégé of Max Weber, systematically challenged this approach to democracy in his classic work, *Political Parties* (1962). Michels, arguing from the experiences of large private organizations, sought to document that inherent in the separation of officialdom and rank-and-file members or voters is control by self-cooptating oligarchies. The summits of all sizable polities are motivated to maintain the perquisites of office, power, and high status, and as part of a superior stratum, develop orientations, interests, which are different from those of the underlings or the rank-and-file. Hence they have distinct opinions and concerns.

In a detailed analysis, stemming from Weber's analyses of the consequences of large-scale organization, Michels presented the ways in which bureaucratic organizational structures give to leadership resources enabling them to dominate, to maintain their power. These involve training in political abilities, such as public speaking, writing, editing, and the like, skills which lesser strata do not have. Control over the organization give to officials the means to reach all the membership or citizenry, favorable publicity for their actions, control over travel funds, etc. The leadership and the bureaucracy are a party; there is usually no formal opposition. Michels formulated a "iron law of oligarchy" which assumes that complex polities can never be democratic, can never be controlled by or reflect the will of the rank and file, of the ordinary electors. There is a host of empirical literature, following in the Michels' tradition, documenting that political parties, trade unions, economic bodies, religious denominations, ethnic associations, have not been democratic internally, that they have been dominated by, and reflect the interests and values of their elites. The studies seem to validate Michels' conclusion that a representative system cannot be truly democratic.

This analytic finding, however, can be challenged by reference to the role and function of multi-party elections in societies as well as organizations. Joseph Schumpeter, an Austrian-born economist and sociologist, suggested in the 1930s that democracy in complex polities can exist, but only as a system in which the populace, the electorate, can choose between alternative candidatures for office, i.e. among parties competing for office.

Parties make for institutionalized rivalry. Such competition for Schumpeter is the essence of democracy in macro polities. The citizenry, the membership, may affect, determine, policy by their ability, their right, to choose between opposing approaches to governance. The presence of an opposition limits the power of incumbents. The alternative government looks for issues which will give them popular support, seeks evidence of malfeasance and/or incompetence by the administration. It presents a different program, which may reflect ideological variations.

To repeat, democracy in mass polities requires institutionalized parties. Institutionalization assumes a supportive culture, the acceptance of the rights of opposition, of free speech and assembly, of the rule of law, of regular elections, of turnover in office, and the like. The requirement for the acceptance by incumbents of turnover is the most difficult to institutionalize, particularly in poor nations. But at least as difficult is the need which parties have for almost unquestioning commitment by a significant segment of the polity, by a base. If a party lacks such loyalty from its following, it may be eliminated by visible policy errors, by malfeasance by leaders, or by the collapse or withdrawal of alternative leadership. Parties in new electoral democracies will be inherently unstable unless they become linked to deep-rooted sources of cleavage, as the parties in the older institutionalized western democracies have been.

Cleavages

Over three decades ago, in *Party Systems and Voter Alignments* (Lipset and Rokkan 1967a), Stein Rokkan and I sought to specify the way in which the parties in the Western European polities emerged and stabilized around basic social cleavages. We pointed to four sources of such divisions, each of which has continued to some extent today. The first, the most general, is class, as noted in my conclusion in *Political Man* (Lipset 1960): "in virtually every economically developed country the lower income groups vote mainly for the parties of the left, while the higher income groups vote mainly for the parties of the right." Class conflict has been a reality everywhere. It has been reflected in election contests which I described as the "democratic class struggle."

The great thinkers of the nineteenth century emphasized its role. Alexis de Tocqueville wrote of the inherent conflict between "aristocracy" (the privileged orders) and the poor, those without property: "I affirm that aristocratic or democratic passions may be easily detected at the bottom of all parties." In *Democracy in America,* he concluded that endemic to stratification was rejection of inequality by the underprivileged. "There is, in fact, a manly and lawful passion for equality . . . which impels the weak to attempt to lower the powerful to their own level . . ." (1956, 53). He anticipated their ultimate triumph once the idea of equality emerged, for there were many more of the economically deprived than of the advantaged. Still, Tocqueville recognized a constant tension in free communities between forces that aimed at limiting the authority of the people and those that served to extend it. Karl Marx, who much admired Tocqueville, obviously emphasized the continuing nature of the class struggle, but, unlike Tocqueville, he called attention to the ways that the power and cultural hegemony of the upper strata would produce "false consciousness," acceptance of values derived from the privileged by the downtrodden.

An emphasis on class as the only important determinant of political cleavage, past, present and future is, of course, wrong. However class is defined, it has never accounted for more than part of the causal mechanism, of the variance, involved in partisan differentiation. Recognizing this, Rokkan and I pointed to the emergence of three other historic cleavages, in addition to class, underlying the diverse character of European party systems. We suggested they were the outgrowth of two upheavals, the National and the Industrial Revolutions.

These transformations produced various social struggles which became linked to party divisions and voting behavior. The first, the political revolution, resulted in a *Center–periphery* conflict between the national system and assorted subordinate ones, for example, ethnic, linguistic or religious groups, often located in the peripheries, the outlying regions, and a *church–state* tension between the growing state, which sought to dominate, and the church, which tried to maintain its historic corporate rights. The economic revolution gave rise to two class conflicts: a *land–industry* fight between the landed elite and the growing bourgeois class, followed by the cleavage Marx focused on, that between *capitalists and workers*.

These four sources of cleavage, each of which has continued to some extent into the contemporary world, have provided a framework for most of the party systems of the democratic polities. But as Rokkan and I noted, class has been the most salient source of political conflict, of party support and voting, particularly after the extension of the suffrage to all adult males. The partisan expressions of the four cleavage models obviously have varied internationally. They have been most fully developed in multi-party systems and condensed into broad coalitions in two-party ones such as those of the United States or Australia. Given all the transformations in Western society over the twentieth century, it is noteworthy how little the formal party systems have changed, though their programmatic content is different. Essentially the cleavages have been institutionalized. The contemporary party divisions still resemble those of pre-World War I Europe. The main post-war changes relate to the rise and disappearance of fascist movements, and to the division of the working-class parties into two in some countries. The latter split has largely disappeared since the collapse of the Soviet Union.

Some critics of the four cleavages model have argued that it assumes too much rigidity, since it largely derives party systems from structure. But as a discussion by three political scientists, Russell Dalton, Scott Flanagan and Paul Beck, notes that it permits flexibility since we understand that events can modify structurally determined linkages.

Although the Lipset–Rokkan model emphasized the institutionalization and freezing of cleavage alignments, the model also has dynamic properties. It views social alignments as emerging from the historical process of social and economic developments. New alignments develop in response to major social transformations such as the National and Industrial revolutions. While the structure of cleavages is considered to be relatively fixed, the political salience of the various cleavages and patterns of party coalitions may fluctuate in reaction to contemporary events.

New cleavages

The Western world appears to have entered a new political phase which roughly dates from the mid-1960s, with the emergence of so-called post-materialistic issues – a clean environment, use of nuclear power, a better culture, equal status for women and minorities, the quality of education, international relations, greater democratization, and a more permissive morality, particularly as affecting familial and sexual issues. These have been perceived by some social analysts as the social consequences of an emerging third "revolution," the Post-Industrial, which introduced new bases of social and political cleavage. The underlying economic analysis has been associated with the writings of Daniel Bell, while the emphasis on new political controversies is linked to the work of Ronald Inglehart. Essentially Bell and others have sought to document the effects on the culture of structural shifts which have sharply increased the importance of occupations linked to high-tech, information knowledge, and public service industries, and require greater reliance on universities and research and development centers, while the production-focused positions located in factories have been declining. Inglehart and others have pointed to new lines of cleavage between those involved in industrial society's concern with production related issues (materialist) and an increasing number employed in the post-industrial economy, often recipients of higher education, who place more emphasis on quality of life issues, and have liberal social views with respect to ecology, feminism, and nuclear energy (post-materialist). Such values are difficult to institutionalize as party issues, but groups such as the Green parties and the New Left or New Politics educated middle-class tendencies within the traditional left parties have sought to foster them.

Issues and cleavages derivative from those of industrial society, however, remain the more important source of policy division and electoral choice, since the materialistically oriented workers and the self-employed constitute much larger strata than the intelligentsia. The biggest change results from the perceived failure of the social democratic welfare state to solve key problems, which has produced a renewal of the appeal of classic liberal (free market) approaches, sometimes presented by their spokespersons in the context of solutions to quality of life concerns as well.

While the older democratic polities of Europe, North America and Australasia remain stable and strong, the formerly authoritarian and colonial systems have had a disparate record. At the beginning of the 1970s, two thirds of the members of the United Nations were classified as non-democratic. The third wave of democratization, which began in

Portugal, Spain and Greece in the mid-1970s, was followed by a rapid diffusion to Latin America, and gradually to a number of African and East Asian states. With the breakup of the Communist regimes, including the Soviet Union, the list of aspiring electoral democracies, which have open competitive elections, has grown enormously, although Russia and the Ukraine have been unstable. Few of the over three dozen Islamic societies can be classified as democratic.

Russia and the Ukraine are, of course, the most important ex-Soviet nations. Both have competitive elections, but are extremely shaky as polities. They lack a stable party system. The Communists are the only institutionalized national party. Other groupings rise and fall from election to election. Some are personal followings; others are regional which do not offer candidates outside their areas. For the most part the non-Communist efforts have been unable to tie into basic cleavages.

Linking class or socio-economic divisions to parties is difficult in the former Soviet Union because the Communists are not only the party of the old ruling class, the nomenclatura or bureaucracy, they also appeal to the masses. They proclaim themselves ideologically as the representatives of the workers and peasants, the trade-unions and mass farm organizations. In the older democratic polities which arose in Europe in the nineteenth century, the conservatives possessed the national summits, generally including monarchy, the church, high status and the land. They tried to preserve strong state authority, e.g. mercantilism. They were challenged by the liberals, based on the rising business strata, who sought to dismantle the power of the state, e.g. free(r) trade, voluntary religion. The masses, urban and rural, were outliers, and eventually formed their own parties, after the once entrenched conservatives and the bourgeois liberals, looking for allies enlarged the franchise, and sought support from the lower orders.

The new rulers of the post-colonial world, followed by those in the post-Communist nations, linked power to leftist or equalitarian ideologies. This has made it difficult to develop the "democratic class struggle." Who are the conservatives, the defenders of traditional authority and privileged interests in Russia? The new higher strata are part of political tendencies, which appeal to the masses, tie up with labor unions. Hence, there is as yet no institutionalized class conflict.

As noted, to endure, political parties require a base which is uncritically loyal, which will work or support them even when conditions go bad. The Communists in the former Soviet Union have such a base, their opponents do not. This pattern is not unique to the former Soviet Union, Mexico offers a good example of a similar system. Until fairly recently, the PRI, the Party of the Institutional Revolution, incorporated the economically privileged, the trade unions and workers, the peasant leagues and most of the rural population in one electoral bloc. It has taken 60 years for relatively strong parties appealing to the urban business and professional classes on the right and the proletariat on the left, to establish their separate bases of support.

This pessimistic analysis may be challenged by reference to the emergence of an institutionalized, regularized multi-party system in the East European, formerly Communist, nations, as well as in the Baltic states, which were part of the USSR. Most of these countries differed from the other ex-Soviet ones in having had a pluralistic party system and independent class organizations *before* they became Communist controlled. The Poles, the Czechs, the Hungarians and many of the others had social/democratic, peasant, Christian, Liberal parties before World War II, groups which were still remembered and able to revive after the downfall of Communism. Hence, although Communist parties have continued in these countries after losing power, they have not dominated the polity ideologically. The post-Communist electoral democracies rest on a revived political pluralism. And in addition to class, other structural cleavages, clerical–anti-clerical, ethnic and regional forces, have become linked to parties which have been able to find loyal mass followings.

In the long history of independent Latin American nations, structural cleavages have given rise to parties, but most of them have rarely been able to form enduring uncritical support bases. They have repeatedly broken down in response to crises. The Third Wave of the 1980s has given them a renewed opportunity to sink roots in the polity. But as yet, they had not done so in many countries. Hence we must consider the bulk of the Latin American polities as at best unstable democracies.

India, the great exception to most of the empirical generalizations about the social conditions for democracy, has remained democratic without stable national parties. Congress is a partial exception. What appears to stabilize India is major cross-cutting cleavages – caste, race, ethnicity, religion, economic class, language – which provide the underlying structures for long-term conflicting relationships, as well as alliances. These persist even after party allegiances break down. The continued strength of British political traditions, especially within the political class, including the civil service and the judiciary, also contributes to democratic stability.

In the Western democracies, the post-industrial cleavages foster new parties and/or rearrange bases of support. But the old cleavage lines, particularly those which Tocqueville saw as most important, class and religion, continue. Hence the Lipset–Rokkan cleavage model is still viable.

Theoretical and
analytical developments

2 *Party Systems and Voter Alignments* in the tradition of political sociology

Erik Allardt

Problems of political power, social order and authority have since ancient times been central concerns for mankind. In the search for the roots of political sociology it seems possible to select many different centuries as the time of beginning. Most common are references to the second half of the nineteenth century and the first decades of the twentieth century. In the Western nations this was a period of rapid industrialization and the beginnings of political democracy. It was also the time of birth of an academic social science. There is often an element of romanticization in the way in which the social science of this period is described.

In a recent volume on *Political Sociology at the Crossroads* the editor Baruch Kimmerling (1996, 152) lists in passing Tocqueville, Spencer, Mosca, Pareto, Schumpeter, Marx and Max Weber as intellectual founding fathers of political sociology. Yet, there are good grounds for saying that many, perhaps almost all of them, became more important and better known in academic circles during the decades after World War II than they ever were during their lifetime. They were raised to their position partly by political sociology, and more generally by the post-war sociology and political science oriented toward an empirical study of societies. Until the post-World War II period the great intellectual and academic names in the analysis of master processes in politics were philosophers such as Plato, Aristotle, Machiavelli, Hobbes, Locke, Rousseau, Hegel, John Stuart Mill, Auguste Comte, etc.

The distinctiveness of the post-war era

The assertion that the positions of the nineteenth-century founding fathers of political sociology were a product of the post-war social science does not imply any denial of their importance as sources of inspiration for later scholars. The intention here is to point out how in the study of the rise of post-war political sociology, an approach related to the history of ideas has to be supplemented by a description of the predicament of the social sciences in the period subsequent to World War II. The study of the history of ideas has to be replenished with the point of view of the sociology of science of the era itself. As a more or less institutionalized discipline political sociology was born after World War II. Part of its roots has to be sought within itself, and particularly in the conditions of research and higher education emerging after World War II.

Party Systems and Voter Alignments: Cross-National Perspectives (Lipset and Rokkan 1967a) was in many senses a landmark in the empirical study of mass politics. It constituted a final point of a short, but intensive, period of the birth of political sociology as a discipline. It contained the germs of new approaches, and, as a sad inquiring question, it perhaps also marked the culmination of the development of an academic political sociology? Its position among the social sciences can be highlighted by a reference to the state of the social sciences in the post-war period.

The social sciences belonged to the most rapidly expanding academic fields during the two first decades after the end of World War II. Great optimism was attached to the possibility of building a better world with the aid of social science and research. Before World War II the scope of the social sciences within the universities and other academic institutions had indeed been minimal. Empirical social research had not been regarded as an entirely respectable scientific activity, perhaps with the exception of economics which, although dismal, nevertheless was a science. Social science had had important forerunners that now became its founding fathers, but after World War II the social sciences became something of an industry.

The rapid post-war development of the social sciences occurred in a situation, in which what little there had been of a European academic study of social and political affairs was in shambles. This was in particular the case in continental Europe, and especially in Germany, from which many of those now defined as founding fathers had come. They were primarily both discovered and rediscovered in the US which also during the same time period was completely dominating within the realm of the social sciences. The American dominance of the social sciences in general, and political sociology in particular, in the 1940s, 1950s and still in the 1960s is an important fact to consider in all analyses of the development of the social sciences. In a revealing essay about political sociology in the Federal Republic of Germany, Birgitta Nedelmann (1997, 159–61) shows how the story of Nazi Germany was completely removed from the reestablishment of sociology and political sociology in post-World War Federal Germany. The German sociologists took as their point of reference in defining the national situation not the years 1933 or 1945, but 1949. The Nazi rule, however, was not removed from American political sociology. To mention some examples, both William Kornhauser's *The Politics of Mass Society* (1959), and Lipset's *Political Man* (1960) relied heavily on data about the growth and support of Nazism in Germany.

The institutionalization of political sociology

As an international scientific endeavor, political sociology was institutional-ized through the founding of the Committee of Political Sociology in September 1959. It occurred under the auspices of the International Sociological Association, but the Committee was later also recognized as a Research Committee by the International Political Science Association. The Committee's first Chairman, Seymour Martin Lipset had already published several innovative books in political sociology, and its first Secretary, Stein Rokkan had started to develop archives and sources for systematic cross-national research. The year 1959 represented in many senses an important landmark in the development of political sociology. In 1959 Lipset established the copyright for his *Political Man* (1960) which indeed can be considered the leading text of the period of birth of political sociology. Its subtitle *The Social Bases of Politics* announced what it was about. Earlier studies and discussions about the background of political decisions and parties had very much centered on ideological issues and relied strongly on political philosophy. Now the study of the social background of politics came into the foreground. Some empirical studies had been conducted already before and during World War II by scholars such as André Siegfried, Herbert Tingsten, and Rudolf Heberle. Their studies represented outstanding efforts by single individuals. Now at the end of the 1950s political sociology had grown into a small industry with young researchers all over the developed industrial world digging up data about the social bases of politics. This pattern can also be observed in the notes to Lipset's *Political Man*. In most European and Anglo-Saxon countries he had acquaintances, associates and students able to produce useful data for a comparative treatment of political behavior. Simultaneously Stein Rokkan was painstakingly building both personal networks of political sociologists and comparable data files.

The founding of the Committee of Political Sociology clearly also established a new kind of cooperation between sociology and political science. The Committee of Political Sociology became a home for re-searchers from both fields. The empirical study of the social bases of politics had earlier been alien to political science. This was perhaps particularly typical for the German-speaking countries and nations in the zone of German intellectual influence such as the Nordic countries. In this region a kind of *Begriffsjurisprudenz* had very much dominated the *Staatswissenschaft*. The Committee and its meetings became a gateway for political scientists who wanted to conduct empirical studies of the social bases of politics, and transform the *Staatswissenschaft* into a *politische Wissenschaft*.

Party Systems and Voter Alignments as a breakthrough of new ideas

There was only a short interval of eight years between the founding of the Committee in 1959 and the appearance of *Party Systems and Voter Alignments* in 1967. In practice the interval was even shorter, because the volume had not only been planned and conceived, but also to a great extent written many years before it appeared in bookstores. At any rate, there had been a very rapid development in the ideas of the committee members and in the content of political sociology. The easiest way to describe the development is to compare the contents of *Political Man* with *Party Systems and Voter Alignments*. In *Political Man* the stratification based on social class was a very dominant cleavage, and social class a central explanatory variable. This is also very openly announced in the book as elections are characterized as "the expression of the democratic class struggle." Simultaneously it seems important to warn against overinterpretations. When *Political Man* appeared, it was novel and radical to emphasize class voting and social class as a variable explaining voting patterns. Lipset's analysis deals in fact also with a number of other cleavages, but the expression of elections as an expression of the democratic class struggle was at its time a very well-found characterization announcing a new kind of paradigmatic orientation.

Nevertheless there is a clear new development to be discerned in *Party Systems and Voter Alignments*. A number of cleavages other than those related to social class were not only treated, but they were also theoretically justified. A systematic attempt to relate political cleavages to current theory building was presented in Lipset's and Rokkan's lengthy introduction *Cleavage Structures and Voter Alignments* (1967b, 1–64). The dimensions of cleavage were related to the functional requisites and necessities of social systems in terms of the well-known A-G-I-L scheme developed by Talcott Parsons (1971).

It may be recalled that in addition to the theoretical introduction by Lipset and Rokkan the book contains eleven chapters about single countries, and in some cases groups of countries. Findings and data from the United States, Canada, Great Britain, Australia, New Zealand, France, Italy, Spain, West Germany, Finland, Norway, Japan, Brazil, and West African countries are presented in the book. Most of the country chapters reveal a great number of cross-cutting cleavages and sometimes even political divisions, which are difficult to explain solely in terms of social background variables. Perhaps the clearest case of such a pattern is seen in Juan Linz's chapter on Spain, in which crucial political differences and constellations are described with ideal-types rather than multivariate statistics, although Linz uses crosstabulations in order to illustrate the types (1967a, 197–282). Linz also introduces a new kind of reasoning in that he clearly accounts for different political intentions found in various regional contexts and avoids blind reliance on multivariate statistical analysis. Yet, the main theoretical contribution is found in Lipset's and Rokkan's introduction. Its application of the Parsonian A-G-I-L scheme needs to be briefly described.

The A-G-I-L scheme

To recall Parsons' point of departure, the basic idea in his paradigm is that all social systems and societies have to solve problems of economic adaptation (A), goal-attainment (G), integration (I) and pattern maintenance of latency (L), and that there are specific institutions or subsystems which attend to these four functions. Thus we have the adaptive subsystem=the economy; the subsystem for goal attainment=the polity; the integrative subsystem=churches, voluntary associations, organizations for cultural aspirations; and the pattern maintenance subsystem=schools, households, the web of informal relations in the village community, etc.

Cleavages exist within each of the subsystems: between workers and employers in A, between political parties in G, and between religious denominations in I. Furthermore there are the cleavages and interchanges, both conflicts and cooperation between the subsystems such as, for instance, between the economy (A) and political decision-making (G).

The Lipset–Rokkan introduction is not a passive application of the Parsonian conceptual scheme. It adds dimensions and dichotomies which have been found to be important in studies of politics. Two of them had been of particular importance in European nation-building. One was the opposition between, or the axis of state-building centers and local, often ethnic peripheries, the other is the opposition between economic interests and strivings for cultural hegemony. These two axes can also be placed into the Parsonian scheme, as also was illustrated by many of the graphic presentations in the Lipset–Rokkan introduction. One such graph is presented in Figure 2.1

The lines between the corners in the quadrant of Figure 2.1 describe oppositions and tensions which are of relevance in all crucial processes of societal change. As said, in the process of European nation-building the oppositions between centers and peripheries, and between economic interests and cultural traditions have been central. It is to be noted that almost all grand theories of societal change take their point of departure in local, primarily agrarian societies, here located in the lowest corner of the chart. In the traditional local society there is a very low degree of differentiation in roles, tasks and statuses. The L-functions, that is pattern maintenance and socialization, are the crucial aims of the traditional local society. When the societies begin to differentiate and develop, differentiation occurs on several dimensions.

The central criteria of differentiation are indicated by the other corners of the chart, to which lines can be drawn from the lowest corner, representing the peripheries and the local societies. The line going from the lowest to the left-hand corner represents economic differentiation. It denotes how economic exchange develops, means of transportation are created and cities as centers for economic transaction are built. An elite of merchants, entrepreneurs, and artisans, in short an urban bourgeoisie, emerges. The line drawn from the lowest to the uppermost corner denotes differentiation based on the development of administration and military strength. The larger society begins to be able to enforce uniformity by using physical strength and legal rules. It means the rise of military and bureaucratic

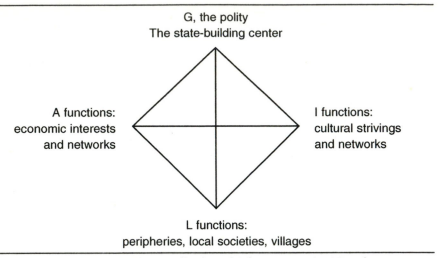

Figure 2.1 The Lipset–Rokkan application of Talcott Parsons' AGIL-scheme.

elites. The line drawn from the lowest to the right-hand corner represents cultural differentiation. Written texts and competence in handling and producing texts become of utmost importance. An elite of clergymen, scribes, and scientists emerges.

The new emphasis on both structure and institutions

The application of Parsons was in the Lipset–Rokkan paper much more elaborate than can be described briefly in this chapter. The reason for not expanding the Parsonian type of reasoning here is that it was mainly a classificatory and taxonomic device fitting in particular Western societies during the post-World War II period. Furthermore the Lipset–Rokkan application of Parsons never led to a substantial following among political sociologists. It was, however, a very useful classificatory scheme in the historical situation in which the work on party systems and voter alignments appeared. Intensive research on politics by both political scientists and sociologists had uncovered a great number of new and complicated cleavages. For summarizing and describing the new mass of information a sophisticated and multidimensional frame of reference such as Parsons' theory was needed.

The Lipset–Rokkan application of Parsons had one more major advantage. During the birth period of the academic political sociology the focus had been, as clearly revealed by Lipset's *Political Man*, in the analysis of how social background factors, such as the social stratification, had influenced politics. By the middle of the 1960s it had become equally important to study the effects of politics on social structure and the societal institutions.

The Lipset–Rokkan application of Parsons represented in a very outstanding manner the combination of a structural and an institutional approach. Even if Parsons' theory has clearly been labeled a sociological one, it became a device for putting political science and sociology on equal footing in the work of political sociologists both inside and outside the Committee. Politics ceased to be a phenomenon which simply could be reduced to its roots and preconditions in the social structure. Politics became so to say both a dependent and an independent variable.

A telling description of the breakthrough accomplished by *Party System and Voter Alignments* was presented as early as 1968 by Giovanni Sartori at the third formal conference of the Committee of Political Sociology held in West Berlin. His conference paper was in a revised form published in 1969 under the title *From the Sociology of Politics to Political Sociology* (1969a, 195–214). Sartori pointed out how one of the advantages of the new Lipset–Rokkan approach was that it paid many-sided attention to different lines of conflicts and cleavages. Sartori went on to show how Lipset and Rokkan in their study of how social structures are translated into party systems avoided the simplifying assumption that there be any direct translation. Many independent political events and processes intervene in the formation of parties. Furthermore, Lipset and Rokkan gave weight to the historical dimension and could thereby avoid historical mistakes made in earlier studies of political sociology. Thereby they had, according to Sartori, definitely surpassed the old-style of the sociology of politics and inaugurated a new political sociology. Politics was no longer a mere projection, as Sartori summarized his analysis.

The A-G-I-L cleavage scheme as a gateway to Stein Rokkan's studies of historical macro changes

There is in the history of political sociology also a third facet of the Parsonian application worth mentioning. It is an informed guess that the use and application of Parsons played a much greater role for Stein Rokkan than for his co-author Marty Lipset. By an informed guess is not meant that I have asked them about their co-authorship. Nor is there any hint about how much each of the two contributed to the actual writing of the introduction. What is meant is that in their subsequent publications and research, the Parsonian thoughts played a much greater role for Rokkan than for Lipset. In his many publications Lipset makes occasional references to Parsons, as many other leading sociologists do, but he does not, as far as I know, base his texts on the theoretical constructions of Talcott Parsons. Rokkan, by contrast, returns in several subsequent publications to the ideas advanced in the Lipset–Rokkan introduction. They are particularly important in his overview articles on nation-building (Rokkan 1970, 11–144), and less explicitly so in the studies about "the conceptual map of Europe" written together with Derek Urwin towards the end of Rokkan's life (Rokkan and Urwin 1983). Yet, even in Rokkan's treatment of the politics of territorial identities in Western Europe (Rokkan and Urwin 1982), roots to the Introduction in *Party Systems and Voter Alignments* can be traced. The Parsonian multifaceted scheme became for Rokkan a device by which he could proceed from his earlier focus on individual voters to studies of nations, basic societal institutions and master changes.

The threefold division of economic, military-bureaucratic, and cultural differentiation and of the corresponding elites is central in Stein Rokkan's European analyses. When Rokkan became increasingly interested in those large-scale processes, which had given birth to the main lines of divisions in present-day Europe, and to his conceptual map of Europe, he introduced new conceptual distinctions and accounted for a growing number of historical nuances. Yet, the opposition between centers and peripheries, and between economic and cultural interests, as well as the three-fold division into economic, bureaucratic-military and cultural differentiation, its corresponding elites and the tensions between them, remained the basic points of departure in all his macro analyses. This is also very well conveyed by Peter Flora's (1992, 81–134) reconstruction of Rokkan's theoretical development. In Stein Rokkan's career as a scholar, *Party Systems and Voter Alignments* was indeed of utmost importance.

The integration theory bias

There is no doubt that *Party Systems and Voter Alignments* was a milestone in the post-war development of political sociology. As such it also brings to the fore certain neglects and biases in the political sociology of the post-war decades. One might even ask whether these biases to an increasing degree came to determine the academic image of political sociology in the 1970s and 1980s. The field of political sociology did not disappear, but it seems fair to say that there was a decline of its relative importance in the community of social scientists. At any rate, the status of the book as a milestone and perhaps also as a culmination, makes it important to try to specify some of its neglects and biases.

It is by now a truism that Talcott Parsons in his theorizing represented what has been labelled the *integration theory of society*. Such a theory conceives of the society in terms of certain patterned and recurrent social functions as those explicated by the A-G-I-L scheme, and it emphasizes integration processes, political stability and normatively structured motives. Its opposite is the *coercion theory* which according to an authoritative formulation by Ralf Dahrendorf looks at the society "as a form of organization held together by force and constraint and reaching continuously beyond itself in the sense of producing within itself the forces that maintain it in an unending process of change" (1959, 159). It is hard to deny that the Lipset–Rokkan Introduction stands out as an exponent of integration theory. It does not only rely on Parsons' functionalism. It also strongly emphasizes how nations become increasingly integrated through processes of political participation, increasing contacts between centers and peripheries, and the rise of consensus based on democratic compromises.

The distinction between integration and coercion theories can be criticized, and it is also obvious that it is not value-free and has a political content. It is also mainly used by those with the ambition to be coercion theorists. Nevertheless, it points out which conditions are accounted for and which on the other hand are neglected. Some important social forces alien to integration theories are simply not treated in the Lipset–Rokkan Introduction nor in the subsequent nation-specific articles.

In the volume in commemoration of Stein Rokkan, edited by Per Torsvik, Charles Tilly has in a paper entitled *Sinews of War* (1981, 121–24) criticized the biases in Rokkan's choice of explanatory factors. What Tilly says applies very much to all authors in the volume edited by Lipset and Rokkan, and to most political sociologists at the time of the publication of the volume. What Tilly misses are, briefly, references to wars and taxes. According to him too little weight is given to warmaking and the interplay between war and the process of statemaking. As a general critique it can be added that economic conditions were not well accounted for in the post-war studies by political sociologists. Economic elites were mentioned but mostly as participants in problem-solving in the favor of political democracy.

In hindsight, I myself as a political sociologist miss in the analyses from the 1950s and 1960s, references to the technological development and the division of labor in particular. Already in the 1950s the industrial workforce had began to decline in the industrially most advanced countries. There was at that time already a strong increase of the service sector, and in the number of women in the labor force, and later on a notable increase in information and computer-related occupations. Due to such changes some of the papers in *Party Systems and Voter Alignments* are somewhat outdated today. This goes for the Alford and Robinson studies of class voting, and for the Dogan and Allardt–Pesonen papers analyzing Communist voting strength in France, Italy, and Finland. The patterns analyzed in these papers hardly disappeared solely because of increased skill in problem-solving or an enhancement of democratic attitudes. At least a contributing factor was by all likelihood the fact that radical changes in the division of labor had made the conditions for class-voting and for Communist voting strength completely different from what they had been before. One may ask why we did not see it at the time when the first tendencies already were emerging.

The bias in the time perspective

Göran Therborn (1996, 2–11) argues in a highly stimulating paper, published in Swedish in a Finnish sociological journal, that time was a crucial element in the semantics of the classical sociology. It was related to modernization. Time proceeded from the past to the future via the present. For some of the founding fathers the present was a threshold to the future, to the fully developed industrial society. But, as Therborn maintains, when the sociological enquiry in the 1940s and 1950s was institutionalized in American sociology by Talcott Parsons and his followers, time was excluded from all reflections. The future had already arrived, and its location was in the US of the 1940s and 1950s. In arguments based on concepts such as values, social norms, social systems, social functions, integration, time is of no importance. The A-G-I-L scheme exists, so to say, in all possible worlds. Therborn says that the post-war sociology, more quietly, but much more efficiently than Francis Fukuyama, had proclaimed the end of history in the rich and developed Western countries. Time and history only existed in the Third World as a pattern of modernization.

Therborn's conception is perhaps a kind of an aphoristic truth, but it gives nevertheless an apt description of some of the aspects of post-war political sociology and the papers in the Lipset–Rokkan volume. The politically central processes in the book are the democratic awakening to political participation, and the rise of political cleavages functional to the further development of national democratic states. The problems to be solved were identified and strategies outlined for handling the existing cleavages. When communism in France, Italy, and Finland presumably was eliminated, a democratic system in Spain inaugurated, and the African states modernized, the world was supposed to be more or less complete. I can not deny that I endorsed and still endorse the goals and values mentioned above, but the problem is that no thoughts are given to what will happen afterwards. A crucial aspect of, and source of richness in social analyses is the capacity to grasp and to understand the intentions and alternatives of action that new social structures and patterns will create and release. This is by and large what Anthony Giddens (1976, 19–20, 156–7) calls reflexivity. Tokens of reflexivity are largely lacking in the Lipset–Rokkan volume. At any rate, there is no pondering about what will follow after successful democratic problem solving, what new intentional configurations it will create, and how the future will look upon the analyses in the book.

The nation-state bias

The decades subsequent to World War II was an era of founding new states, of democratic consolidation of European states strongly disintegrated in the war, and of the rise of an Iron Curtain creating a simple division between states but also bringing about internal oppositions within states. It is no wonder that the Lipset–Rokkan volume both in its theoretical introduction and in its country-specific articles was very strongly centered on nation-states.

Some internal regional differences are, to be true, accounted for in all the country-specific articles in the book. They are, however, mostly related to only one dominant dimension, the distinction between developed centers and undeveloped peripheries. Yet, there are also in all the nation-states studied other regional differences of political importance.

The bias favoring a sole focus on the nation-state is perhaps particularly misleading in large-scale historical studies. Charles Tilly (1981, 122) remarks that most of the organizations which once levied taxes and waged war, and thus also contributed to state-making in Europe, no longer exist. They have been incorporated into larger national states. As Tilly notes, "important powers which sent delegates to the conferences which produced the Peace of Westphalia in 1648, after all, were not only Spain, France and England, but also Brandenburg, Hesse-Cassel, Bavaria, the Palatinate, Saxony, Venice, Lorraine, Savoy, Zeeland, Holland, the Empire, The Hanseatic League and the Papacy." Michael Hechter and William Brustein (1980, 1061–94) show in a paper about state formation in Western Europe how "the geographical distribution of the first modern state structures was largely determined by preexisting regional differences of social and economic organization, differences emanating from the 12th century if not earlier." In Hechter's and Brustein's analysis these regional differences are seen as emanating from different modes of production existing at that early time.

The discussion about a nation-state bias is not here meant as a devastating criticism. During the post-war era there was indeed a human and political call for the study of nation-states. This was the period of proliferation of comparative research, and comparative research came to mean comparisons of nation-states, despite the fact that comparisons are characteristic of all social research. It is, however, important to be aware of the fact that political sociology during the 1950s and 1960s not only was, but also had many reasons to be strongly state-centered.

Yet, it is obvious that there also existed among political sociologists a growing awareness of the multiformity of regional and ethnic differences. It is to be remembered that also Stein Rokkan in the context of his nation-building studies increasingly began to emphasize the territorial identities in the European peripheries (Rokkan and Urwin 1983). It seems to me that those country-chapters in the Lipset–Rokkan volume, which more thoroughly than others analyzed the varying conditions for territorial differences, have sustained most of their freshness. This applies for instance to Mattei Dogan's analysis of France and Italy, and to the study of Spain by Juan Linz. The latter's disposition to dig deeply into the background of territorial differences is very well conveyed by the title of one of his other publications from the same period, that is *Within-Nation Differences and Comparisons: The Eight Spains* (Linz and de Miguel 1966, 267–319).

The neglect of agency

The importance for analyzing the background of territorial differences is in political sociology hardly a token of a simple urge to express territorial interests. The fruitfulness of studying territorial differences in the context of the politics in the nation-states lies very much in that it gives possibilities to analyze and unveil political intentions and motives.

The present popularity of the rational choice theory has in my opinion in the social sciences had some positive, perhaps largely unintended, consequences. Rational choice theory brings to the fore people's intentions and motives, and it has given an additional and fruitful push to attempts to account for human agency and to apply agential explanations.

As Jon Elster (1993, 179–90) has shown quite convincingly, rational choice theory is not a causal, predictive theory, but essentially a hermeneutic one. The construction of rationality, according to Elster, is partly discovery, and partly decision. It unveils the intentions of the actors, and as many methodologists have shown, intentional explanations are not causal ones in which the cause and the effect are logically independent of each other. In intentional explanations the action is already logically contained in its intention.

It appears perhaps far-fetched to introduce rational choice theory into the discussion of past political sociology. Yet, my point is to emphasize how it brings in human agency, and the importance of the study of the motives of the political actors. The agency aspect, the study of political intentions and motives, is very much missing from the country-specific contributions in *Party Systems and Voter Alignments*.

What is typical of most of the explanations offered in the chapters in the Lipset–Rokkan volume is that they aim to be causal, establishing statistical associations between elements of the social structure and the political system on the one hand, and political behavior on the other. The intervening mechanisms, describing why people behave as they do, are largely left out from the analyses. The message from the Lipset and Rokkan introduction did not reach the other contributors to the volume. As emphasized earlier, one of the revolutionary thoughts in Lipset's and Rokkan's introductory chapter was that there is never a direct translation of structural divisions into political action or into party alignments. Between them there are actors and agents with their various motives and political perceptions.

Party Systems and Voter Alignments was produced at a time when it was considered sufficient to establish statistical associations between variables without accounting for the mechanisms connecting the variables. Most of the arguments, but not all of them, in the volume are based on such external associations between variables without further analyses of the intentions of the actors or agents. This is today increasingly insufficient. Simultaneously, intentional explanations are considered increasingly legitimate. Leading analysts of political movements (Touraine 1984) have emphasized how in contemporary political sociology human agents and their motives have to be accounted for.

Is there a new coming of political sociology?

The list of biases presented here is of course an expression of hindsight, and an attempt to indicate what approaches appear important today. The critique can not obscure the fact that *Party Systems and Voter Alignments*, and particularly its introduction, was a pathbreaking contribution. It proved that political sociology at its best can analyze large-scale historical processes and the simultaneous occurrence of political and social change.

During the time interval between the appearance of the Lipset–Rokkan volume and the beginning of the 1990s there was perhaps, as has been hinted here, a decline of the strength and popularity of political sociology. It was at least partly due to the fact that many of the research activities which had been initiated within the Committee of Political Sociology had become incorporated in either political science or sociology.

On good grounds it seems reasonable to inquire whether a revival of political sociology has arrived. One reason is the globalization of the skills needed by political sociologists. Political sociology and the activities of the Committee were earlier strongly centered in Europe and the Americas. There were rapid changes in other parts of the world, but they lacked political sociologists. Today there is a much greater spread of both skills and motivation among social scientists inclined to study both politics and societal changes.

At the same time, European society has during the last decade undergone thorough and dramatic master changes. There are the events of the revolution of 1989, and the growth of the European Union. Problems of democracy, very much discussed during the time of the founding of the Committee of Political Sociology, are again of great interest. Seymour Martin Lipset, the first chairman of the Committee has addressed the problem of the requisites of democracy anew (1994, 1–22).

The present major changes are by no means restricted to political life. The division of labor, both in terms of what kind of work is needed today, and because of the large-scale entry of women into the labor market in many countries, has thoroughly changed the social structure. Technical innovations especially within the information and computer industries have in Europe produced unemployment on an unprecedented scale. A serious question is whether the present unemployment is a qualitatively new phenomenon, and as such is a symptom of a new type of society. At any rate, there exists an abundance of large-scale societal problems and master processes which used to be and are the prime object of political sociology.

There are presently considerable ongoing changes in the party systems and especially in the patterns of voter alignments. One of the specific hypotheses in the Lipset and Rokkan Introduction was the thesis about the "frozen party system", in other words the proposition that despite considerable changes in the social structure of societies, the institutionalized party systems have remained more or less intact. The notion of the frozen party system is and has been criticized on both conceptual and empirical grounds. One of the first and important criticisms was presented by Giovanni Sartori in the article mentioned above (1969a, 195–214), when he maintained that the frozen party system hypothesis is interesting only as long we treat the party system as a dependent variable. The hypothesis loses much of its fascination as soon as we go on to analyze how the party system in itself transfers and molds the social and political world.

Despite the criticisms of the concept of the frozen party system it has through the years had a great sensitizing effect. It has stimulated many studies of the degree of stability in party systems and voter alignments. Presently there are many indications of considerable losses both in the stability of party systems and in voter alignments. Some of the most crucial ones are the decreases of political party involvements and voting participation among young people in many countries. Another is the rapidly changing content and meaning of the cleavage between left and right. These are problems studied intensively today. Political sociology thrives in times of great social and political transformations.

3 The freezing hypothesis
An evaluation

Peter Mair

Introduction

Despite more or less thirty years of close reading by countless scholars in a variety of different fields, and despite what is now a genuinely voluminous literature seeking to explore and often test the ramifications of the so-called "freezing hypothesis", there still remains a marked degree of confusion about what precisely was believed by Lipset and Rokkan to have settled into place by the 1920s. On the one hand, the conclusion of the original authors (Lipset and Rokkan 1967a, 50) might be read as unequivocal, in that it was the "party systems" which had reflected a more or less unchanging history over the previous forty or so years, with their constituent "party alternatives" becoming "older than the majorities of the national electorates". What appeared frozen, therefore, were the parties and the systems that they constituted. On the other hand, the principal burden of the rich and lengthy Lipset–Rokkan essay was not so much concerned with parties or even party systems as such, although this was certainly one of the recurring themes, but rather with cleavages and cleavage structures. Indeed, the subsequent continuity or freezing of the party systems into the 1960s was actually defined in terms of their still reflecting the original "cleavage structures" of the 1920s. Following this latter reading, what appears to have been frozen was the cleavage system, with the parties and party systems being simply the outward manifestation of that particular stasis.

This central confusion continues to mark many of the contemporary commentaries on the freezing hypothesis. From the perspective of one approach, the Lipset–Rokkan argument continues to receive backing by virtue of the continuing and often still dominating presence in contemporary competitive politics of many of the traditional party alternatives, as well as by virtue of the evidence of long-term party organizational continuity over time. From the perspective of a second approach, however, the continued validity of the thesis depends on being able to establish that cleavages persist, and that contemporary mass politics continues to be grounded among traditional social oppositions.

Each of these approaches may be seen as reasonably valid in its own right, of course, but precisely because they are concerned with markedly differing interpretations of the freezing hypothesis, their conclusions often tend to talk past one another. For one group of scholars, much of the evidence suggests that the freezing hypothesis continued to remain more or less valid even through the decades subsequent to the Lipset–Rokkan formulation. For the other, the weight of evidence suggests it is no longer valid, and that it has long passed its useful sell-by date. The real problem here, however, is that each set of findings is actually reasonably correct, and even mutually compatible, in that both of these ostensibly contradictory conclusions rest on what is, in fact, a largely confused – and confusing – assertion. In the following two sections of this chapter I will therefore offer a brief review of each of these approaches, before going on in the remaining sections to discuss the relevance and meaning of the freezing hypothesis itself, and to suggest how, at least at the systemic level, it might even be taken for granted.

Testing the hypothesis: cleavage change

Most of the explicit efforts to test the Lipset–Rokkan thesis have focused primarily on the relationship between social structure and voting behaviour. This is hardly surprising, especially since the most intuitive sense of the term "cleavage" is one in which particular social strata are conceived to be consistently aligned with particular party alternatives. Hence, from Rose (1974) onwards, and most especially in the more recent work by Franklin *et al.* (1992), we see powerful attempts to evaluate the continuing validity of the Lipset–Rokkan thesis in terms of the relationship between social structure and party preference. In a related vein, in work ranging from Inglehart (1984) to Knutsen and Scarbrough (1995) and, most recently, Kriesi (1997), we see a more nuanced approach being adopted, in which social structural determinants of voting preferences are combined with or even ranked against determinants deriving from value conflicts. Moreover, and with the possible exception of the conclusions derived from that relatively early work by Rose and his colleagues, we also gain from all of these analyses a more or less profound sense that things now have changed.

Franklin *et al.*, for example, in what is perhaps the most exhaustive systematic cross-national comparison to date, effectively conclude not only that many party systems had already freed themselves of the "straitjacket of traditional cleavage politics" (1992, 404) by the mid-1980s, but also that most of the remaining countries, where social structural determinants continued to exert a powerful role, were likely to follow suit in the near future. In other words, with time, we were witnessing the gradual decay of cleavage politics, at least in this social-structural sense of the term, and the only question which remained was the extent to which this effectively inevitable process was either accelerated or delayed. And although Knutsen and Scarbrough (1995) were unable to confirm this conclusion, at least at a more general level, they nonetheless sustained it in part by the enhanced role which they attributed to what they call "value voting", especially in the advanced industrial democracies. Kriesi (1997) also highlights change, particularly insofar as the decline of traditional cleavages are concerned, although here too, as with Knutsen and Scarbrough's analysis, social divisions continue to emerge as an additional important determinant of party choice (see also Goldthorpe 1996).

But for all the qualifications which might be derived from a more sensitive application of "traditional" cleavage variables, including attitudes and values as well as more objective social determinants, and for all the precision which might be derived from a more nuanced and differentiated notion of social class and its impact on voting behaviour (see especially the work of Goldthorpe and his colleagues, e.g. in Evans 1998), we still continue to be confronted in these sorts of studies with evidence of change, and with the argument that we need to revise or even abandon the freezing hypothesis when it comes to the understanding of contemporary voter alignments. Few of the scholars involved in this sort of work would deny both the relevance and accuracy of the Lipset–Rokkan diagnosis insofar as the voting patterns which prevailed through to the late 1960s and even the 1970s are concerned – indeed, Franklin and his colleagues are often at pains to emphasize the sheer strength of the cleavage politics in that earlier period. Once more contemporary patterns come to be analyzed, however, an alternative picture emerges, with traditional cleavage alignments being seen to have fractured or even dissipated, and with the notion of freezing being no longer easily, or adequately, applicable.

We need not be surprised at this conclusion. As almost all studies of party politics since the time of Kirchheimer (1966) have emphasized, the party end of the traditional cleavage linkage has been substantially transformed over the past thirty years or so, with a loosening of organizational ties to the electorate, and with a more catch-all approach to electoral campaigning. Few if any parties are now content to restrict their appeal to a narrowly defined set of voters, and those that do so are often restricted to the margins of mass politics. As voters begin to choose, to adopt the phrasing of Rose and McAllister (1986), the parties themselves become less choosy, seeking votes whenever and wherever they can be obtained.

At the same time, and perhaps more crucially, the social-structural end of the traditional cleavage linkage has also been subject to a dramatic transformation. Both class and religious identities have clearly been eroded in the past thirty years, for example, the one through the increased advance of post-industrialism, and the other through the steady advance of a generalized secularism. Collective identities more generally have become substantially more fragmented in the thirty years which have elapsed since the original formulation of the Lipset–Rokkan thesis, and voting behaviour, in consequence, and to adopt the terms of Franklin *et al*. (1992, 406–31), has become more particularized. If the validity of the freezing hypothesis depended on the existence of close ties between broadly recognizable and politically relevant social strata, on the one hand, and specific class- or religiously oriented party organizations, on the other, then clearly the conditions for such a politics have by now been significantly undermined.

As against this, however, it can be argued that this view reflects quite a restricted conception of the freezing argument, since it implies, as I have suggested elsewhere (Mair 1993), that the Lipset–Rokkan thesis could be valid only in what is an essentially frozen *society* – and this is clearly an impossible precondition. Class structures change both inevitably and inexorably, while religious identities are also far from fixed or preordained, and to the extent that the freezing argument depends upon social stasis then it could be deemed as almost irrelevant from the beginning. No society is, or has been, frozen, and hence if political alignments are stabilized, this process must be due to something else, or to something more. To put it another way, if the freezing hypothesis is to carry any weight, either now or in the past, then it must refer to something other than, or, at least, to something more than, the immediate linkage between social strata and party preference. Both ends of this equation – the social structure, on the one hand, and the party organizational and electoral identity, on the other – are simply too vulnerable and too contingent to sustain such a potentially powerful hypothesis on their own.

Of course, it is always possible to remain more or less within these terms of reference and yet build a more robust and accommodating model. It might be possible, for example, to avoid the immediacy of the contingent social structure–party preference linkage by building in a notion of partisan loyalty or partisan identity which can be transmitted through generations, and which, while not dependent on there being a frozen society, never-theless harks back in the end to a particular social alignment. Such loyalties might therefore persist, and so continue to validate the freezing thesis, notwithstanding social mobility and restructuring. At the same time, how-ever, this idea of autonomously persisting identities is always difficult to test and to verify, and it probably requires a more refined definition of cleavage politics in order to embrace both a normative and an organizational dimension (see Bartolini and Mair 1990). In distinguishing value orient-ations from social structural features both Kriesi (1997) and Knutsen and Scarbrough (1995) go some way towards applying such an approach at the empirical level, and it is therefore interesting to note the extent to which they witness stability as well as change. But this is inevitably a difficult and contentious terrain.

Finally, it might also prove possible to develop an analysis along the lines suggested by Inglehart (1984), and to posit the emergence of new post-industrial cleavages which are more in tune with the contemporary social structural realities than the more traditional cleavages originally identified by Lipset and Rokkan. This approach is also problematic, however. In the first place, it may be doubted whether we are comparing like with like, in that the principal cleavages discussed by Lipset and Rokkan reflected very long-standing divides which were politicized and then institutionalized within clearly identifiable conjunctures of long-term political development. The newer and more contemporary "cleavages", on the other hand, are, at least as yet, necessarily more ephemeral and short-term, and for now may more usefully be seen as reflecting simple issue divides or even value conflicts. Second, even if it can be argued that these new divides constitute real cleavages which are equivalent to those long-standing alignments identified by Lipset and Rokkan, this still casts uncertainty over the whole notion of the freezing hypothesis. Cleavage politics in this new sense might well be relevant, but since the cleavages involved have been substantially transformed, it hardly seems appropriate to speak of a freezing process as such.

Testing the hypothesis: electoral and partisan stability

The second principal approach to evaluating the continued validity of the Lipset–Rokkan argument takes as its focus the broad patterns of electoral stability and instability, with these usually being measured at the aggregate level in order to tap into longer term (i.e. including pre-mass survey periods) trends. In this case, and again reflecting the ambiguity and confusion in the original formulation by Lipset and Rokkan, the emphasis is less on the persistence of cleavages as such, and rather more on the persistence of parties and party systems. Should these have been frozen, so the argument goes, we would then witness quite pronounced electoral stability – even if only at aggregate level – as well as an evident organizational longevity at the level of the parties involved.

Beginning with the classic study of Rose and Urwin (1970), therefore, which was completed very soon after the publication of *Party Systems and Voter Alignments,* and going on through the work of Pedersen (1979), Maguire (1983), Shamir (1984), and Bartolini and Mair (1990), a host of studies have sought to measure aggregate levels of electoral stability and instability and to relate these to the freezing hypothesis. It should be added that these studies have also employed a variety of different indicators, including vote trends, volatility levels, as well as indicators based on the performances of individual parties and blocs of parties.

What is most striking here, however, and what stands in relatively sharp contrast to the general consensus underpinning many of the studies on cleavage politics, is a tendency to prove quite supportive of the Lipset–Rokkan conclusion, with the evidence of sporadic and unevenly distributed levels of instability – at least through to the late 1980s – being generally outweighed by the more consistent emphasis on continuities and persistence.

Elections certainly can prove volatile, and sudden and sometimes even very dramatic shifts in the partisan balance have been recorded, but almost all observers continue to remain impressed by the sheer staying power of many of the traditional alternatives, even during the past thirty years. Moreover, as has been argued elsewhere (Bartolini and Mair 1990), and notwithstanding partisan fluctuations, the stabilization of alternatives appears particularly pronounced when these are aggregated into broad "cleavage" blocs of left and right, a pattern which seem particularly telling as far as the continued validity of the Lipset–Rokkan argument is concerned.

Even here, however, at least some members of the jury are still out, and will probably always remain out. Four important doubts can be, and have been expressed. In the first place, the fairly consistent evidence of aggregate electoral stability over time, which seems to invoke an essential feature of the freezing proposition and which therefore appears to confirm the continued validity of the Lipset–Rokkan hypothesis, is often countered by more in-depth evidence of substantial fluctuations at the level of the individual voter, which appear to run counter to the freezing idea. Hence it is often argued that only a partial picture is being obtained through the use of aggregate data, even though these have the definite advantage of allowing tests of stability to be extended all the way back to the beginnings of mass democratic politics. Aggregate continuities may therefore conceal significant individual-level flux, or so it is argued, and hence may disguise the real extent of unfreezing.

Second, and particularly insofar as measures of electoral volatility are concerned, it is often suggested that the evidence of stability in the short-term (that is, volatility from one election to the next) may actually conceal longer-term processes of decline and realignment, and it is these latter processes which are seen to be of greater relevance to the Lipset–Rokkan argument. Thus even though the electoral balance may not change substantially across any given pair of elections, viewing the longer-term trends actually cautions against any easy acceptance of the freezing idea.

Third, it is sometimes argued that both aggregate and individual measures of electoral change are in fact far too insensitive to tap into the more crucial question of party system stability, since not all electoral changes matter equally, and since some changes may have more systemic implications than others. What matters, therefore, is not the extent of any change as such, but rather its location, and the way in which it may impact on the core of the party system itself (see Mair 1983, and Smith 1989). Thus even when fairly low levels of change are recorded, these nevertheless might well be sufficient to challenge the notion of freezing.

Finally, and even gainsaying all of the above criticisms, it can now also be suggested that whatever the patterns of aggregate electoral stability which prevailed through to the end of the 1980s, the last five or six years have suddenly witnessed a major new upsurge in volatility, with record high levels of aggregate electoral change being recorded in the early to mid-1990s.

The dramatic changes in Italy – which, by any standards, must represent a clear "unfreezing" – offer one case in point, with less striking but none-theless substantial electoral shifts also being recently and quite suddenly manifested in the Netherlands, France, Ireland, Norway and Sweden (e.g. Lane and Ersson 1997). Thus even if it were to be accepted that the freezing hypothesis had continued to hold sway through to the end of the 1980s, it is now believed to have become increasingly vulnerable.

How relevant is the freezing "hypothesis"?

Arguments concerning and surrounding the two approaches summarized above have now occupied a very substantial part of the recent literature of electoral change and party system change, much of which is explicitly based on, and often begins with, the Lipset–Rokkan hypothesis. Moreover, and as noted, the findings of these two approaches often appear to contradict one another, with the cleavage-based argument increasingly asserting the contemporary redundancy of the freezing proposition, and with the party-based argument tending mainly to confirm it. In fact, as we have seen, there is really no contradiction here, since each actually maintains quite a different interpretation of what "freezing" implies. In this sense, albeit while talking past one another, both conclusions are probably compatible with one another, and, at least within their own terms of reference, both are probably also correct.

But this is by the way, for the more important question which remains is whether either really offers an appropriate test of the original proposition, and of what is implied by that proposition. To the extent that the continued validity of the freezing hypothesis depends on the existence of a more or less frozen society, for example, then, as noted above, the argument is almost trivial, and is not really worth pursuing. To the extent that it depends on evidence of the stabilization of (aggregate or individual) voting patterns, on the other hand, problems are also presented, particularly since it remains unclear to many observers precisely how stable is stable, and to what extent the inevitable fluctuations which occur may still be accom-modated within the assumptions of the original proposition (see also Shamir 1984). In this sense, Lybeck's (1985) brief but powerfully argued assessment remains highly apposite: the hypothesis may not be testable at all, and was probably not intended to be testable. Hence there is perhaps a prior question that is begged: *How relevant is the original formulation?* More to the point, and returning to the observation at the beginning of this chapter: *What precisely is supposed to have been frozen?*

In fact, as I have suggested elsewhere (Mair 1997, 3–16; Mair and Sakano 1998, 177), what we tend to think of as the freezing "hypothesis" was not really a hypothesis at all; rather, it was an empirical observation. Lipset and Rokkan were certainly concerned to explain the ways in which the different constellations of party forces had finally settled into place in the 1920s, and they also clearly sought to make sense of the both the diversity and the commonalities which had become evident in the world of European party politics at the beginnings of mass democracy. But evidence of subsequent stability received relatively little attention within their lengthy and powerful analysis, and although many later readers have since tended to focus in on the question of the freezing of cleavage structures and/or party systems through to the 1960s and beyond, this particular element constituted little more than a postscript to what had been a very differently oriented analysis. In fact, there was hardly any effort made in that original article to elaborate specific arguments or theories as to why or how the tendency towards stability was maintained in the later practice of mass democracy. In other words, and despite the preoccupations of later generations of scholars, the question of the extent to which party systems were genuinely frozen after the 1920s appears to have had little fundamental bearing on what Lipset and Rokkan were primarily concerned to explain. Moreover, and precisely because it proved to be so marginal to their overall argument, the validity or otherwise of the freezing proposition has little or nothing to add to the value of their core analysis.

There are two reasons which can be suggested to explain why Lipset and Rokkan chose to devote so little attention to the mechanics of the freezing process in that original essay. The one is relatively trivial, the other perhaps more important. The more trivial reason is that the authors were simply not particularly concerned or interested to develop an analysis of the post-1920s patterns, at least in this context. The burden of the original essay was devoted to an understanding of how the constellations of the 1920s had come about; it was not about how these had subsequently unfolded. The focus was on the genesis of modern European party systems, and not on their subsequent trajectories or performance. With more time, or perhaps with the more generous scope which might have been afforded by a monograph, these latter developments might have been explored more completely. In this particular context, however, attention to the dynamics of fully mobilized party systems was almost by the way and was therefore seen to be of little concern. Nor was the original volume as a whole really intended to deal with these questions: instead, it was designed as an inquiry into "[first] the genesis of the system of contrasts and cleavages within the national community . . . [second] the conditions for the development of a stable system of cleavage and oppositions in national political life . . . [and third] the behaviour of the mass of the rank-and-file citizens within the resultant party systems" (Lipset and Rokkan 1967a, 1–2). In other words, in both the original Lipset–Rokkan essay, as in the volume from which it is drawn, the primary concern were to explain how the patterns which had taken shape by the 1920s might best be understood, with an additional focus of attention directed towards the implications of these patterns for the political behavior of individual voters. How the party systems themselves subsequently developed was therefore secondary to these broad lines of inquiry.

The second and more interesting reason which can be suggested is that the authors, and, perhaps, most analysts, could actually take post-1920s persistence, or freezing, for granted. To put it another way, if a freeze did set in, then this was hardly surprising. Indeed, it may well be argued that party systems enjoy an inherent bias towards stability (see Mair 1997, 7). Once electorates had become fully mobilized, and once the institutional structures of mass democracy had become consolidated, a crude equilibrium became established; thereafter, and at least to a large extent, the laws of inertia could take over (Sartori 1969b, 90). To adopt an analogy from space exploration, we might therefore read Lipset and Rokkan as having devoted their attention to how a satellite comes to be launched into orbit rather than to how that orbit might subsequently be maintained. Indeed, this was also the more challenging problem; the orbiting itself could be taken as given.

Freezing and institutionalization

Although this notion is intuitively appealing, it does need to be specified more carefully, and particularly with reference to what precisely was believed to have been frozen into place in the 1920s. In fact, and building from the discussion in the earlier sections, there are three distinct ways in which the freezing process can be conceived. First, there is the possible freezing of cleavages, in which more or less the same social forces combine and compete in alignment with more or less the same party alternatives. Second, there is the freezing of the party alternatives themselves, whether these be still based on the original social forces which 'created' them, or whether they survive in a much adapted form. Third, and most importantly, there is the freezing of party systems as such, which are conceived here as involving a set of patterned interactions between the different party alternatives and a stable structure of inter-party competition (Sartori 1976, 44; see also Smith 1966; Eckstein 1968; Bardi and Mair 1997). Let us look at these three in turn.

To begin with, it seems obvious that cleavages cannot easily be taken as a given, even within a more robust conception that involves not just the differentials of social stratification, but also the more general sense of collective identity, as well as the role of organizational intervention (on this three-fold conception of cleavage, see Bartolini and Mair 1990, 212–25). As noted above, social structure itself is highly mutable, while collective identities are inevitably susceptible to fragmentation and realignment. And although we learn from Lipset and Rokkan that the principal cleavages in Western societies are both deeply rooted and enduring, it is also clear that we can never simply take their perpetual freezing – or salience, or exclusivity – for granted.

Nor can we afford to take the parties themselves for granted. Indeed, if there is a single lesson to be drawn from the wealth of party studies which have been conducted over the past thirty years, as well as from Rokkan's own pioneering work on Norway (e.g. Rokkan 1966a) and the contemporaneous insights afforded by Kirchheimer's (1966) theories of the catch-all party, it is that parties have an almost inexhaustible capacity to adjust and to adapt, and hence to survive through transformation. In this sense, the parties of the 1990s are clearly very different from those of the 1960s, and, as both Lipset and Rokkan knew all too well, the parties of the 1960s were very different from those of the 1920s. Parties are marked by continuous processes of adaptation, in which principles, programmes, and policies are modified to meet new and ever-changing circumstances, and in which both their organizational character and electoral base are constantly trimmed and tucked. Above all, parties are dynamic structures: were they to be wholly frozen or petrified it is unlikely that they could survive. They are now different parties than before, and to allow this inevitable plasticity to be accommodated within an assumed notion of party freezing is to risk stretching that notion to a degree where it becomes almost banal.

This therefore suggests that it is really only within the third conception of freezing, the freezing of party systems as such, that stasis might be meaningfully assumed, for party *systems*, defined as such by the existence of a patterned set of interactions, and by an identifiable structure of competition, and as noted above, could be seen to enjoy an inherent bias towards stability. This would not be a surprising conclusion; but neither is it trivial. Indeed, it follows from the very notion of systemness, in that all systems, by definition, have "a tendency towards a state of equilibrium, i.e., the system tends to maintain itself through various processes whenever it is disturbed" (Mitchell 1968, 473). Or, as Sartori (1994, 37) puts it, "when the electorate takes for granted a given set of political routes and alternatives very much as drivers take for granted a given system of highways, then a party system has reached the stage of structural consolidation qua system". In other words, and turning back to the original theme of this chapter, Lipset and Rokkan can be read as having been more concerned with how party systems became structured or institutionalized (in or around the 1920s) – this being the result of the interplay between cleavage structures, institutional constraints and patterns of social and political mobilization – and as having been understandably less concerned with how this institutionalization was subsequently maintained, since this, virtually by definition, required little explanation. Party systems, as systems, freeze themselves into place. They acquire their own momentum. This is, in fact, precisely what Jepperson has identified as being entailed in the concept of institutions more generally, in that they embody "those social patterns that, when chronically reproduced, owe their survival to relatively self-activating social processes . . . [Institutions] operate as relative fixtures of constraining environments and are accompanied by taken-for-granted accounts" (Jepperson 1991, 145, 149).

But how easily may we take accounts of party system "freezing", or, perhaps better still, "institutionalization", for granted? To return to an earlier analogy, should we regard the maintenance of an orbit as given, and, like Lipset and Rokkan, focus our attention instead on how the satellites are launched, or on how they are constructed? In other words, should we study orbital patterns only when they break down or become erratic?

On the one hand, the degree of persistence in party systems appears to be such that it is only the infrequent cases of change which seem to demand explanation. However specified, the exceptions to party system stability still appear to be few – if also significant (Lipset and Rokkan 1967a, 50). In addition to the rare cases noted by Lipset and Rokkan themselves, we can now most obviously add that of Italy in the early 1990s, as well perhaps as that of Ireland during the same period, and the increasingly likely case of Austria. Beyond this small group of countries, however, and it is worth underlining that their potential transformations are all of a very recent origin, the patterns which continue to assert themselves in Western Europe are still largely familiar: the two, or two-and-a-half party format in Germany and the UK, the bipolar socialist-bourgeois opposition in the Scandinavian countries, and the fragmented multi-party patterns in the old consociational democracies. There is little about the party systems in such countries which might now lead an observer returning after thirty years to be taken aback.

On the other hand, even institutions themselves, and institutional reproduction in particular, merit some attention, for it is really only by understanding how systems are maintained that we can become aware of how they may change. Institutional reproduction, and hence, in this case, the freezing of party systems, may not require much formal "action", to use another term from Jepperson (1991, 145) – that is, it may not require "recurrent [electoral] mobilization" – but this should not prevent us from seeking to identify and analyse which factors are likely to prove supportive of this process and which are likely to prove destructive. Before turning to this question, however, it is perhaps useful to specify more precisely what is entailed in a party system, and how party systems may differ from one another in terms of both their "systemness" and stability, or, as I will suggest, predictability.

As noted above, a party system may be understood as a system of interactions that are defined by the pattern of competition between the parties involved (Sartori 1976, 44). Two points immediately follow from this. First, and more marginally, not all parties may have a bearing on the system itself, in that smaller parties, or those whose behaviour has little or no impact on their ostensible competitors, may be deemed irrelevant (Sartori 1976, 121–5). They may come and go, or even persist over the long term, without having any systemic importance. The various Northern Irish parties in the United Kingdom may be regarded in such a light, or

even the more prominent British Liberal Party. Second, and more importantly, some "systems" of parties may not be party systems at all (see Eckstein
1968; Bardi and Mair 1997), in that the parties may not compete with one
another, or, while competing, they may reveal no clear set of patterned
interactions. The one case might be typified by a classic and pronounced
pattern of segmentation or *verzuiling*, in which each of the ostensibly
competing parties exists within its own universe, being content to mobilize
only among its own potential and self-enclosed electorate. No two parties
would be seeking the same voters, and no interaction would occur. Hence
no party system as such would exist. The other case is most evidently
typified by newly emerging party systems, in which party identities and
electoral alignments are so inchoate and unstructured that no systemic
logic has yet become discernible: neither the parties nor their erstwhile
supporters are in any sense predictable, and hence no party system has yet
become institutionalized.

The degree of party "systemness" therefore differs from country to
country, as well as over time. To put it another way, there is a more or less
considerable variation in the extent to which party "systems" are structured,
or institutionalized. The key element here is probably predictability, with
strong party systems being highly predictable, and with weak or feebly
structured party "systems" being highly unpredictable. Predictability then
becomes a surrogate of structuration: the more predictable a party system
is, the more it is a system as such, and hence the more institutionalized it
has become. This is also what freezing is about.

Institutionalization and prediction

Party systems may be characterized in a variety of different ways, and
according to a variety of different indicators. These include the number of
competing parties, the relative electoral and/or parliamentary weights of
the competitors, the ideological distances which separate them, and so on.
Categories can include two-party systems and multi-party systems, party
systems with dominant parties and those without dominant parties, even
and uneven multi-party systems, or systems of polarized pluralism and
systems of moderate pluralism. For the purposes of this discussion,
however, and building from an earlier and related analysis (see Mair 1996),
I find it more useful to narrow the focus down to just one dimension, that
is, the competition for government.

The core of any definition of a party system obviously revolves around
the notion of competition: the system itself is constituted by the
interactions between the parties and by the ways in which they relate to one
another. But although it may be argued that these interactions take place in
a variety of different arenas, including the electoral arena, the parliamentary arena, the governing arena, and so on (Laver 1989), it is the way in
which government is contested which, albeit often implicitly, clearly

underlies almost all of the accepted characterizations. Two-party systems may be distinguished from multi-party systems, for example, not just in terms of the number of parties – of which there are rarely just two – but also and more meaningfully in terms of the way in which governments alternate. Multi-party systems with a dominant party differ from what are sometimes defined as "even" multi-party systems not only in terms of the relative size of the parties involved, but also by virtue of the capacity of the dominant party in question to form single-party governments. Polarized pluralism differs from moderate pluralism because of the extremes of ideological opinion, but also, and perhaps even more usefully, because the permanent occupation of government by centre parties may be distinguished from a tendency towards alternating and sometimes overlapping coalitions. Party systems are defined by their patterns of competition, and the particular pattern which weighs most heavily here is the competition for government.

If party systems are to be predictable, therefore, then it is at this level that the predictions are likely to apply. In other words, the more structured a pattern of competition, the more likely it is that the potential governing alternatives will not only be identifiable, but also reasonably familiar and predictable. Conversely, the more unstructured the system, the more likely it is that voters will vote in the dark, that is, and at least in this sense, without having any clear expectations as to the alternative governments on offer. Although the limited scope of this short chapter prevents a full elaboration of the guidelines for specifying these differences in practice, these are all clearly related to the historical patterns of government formation and alternation in any given system. Putting it very briefly, and summarizing a discussion sketched out in an earlier paper (Mair 1996, 89–97), a strong or closed structure of competition is one likely to be characterized by: (a) a tradition of wholesale alternation in government, whereby any changes which occur involve the complete defeat of the existing incumbent government and its replacement by a government composed of a party (or parties) which was (or were) previously in opposition; (b) a lack of innovation, whereby previously untested governing formulae (new combinations of parties, new single-party governments) rarely if ever emerge; and (c) limited access, whereby newly emerging and previously non-governing parties find it very difficult to break through the threshold of executive power. In unstructured systems, by contrast, turnover in government is likely to be exclusively partial in character, or at least to reflect a mix over time of partial and wholesale alternation; innovative formulae are likely to occur with relative frequency; and few obstacles are likely to stand in the way of the access to government of newly emerging parties.

Taking this distinction one step further, when a system is strongly institutionalized, as with the former case, then we can anticipate that voters will be choosing between both parties *and* likely governments; in the latter case, where the system is not strongly institutionalized – at least at the particular level associated with the competition for government – the voters will be largely choosing *only* between parties. In fact, this distinction is not very far removed from one originally drawn by Rokkan (1970, 93), who differentiated between systems of parties in which the protagonists are primarily representative or expressive in orientation as against those whose primary motivation is the competition for office: "In some countries elections have had the character of an effective choice among alternative teams of governors, in others they have simply served to express segmental loyalties and to ensure the right of each segment to *some* representation, even if only a single portfolio, in a coalition cabinet".

In the one case, in short, there is an established party *system*, with a clearly identifiable and predictable structure of competition for government; in the other, there is a "collection" of individual parties, which, at least as far as patterns of government formation are concerned, do not interact with one another in any systematic and recognizable pattern. If we now try to apply the notion of "freezing" or institutionalization to these contrasting cases, then we might conclude that in the former case it is the system that is frozen, or institutionalized, even when this survives some quite fundamental changes in the programmes, electorates, and even the identities of the parties involved in that system. Moreover, it is precisely this type of freezing, occurring at the level of the system qua system, which we can most easily take for granted. In the latter case, on the other hand, it is the individual parties themselves, if anything, which are frozen, while the "system", such as it is, remains malleable and unstructured. This sort of freezing cannot easily be accepted as a given, of course: individual parties are not so likely to have an in-built bias towards inertia.

Specifying the freezing process

This proposal echoes but also clarifies the different conceptions of freezing which were outlined briefly above. That is, it enables us not only to separate the notion of the freezing or party systems from that of the freezing of individual parties, but it also allows us to juxtapose the two into four distinct types of freezing process, as suggested in Figure 3.1, each of which may be associated with a particular country or countries. Type I in Figure 3.1 is the most extreme case of freezing, in which both the party system and the individual parties are strongly institutionalized. The United Kingdom in the post-war period offers the most appropriate example of this, while Italy during the "first republic" would also be a likely candidate for this category, as would post-war (West) Germany. France during the Fifth Republic, as well as good stretches of post-war Ireland and the twentieth-century United States would provide the most useful examples for Type II: all three countries in these periods are characterized by relatively fluid and adaptable parties, yet all three also managed to maintain quite stable party

	Parties: Frozen	Parties: Unfrozen
Party system: Frozen	I	II
Party system: Unfrozen	III	IV

Figure 3.1 Types of freezing.

systems over the longer term – whether this be the two-party system of the USA, the bi-polar two-bloc system of the Fifth Republic, or what might have been typified as the "Fianna Fáil versus the Rest" system in Ireland.

Examples of Type III are less frequently found, the most striking case being perhaps that of the Netherlands, especially during the hey-day of consociationalism, when the parties were deeply rooted within their respective pillars or *zuilen*. What is noteworthy in this case is not any instability as such in the party system qua system, but rather its lack of identity and coherence: almost all of the parties, including most newly formed alternatives, were coalitionable, as were almost all possible combinations of parties. Turnover in government was always partial in character, and no really stable structure of competition was in evidence. Finally, Type IV cases are those which are inchoate at the level of both the parties and the "system" itself. Contemporary Italy clearly verges on this category, if only perhaps temporarily, while, at least in the shorter term, virtually all of the new post-communist democracies could also still be grouped here.

The third conception of freezing identified above was the freezing of cleavages as such, and this can also be related to the distinctions summarized in Figure 3.1. Putting it very baldly, cleavages are primarily relevant to the party end of this process, but not to that of the party systems. In other words, while the freezing of parties may well derive from the prior or even related freezing of the cleavage structure, this need have no direct connection to the freezing of party systems qua systems. This point has already been clearly stated by Smith (1989, 351), who suggests that "as one set of factors shaping electoral alignments, the cleavage structure relates to the social make-up of support for individual parties – not the 'system', not that is if we follow a definition based on interaction. Social cleavages, and changes in them, obviously have important consequences for the system as a whole, but those effects are registered through the individual parties". The discussion of the freezing of cleavages therefore not only needs to be separated from the discussion of the freezing of parties, although a relationship between these might well be hypothesized and even proven, but it also must be separated even more emphatically from the discussion of the freezing of party systems. An indirect effect may certainly exist: cleavages can freeze parties, and the freezing of parties can be associated with the freezing of party systems (Type I in Figure 3.1); but there is no necessary or inevitable relationship between any of these three elements, and the very fact that we can conceive of a frozen party system in the context of relatively flexible and labile parties (Type II), as well as an "unfrozen" party system in the context of quite frozen, stable and, in the early Dutch case, highly cleavage-bound parties (Type III), simply serves to emphasize that different factors are at play.

Although it is beyond the scope of this short chapter to dwell at any length on the particular factors which might promote the freezing of party systems qua systems, and which may therefore enhance predictability in the patterns of competition for government, there are some indications that might be considered briefly. As is the case with explanations of the strengthening of partisan identities (Converse 1969), for example, the simple matter of time is obviously important here, since the cumulating daily practice of politics may lead both voters and party leaders to become used to thinking within a particular, and hence institutionalized, set of terms of reference. Time and experience also play a crucial role in what Schattschneider (1960, 69) has otherwise referred to as "the mobilization of bias", and if the range of alternatives has been limited in the past, then this is likely to encourage both observers and participants to believe that they may also be limited in the present. If, to cite the Irish example, previous governments have been formed only by either Fianna Fáil on its own, on the one hand, or a coalition of more or less all other parties, on the other hand, then it is unlikely that voters will be easily persuaded to think in terms of any alternative constellations. It is in this sense that a system becomes predictable and even taken for granted: the alternatives appear to be constrained. Moreover, since predictability – and hence systemness and freezing – may be associated with specific patterns of turnover in government, levels of innovation in governing formulae, and the degree of ease of access to executive power (see above), it will also depend on elite choices and elite political culture, with the leaders of the established parties being keen to promote the maintenance of those particular alternatives which have served to guarantee them success in the past (see Schattschneider 1960, 60–74).

The nature of the wider institutional structure within which the party system is located can also serve to enhance the freezing process. In the first place, this wider institutional context will help to define and hence to limit the potential alternatives which are seen to be available. Bi-polarity in the party system of the Fifth French Republic, for example, was clearly facilitated by the institution of the presidency, and by the way in which the parties learned to compete within the presidential arena. In Switzerland, the maintenance of the 'magic formula' has been partly made possible through the displacement of decision-making power to realm of the popular referendum. In the United States, the survival of the two-party system owes a great deal to the restrictive practices in electoral registration and ballot-paper access. In the United Kingdom, two-partism is helped significantly by the combination of a plurality system of elections and the pronounced party discipline in Westminster. Echoing Mary Douglas (1987, 99), who once asked "How can we possibly think of ourselves in society except by using the classifications established in our institutions?", it might therefore be suggested that it is the institutions in politics which provide us with the means and the language for thinking about political alternatives. This holds true for institutional structures in general, including the party system, as well as for those institutions which work *through* the party system. They help to impart a language of politics which, when learned, is likely to become taken for granted. This is certainly part of the bias towards inertia. As Lipset and Rokkan (1967a, 53) noted, "the voter does not just react to immediate issues but is caught in an historically given constellation of diffuse options for the system as a whole".

In addition, party system freezing will also be facilitated by the sheer stability of the wider institutional order within which it is nested. A party system, as Jepperson (1991, 151) notes of any given institution, "is less likely to be vulnerable to intervention if it is more embedded in a framework of [other] institutions". And if these other institutions are themselves relatively "frozen", then it follows that the party system is more likely to remain intact. Indeed, this was also one of the key findings from a broader study of the stabilization of electorates in twentieth-century Europe, in that the two crucial determinants of stability that were identified were those of cleavage strength, on the one hand, and institutional incentives, on the other, with institutional change tending to counteract cleavage influence and hence serving to encourage electoral flux, and with institutional persistence working together with cleavage strength to promote aggregate electoral stability (Bartolini and Mair 1990, 279–307). Much as stable institutional structures, including the party system, are therefore likely to lead to electoral stability, so too will persistence of the wider institutional framework within which the party system is embedded facilitate the stabilization or freezing of the party system itself. The predictability and taken-for-granted character of party systems is therefore also derived from the predictability of the wider institutional order within which they operate.

Conclusion

In their original and path-breaking analysis, Lipset and Rokkan chose not to devote much attention to the freezing process. In part, as I have suggested, this was because they were concerned with other matters, and most particularly with what came before the 1920s, rather than what followed on from there. In part also, however, it was because they could afford to take freezing more or less for granted, particularly when this notion was applicable to the world of party systems qua systems. In this sense, freezing is not really intriguing: it is what we should assume.

That said, and thirty years on, we can now come closer to identifying those factors which might serve to disturb systemic inertia, and which might disrupt the long-prevailing equilibria. Two of these factors in particular merit a brief mention. First, and perhaps most importantly, we can now see some indication of a weakening in the predictability associated with patterns of competition for government in many of the West European democracies: innovative governing formulae are now becoming much more prevalent than was the case thirty years ago; new parties are emerging and gaining access to office in ever larger numbers; and the increasing coalitionability of almost all competing parties has led to a major increase in the level of promiscuity in government formation. While it is difficult to specify the reasons for these recent changes – although parties may well be motivated by the increased attractiveness of short-term office benefits and by the decline in their programmatic distinctiveness – their reality is beyond major doubt. As the game of government formation becomes ever more open, therefore, the old certainties become eroded, as does the degree of predictability.

Second, we can also witness the potentially related willingness to consider and experiment with institutional reforms, although in practice, and within Western Europe, the significant moves in this direction are still limited largely to Italy, Belgium, and the United Kingdom. Nevertheless, should institutional reform figure more prominently and pervasively on the agenda of the West European polities, not least as a result of the increased Europeanization of domestic politics, then this might well disturb the otherwise stable context within which party systems are nested. Here too, then, predictability may be undermined.

In the end, however, what particularly needs to be underlined is that it is precisely these changes at these levels, that is, changes in the pattern of competition for government, as well as changes in the broader institutional setting, that are most likely to discourage us from taking continued freezing for granted. The weakening expression of decaying cleavage structures are certainly important, but if party systems are to become more fluid, then it is at the level of institutions that the key explanations are most likely to be found.

Acknowledgements

I would like to thank the participants in the Bergen Conference on "Party Systems and Voter Alignments: Thirty Years After", including Erik Allardt, Mattei Dogan, David Farrell, Piero Ignazi, Lauri Karvonen, Stein Kuhnle, Kay Lawson, Juan Linz, Birgitta Nedelmann and Pertti Pesonen, for their various comments on an earlier version of this chapter.

4 How bright was the future?

The study of parties, cleavages and voters in the age of the technological revolution

Lauri Karvonen
Jostein Ryssevik

Introduction

The establishment of the Committee of Political Sociology in 1959 was part of a larger process of activation and expansion in international social science. For the study of politics, this trend meant a number of profound improvements. It gave rise to a genuine cross-national exchange, bringing together sociologists and political scientists from around the globe long before "internationalization" became the pet word of national research councils and academic bureaucrats. It brought about a stronger emphasis on theory by linking empirical research with abstract models. It shifted the focus towards comparative empirical analysis, thus reducing the element of parochialism that had been all too evident in much of earlier research on government and political sociology.

The scholars who constituted the Committee during its early years were keenly interested in systematic empirical documentation. Their interests therefore also converged on questions related to empirical research methods and the quality and accessibility of data (Rokkan 1964a, 17–18). Consequently, many of the founding fathers and early members of the Committee were found at the forefront of the international "data archive movement" which gained prominence among social scientists in the 1960s. Many committee members were involved in this movement, but it is probably safe to say that Stein Rokkan was the leading activist in this field.

Today, an extensive network offering social science data services stands as a result of the work of these pioneers. To evaluate to what extent these institutional structures have lived up to expectations is a task that would be as demanding as it would be interesting.[1]

The present chapter has, however, a more limited aim. The focus is on the theme of *Party Systems and Voter Alignments*. Briefly, we wish to illustrate the change brought about by the increased availability of data and the development of computer-based research methods and technologies. Have the institutional growth and the technological revolution altered the landscape of the research on parties, voters and cleavages radically, or have they simply led to "more of the same" in this field? In a word, how bright was the future envisaged by those who pioneered the work on international archives and data services?

Although based on some systematic data, this chapter is not primarily a substantive empirical report either in terms of an independent research contribution on parties and voters or in terms of an analysis of "the state of the art" of party and election research. Rather, empirical data are used to illustrate how the development of data and archival services, the revolution in communications technology and new methods of data analysis and presentation have altered the *conditions* of research and researchers.

Given the focus of research as presented in the 1967 volume, where can researchers today turn for empirical evidence? What is the availability and comparability of relevant data? What do data cover in time and space and how reliable are they? In what form are they accessible, i.e. what must a researcher do in order to get hold of the data he needs? What are the main methods of analysis available for the use of these data today? How would a contemporary researcher present his findings, i.e. what changes in the techniques of presentation can be noted during the thirty-year period which has elapsed since the publication of *Party Systems and Voter Alignments*?

The growth of data services

It would certainly be incorrect to attribute the emergence and expansion of social and political science data services to a single cause or actor, such as the work of the International Social Science Council. In fact, many of the institutions that were to develop into specialized data services and archives existed in the form of research projects, data sets or sections at university departments years before the Council launched its long-term program for comparative cross-national research (Henrichsen 1992, 431–2).

Nevertheless, thanks to the work under the auspices of the Council – especially the Conferences on Data Archives held from 1963 on – the national efforts to develop specialized social science data services were firmly linked to a broader international effort to foster international research cooperation (Rokkan 1966b, 11–32). These early contacts at the international level helped develop existing national projects in a more cooperative spirit. Equally important, newly emerging institutions met an atmosphere where international collaboration was seen as something self-evident.

The first clear wave of institutional expansion occurred more or less parallel to the International Conferences on Data Archives. Starting with the creation in 1960 of the *Zentralarchiv* at the University of Cologne, the 1960s witnessed the establishment of a number of important institutions: ICPSR (Inter-university Consortium for Political and Social Research, Ann Arbor, Michigan, 1962), Steinmetz (Amsterdam, 1967) and UK Data

Archive (Essex, 1967) were among these. In the 1970s and 1980s, institutions were created in Scandinavia, Austria, France, Hungary and Australia; in the 1990s, Israel, New Zealand and South Africa have followed suit.

Today, nearly thirty organizations form an international network offering specialized social and political science data services. However, this is still largely a West European and North American phenomenon. Of the former Warsaw Pact countries, only Hungary has created a specialized social science data service (TARKI, The Social Research Information Center, 1985) with an established role in the international network. In the Third World proper the institutional development is still in its infancy.

As to the substance of the materials stored by these institutions, data on voters, elections and parties have always been very much at the core. Space only permits rather sweeping generalizations here. As for individual-level data the institutions endeavor to provide access to all major electoral surveys carried out in their country. The extent to which such surveys exist varies from country to country. In a fairly large number of cases, surveys have been carried out at regular intervals for several decades, with a set of core questions included.

As to aggregate electoral statistics, national-level data for the industrialized West are normally available via these institutions. In some cases, these data cover large parts of the post-war era, sometimes even earlier periods. For highlighting the development of structural cleavages underlying political change, most of these institutions can offer census data to match these electoral statistics. However – and this is a considerable limitation from the point of view of ecological studies – data on the *regional* level (constituencies, provinces, municipalities) is only available for a few countries. In fact, it seems that over time the emphasis has been less and less on aggregate data and increasingly on individual-level data.

Several of the institutions store data from different countries to help comparative research. Even more important, cross-national efforts have provided increasing amounts of relevant data for comparativists. The *Eurobarometer* has collected public opinion data in Europe for over two decades at regular intervals; many of the recurrent questions in these surveys are of central relevance to electoral research. Similarly, the three rounds of *European Value Study/World Value Study* have produced a wealth of empirical materials depicting attitudes and belief systems of importance to the student of parties, voters and cleavages. Moreover, the creation in 1989 of the International Committee for Research into Elections and Representative Democracy (ICORE) marks a new phase in international cooperation. The specific goal of this undertaking is to bring together academically directed national programs of electoral studies and to create an international data center in this field (NSD Katalog 1997, 112–19).

Naturally, the bulk of the data on parties and elections still concerns Western Europe, North America and the most advanced of the former British possessions. Efforts to expand the geographical scope of the data archives are taking place. The launching of the *Latinobarometer* is one important step during recent years. Still, it would seem that the creation of a permanent institutional structure for data collection, processing and services outside the advanced industrial part of the world is a necessary prerequisite for a genuine globalization of social science data supplies.

The rapid technological advances at both the producer's and the user's end have made it dramatically easier to gain access to and use social science data archives. Practically all data are now in machine-readable form. Information about existing files is abundant on the Internet as well as in the form of printed materials. Although some data services give preference to local users, most of the data relevant to the study of parties and voters are available to all researchers. Costs may be involved but they are rarely high. Researchers may gain access to foreign data services through their national institutions. To an increasing extent, data can also be retrieved directly over the net.

Again, technological advances as such would not be sufficient to enhance the accessibility of social science data. The creation of such international structures as the International Federation of Data Organizations for the Social Sciences (IFDO) and particularly the Council of European Social Science Data Archives (CESSDA, est. 1976) have been crucial in the coordination and integration of data bases and in making them universally available for research (Tanenbaum and Mochmann 1994, 499–511).

Indeed, the landscape for the empirically oriented researcher in the field of parties and elections has changed a great deal during the past two decades. Construction of data files from printed statistics as well work "out in the field" and in libraries can increasingly be replaced by perusals of data catalogues and the web pages of data services.

The following couple of illustrations give an idea of the possibilities available today. Figure 4.1 shows the web page of the WWW gateway to social science data archives around the world. In addition to access to the various European archives there are links to North American archives as well as to data services elsewhere in the world. Figure 4.2 contains the Query Form of the integrated on-line data catalogue for the CESSDA archives. This catalogue allows for data search across national archives specified according to substance, time periods and countries covered.

The next major step is a development project called NESSTAR (Networked Social Science Tools and Resources) and headed by the British, Norwegian and Danish data services. It will provide a common WWW gateway to social science data resources in Europe. Search for data across the holdings of all data archives will be made possible, as will on-line browsing of full-text data documentation, including references to publications and links to researchers. On-line data browsing, analysis and visualization will also be made available. Moreover, it will be possible to download data for further analysis at a local computer in the format desired by the local user.

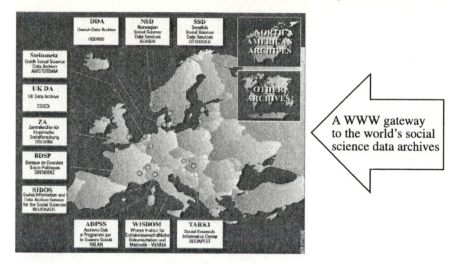

Figure 4.1 The European data archives web page.

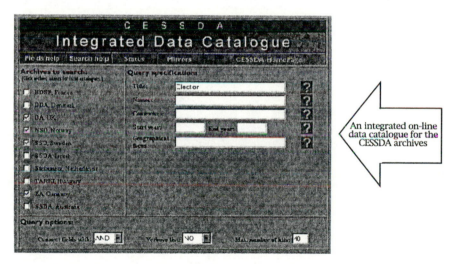

Figure 4.2 The Query Form of the CESSDA integrated data catalogue.

Patterns in party research during a quarter century

The conditions for empirical research on parties, voters and elections have changed, but has research itself changed accordingly? This is a complex problematique, and in fact one where causal links are virtually impossible to demonstrate. Even if it were possible to define a literature which is in some sense representative of this research at large, and even if clear patterns of change over time could be pinpointed, it would still be very difficult to attribute these changes convincingly to the kinds of developments that have been discussed in the previous sections of this chapter.

These caveats should be borne in mind when examining the data that will be presented in the following. The data do not pretend to present any sort of conclusive "proof" of an empirical change that has in fact taken place. They simply offer an illustration of possible changes in this research field.

Briefly, the data presented in this section originate from six political science journals in the period 1970–96. The 1970, 1980, 1990 and 1995 volumes of *American Political Science Review* (APSR) and *Political Studies* (PS) were examined. Two regional journals which started to appear in the 1970s – *European Journal of Political Research* (EJPR) and *Scandinavian Political Studies* (SPS) – were examined for 1980, 1990 and 1995. In addition, two more recent special journals in party and election research were included. The 1990 and 1995 volumes of *Electoral Studies* (ES) as well as the very latest (1996) volume of *Party Politics* were surveyed.

It goes without saying that no selection of sources can be entirely satisfactory given the vastness of the field. Moreover, we readily admit to a certain northwest European bias in our selection. Still, the journals selected represent fora of the kind where one would expect changes in mainstream political science research to be portrayed.

The first interesting question is how the relative share of *articles dealing with parties, voters and elections* has evolved over the years. The answer naturally depends on how this field is defined. The following criteria were applied in order to outline a group of *relevant articles*:

- only articles and research notes, but not, for instance, book reviews and short communications were included[2]
- only articles that contained a clear empirical contribution were included
- articles dealing with presidential and gubernatorial elections were omitted
- articles dealing with representative assemblies were included only if there was a clear emphasis on the "party aspect"

Naturally enough, there was only a handful of articles in the two special journals (ES and PP) which did not meet these criteria. Table 4.1 shows the share of relevant articles in the four general political science journals.

These data would seem to suggest that the share of relevant articles has, if anything, declined over time in APSR and PS (especially in the latter). Less than 10 percent of the articles have dealt with parties etc. in the 1990s. The two European regional journals present a different picture. Here, research on parties and elections is clearly a very central field indeed. Whether party researchers have consciously begun to favor journals

Table 4.1 Articles on parties, voters and elections in four political science journals, 1970–95

Journal	Year	Total no. of articles	Relevant articles	% Relevant articles
APSR	1970	52	8	15
APSR	1980	46	5	11
APSR	1990	52	4	8
APSR	1995	51	5	10
PS	1970	34	8	24
PS	1980	36	3	8
PS	1990	43	2	5
PS	1995	38	3	8
EJPR	1980	29	8	28
EJPR	1990	34	15	44
EJPR	1995	32	7	22
SPS	1980	19	5	26
SPS	1990	18	5	28
SPS	1995	13	6	46
N		497	84	av. 17

other than APSR and PS is difficult to say, but it is possible that the appearance of specialized journals has had such an effect. Also, the decline in the number of relevant articles in PS may partly be due to the appearance of EJPR as an alternative forum. All in all, therefore, one can not speak of any unambiguous trend in light of these data.

In addition to the 84 relevant articles from the four general political science journals, there were 23 articles in *Electoral Studies* (the 1990 and 1995 volumes) and 19 articles in the 1996 volume of *Party Politics* that were classified as relevant. The total number of articles examined in the following is, consequently, 126.

The following variables were used to analyze these articles:

- *Design*: is the study comparative (extensive treatment of two or more countries) or non-comparative?
- *Time perspective*: are the data cross-sectional or longitudinal?
- *Type of data*: are individual-level or aggregate data used, or does the study combine both types of data, or perhaps use some other type of data?
- *Number of variables/dimensions*
- *Illustrations*: do the studies use illustrations other than tables?
- *Use of social science data services*: have the data or parts of them been obtained from social science data archives or corresponding institutions?

Over time, the number of comparative articles increases thanks to the increase in the number of journals examined (see Table 4.2). The relative

Table 4.2 Comparative and non-comparative articles by journal and year
(percentages)

	Comparative	Non-comparative	N
Journal			
APSR	9	91	22
PS	13	87	16
EJPR	60	40	30
SPS	25	75	16
ES	13	87	23
PP	42	58	19
Year			
1970	13	87	16
1980	48	52	21
1990	29	71	38
1995/96	27	73	51
N	37 (29%)	89 (71%)	126

share of comparative articles in our sample peaked in 1980 thanks to the high share of comparative studies in EJPR.

APSR and PS are the least comparatively oriented journals in this field; ES also has a low share of comparative studies. SPS comes close to average, whereas PP seems to include a fair number of comparative articles. EJPR nevertheless stands out as the comparative journal *par excellence*. All in all, one can not speak of a linear growth in the share of comparative studies among the articles on parties etc. in these journals.

Most of the early studies used time series data. In 1980, there was a clear predominance of cross-sectional data; notably, seven of eight articles in EJPR utilized cross-sectional data. Since then, there has been an increasing predominance of time-series data in all journals (see Table 4.3).

As for the next three dimensions – type of data, number of variables/ dimensions, and use of illustrations – details can be found in Appendices 1–3.

Save for *Party Politics*, where aggregate-level data predominate, there is a relatively even distribution between individual- and aggregate-level data across journals. Towards the middle of the period studied, the share of studies using individual-level data increased clearly. This is largely attributable to the orientation of EJPR and SPS at that time. In the 1990s, there is possibly a reorientation towards aggregate data again. The "other" category contains articles dealing for instance with party strategies or programs and manifestos (see Appendix 1).

Over time, there has been a tendency to include an increasing number of variables or dimensions in the studies published in these journals. Again, however, the trend is not linear. Also, once again we find that EJPR has a

Table 4.3 Cross-sectional and longitudinal studies by journal and year (percentages)

	Cross-secional	Longitudinal	N
Journal			
APSR	36	64	22
PS	38	62	16
EJPR	37	63	30
SPS	31	69	16
ES	43	57	23
PP	16	84	19
Year			
1970	38	62	16
1980	76	24	21
1990	26	74	38
1995/96	22	78	51
N	43 (34 %)	83 (66 %)	126

special profile; studies published in this journal frequently employ a large number of variables and dimensions (Appendix 2).

The use of illustrations other than tables has increased in a relatively clear and linear fashion over the period studied. However, this increased frequency has not necessarily led to a qualitative change in the kinds of illustrations used. Simple graphs and diagrams seem to be the typical form of illustration throughout the period. Naturally, with computer-based graphics even simple illustrations attain a higher quality than a quarter of a century ago. Still, given the vast opportunities offered by available technology one is struck by the relatively limited range of illustrative techniques employed today. Most notably, only two studies contained *maps*. Incidentally, both of these appeared in *Electoral Studies* (in 1990 and 1995). This is rather striking given the relative frequency of aggregate-level analyses among the studies and the enormous advances in cartographic techniques during recent decades (Appendix 3).

Around 1970, the number of institutions offering specialized data services to social scientists was much smaller than during recent years (see Table 4.4). Therefore, the low percentage of articles reporting data obtained from such institutions comes as no surprise. All the more astonishing is the fact that the use of such services seems to have been much more frequent around 1980 than today. Merely 12 percent of the articles in 1995/96 report having used these services, while the figure for 1980 is 48 percent. Again, this is to some extent a result of the selection of journals for the various years. For 1995/96 the result is clearly affected by the fact that not a single one of the 19 articles in PP reported to have used these services. But a few other features should be noted as well. As for APSR,

Table 4.4 Use of social science data services by journal and year (percentages)

	Yes	No	N
Journal			
APSR	27	73	22
PS	6	94	16
EJPR	33	67	30
SPS	38	62	16
ES	17	83	23
PP	0	100	19
Year			
1970	6	94	16
1980	48	52	21
1990	26	74	38
1995/96	12	88	51
N	27 (21 %)	99 (79 %)	126

there was a clear peak in 1980 when four out of a total of five articles reported use; for 1970 the corresponding figures were 1/8, for 1990 1/4 and for 1995 0/5. Of the 16 relevant articles published in PS during the entire period, only one (in 1990) reported use. EJPR and SPS, the two regional journals in Europe, stood out as the most consistent users of social science data services. Throughout the period 1980–95, reported use ranged between 20 and 50 percent here.

Once again, limitations in the scope and representativeness of the sources used here should be emphasized. Any conclusions must be seen as tentative reflections rather than as established facts. Nevertheless, one possible interpretation is that the propensity to use social science data services – once these services began to be more generally available – was greater among established party researchers as long as these services were a new phenomenon. It is even possible that the availability of processed machine-readable data for a while had a certain steering effect on the choice of empirical foci. As the data services with the passage of time became part of the "normal routine" surrounding day-to-day research work, they perhaps lost some of this role as a beacon for new research.

Furthermore, the picture may reflect the more general development of party research itself. The first two decades comprised by our data can perhaps still be ascribed to the "Golden era" of party research, to the period which produced landmark volumes by, i.e., Duverger (1956), Key (1949), Epstein (1980), Lipset and Rokkan (1967), and Sartori (1976). This research directed a great deal of attention to cleavages, patterns of mobilization and organization, and the corresponding structuring of the vote and of party systems. The services of social science data institutions placed a great deal of weight on these kinds of data. When these services became more generally available in the course of the 1970s, research began to use them actively.

Later on, however, the focus of research has shifted towards the output side of politics, creating a need for new kinds of empirical evidence. Therefore, students of these aspects of parties and elections may have had less use for existing data files and archives.

This interpretation is an optimistic one in the sense that it sees the development and expansion of data services as a *research-driven* process. New research has to point the way for data services which will then follow up with data collection and services in due course.

Finally, it may well be that technological change may have reduced the *propensity to report* use of social science data services. In fact, in many cases a user may not even be *aware* of the fact that his is using a product or a service supplied by one of these institutions. Data obtained over the net may be stored by the user and later be used by others who perhaps view them as the property of their local department. The increasing availability of data processed by data services on CD-Rom may have a similar effect. For instance, American National Election Studies 1948–95 have been made available on CD-Rom by ICPSR, and National Election Studies by UK Data Archive in Essex.

After these reflections, some words about our findings are nevertheless in order. On average, studies which have utilized data services deviate rather clearly from the other articles. They clearly more often have a *comparative design* than do other studies. They use *cross-sectional data* much more frequently than the rest of the studies do. *Individual-level analyses* are also much more common here. Finally, these studies tend to employ a *larger number of variables* than other studies.

None of this is really surprising. It is quite evident that the cumbersome process of comparative survey analysis stands to gain a great deal from the services and international cooperation of the data institutions. Such studies naturally employ individual-level data which of course more often than not tends to be cross-sectional rather than longitudinal.

The results of this modest survey of political science journals can be summarized in the following way:

- The relative share of articles dealing with parties, voters and elections has tended to decline in *American Political Science Review* and in *Political Studies*. In the two European regional journals it remains high throughout the period examined. The rapid expansion in the field of scholarly journals, including the appearance of specialized journals for parties and elections, makes any definite conclusions about the relative status of this research field very difficult.
- Comparative studies were more common at the end than at the beginning of the period examined. However, the peak was reached in 1980

largely thanks to the strongly comparative orientation of *European Journal of Political Research*.

- Longitudinal studies have always been more common than cross-sectional ones. However, for 1980 an increase in cross-sectional studies was noted, again mainly because of EJPR.
- The number of studies using individual-level data is roughly equal to the number of aggregate-level analyses. EJPR and *Scandinavian Political Studies* are characterized by a fairly large share of individual-level analyses.
- Over time, studies using relatively large numbers of variables and dimensions have become more common; however, the trend is not entirely linear. Again, this is most pronounced for EJPR.
- Illustrations other than tables have become more common over time. However, the variation in the types of illustrations used is still surprisingly limited. Maps are next to absent in these texts.
- A little over one-fifth of all articles reported use of social science data services. Somewhat unexpectedly, the frequency was lower in 1995/96 than in 1980 and 1990.

The overall impression is certainly not one of dramatic change. To be sure, in absolute terms there are more party studies and party researchers in the mid-1990s than in 1970. Given the expansion of the academic research sector and the fora for publication, the relative status of party research is certainly not stronger today than three decades ago. There is more comparative research over time, there are more studies using a large number of indicators, and there is more survey material being used. However, given the availability of data and advanced methods for analysis and presentation today, an article from 1995 and one published in 1970 look surprisingly alike.

Problems and challenges

Ecological studies

> Even in a system of completely "nationalized" politics, therefore, any analysis of electoral behavior will be incomplete as long as it has not traced the effects of differences between communities and changes over time in the ranges and characteristics of the alternatives presented to the electorate.
>
> (Rokkan 1964b, 52)

The use of aggregate data has been common in the journals examined throughout the period. To a very large extent, however, the data used portray aggregate *national* statistics. Our impression is in fact that ecological studies based on data at the level of regions and municipalities are increasingly uncommon. If this observation is more generally valid, it should give cause for concern. Ecological data at this level offer avenues into the study of *contextual effects* in politics, while at the same time allowing for a longitudinal perspective. This is an important field of empirical research which can hardly be replaced by other types of analyses (Ranney 1964; Eulau 1969; Dogan and Rokkan 1967, 1974).

Above it was noted that this is an area where – despite some notable exceptions – the services of the social science data institutions are not particularly well-developed. Survey data are predominant, and aggregate statistics are usually at the national level. This stands in clear contrast to Rokkan's wish to create a network of "ecological files [that] would help to bridge the gap between archives of individual . . . and . . . aggregate data" (Brosveet *et al*. 1981, 44).

In fact, even the virtual absence of maps noted in our survey of the journals may be explicable in these terms. If intermediate-level analyses are uncommon and if data of this type are not readily available from the data institutions, then fewer scholars will need maps as an indispensable tool of presentation. As a consequence, the possibilities created by new techniques of cartographic presentation may be under-utilized.

It is an urgent task to secure continued research on parties and elections at the intermediate level. Proud traditions from Siegfried (1913), Goguel (1946), Heberle (1963), Rokkan, Dogan and many others must be carried further.

Having said this, we must mention some institutions that indeed have made important contributions to this field. The Norwegian Social Science Data Services (NSD) has created a Nordic Data Base on Regional Time Series (NDRT) at the level of counties; the time period covered is 1945–94. ADPSS in Milan has been particularly active in documentation at the municipal (communal) level. A comprehensive data base with the 8,000 Italian Communes as units gives great opportunities for a contextual analysis of Italian politics (NSD Katalog 1997). The Mannheim Centre for European Social Research (MZES) has a library specializing in European regional data. Moreover, this institution is currently constructing a regional data base for entire Europe based on electoral and census statistics since 1945.

Comparability

Rokkan's intention seems to have been for a supra-national archive, perhaps servicing a west European constituency. The archive movement however took a different development tack and concentrated on building national infrastructures.

In describing early German developments, for example, Scheuch and Brüning (1964) argued that most use would be within-cultural rather than cross-cultural. Thus when planning the Zentralarchiv in Cologne, although they hoped that the data held there would support cross-cultural analyses, they thought the most effective means of

ensuring this was to build strong domestic collections which could
then join in '. . . a system of co-operation between archives organized
according to language areas or countries'. This is in fact what has
happened.

(Tanenbaum and Mochmann 1994, 501;
cf. Brosveet *et al*. 1981, 45)

International impulses and models were central and international cooperation a necessity when the national structures for social science data
services started to emerge from the 1960s on. However, as the above
quotation shows, some of the transnational ambitions of Rokkan and other
founding fathers were not realized. This is a major explanation of the
problem of comparability which will be evident to anyone trying to utilize
national data sets within a comparative framework.

In the absence of a central authority (a "supra-national archive") many
things can go wrong from the point of view of the comparativist. In survey
studies, several practical problems are quite common. The formulation of
questions may vary. The order in which questions are put to the respondents may be different. Response alternatives may be defined differently;
varying response scales may be used. Sample designs may also vary.

These problems – the list could be made considerably longer – mean
that there are no guarantees for linguistic and conceptual equivalence
across national data sets. Standardization of data sets is often possible, but
it is usually a very cumbersome undertaking indeed.

For aggregate data, there are also some special problems. The oldest
data are often available in the form of printed materials only. Definitions of
concepts and units must frequently be accepted as such and can not be
altered ex post facto. Also, studies at the regional level will have to live with
the fact that "region" means widely varying things from country to country.

The picture is not, however, entirely gloomy. For one thing, there are
important data sets that have been constructed in a comparative fashion
from the beginning. The Eurobarometer and the European/World Value
Study have been mentioned previously. The Luxembourg Income Studies
Archive (LIS) and the project Beliefs in Government (BIG) are additional
examples of undertakings which have successfully created data sets comparable across nations. Based on experience gained through BIG, a large
European Social Survey is currently being planned.

Particularly important from the point of view of this chapter, the ICORE
project is now undertaking the demanding task of standardizing national
election studies. Finally, although in many ways still in its infancy, an
ambitious effort to build an integrated European socio-economic data base
has been proclaimed (Tanenbaum and Mochmann 1994).

None of the efforts so far have been unproblematic. Generally speaking,
the creation of comparative cross-national archives and data sets is
frightfully expensive and time-consuming. It is vital that the ground work is

done correctly and successfully. If that is the case, the updating of the data sets will be simpler and demand smaller resources. This calls for an active participation on the part of academic researchers as well as experts on computer technology starting with the very first phase of the cooperative efforts.

Information overflow?

Finally, a few words on a more speculative note. According to a cliché, the availability of information technology and the ensuing abundance of information tend to make people passive and reduce their receptivity. The question is whether the past three decades have not witnessed a similar development in the habits of social scientists as well. Faced with massive amounts of readily available data, scholars may react with resignation rather than an active interest.

In an underdeveloped and closed society researchers may have difficulty in obtaining any kind of information needed for research (1 in Figure 4.3). Before the revolution in information technology, researchers in open societies often had to construct their data bases "from scratch"; the relevance of data thus obtained was, however, often high (3). This was still largely the case when the work on the 1967 volume by Lipset and Rokkan was carried out.

From that situation, we have gradually moved towards (2) and (4). There is a wealth of empirical data of little interest to research available; at the same time, there is also a growing abundance of relevant material at our disposal.

To master this *embarras de richesse* so as to maximize the use of actually available relevant data is a major challenge to the research community, as well as to the specialized data institutions. Routines for specific data search resulting in exactly what the researcher is looking for (and nothing but that) must be developed. It is imperative that scholars not shy away from existing data bases simply because of the immensity of the result of each data search.

The fact that the data revolution has coincided with a rise of speculative, non-empirical or pseudo-empirical currents in social science is undeniably somewhat disconcerting.

		Access	
		Difficult	*Easy*
	Low	1.	2.
Relevance			
	High	3.	4.

Figure 4.3 Access to data and data relevance: four situations.

Concluding remarks

The scholars who produced *Party Systems and Voter Alignments* were active in an empirical field where the transition from agrarian to industrial society was very much the key issue. Lipset, Rokkan and several of the other scholars left a permanent mark in the study of the political aspects and effects of this transformation. The outstanding characteristic of these scholars was that their contribution was theoretical and empirical at the same time. They contributed heavily to theoretical development while simultaneously presenting systematic empirical data and endeavoring to improve the quality and accessibility of empirical evidence.

Today, party research faces the challenge presented by a new transition, that from an industrial to a post-industrial society. Unfortunately, the scholarly community is much more fragmented today. Much of the empirical research done is in the form of surveys, often miles away from those purportedly theoretical works that claim to present an understanding of post-industrial and post-modern reality. The representatives of the latter genre frequently look upon the data gathering empiricist with suspicion.

In order to come to grips with this challenge, research on parties and voters must again place more emphasis on the interplay between general theory and systematic comparative evidence. Between esoteric post-modernist theorizing and atomistic survey research, a gap needs to be filled with research once again stressing the importance of *contextual* factors for any change in political behavior and voter alignments. Great changes have taken place in the local and regional environments in which voters live their daily lives; migration and immigration, urban decay and renewal, mass unemployment and new forms of trade and production have left their mark on our physical and social milieux. Contextually based theory is in need of development, refinement and expansion to meet these challenges.

It is here perhaps more than anywhere else that we see a need of deepened cooperation among party researchers and a development of comparative social science data services.

Acknowledgments

We thank Ulf Lindström and Stein Kuhnle for their helpful comments in the course of our work on this chapter.

Notes

1. Among other things, given the fact that the Norwegian Social Science Data Services, one of Rokkan's many important institutional achievements, has recently celebrated its 25th anniversary.
2. For Electoral Studies, the quite numerous "Notes on Recent Elections" were omitted. These were mostly short reports based on basic electoral results from newspapers or official statistics, and they rarely had the character of independent research reports.

Appendices

Appendix 1 Use of different types of data by journal and year (percentages)

Journal	Indiv.	Aggr.	Combin.	Other	N
APSR	41	41	5	13	22
PS	38	44	6	12	16
EJPR	40	37	10	13	30
SPS	63	37	0	0	16
ES	39	52	9	0	23
PP	11	58	11	20	19
Year					
1970	25	56	13	6	16
1980	57	29	5	9	21
1990	39	45	8	8	38
1995/96	33	47	6	14	51
N	48 (38%)	56 (44%)	9 (7%)	13 (11%)	126

Appendix 2 Number of variables/dimensions by journal and year (percentages)

Journal	1–5	6–10	11–>	N
APSR	0	59	41	22
PS	50	31	19	16
EJPR	27	23	50	30
SPS	31	38	31	16
ES	39	48	13	23
PP	42	47	11	19
Year				
1970	25	63	12	16
1980	33	24	43	21
1990	27	39	34	38
1995/6	35	41	24	51
N	38 (30%)	51 (41%)	37 (29%)	126

Appendix 3 Use of illustrations other than tables by journal and year (percentages)

Journal	Yes	No	N
APSR	45	55	22
PS	6	94	16
EJPR	37	63	30
SPS	31	69	16
ES	35	65	23
PP	26	74	19
Year			
1970	19	81	16
1980	24	76	21
1990	34	66	38
1995/96	37	63	51
N	40 (32%)	86 (68%)	126

Revisited themes

5 Are cleavages frozen in the English-speaking democracies?

Richard S. Katz

It would be hard to overstate the influence of *Party Systems and Voter Alignments,* and particularly of the introductory chapter by Seymour Martin Lipset and Stein Rokkan (1967a), on the study of political parties and party systems, or on the study of electoral behaviour, in Europe. Thirty years after its publication, it is still widely cited, and indeed if one traces the provenance of other citations, there are not many works on the subject that are not directly or indirectly indebted to this essay. It has proven to be a seminal work in the fullest sense of the word.

The chapter is extraordinarily rich, moving from the high-level abstraction of Talcott Parsons' four-fold paradigm for the analysis of societal interchanges, to the concrete details of the historical experiences of individual countries. It can be read and re-read with profit from many perspectives, and for the insights and suggestions it offers on many important questions. Nonetheless, if there is one key contribution, one key finding or conjecture, that assures the essay its place on the required reading lists of students of parties and elections, it is the idea of "frozen cleavages".

At its simplest level, the frozen cleavages hypothesis is simply the observation that *"the party systems of the 1960s reflect, with few but significant exceptions, the cleavage structures of the 1920s . . . the party alternatives, and in remarkably many cases the party organizations, are older than the majorities of the national electorates."* (50, italics in original). This is accompanied by a tentative explanation of why cleavages would have become frozen by the 1920s:

> It is difficult to see any significant exceptions to the rule that the parties which were able to establish mass organizations and entrench themselves in the local government structures before the final drive to maximal mobilization have proved the most viable. The narrowing of the "support market" brought about through the growth of mass parties during this final thrust toward full-suffrage democracy clearly left very few openings for new movements.
>
> (51)

This suggestion that the "support market" was narrowed in the adoption of and adaptation to manhood suffrage can be read in two ways. On one hand, it may refer to the demand side of the market; with the integration of the working class into full citizenship, there were no large groups of potential supporters waiting to be mobilized by a new set of leaders. On the other hand, it may refer to the supply side, suggesting that with the integration of the working class, there were no further cleavages to be made politically relevant. If this second reading suggests that somehow history came to an end in the 1920s, the first suggests that partisan mobilization is a one way street, and that once integrated into the support structure of a political party, a citizen, and indeed his (or once the vote was extended to women, her) descendants are no longer available for competing or newly arising parties. Lipset and Rokkan, of course, recognize the unreason-ableness of these extreme interpretations, and in the concluding paragraphs of the chapter discuss processes that might lead the frozen cleavages to "melt".

That said, the greater part of the chapter is devoted to an account of how the party and cleavage systems found in Europe in the 1920s came to be the way they were. In large measure, this too is observational rather than theoretical. The process is hypothesized to have been driven by elite choices, but while those choices are assumed/asserted to be constrained by a number of logical or historically driven rules, within the broad bounds set by those constraints, there is no attempt to explain why one country's nation-builders or their opponents made one set of choices rather than another. Instead, Lipset and Rokkan "start out with a review of a variety of *logically possible* sources of strains and oppositions in social structures and . . . then proceed to an inventory of the *empirically extant examples of political expressions of each set of conflicts*" (6, italics in original). This approach finally leads to a list of eight potential types of cleavage alignments and an example for each of the closest fitting European party system.

In more detail, the model gives pride of place to two historical "revolu-tions", each of which potentially generated two cleavages. The first revolution is the National Revolution, spawning first a split between the centre and the periphery and then, especially in those countries that remained loyal to Rome at the time of the Reformation, between church and state. The second revolution is the Industrial Revolution, spawning first a split between land and industry and then between owners and workers. Both who allied with whom, and whether the split was in fact actualized, with regard to the first three of these potential cleavages varied among European countries, leading to the eight types; the fourth, the class cleavage, they have in common, and as just suggested, it is the actualization of this cleavage that is claimed to have "frozen" the party systems.

Frozen cleavages in the English-speaking democracies?

Attempting to assess the (continued) utility of this work – both the frozen cleavages hypothesis and the theoretical model/reasoning that underlies it

– for the English-speaking democracies forces one to answer several questions. One concerns the definition of the phrase "English-speaking democracies" itself. There is, of course, the problem of the numerous former British colonies in the Caribbean, not to mention the former colonies in Africa and Asia, especially India. Even among the longer established democracies, some might object to characterizing Canada as "English-speaking", and it is precisely those objections that suggest the political relevance of a language-based or language-reflected cultural cleavage. In this era of political correctness, the "English-speaking" status of the United States is also under dispute, and indeed is *sub judice*. Notwithstanding these problems, in this chapter I am simply adopting the definition of "English-speaking democracies" implicit in the three chapters on that subject in the original volume (Alford 1967; Robinson 1967; McKenzie and Silver 1967), that is the United Kingdom, Australia, Canada, New Zealand, and the United States, with the addition of the Republic of Ireland.

A more significant question is exactly what it is that is being assessed. First, there is the problem of defining cleavage. As Bartolini and Mair (1990, chap. 9) point out in their excellent analysis of the concept, "cleavage" properly refers to more than simple difference, but "has to be considered primarily as *a form of closure of social relationships*" (216). Nonetheless, in this chapter I will use the term merely to refer to social structural differences that might (or might not) be politically charged.

Second, is the frozen cleavages hypothesis to be taken primarily as a hypothesis about parties or primarily as a hypothesis about voters? Taking the class cleavage as the clearest and most relevant example, the politicization of this cleavage should be reflected in the existence of one or more working class parties. But what is a working class party? Is it a party with direct organizational ties to other working class organizations such as, in particular, trade unions, and presumably also with a left-leaning economic programme or ideology and making overtly class-based electoral appeals? Or is it a party that gets the overwhelming proportion of its electoral support from the working class? Or is it the party for which the overwhelming proportion of the working class votes? Presumably in a system in which a fully mobilized class cleavage was the only cleavage, and with parties organized in accord with the model of the mass party of integration (Duverger 1954), the three definitions all would be satisfied simultaneously. Failing this, however, they are likely to lead to different assessments.

This is especially so if one is looking over time to see whether the class cleavage has been frozen, rather than at a single time to see only if it is relevant. Does the freezing of the class cleavage require that the same working class party persist over time, or only that there continuously be at least one working class party? Does it require that the working class party receive a constant share of the vote? A constant share of the working class vote? Or does it require that (*mutatis mutandis* to allow for generational replacement) that the same individuals vote for the/a working class party election after election? Does the freezing hypothesis suggest that the same parties persist, or that the sociological differences that distinguish one party's supporters from those of the other parties remain the same, or simply that the electoral strengths of the parties remain relatively fixed?

A further question is what to make of the countries other than Britain, or perhaps other than Britain and Ireland. The Lipset and Rokkan model is very much an inductive exercise based on European history, looking back to the sixteenth century, if not before. With the exception of occasional references to Ireland in the elaboration of the history of Britain (the point of many of these being that in leaving the United Kingdom, Ireland took the basis of at least one possible cleavage with it), the full model is only elaborated among the English-speaking democracies for Britain (with the rump of Northern Ireland essentially ignored). One can consider that the other English-speaking countries partake in the British experience in truncated form, although one must then observe that often only one side of a cleavage crossed the ocean, or that in the case of the United States and Canada, as well as in the case of Ireland and the United Kingdom, there was a territorial sorting that put opposites sides of a cleavage in different countries.[1]

This suggests at least three possible senses in which the Lipset and Rokkan model can be "applied" to the rest of the English-speaking world. First, one can apply the European cleavage model and see what happens. On one hand, this may mean simply assuming that all these countries are like Britain, and looking for the consequences of a pre-mass-suffrage opposition between a nation-building elite cooperating with a "body of established landowners controlling a substantial share of the total primary production" and an alliance of periphery, dissident religious activists, and "urban commercial and industrial entrepreneurs controlling the advancing secondary sectors of the national economy" overlain with or supplanted by the opposition of labour and capital. In particular, this would mean looking, as the authors of the chapters on the English-speaking democracies in the original volume looked, virtually exclusively at the class cleavage, although one should note even here that while Britain is not regarded by Lipset and Rokkan as one of the "few but significant exceptions", to the observation that the party systems of the 1960s reflected the cleavage systems of the 1920s, the dominance of the class cleavage in British politics, and the strong two-party system that was in the 1960s regarded as particularly strong in Britain, were not established until the election of 1931. On the other hand, application of the European cleavage model to the not-British cases could mean returning to the full eightfold typology of basic political oppositions, to see into which, if any, type each of the cases appears to fall.

Second, one could apply the spirit of the model's emphasis on crises of nation-building to the particular histories of the countries in question. In this case, rather than focusing on alliances made at the time of the Reformation or French Revolution, one would look particularly at elite alliances at the time of such events as the American and Irish civil wars, the British conquest of French Canada and the Quebec Act, the formation of the Australian Commonwealth, or the Treaty of Waitangi. Moreover, a focus on the individual histories of the countries allows one more explicitly to address a major theoretical problem with an application of the frozen cleavages hypothesis to the United States, Australia, and New Zealand (and to a lesser extent to Canada as well). The relative timing of the formation of parties embodying the pre-working class cleavages and the advent of mass suffrage is central to the Lipset and Rokkan analysis. But in these countries, suffrage came much earlier relative to widespread industrializ- ation, in part because they were part of the periphery of the world economic system, and in part simply because mass suffrage came earlier than it did in the United Kingdom, or in most of the rest of Europe.

Although suffrage expansion occurred simultaneously in Ireland and Britain (because Ireland was still part of the United Kingdom), and the various income and property restrictions applied in the Canadian provinces were eliminated gradually during the period of 1888 to 1920, universal adult suffrage was introduced in Australia in 1902; universal manhood suffrage was introduced in New Zealand in 1879, with women given the vote in 1893; and although legal guarantees of black suffrage often were ignored through the 1960s, universal manhood suffrage was the rule in the United States from the 1860s, with women enfranchised between 1867 and 1920. While this aspect of the problem will not be pursued here, one possible implication is that if one were to test the frozen cleavages theory in these cases, the key date would not be the 1920s, but several decades earlier.

Finally, one could simply apply the model's most general orientation, that politics reflects social structure. Pursuing this line would mean looking, on the one hand, for organizational ties with, and appeals directed to, social structural groups, and on the other hand for clear differentiation between the voting behaviours of members of different social structural groups. If such ties between politics and social structure are found to persist over time, this could be taken as support for the hypothesis that socio- political cleavages are frozen, with the differences found defining induc- tively the politically relevant cleavages.

This full list of possibilities describes an agenda far too extensive for a single chapter. Nonetheless, by specifying alternative approaches and under- standings, I hope to make clear the limitations of what will be presented here. In particular, this chapter, like the chapters on the English-speaking democracies in the original volume, will concentrate primarily on electoral choice, and draws its data primarily from national election surveys. The first question to be addressed is that of the persistence, and indeed the original status, of the class cleavage as the main organizing principle of politics. I then look at the possible persistence or re-emergence of other social structural cleavages in the spirit of the Lipset and Rokkan analysis.

Revisiting the class cleavage in the English-speaking democracies

In adapting the work that he had published earlier (Alford 1963) in *Party and Society*, Alford juxtaposed the model of class voting against the view "that parties need not be representatives of social classes. [And indeed] need not represent . . . set of interests consistently, but need only be alternative sets of leaders . . ." (67). This view, which Alford associated with Joseph Schumpeter, is also an integral part of Kirchheimer's (1966) ideal type of the "catch-all party", advanced in a book published the year before *Party Systems and Voter Alignments*. As the existence of Christian parties, agrarian parties, etc. in many parts of Europe attests, it is not self-evident that the alternative to *no* ties between social groups and parties is precisely a tie between social classes and party, although that such a tie will at least be one among other connections between social structure and party certainly is implicit in Lipset and Rokkan's "fourth step" of their developmental model.

This said, the concentration on the class cleavage in the original chapters appears to have a two-fold justification. The first was the claim that a division of interest between the "haves" and the "have-nots" not only is universal, but is universally the basis of conflict in the political arena. That this naturally translates into conflict between manual workers and others appears to have been taken for granted.

The second justification was the apparent nature of the party systems of the Anglo-American democracies. In particular, that "Each of the Anglo-American countries tends toward a two-party system, although three of the four have more than two parties actually running candidates . . ." and that "Their political parties fall along the classic Left–Right continuum" (72) furthered the idea that politics would be characterized by one cleavage, and that it would be social class. And this then could be reinforced by the existence of political parties with explicit ties to organized labor in the United Kingdom, Australia, and New Zealand (and similarly in Ireland, although it was not considered in the original chapters), plus the less formal ties between the post-New Deal Democrats and organized labor in the United States.

Two-party/left–right politics

The first question one might ask is how this two party-ism has persisted, and the first part of an answer is to observe that one has to make several significant concessions in the definition of two-party politics even to make it fit in the 1950s. The "two-party" Australian system was then, and continues to be now, bipolar, but one of the poles is a semi-permanent coalition of two parties, which "is the closest relationship that the parties have [and one] which they achieve with constant strains, and then in only three states and the national parliament" (Jaensch 1994, 7). Similarly, Ireland only approximates bipolarity if one abandons the centrality of a class cleavage and defines the two poles as Fianna Fáil on one side and either everyone else (which is then tautologically but uninterestingly bipolar) or Fine Gael plus Labour on the other. Finally, as will be suggested below, while the relative dominance of Liberal and Conservative parties as the only two potential governing parties in Canada was clear in the 1950s and 1960s (albeit one of the parties actually won a majority in the House of Commons in only three of the seven general elections of those two decades), that they represented opposite sides of any kind of class cleavage was far from clear.

With these qualifications, the fit of a "two-party" characterization of politics accorded reasonably well with reality in the 1950s in four of the six Anglo-American democracies, as shown in Table 5.1. This table describes the party system of each country in two ways, each based on the average of the general elections (presidential in the United States; lower house of the national parliament in the other countries) held in each decade. The first measure is the percentage of the popular vote won by the two major parties (three in Australia and Ireland), the other is the "effective number of parties" (E) (Taagepera and Shugart 1989, 78–80). While Australia, New Zealand, Britain and the United States show at least one of over 90 per cent of the vote going to the dominant competitors or an effective number of parties under 2.5, in Canada and Ireland, the dominant competitors won no more than 85 per cent of the vote in the average election and the average effective number of parties was closer to three than to two.

More important than the fit of the two-party characterization at the beginning of the period, however, is the change over time. Although only in the Canadian case (and that based largely on the 1993 election) would the term "collapse" seem appropriate, in every one of the six countries the share of the vote received by the parties that defined the "two-party" system of the 1950s and 1960s has declined substantially, while the effective number of parties has increased. Indeed, looking only at the average effective number of parties for the 1990s would lead one to characterize all of these countries, with some possible hesitancy in the case of the United States, as three- or four-party systems. While it is too early to tell whether this trend will continue – the American figures are influenced by the votes for Ross Perot's Reform Party, which was significantly weaker in 1996 than in 1992; the British figures by the rise of the Liberal Democrats and their predecessors, which now appear to be declining; the Canadian figures by the collapse of the Conservatives, which may or may not be reversed in future elections[2] – both the length of time during which the trend has persisted, and the coincidence of events which suggests that the particular

Table 5.1 Major party vote percentage and effective number of parties (E) by decade

	1950s			1960s			1970s			1980s			1990–1996		
	Vote	E	n	Vote	E	n	Vote	E	n	Vote	E	n	Vote	E	n
Australia (Labor and Liberal+National)	94.1	2.7	4	90.5	3	4	92.3	2.8	4	92.4	2.8	4	86.2	3.1	3
Canada (Liberal and Conservative)	82.3	2.8	3	74.6	3	4	76	3.1	3	76.6	2.9	3	57.3	3.9	1
Ireland (Labour, Fine Gael and Fianna Fáil)	85	3.3	3	93.8	3	3	93.9	2.8	2	88	3	5	82.9	3.9	1
New Zealand (Labour and National)	93.4	2.3	3	89.8	3	4	85.8	2.6	3	82.9	2.7	3	71.7[a]	3.6[b]	3
United Kingdom (Labour and Conservative)	93.9	2.3	4	88.7	3	3	80.1	2.9	4	71.6	3.1	2	76.8	3	2
United States (Democrat and Republican)	99.5	2	2	95	2	3	98.2	2	2	96.7	2.1	3	85	2.6	2

Source: Mackie and Rose, 1991; European Journal of Political Research: Political Data Yearbook, various issues.
Notes: [a]76.4 if the 1996 election, held under the Mixed Member Proportional electoral system is eliminated.
[b]3.1 if the 1996 election, held under the Mixed Member Proportional electoral system is eliminated.

events in the various countries may be responses to a general phenomenon rather than idiosyncratic coincidence, indicate that there has been a real and substantial change in the party systems of all six countries.

Before interpreting this change as evidence that social cleavage/party alignments frozen in the 1920s have started coming unstuck in the period since the 1950s, two problems concerning the degree to which those alignments were frozen even in the 1950s must be raised. First, as already noted, the establishment of the working class/Labour Party versus middle class/ Conservative Party conflict as the central theme of British politics only found electoral reflection after 1931. If one replicates the analysis in Table 5.1 for the first two elections of the 1930s, it appears that the two-party model fit better in the 1950s than it did two decades earlier. Moreover, as will be indicated below, there was not simply an overlaying of class on to the pre-existing system, with the ties between party and social grouping within the "bourgeois" block remaining intact; instead, the social basis of the Liberal party and its successors is in many respects the opposite of that suggested by the cleavage structures of the 1920s. In this case, even if the party persisted, it is not clear that the cleavages which it presumably was instrumental in freezing persisted.

As the phrase "and its successors" indicates, however, there is also a problem of organizational continuity. Lipset and Rokkan talk not only about "working class parties" or "farmers' parties", but about specific organizations that had managed to "entrench themselves". The replacement of the Liberal Party by the Liberal Democrats involved far more than a simple change of name, and would raise the question of whether it confirms or disconfirms the frozen cleavages hypothesis even if its social basis had not changed. Similarly (and more significantly, given its greater electoral weight), one can question whether Fine Gael in Ireland is simply a renamed Cumann na nGaedheal. Even more, the New Zealand National Party only was formed in 1938, and the Australian Liberal Party did not exist until 1946. Thus the second problem is the possibility that a cleavage (and in the Australian and New Zealand cases, party historians are agreed that it was class, or at least pro- versus anti-Labour) remains significant, but that the parties change.

This problem of organization continuity also bears on another question raised by the original chapters. This concerns the organizational ties between the parties of the left and the trade union movement, and the commitment of those parties to a generally left wing, or socialist, ideology. There can be no doubt that these have weakened in three of the four countries with labour parties, and doubt is raised in the fourth (Ireland) only by the fact that these ties were so weak in the first place. The best known example is the organizational reform of the British Labour Party, including reduced voting power for the trade unions in party bodies and the elimination of Clause Four from the party's constitution, that have been in progress throughout the 1990s (Webb 1992, 33–5; 1994, 114–15). Similar developments, in which the parliamentary party claims increased independence from its extra-parliamentary supporters, and the trade union movement in particular, and then adopts economic policies more traditionally associated with the right, have also been taking place in Australia and New Zealand (see Beilharz 1994, Mulgan 1994, 212, 236–9). In the United States, the tie between labour and the Democratic party reached its nadir in 1972, when the AFL-CIO declined to endorse the Democratic candidate and the Teamsters Union went so far as to endorse the Republican, but the retreat of the Democratic party from traditional left policies has continued.

From both these perspectives – aggregate party strength and organizational ties – the evidence so far suggests that however well the frozen cleavages hypothesis fit these cases in the 1950s, it fits them less well today.

Stability and volatility

The idea of frozen cleavages has often been associated with expectations regarding electoral volatility, with "high or growing levels of total volatility . . . taken as indicators of a decline in the hold of traditional cleavages and party alignments" (Bartolini and Mair 1990, 35–6). What has been the pattern in the English-speaking democracies?

As Bartolini and Mair go on to say, the equation of volatility and cleavage strength is problematic, both because of the possibility of volatility among parties all of which are on the same side of a cleavage, and because cleavage strength is not the only contributor to total volatility. The second of these caveats can only remain as a warning against reading too much into the data to be presented next; the first can be dealt with here, as it was in their book, by looking at block volatility (BV), the magnitude of changes in the total level of voting for all parties on one side of a cleavage versus the other, as well as at total volatility (TV). Moreover, with the narrower temporal and spatial foci of this chapter in comparison to the Bartolini and Mair book, it is possible to look at individual level shifts in vote choice between elections directly on the basis of survey data, rather than relying solely on inferences from aggregate electoral returns.

Table 5.2 shows the total and block volatilities for each election between 1950 and 1996 based on national vote totals, and where data allow based on survey research as well.[3] For the aggregate data, TV is one-half the sum of the absolute differences between the vote percentage a party received in the relevant election and the vote percentage it received in the previous election; when party coalitions presented candidates jointly, the comparison was to the sum of the votes received by the allied parties when they ran candidates separately; votes cast for "independents" and "others" were counted as if they had been cast for parties of those names. BV repeats the exercise, but treating all parties on the left (as identified in the table) as if they were a single party, and all other parties as if they were its only competitor. The survey based figures report the proportion of respondents

Table 5.2 Total and block volatilities

Australia

Year	Aggregate data TV	BV	Survey data TV	BV
1951	8.35	6.0	0.0	0.0
1954	10.25	9.6		
1955	6.3	5.4		
1958	5.7	2.5		
1961	5.2	5.1		
1963	4.1	2.3		
1966	5.8	5.7		
1969	8.2	6.7	21.6	14.2
1972	5.0	2.6		
1974	5.2	0.4		
1975	9.5	6.4		
1977	9.6	3.1		
1980	5.8	5.4		
1983	4.8	4.4		
1984	2.4	2.1	13.9	12.2
1987	2.5	1.7	17.7	12.8
1990	9.6	6.4	28.4	26.3
1993	8.9	5.5	23.3	23.6
1996	7.1	6.2	20.2	14.3

Canada

Year	Aggregate data TV	BV	Survey data TV	BV
1953	3.5	2.3 / 1.6	0.0	0.0
1957	9.5	9.5 / 1.6		
1958	14.7	8.5 / 7.6		
1962	16.7	7.6 / 4.0		
1963	4.8	4.1 / 4.0		
1965	10.2	3.3 / 4.8	15.8	10.7 / 6.4
1968	5.4	4.4 / 0.9	20.1	14.8 / 6.8
1972	11.4	6.3 / 0.7	37.9	28.3 / 10.5
1974	5.1	2.4 / 2.3	21.7	17.3 / 7.7
1979	3.6	0.6 / 2.5		
1980	6.6	6.1 / 1.9		
1984	19.0	17.3 / 1.0	30.8	25.3 / 8.0
1988	8.9	5.5 / 1.6	24.7	19.3 / 11.6
1993	42.3	4.2 / 13.6	53.4	46.0 / 12.0

Ireland

Year	Aggregate data TV	BV	Survey data TV	BV
1951	11.8	0.1		
1954	7.1	0.7		
1957	11.2	3.0		
1961	8.1	2.5		
1965	9.7	3.8		
1969	2.8	1.6		
1973	3.4	2.2		
1977	7.5	1.5		
1981	8.9	1.3		
1982	4.3	0.7		
1982	3.9	1.4		
1987	16.2	2.5		
1989	7.8	4.3		
1992	12.9	8.3		

New Zealand

Year	Aggregate data TV	BV	Survey data TV	BV
1953	2.2	1.7		
1954	11.5	1.6		
1957	4.2	4.2		
1960	4.9	4.8		
1963	1.2	0.4		
1966	6.7	2.5		
1969	5.6	2.7		
1972	6.2	4.2	1.3	1.3
1975	10.1	8.8	9.9	7.6
1978	10.6	0.8		
1981	5.1	1.4	19.1	14.0
1984	16.4	4.0		
1987	14.0	5.0	30.1	22.7
1990	17.2	12.9	25.4	17.4
1993	13.9	0.4	35.9	22.1
1996[a]	16.4	6.4		

United Kingdom

Year	Aggregate data TV	BV	Survey data TV	BV
1950	3.4	2.0		
1951	7.3	2.5		
1955	2.4	2.4		
1959	3.4	2.6		
1964	6.0	0.4	14.7	9.3
1966	4.3	3.9	10.1	7.0
1970	6.0	5.0	11.7	8.7
1974	15.0	5.9	21.3	13.1
1974	3.4	2.1	15.3	8.1
1979	8.7	2.4	19.1	12.9
1983	12.0	9.4	23.5	15.0
1987	3.6	3.2	19.6	8.5
1992	5.6	41	17.2	7.8

United States

Year	Aggregate data TV	BV	Survey data TV	BV
1952	10.2	5.5	20.4	19.8
1956	2.7	2.3	14.5	
1960	7.9	7.7	18.6	
1964	11.4	11.4	18.0	
1968	18.5	4.9	21.9	12.2
1972	17.3	17.3	27.3	25.2
1976	14.1	11.3	22.8	21.9
1980	10.2	9.3	27.6	
1984	8.1	0.4		
1988	5.6	5.0	13.9	
1992	19.1	2.7	33.8	20.9
1996	10.9	6.3		

Note: [a] There was a change of electoral system from FPTP to MMP.

reporting a party vote (or intended party vote, as indicated in the table) for the current election *and* recalling a party vote in the previous election who changed parties (TV) or who changed from a party on one side of the left–right divide to a party on the other (BV).

Looking first at the volatility measures based on aggregate returns, one is immediately struck by the fact that there is no simple trend observable. Rather, in each country the pattern in TV has been one of flurries of high volatility alternating with periods in which aggregate election returns are more stable. Nonetheless, it does appear to be the case that in each country both the peaks and the valleys are a bit higher in the 1980s and 1990s than they were in the late 1950s and 1960s. The same is true for BV except in the United States; because Perot was classified as a "non-left" candidate, BV did not soar along with TV in 1992. Overall, while these data are inconsistent with a deeply frozen cleavage system, except for New Zealand they show only weak evidence of a "melting" relative to the departure from a rigid class-based cleavage system that was already observable in the 1950s.

This picture is both qualified and modified in important ways when the survey-based figures are considered. There are two qualifications. First, the survey data show levels of volatility that are dramatically higher than suggested by a naive reading of the aggregate data, and indeed because these figures are based on recall of previous vote, which is likely to be biased in favour of consistency with current vote (intention), and because they exclude those who move in and out of the electorate (either because of coming of age/death or simple failure to vote in one of the two elections), the real level of individual volatility is likely to be significantly higher still. Second, although there is an obvious correlation between volatility measured at the aggregate and individual levels, the correlation is far from perfect. While the correlation between the two series of TV for Australia is over 0.89, for the United States it is only 0.78, for New Zealand, 0.69, and for the UK, 0.67; the correlations for BV are uniformly lower, and indeed for New Zealand the correlation is negative. Thus, although the aggregate figures may indicate something important, and while the series may be comparable over time and possibly across space as well, one must be circumspect in drawing conclusions about individual-level behaviour from these data.

The modification is that with the individual-level data the evidence of increasing volatility is much clearer, especially with regard to TV. The electorates of each of the countries appear to be increasingly composed of individuals who change parties between one election and the next, and indeed are increasingly composed of individuals who shift their support from one side to the other of the class-electoral cleavage. Again, if there was a frozen class/party cleavage in the 1950s, it appears to be less frozen in the 1990s.

Class voting

The major concern of the chapters on the Anglo-American democracies in the original volume was to assess and account for the levels of class voting in the five countries considered. The measure used was the Alford index of class voting (A), that is the percentage of the working class reporting voting for a party of the left minus the percentage of the middle and upper classes reporting voting for a party of the left. Although there was some variation from survey to survey in the level of class voting found within each country, there was very little overlap of the distributions between countries; the lowest value observed for Britain was only two points below the highest value observed for Australia, the lowest Australian value was higher than the highest American value, and the lowest American value was only four points below the highest Canadian value. The average score reported for these countries, plus a marginally comparable score for New Zealand reported by Alford elsewhere (1963, 105), are reproduced in the first data column of Table 5.3.

The rest of Table 5.3 reports the index of class voting based on surveys from the 1960s through the 1990s. These figures differ from those computed by Alford in that (with the exceptions specified in the footnotes) they are based on subjective class identification rather than on occupational class. This facilitated the construction of the table in several ways: it made classification of occupations between manual and non-manual unnecessary; it obviated the problem of classifying respondents from households with more than one employed person; it suggests, at least on the surface, a comparable classification across countries and over time. At the same time, it must be recognized that subjective class identification is not identical to occupational class, and that much of the theory upon which a focus on social class often is based draws specifically on the employment conditions of industrial workers – regardless of whether their more general life circumstances lead them to identify themselves as members of an everexpanding middle class.

A second significant difference that should be noted between my analysis and that of Alford relates to the classification of parties, particularly in the Australian and Canadian cases. The Australian problem concerns Democratic Labor, which Alford classifies as a potential working class party. While this party was a break-away from the Australian Labor Party, and in that sense might be regarded as still on the working-class side of any class cleavage, its primary *raison d'être* was to keep the ALP out of office, and in that more significant sense it is inappropriate to regard votes for the ALP and for the DLP as equally supportive of a potential government of the left. Accordingly, the Australian figures reported after the first data column of Table 5.3 (as were the block volatility figures in Table 5.2) are based on classification of the DLP with the parties of the right.[4] For Canada, Alford divided the political spectrum between the Liberals plus the NDP on the

Table 5.3 Index of class voting (A)

	Alford	1950s Year	1950s A	1960s Year	1960s A	1970s Year	1970s A	1980s Year	1980s A	1990s Year	1990s A
Australia (Labor, Communist, Lang Labor v. others)[a]	33									2.0e+11	20.5 / 21.1
Canada (Liberal & NDP v. others)[b]	8			2e+07	-6.3 / -2.0			2e+07	4.6 / 8.0[b]	2.0e+07	1.7 / -2.1
Canada (NDP v. others)	8			2e+07	3.1 / 8.9	3e+07	1.2 / 4.4	2e+07	10.7 / 8.4	2.0e+07	7.1 / 0.1
Ireland (Labour, Workers Party, Democratic Left v. others)[c]				1969[d]	20.6	1973 / 1977 / 1977[c]	11.6 / 14.6 / 8.8	2e+19	21.1 / 13.7 / 11.7 / 17.2 / 14.6	1992	14.9
New Zealand[e] (Labour, NewLabour, Communist v. others)	[40][f]			1963	[30]	1972[g] / 1975	38.3 / 19.6 / [19]	1981 / 1984 / 1987[h]	24.4 / [16] / [15] / 1.2 / [9]	2.0e+07	18.3 / [5] / 24.2 / [10]
United Kingdom (Labour, Communist v. others)	40			1964	43.1	1970 / 1974[f] / 1974[o]	27.9 / 31.0 / 30.9 / 31.0	2E+07	24.3 / 24.0	1992	29.3
United States (Democrat v. others)	16	2e+07	25.0 / 12.6	2e+11	19.8 / 22.1 / 9.5	2e+07	3.2 / 20.4	2e+11	17.6 / 11.6 / 16.1	1992	5

Notes: [a]Excludes the DLP on the grounds that "Its original raison d'être was to keep Labor out of office." [Jaenisch 1994, 34]. If it is included with Labor, the Alford index in 1969 is 30.
[b]Occupational class and expected vote.
[c]1969–87 figures based on occupational class.
[d]Based on Gallup survey of April 1969 as reported in Manning (1972, 114).
[e]Figures in brackets based on manual v. nonmanual occupation and are from Vowles et al. (1995, 21).
[f]Based on the single constituency of Dunedin Central.
[g]Sample (n=106) from Lyttelton Electoral District only.
[h]Sample restricted to 5 urban regions.

left and the Conservatives plus Social Credit on the right. While not disputing that the Liberals may have been in some reasonable sense to the left of the Conservatives, to translate that into an expectation that the Liberals would be the party of the working class does considerable violence to Canadian political history (Jackson *et al*. 1986, 436–44). That this is so is reflected in the fact that the Canadian scores reported by Alford are not just very low, but indeed sometimes are negative, indicating that a higher proportion of middle-class than of working-class voters supported the parties of the so called left. While the values of A computed on the basis of this classification are reported in Table 5.3 for the sake of comparability, my attention will focus primarily on values of A computed on the (itself questionable) assumption that only the NDP should be classified as a potential party-of-the-working-class in Canada.[5]

This reclassification of the Canadian parties raises one more point. While distinctive voting patterns are a necessary condition for the importance of the class (or any other) cleavage, they are sufficient only to one sense of "importance". In particular, if there is a relatively small party whose electoral support is drawn very disproportionately from the working class, the result will be a moderately high index of class voting (the working class far more likely than the middle class, although still not terribly likely, to vote for that party) and a party whose support is heavily working class (a working class party), but at the same time there will not be a party of the working class (because the majority of the working class vote for other parties) and a system in which the class cleavage is relatively unimportant (because the working class party, by virtue of its small size, is itself not very influential). This is particularly significant in interpreting the Irish data, for which the moderate (by the evolving standard of the 1980s and 1990s) values of A reflect the highly working class composition of the Irish Labour Party's electoral support, notwithstanding that upwards of three out of every four working class voters support a non-working class party.

Bearing these points in mind, the trend evident in Table 5.3 is striking. In each of the countries considered, class voting has declined substantially over the decades from the 1950s to the 1990s. In Australia and New Zealand, the levels of class voting are about half of what they were at the beginning of the period, indeed rather less than that if one focuses on occupational class. In the United States, the 1992 figure suggests the virtual disappearance of class as a basis for party choice; although it is likely that 1992 will prove to have been an aberration, however, there is no reason to suppose that the index of class voting will rebound even close to what it was in 1952, 1960, or 1964. Even in Britain, Peter Pulzer's (1975, 102) often cited observation that "Class is the basis of British party politics; all else is embellishment and detail" no longer rings so true – and although fully comparable data are not yet available, data from exit polls suggest that the level of class voting in 1997 was substantially below that shown for the three previous elections.[6] Overall, if the Lipset and Rokkan frozen cleavages hypothesis as applied to the English-speaking democracies translates into a prediction of bipolarity and class-based voting, then it clearly holds significantly less well in the 1990s than it did in the 1950s and 1960s.

Although a thorough explanation of the decline in class voting is beyond the scope of this chapter, which is instead limited to an assessment of the degree to which the Lipset and Rokkan frozen cleavages hypothesis can be sustained in the English-speaking democracies at the end of the twentieth century, several potential explanations can be listed briefly.

One possible explanation is the decline in the size of the working class itself. For example, between the 1952 and 1992 American National Election Studies, there was a decline of roughly 10 per cent in the proportion of respondents identifying themselves as "working class". The industrial working class is declining as manufacturing jobs are shipped off-shore or replaced by automata. The proportion of the workforce that is unionized is declining in many countries (Western 1993). While none of this means that the remaining working class need be less solid in its partisan choice – indeed, one might expect a tendency of a beleaguered rump to "circle the wagons" – it suggests that a strategy of appealing directly to the working class might prove decreasingly attractive to party leaders.

A related possibility stems from the fact that the working class not only is declining in magnitude, but also in distinctiveness. The progressive opening of educational opportunities, the success of programs of social insurance, the rise of the mass media, the improved living conditions of workers all mean that the life conditions and life chances of members of the working class are less different from those of the middle class than they once were. One might, therefore, expect lesser feelings of class solidarity, and that class would play a lesser role in the self-identity of citizens.

A third potential reason for the decline of class voting is the abandonment of traditional left-wing policies by the parties nominally of the working class. Given the period of "Rogernomics" in New Zealand; the "Accord" between the Australian Labor Party and the Australian Council of Trade Unions; the emphasis by President Clinton on a "middle class tax cut", bringing the Democratic party into the "center" and "ending welfare as we know it"; the policy shifts in the British Labour party advanced by John Smith, and even more vigorously by Tony Blair, it becomes less obvious why the working class should support the parties of the so-called left. Indeed, the 1997 British Labour Party manifesto mentions conflict between the middle and working classes only once, and that to declare the conflict "of no relevance whatsoever to the modern world".

And, of course, a fourth possibility is that the class cleavage is becoming less important because something else is taking its place. On one hand, it could be that voters are, in Rose and McAllister's (1986) phrase, beginning to choose, that voters increasingly think of themselves as autonomous individuals rather than primarily as members of social groupings, and that the influence of social position on political behaviour is mediated by an increasingly complex and individually variegated set of attitudes, opinions, and preferences. On the other hand, the class cleavage could be losing its importance because other social cleavages are asserting or reasserting themselves.

Other frozen cleavages?

According to the analysis of Lipset and Rokkan, the British party system before the rise of the class cleavage and the Labour party was characterized by a division between the party of England, agriculture and the Church of England (the Conservatives) and the party of the Celtic fringe, Protestant dissenters and Catholics, and industry (the Liberals). It is possible that any or all of these territorial, religious, and economic-sectoral cleavages are being reasserted, either through a reinvigoration of the Liberals as a non-class-based party of resistance to Conservative hegemony or through the rise of new parties on the anti-Conservative side of those cleavages. In support of the first possibility, one can observe that average vote for the SPD/Liberal Alliance and the Liberal Democrats (assuming one accepts them as the lineal descendants of the Liberals) in the four British elections since 1980 is more than four times that received by the Liberals in the four elections of the 1950s; in support of the second, one can point to the even more dramatic rise (in proportional terms) of the vote for the Scottish and Welsh nationalist parties. Finally, it is also possible that these cleavages have been reinvigorated by the reorientation of the Labour party itself to become a cross-class party of peripheral resistance.

While some elements of the British analysis clearly are not directly applicable to the other English-speaking democracies – none has a Celtic fringe unless one considers the Irish Gaeltacht as the ultra-Celtic fringe of a Celtic country; none except for Ireland had the concentration of owner-ship of land typical of post-feudal European societies (and in the Irish case it was absentee ownership); none has an established Protestant church – the more general idea might be applicable to them.[7] Thus, one might look for evidence of a cleavage between the dominant culture and a territorially based subject culture; among religious denominations, especially "main-stream" Protestant versus Roman Catholic, Orthodox, non-Christian and non-mainstream Protestant sects; and between the primary and secondary sectors of the economy. And as with Britain, these cleavages might be manifested in support for a party that pre-dates the hypothesized water-shed of the 1920s, by a newer party representing some social segment, or by the reorientation of an older party.

Table 5.4 summarizes the specific distinctions through which the basic cleavages discussed by Lipset and Rokkan might be manifested in the English-speaking democracies. The American parallel to the British cleavage between the Celtic fringe and England is the cleavage between the states of the Confederacy and the rest of the country; in the wake of the period of

Table 5.4 Other "traditional" cleavages

	Center–Periphery	Religion	Urban–Rural	Other
Australia		Protestant v. other	Urban v. rural	
Canada	1. French v. English Canada 2. Ontario v. rest of English Canada	Protestant v. other	Urban v. rural	
Ireland	East v. west	Practicing Catholic v. other	Urban v. rural	
New Zealand	South Island v. North Island	Protestant v. other	Urban v. rural	Maori v. Pakeha
United Kingdom	Celtic fringe v. England	Episcopal v. other	Urban v. rural	
United States	South v. "north"	Protestant v. other	Urban v. rural	Black v. white

reconstruction imposed by the northern Republicans, the south became solidly Democratic.[8] The most directly parallel Canadian cleavage is that between French and English Canada; as with the British Celtic fringe and the American south, this cleavage is ultimately based on military conquest and the perceived imposition of one culture on another. The English side of the French Canada versus English Canada cleavage is further divided, however, by a cleavage between Ontario and "peripheral" Canada (the Maritimes, Manitoba, Alberta, Saskatchewan plus British Columbia). In the Irish case, one can hypothesize an analogous socio-cultural division between Dublin and its environs and the west; Garvin's (1974) characterization of this division as east versus west, operationalized by the pattern of farm sizes in the 1930s, is employed here.[9]

The British distinction between the Church of England (operationalized here to include the Episcopal church in Scotland) and other Protestant denominations does not resonate with traditional understandings of the relationship between religion and politics in the other English-speaking countries, although in recent years the distinction between fundamentalist and born-again Protestants versus the others has received greater attention. For Australia, Canada, New Zealand, and the United States, the cleavage investigated here is between mainstream Protestant denominations as the dominant religion, on one hand, and Catholicism, Orthodox Christianity, Judaism, and other religions, on the other; where small non-mainstream Protestant sects could be distinguished, they were included in this latter category, but the numbers of adherents of these denominations among the actual survey respondents is so small as to make no significant difference to the results reported. In the Irish case, the closest equivalent cleavage is between practising Catholics (those attending church at least once every week) and nominal Catholics plus all others.

The cleavage between primary and secondary economic sectors is operationalized here for all countries as an urban-rural cleavage, for three basic reasons. First, particularly in Britain, there simply are too few citizens directly engaged in agriculture either to serve as the basis of party conflict or to appear in sufficient numbers in a national survey to be analysed. Second, if there is a sectoral cleavage, then the primary "side" includes not only those directly involved in agriculture, but all those in their communities who depend indirectly on the agricultural economy for their livelihood. Third, although the cleavage between those dependent on the primary and secondary economies can be characterized in terms of economic interests, it is also about different life styles and value systems.

Finally, in the cases of the United States and New Zealand it is possible to consider the possibility of a racial cleavage. In the American case, this would be a division between black and white; in New Zealand, a division between those of European descent (Pakeha) and all others (primarily Maori).

Analyses of the strength of these cleavages are reported in Tables 5.5a through 5.5f. In each case, the statistic reported is analogous to the Alford index – the percentage of respondents on one side of the hypothesized cleavage reporting themselves to have voted (to be intending to vote) for the party or parties associated with that side of the cleavage minus the percentage of respondents on the other side of the cleavage voting for those parties. As this implies, and as is indicated in the tables, the partisan divisions associated with these cleavages need not be the same, nor need they be the same as the partisan division associated with the class cleavage. Nonetheless, both to parallel Alford's analysis in the original volume and because the parties associated with the class cleavage are overwhelmingly the strongest parties in most of these countries, the cleavage differentials are also reported within each of the social classes. Looking first at Table 5.5a, the British data strongly confirm the suggestion that the decline in class voting observed earlier might be associated with increased salience of other cleavages. In particular, these data show a marked increase in the importance of the regional cleavage, with Scottish and Welsh voters more than 26 per cent more likely to vote Labour or nationalist in comparison with English voters. More detailed analyses (not shown) indicate that the bulk of this difference comes from differential rates of Labour voting, although the nationalist vote (which is constrained by the lack of candidates to be zero in England) does make a significant contribution. Liberal voters, however, are very much like Conservative voters. Moreover, the regional difference (as well as the religious difference with which it is highly correlated) remains strong even when class is controlled. While these data attest to the continued importance of the societal cleavages that Lipset and Rokkan addressed, they undermine the hypothesis that the relationship between those cleavages and political parties would remain fixed. On one hand, the Liberal party appears effectively to have changed sides, while on

Table 5.5a Cleavage differentials, United Kingdom

	Scotland and Wales [Labour, Plaid Cymru, Scots Nats] v. England [Conservative, Liberal]			Episcopal [Conservative, Liberal v. other Wales [Labour, Plaid Cymru, Scots Nats]			Rural [Conservative, Liberal] v. urban[a] [Labour]		
	Overall	Within working class	Within middle class	Overall	Within working class	Within middle class	Overall	Within working class	Within middle class
1964	9.2	12.4	0.0	7.6	9.8	3.0	7.9	9.0	0.9
1966	3.8	0.0	6.8	6.4	5.2	5.6			
1970	9.7	11.0	−0.3	9.0	4.0	9.5			
1974f	20.7	16.0	19.3						
1974o	27.0	34.9	21.3	17.5	15.1	14.4			
1979	21.8	25.2	11.7	12.5	8.2	12.9			
1983	16.3	17.0	6.0	11.4	9.6	9.8			
1987	19.5	22.8	7.0	12.6	13.8	10.5			
1992	26.3	21.2	22.3	17.8	17.9	12.3	16.8	15.1	9.8

Notes: [a]1964: Cities and urban areas v. mixed and rural areas.
          1992: English Metropolitan counties, Strathclyde and Lothian v. other.

Table 5.5b Cleavage differentials, Australia

	Protestant [Liberal, Country/ National] v. other [Labor, Democratic Labor]			Rural [Country/National] v. urban [Labor, Democratic Labor, Liberal]		
	Overall	Within working class	Within middle class	overall	Within working class	Within middle class
1967	18.9	5.3	24.5	15.7	15.1	15.6
1969	15.9	6.5	20.5	27.9	22.4	33.6
1984[a]	8.6	7.3	9.3			
1987	8.4	4.2	15.3	14.8	10.3	18.2
1990	7.4	2.0	9.0			
1993	13.8	8.8	19.3	11.3	8.9	13.7
1996	13.7	10.1	16.5	10.7	12.8	7.6

Note: [a]Vote asked in urban sample only.

the other hand the Labour party has broadened its appeal to represent not only the working class, but also those societal constituencies formerly associated with the Liberals.

The pattern for Australia (Table 5.5b) is quite different. There the decline in class voting has been accompanied by a modest decline (from a modest initial position) in the importance of the other social cleavages considered as well. In contrast to the British case, these additional cleavages appear to have a more pronounced effect in the middle class. This reflects the importance of the Labor party as the primary point of

Table 5.5c-1 Cleavage differentials, all Canada

	Quebec [Liberal and nationalist (BQ only in 1993)] v. English Canada [Conservative, NDP, Social Credit]			Protestant [Conservative, NDP, Social Credit] v. other [Liberal and nationalist]			Rural [NDP, Social Credit] v. urban [Liberal, Conservative]		
	Overall	Within working class	Within middle class	Overall	Within working class	Within middle class	Overall	Within working class	Within middle class
1965	17.4	14.8	19.4	27.1	26.7	29.3	−6.6	−11.4	−4.9
1968	23.9	25.0	20.9	26.9	32.0	23.0	2.4	−7.8	−0.5
1972	14.9	11.6	16.1	16.2	16.3	17.3			
1974	23.2	19.7	26.1	24.4	26.0	14.5	−0.1	−2.9	0.6
1984	8.4	14.9	5.5	11.0	12.1	8.4	−2.5	−5.3	−2.7
1988	−4.8	3.9	−8.0	7.3	8.8	6.9			
1993	53.5	63.5	47.0	32.4	37.4	28.6			

Table 5.5c-2 Cleavage differentials, Canada excluding Quebec

	Ontario [Liberal v. peripheral Canada [Conservative, NDP, Social Credit]			Protestant [Conservative, NDP, Social Credit] v. other [Liberal]			Rural [NDP, Social Credit] v. urban Conservative]		
	Overall	Within working class	Within middle class	Overall	Within working class	Within middle class	Overall	Within working class	Within middle class
1965	−11.8	−11.8	−14.5	30.3	29.5	35.2	−9.2	−16.8	−5.3
1968	−9.6	−9.1	−8.1	25.1	32.1	20.7	−4.1	−11.3	−0.6
1972	1.5	6.0	−0.5	15.6	16.4	16.8			
1974	−1.9	−4.89	−15.5	21.2	24.2	20.2	−3.7	−9.6	−2.2
1984	−11.8	−13.0	−10.9	10.5	9.9	8.4	−1.8	−4.8	−1.8
1988	−10.3	−6.6	−12.0	12.7	10.8	13.2			
1993	−1.8	4.9	−6.4	6.3	2.5	9.7			

reference in Australian party politics, and moreover is consistent with the idea that these cleavages, reflecting social conflicts that predate the rising of the industrial working class, would be relevant primarily on the non-working-class side of the class cleavage. In this sense, one might suggest that the Australian evidence is more consistent with the Lipset and Rokkan model for Europe than is the British.

Canada (Tables 5.5c-1 and 5.5c-2) presents the most complicated pattern, potentially revealing a major realignment. Looking first at the data for Canada as a whole, one sees the decline of the cleavage pattern aligning

Table 5.5d Cleavage differentials, Ireland

	Periphery [Labour, Workers, Democratic Left, Sinn Fein] v. core [others]			Practicing Catholic [Fianna Fáil] v. other [other]			Rural [Fianna Fáil, Fine Gael] v. urban [other]		
	Overall	Within working class	Within middle class	Overall	Within working class	Within middle class	Overall	Within working class	Within middle class
1973				25.3	41.7	19.3	11.0	11.0	8.2
1977		8.1	7.6	13.8	6.4	16.6			
1981				28.7	30.1	22.6	12.1	9.9	7.4
1982							11.9	14.6	6.3
1982							6.8	−0.7	10.9
1987	3.3	0.8	2.3				11.3	6.3	9.7
1989	10.3	7.4	5.3	17.5	13.6	27.2	15.5	27.0	13.5
1992	15.1	21.3	6.2	16.0	21.3	15.3	19.6	26.8	10.5

Quebec with the federal Liberal party. This alignment, which dated from 1887 when Wilfrid Laurier became leader of the party and then French Canada's first federal prime minister, received a boost from the accession to the leadership and premiership of Pierre Trudeau in 1968, but thereafter declined, so that by 1988 the cleavage differential index actually became negative, indicating that the Quebec voters (particularly in the middle class, as the class breakdown reveals) were less likely than other Canadians to vote Liberal. Had the data series stopped then, one might have concluded that this regional cleavage had lost its partisan relevance. This did not reflect a decline in the political importance of the cleavage, however, but rather an inability of the existing party system to represent it. This problem was "cured" in 1993 with the rise of Bloc Quebecois. As in Britain, an old cleavage reasserts itself, but this time through the rise of a new party instead of the reorientation of an old one.

The French/English cleavage is so strong and so highly correlated with religion that it is not useful to talk about the other cleavages in the context of Canada as a whole. Looking only at Canada other than Quebec, one sees a marked decline in a once significant religious cleavage. A cleavage between Ontario and the rest is apparent, but quite weak. As with the question of Quebec, but on a smaller scale, this does not indicate the political unimportance of the cleavage, but rather its detachment from federal partisan divisions. Instead of forming the basis for parties with a strong regional orientation competing at the national level (as was the case with Social Credit and the NDP), the cleavage increasingly has been accommodated within each of the major parties – including, one might add, in the Reform party, which attracted many votes in Ontario.

As is shown in Table 5.5d, the "societal" cleavage with the greatest connection to party choice in Ireland is that between practising and more secular Catholics. The inverted commas are necessary because regularity of

Table 5.5e Cleavage differentials, New Zealand

	South Island v. North Island			Protestant v. other			Rural v urban			Maori etc. v. white		
	Overall	*Within working class*	*Within middle class*	*Overall*	*Within working class*	*Within middle class*	*Overall*	*Within working class*	*Within middle class*	*Overall*	*Within working class*	*Within middle class*
1972[a]				16.7	7.6	26.6						
1975				7.6	0.3	8.2				35.7	46.6	19.6
1981	9.0	10.0	7.2	2.2	1.1	-2.6						
1987[b]	6.6	15.3	3.2				-4.3	-4.6	-2.6	26.7	31.5	17.8
1990				14.0	3.6	17.8				26.6	20.5	45.6
1993				8.0	6.7	8.9	7.7	12.9	5.1	29.3	22.3	22.9

Notes: [a]Sample (*n*=106) from Lyttelton Electoral District only. [b]Sample restricted to 5 urban regions.

Table 5.5f Cleavage differentials, United States

	South v. north			Protestant v. other			Rural v urban			Black v. white		
	Overall	*Within working class*	*Within middle class*	*Overall*	*Within working class*	*Within middle class*	*Overall*	*Within working class*	*Within middle class*	*Overall*	*Within working class*	*Within middle class*
1952	9.1	4.3	25.0	18.4	17.4	13.1	3.8	8.7	0.3	40.4	30.9	48.4[a]
1956	14.7	17.5	14.8	15.2	10.2	19.2	0.0	-3.8	6.2	24.2	18.6	26.7[a]
1960	5.4	-2.1	14.7	43.7	40.1	47.0	9.2	14.9	2.1	23.0	15.0	64.4[a]
1964	-5.7	-5.1	-8.2	16.8	7.9	30.9	4.3	8.0	3.3	35.1	24.6	43.1
1968[b]	13.6	21.4	-0.7	17.7	13.5	24.3	5.5	7.4	6.7	48.6	41.8	56.8
	-3.6	-3.1	-7.6	23.1	17.4	29.7	11.6	16.0	10.6	60.9	58.2	65.1
1972	-3.1	0.2	-10.0	10.8	7.9	12.9	12.5	15.9	9.4	57.0	49.6	50.5
1976	7.5	6.0	2.7	8.7	6.6	12.6	6.8	13.6	4.0	48.2	42.3	43.8
1980	3.2	8.5	2.3	1.7	-2.1	9.0	14.0	18.8	7.0	57.0	49.9	52.8
1984	3.2	3.2	1.4	10.8	6.6	13.9	11.8	13.7	11.5	54.1	51.0	56.6
1988	2.4	0.7	-3.6	10.9	9.4	16.0	11.6	12.3	11.4	50.8	49.2	38.2
1992	6.0	15.9	-3.4	10.5	5.7	14.9	9.1	21.3	12.5	49.9	49.0	51.3

Notes: [a]*n* <10. [b]**Row 1**: George Wallace included with Democrats. **Row 2**: George Wallace included with Republicans.

church attendance reflects as much an attitudinal as a social distinction. It is also important to note that religious practice is likely to be highly correlated with family traditions which in turn are strongly related to what has generally been regarded as the primary basis of Irish party politics – the pro- and anti-treaty forces of the Irish civil war. The survey data available do not allow this question to be pursued here, and in any case it points to a distinction of a different genus from those on which this chapter (and the Lipset and Rokkan book) focus. In this sense, the decline in the importance of the religious cleavage shown in the table may be an additional bit of evidence that the civil war is fading in partisan importance, and that politics in Ireland is coming more into line with politics in the rest of the industrial world.[10] Whether or not this is the case, however, these data lend no significant support to a hypothesis that either the "standard" British cleavages, or the idiosyncratic Irish cleavages, were set in the early days of the state and have remained frozen since then.

Serious survey research is a relatively recent arrival in New Zealand, making it difficult to discern trends. To the extent that one can, however, Table 5.5e suggests a modest decline in the religious cleavage, and a similarly modest decline in the racial cleavage, which although stronger as an inter-group difference is less important politically because of the relatively small number of non-Europeans.

The data from the United States (Table 5.5f) show a number of interesting trends. First, one sees the last vestiges of the south as a solidly Democratic stronghold. This development began at the presidential level before the start of the data series available here (in particular with the States Rights candidacy of Strom Thurmond in 1948) and proceeded much farther at the congressional level. Nonetheless, the decline in the relative Democratic preference (ultimately becoming a "dispreference") of the southern middle class is striking. Paralleling this, and reflecting many of the same forces, is the dramatic increase in the cleavage differential for race; this index, in effect, is capped by the facts that blacks cannot be more than 100 per cent Democratic, and are not sufficiently numerous or concentrated geographically to form an effective party of their own analogous to the Bloc Quebecois. These data show a modest decline in the partisan significance of the religious cleavage, particularly in the working class; not explored here is the replacement of the traditional Protestant versus other cleavage by a fundamentalist (Protestant, Catholic, and Jewish) versus other cleavage. Finally, there is an evident increase in the partisan relevance of the rural–urban cleavage. Assuming that the correct reference point in the United States is the New Deal realignment of the early 1930s, these cleavages present a mixed picture with regard to a hypothesis of continued freezing. The north–south cleavage has disappeared, perhaps replaced by different regional differences. These, however, do not have the grounding in major social upheavals (revolutions) associated with the cleavages with which the Lipset and Rokkan argument is concerned. On the other hand, the racial cleavage, which does have these characteristics, has become even deeper, and more solidly frozen. The possibilities that the Protestant versus other cleavage has been replaced by a division between fundamentalists and others, and that the rural versus urban cleavage may have been supplanted by a division between suburbanites and others would be consistent with the continued importance of social differences for politics, but not with the idea that the differences that would be relevant were somehow defined for all time with the advent of mass suffrage.

Conclusions

In the simplest of terms, the conclusion of this analysis must be to raise considerable doubt about the validity of the usual understanding of the frozen cleavage hypothesis for the English-speaking world. That under-standing emphasized the class cleavage as the primary basis for partisan alignments, and the class cleavage appears to have weakened in political significance everywhere. Taking a broader understanding of the frozen cleavage hypothesis, however, the data show remarkable persistence, and even strengthening (or deepening) of cleavages that might be described as being of the Lipset and Rokkan type, although they were not mentioned by Lipset and Rokkan because they do not appear in Europe. In particular, the racial cleavage in the United States and the French–English cleavage in Canada are reflected in intergroup differences in party preference that dwarf the British interclass difference in the period when those differences were presumed to define British politics.

The analysis also raises questions and doubts that call for further analysis. This chapter has barely scratched the surface of the research agenda mapped in its opening sections. We need to explore the possible signific-ance of new cleavages. We also need a more detailed analysis of the ways in which the political histories of these countries might map into politically mobilized cleavages.

Thinking about this map raises a number of questions. Neither Canada nor Ireland nor New Zealand nor Australia had significant industrial working classes in the early days of the twentieth century, yet labour parties estab-lished themselves as the main pivots of the national party systems in the last two, only as a minor player in the second, and not at all in the first. Why?

Why does the United States appear to be the only country to have experienced what might properly be described as a real electoral realignment, in which significant social groups appear to have moved over a relatively short period of time from one party to another in a way that not only altered their relative strengths, but fundamentally changed the basis on which they compete with one another?

Perhaps most fundamentally of all, how deep, and how deeply frozen, were political cleavages in the first place? There can be no doubt that the parties that existed in the English-speaking democracies in the 1920s and

1930s were still around, and indeed still dominant, in the 1960s and 1970s – and indeed with the possible exception of the Canadian Progressive Conservatives there is every reason to expect that they will still be dominant into the twenty-first century. But whether their organizational persistence reflects the persistence of the social structural basis of these parties is an open question. And if the answer to that question now is "no", we need to ask to what extent it ever was "yes".

Notes

1. As the one-time Chief Justice of British Columbia wrote (and later repeated as a member of the Supreme Court of Canada), "Our forefathers did not rebel against the English tradition of democratic government as did the Americans . . ." *Dixon v. British Columbia (Attorney-General)* 59 D.L.R. 4th 247 (1989); *Ref. re: Electoral Boundaries Commission Act, ss. 14, 20 (Sask.)* 81 D.L.R.4th 16 (1991).
2. While the Conservative vote in Canada went up slightly in 1997 this was almost exactly compensated by a decline in the Liberal vote, leaving the Liberal plus Conservative share unchanged at 57.3 per cent. The 1997 British election shows a further decline in the Labour plus Conservative share of the vote, to only 73.8 per cent.
3. Survey data used in this chapter are listed below. The data were provided by the Inter-university Consortium for Political and Social Research, the Social Science Data Archive of the Australian National University , and the Data Archive of the University of Essex as indicated for each study. Neither the archives providing these data, nor the original investigators, bear any responsibility for the analyses and interpretations presented here.
   > Vowles, J. *et al.* (1991) *New Zealand Election Survey, 1987* [computer file]. Canberra: Social Science Data Archives, The Australian National University.
   > Roberts, Nigel *et al.* (1990) *New Zealand pre-Election Survey, 1975* [computer file]. Canberra: Social Science Data Archives, The Australian National University.
   > Vowles, J. and Aimer, P. (1992) *New Zealand Election Survey, 1990* [computer file]. Canberra: Social Science Data Archives, The Australian National University.
   > Bean, Clive *et al.* (1983) *New Zealand Voting Survey, post-Election 1981* [computer file]. Canberra: Social Science Data Archives, The Australian National University.
   > Roberts, Nigel *et al.* (1991) *New Zealand pre-Election Survey, 1972* [computer file]. Canberra: Social Science Data Archives, The Australian National University.
   > Levine, Stephen and Robinson, Alan (1991) *New Zealand post-Election Survey, 1975* [computer file]. Canberra: Social Science Data Archives, The Australian National University.
   > McAllister, Ian *et al.* (1990) *Australian Election Study, 1990* [computer file]. Canberra: Social Science Data Archives, The Australian National University.
   > *1952 American National Election Study.* Ann Arbor: Inter-university Consortium for Political and Social Research.
   > *1956 American National Election Study.* Ann Arbor: Inter-university Consortium for Political and Social Research.
   > *1960 American National Election Study.* Ann Arbor: Inter-university Consortium for Political and Social Research.

1964 American National Election Study. Ann Arbor: Inter-university Consortium for Political and Social Research.

1968 American National Election Study. Ann Arbor: Inter-university Consortium for Political and Social Research.

1972 American National Election Study. Ann Arbor: Inter-university Consortium for Political and Social Research.

1976 American National Election Study. Ann Arbor: Inter-university Consortium for Political and Social Research.

1980 American National Election Study. Ann Arbor: Inter-university Consortium for Political and Social Research.

1984 American National Election Study. Ann Arbor: Inter-university Consortium for Political and Social Research.

1988 American National Election Study. Ann Arbor: Inter-university Consortium for Political and Social Research.

1992 American National Election Study Enhanced File [1990–1991–1992]. Ann Arbor: Inter-university Consortium for Political and Social Research.

Irish Election Studies, 1977. Colchester: The Data Archive, University of Essex.

Canadian National Election Study, 1988. Ann Arbor: Inter-university Consortium for Political and Social Research.

1974 Canadian National Election Study. Ann Arbor. Inter-university Consortium for Political and Social Research.

1965 Canadian National Election Study. Ann Arbor: Inter-university Consortium for Political and Social Research.

1984 Canadian National Election Study. Ann Arbor: Inter-university Consortium for Political and Social Research.

Canadian National Election Study, 1972. Ann Arbor. Inter-university Consortium for Political and Social Research.

Canadian Federal Election Study, 1968. Ann Arbor: Inter-university Consortium for Political and Social Research.

Canadian Election Study , 1993: Incorporating the 1992 Referendum Survey on the Charlottetown Accord. Ann Arbor: Inter-university Consortium for Political and Social Research.

European Communities Studies, 1970–1992: Cumulative File. Ann Arbor: Inter-university Consortium for Political and Social Research.

4. Recomputation of the Australian figures with the DLP classified on the left suggests that this choice makes very little difference to the results obtained.
5. As Meisel (1975, 16), citing Lipset, described it, "The New Democratic party is the lineal descendant of the Co-operative Commonwealth Federation (CCF), Canada' s major social democratic party, which emerged in the thirties partly as a western regional protest movement and partly as the instrument of labor."
6. On the debate over the decline of class voting in Britain, see Heath *et al.* (1985), Crewe (1986), and Dunleavy (1987).
7. This statement needs to be qualified by the recognition that the formation of a single state, the driving question of the Lipset and Rokkan model in the broadest terms, was never problematic in New Zealand or in the 26 countries of the Republic of Ireland.
8. More accurately , southern whites became solidly Democratic, while southern blacks generally were excluded from electoral participation. Where they could vote, southern blacks generally were Republicans at least until Franklin Roosevelt, and eventually they became virtually the only Republicans in the south. (Key 1949, 286).
9. The actual operationalization is constrained by the coding scheme of the Eurobarometer series. The "west of Ireland" as used here means counties Donegal, Sligo, Leitrim, Mayo, Galway, Cork, and Kerry.

10. While the decline in the association between religious practice and Fianna Fáil voting shown in the table may reflect a weakening of a traditional versus secular culture division (see Mair 1987, 220), the very fact of any positive association indicates the weakening of the legacy of the civil war. As Ayearst (1970, 217) observes, in the early days of the Free State, Cumann na nGaedheal received more clerical votes than did Fianna Fáil.

6   Class, religion, party

Triple decline of electoral cleavages in Western Europe

Mattei Dogan

During the twentieth century, more than in any previous century, Europe has been the theatre of enormous social, economic, cultural and political experimentation. In 1920, on the ruins of four empires, the old continent counted twenty-four competitive democracies, from Lisbon to Warsaw. Between 1922 and 1939, fifteen of these democracies collapsed, and four others were suppressed in 1940 by military occupation. In 1944 Europe was a cemetery of nineteen democracies and a devastated continent.

During the second half of the century, however, Western Europe, the United States, Japan and a few other countries achieved a greater economic growth than during the previous three centuries. This rapid change has been labelled variously: "the three glorious decades" (Fourastié 1979), "the second French revolution" (Mendras 1995), "the German economic miracle", "the second Italian Renaissance", "the golden epoch", "the silent revolution", etc.

Today, the Western democracies are post-industrial societies, as coined by Daniel Bell in 1976, nine years after the publication of *Party Systems and Voter Alignments*. The concept of post-industrial society implies that group solidarities and stratifications derived from the previous industrial revolution are, today, largely obsolete.

In spite of this tumultuous history, the imprints of the past are still visible. The contemporary map of Europe reflects somehow the confessional segregation generated long ago by the principle of *Cujus regio, ejus religio*. An economic regional diversity inherited in part from the first industrial revolution is still visible. The ancient linguistic cacophony of thirty languages persists. Social inequalities in the 1990s are partly inherited from previous generations. Nevertheless, the social upheavals and the impact of recent history have weakened the old roots of the political cleavages and political parties.

This chapter focuses on the social and political changes which have occurred during the last half of the century, particularly during the last three decades, since the publication of *Party Systems and Voter Alignments*.

Metamorphosis of the society

During the last half of the century, technological progress and new sources of energy have generated profound social transformations. The replacement of coal by oil, gas and hydraulic energy, and later by nuclear energy have marked the passage from the industrial society to the post-industrial society. The automobile industry, considered yesterday as a fortress of the working class, has become by the spread of automation an industry where more than half of the employees are white-collar workers or polyvalent technicians. The railway, in the first half of the century a carrier of revolutionary ideals, has by the electrification of the network, suppressed three-quarters of the jobs in most Western European countries without diminishing freight and passenger traffic. Simultaneously, the number of lorry-drivers has increased and is today as large as was the number of railwaymen yesterday. As attested to by various surveys, lorry-drivers and railwaymen display different patterns of political behaviour. The first are conservative and individualist, the second, unionized with leftist tendencies.

Not long ago industrial plants were concentrated in cities. In Europe, many metropolises were encircled by "red belts". At the beginning of the century Marxists could not foresee that the increasing suburbanization would "expel" industrial workers from cities. The proportion of industrial workers employed in large plants has decreased everywhere during the last two decades.

In France, the number of farmers declined from 42 per cent in 1946 to 7 per cent in 1992, and the number of industrial workers from 40 per cent to 27 per cent during the same period. In 1947, there were one million workers in France working in coal mines and on the railways and 100,000 students. In 1995, there are 2,300,000 students, 90 per cent of them over eighteen and with the right to vote. On the other hand, there are only 100,000 blue-collar workers on the railways, and the coal mines have all been closed down. In 1946 there were a million domestic servants in France. By 1964 kitchen appliances had reduced their number to less than one-tenth. Similar changes took place in all European countries.

The share of GNP collected and redistributed by the state has doubled in two decades, except in Switzerland, so that Western Europe may now be considered to have mixed economics – half capitalist, half socialist.

The reduction of the working class has been accompanied by a well-known phenomenon: the growth of the middle classes. There is no need to discuss here the distinction between the two categories of middle classes: independent and salaried, new and old. This neo-Marxist debate is sufficiently clarified elsewhere.

In the 1980s, for the first time since the industrial revolution, several European countries have imported more manufactured products than they have exported. The decline of heavy industry involved a decline of number of workers in large industrial complexes.

Unionized workers in strategic positions as locomotive drivers, overseers of electric plants, air traffic controllers, etc. have the power to paralyse an entire country by strike. But today this "aristocracy of the labour force" is less motivated than yesterday to take the lead in social unrest, because politicians and managers have wisely allowed it substantial privileges. So, the upper strata of the working class have been detached from the base of the pyramid.

Two recent changes in the structure of the working class need to be pointed out, one caused by structural unemployment and the other by immigration from non-European countries, mostly from Southern Asia, North Africa and Black Africa. For about the last ten years unemployment in Western Europe has averaged 12 per cent (with Spain in the lead at 20 per cent in 1994). This figure concerns the active population as a whole, but is higher for the working class: it is as much as 25 per cent in some industrial sectors. This structural unemployment is not just a short-term problem but a durable phenomenon, the result of technological progress and higher productivity. Though economically inactive, the unemployed persons are still voters.

In the span of a single generation, the working class has shrunk by a third in most Western European countries. Part of the remaining two-thirds has changed ethnically as a result of the upward mobility of the indigenous workers and their replacement by immigrants in the hardest, least skilled and lowest paid jobs, those that many nationals no longer want. Most of these immigrants have no citizenship or voting rights, as in Germany and Switzerland.

Thus, the working class is also fissured at its base by a change of its ethnic composition, resulting from a non-European immigration. Immigration has gone through two phases. In the boom years, industry needed cheap, unskilled labour. German and French firms in particular went recruiting all around the Mediterranean. As the British Empire crumbled, Britain had to accept immigration from southern Asia. After a time technological progress and automation turned the manpower shortage into a manpower surplus. Meanwhile, however, immigrants had put down roots, and their children had acquired the nationality of the host country, particularly in France under the *droit du sol*. These immigrants' children, in their turn, came on to the labour market at a time when millions of workers of European origin were losing their jobs. The first generation of immigrants were quiet people, content to lead humble and unassertive lives. Their children, however, demand recognition as fully fledged citizens. The social unrest is greatest in the highly populated areas where there are large numbers of non-European immigrants, rather than in the richer middle-class districts. Here we see the effect of the social context, of which too little account is taken in the surveys, because they consider only individual attributes.

Increasing social mobility and improved living standards have eroded class awareness among autochthonous workers. The gap between them and immigrants has widened, and class solidarity is now mere trade-union rhetoric.

To refer nowadays to the "working class" in the singular is sociologically inappropriate. It has to be recognized that the numerical shrinkage of this working class has been accompanied by the growth of poverty as result of unemployment, social exclusion and reduction of income. This poverty is creating a new social stratum, a sub-proletariat, a significant proportion of which is ethnically different from the majority of the population. Compared with this sub-proletariat, the old working "class" is becoming a relatively privileged category. Such changes in society have repercussions on voting motivations and on the role of the political parties.

Crosscutting cleavages in pluralist democracies

Contemporary pluralist democracies are complex societies characterized by many cleavages. Their equilibrium is founded on the criss-crossing of economic, social, religious and cultural cleavages. There are two types of cleavages. Vertical cleavages divide society according to cultural criteria, such as religion, language, ethnicity and social memory. Horizontal cleavages relate to economic and social layers, such as social class, income, level of education, urban or rural environment, type of job, etc.

In their model of evolution of the European party systems, Lipset and Rokkan introduced seven "actors" into the political game (Lipset and Rokkan 1967a, 36). Four of them are referring to vertical cleavages ("ecclesiastical body", "religion", "periphery", etc.), the others, to horizontal cleavages ("landowners", "urban entrepreneurs"). But during the twentieth century these cleavages have deeply evolved, with some new cleavages gaining in importance and some older cleavages losing ground. For instance, when the elites in Belgium signed the school pact they had in fact decided to renounce the battle on the religious front. This decision opened the road to confrontations elsewhere, giving priority to the linguistic issue.

All European countries have long had both horizontal and vertical cleavages, though in varying proportions. Within each country these cleavages intersect in a particular way which forms the originality of each nation. A country in which there were only vertical cleavages would lose its unity. If a large number of horizontal cleavages were superimposed without counterbalancing vertical cleavages, the society would experience social unrest. The fabric of a well-established democracy is formed by the weave of cleavages. The best research on electoral sociology is focused precisely on these clusters of cleavages.

Horizontal conflicts are much easier to resolve than vertical conflicts. Many political events – election results in particular – may be explained by this unequal capacity to resolve socio-economic conflicts and cultural conflicts. Over a long period vertical cleavages predominated over horizontal cleavages in most countries, but today the two seem to have found some kind of balance.

On economic, social or financial problems compromises are possible. Decisions may be good or bad: a high increase in wages can cause economic imbalance as can too great a reduction in working hours. Decisions may have fortunate or unfortunate effects. But here we are not concerned with the consequences of compromises, but with the possibility of negotiation. A particular social or economic reform can progress or be held back; a particular social group may or may not be advantaged, depending on the clout of the forces at work, on the strategy of the pressure groups, the skill of their leaders and on the current economic climate; but dialogue is possible and so is agreement, though the cost may be high. By contrast, arriving at a compromise on cultural problems is difficult and sometimes impossible. You cannot ask a Flemish person to speak French part of the time or a Calvinist to be partly Catholic. People are Catalan or Basque rather than Spanish, Slovenian or Croat rather than Yugoslavian. If you are born in Tuscany you have four centuries of anti-clericalism behind you, whereas in Veneto you are more likely to take the Catholic view of things. And what about Ulster and Cyprus? The two World Wars had ethnic pretexts: Sarajevo and Danzig. In the history of France during the last century the problems causing the deepest divisions in public opinion were cultural: the Dreyfus affair which split the country in two, or the separation of church and state. In many countries there is no agreement on freedom of divorce and of abortion.

It is true that Belgium's recent religious and linguistic history displays nothing but a series of compromises and agreements. The way in which educational relations have been formed and reformed, the use of the two languages in government and administration, the recognition of certain rights and the shifting of linguistic boundaries have been resolved by negotiation. It is not so much compromise as mutual tolerance. But there are very few real consociational democracies in the world, and it is by no means certain that the consociational model (Belgian – Dutch – Swiss – Austrian – Canadian) could be transplanted to many other countries.

There can be no real democracy without some intersection of cleavages. In normal times the configuration of these cleavages changes slowly; in case of historical upheavals, they may be modified substantially. Cleavages have been "frozen" for long periods only in a few countries.

The hypothesis of "frozen cleavages" is treated by Lipset and Rokkan toward the end of their essay, in a few lines (1967, 50), suggesting that their analysis of the gestation of party systems, which stops "to some point in the 1920", in the "wake of the extension of suffrage" may be reflected in the party system of 1960s. This freezing hypothesis cannot be extended to the three decades since the publication of *Party Systems and Voter Alignments* because of the generational dynamic, the importance of which has been revealed by the recent international surveys on values.

A fallacious model: social class on a pedestal

For a long time, two sociological indicators – social class and religious faith – were jointly sufficient to explain a significant part of electoral variance. Their cumulative effect gave them a capacity to explain part of the electoral results. But the relative shares of each – class and religion – was not the same everywhere. In this respect countries fell into two categories: in the first, by far the larger numerically, the religious factor predominated; in the other, confined to relatively few countries, social class played the leading role (see Figure 6.1).

In electoral studies, social class was, so to speak, put on a pedestal. The assertion of the paramount role of social class in electoral behaviour can be found in dozens of books on Western Europe, particularly and curiously enough, in the work of some Americans scholars. But this hazardous generalization was contested by other scholars: Dogan 1960; Rokkan 1969; Sartori 1969b; Rose and Urwin 1969; Rose 1974, 1982; Rose and McAllister 1986; Lijphart 1968, 1973, 1976; Rogowski 1981; Lipset 1981, 1991; Inglehart 1990, on a comparative basis, and many others in relation to individual countries.

It is time to get rid of this deeply rooted assumption, upheld even by non-Marxist authors, and based in the 1950s and 1960s on a handful of countries where research on electoral sociology began just after the war: the United States, Britain and the Scandinavian countries, all of which are

Vertical cleavages

		Strong	Weak
Horizontal cleavages	**Strong**	Germany Austria Belgium	England Sweden Finland Denmark Norway
	Weak	France Italy Netherlands Spain Portugal Switzerland Northern Ireland Canada USA	Ireland Greece

Figure 6.1 Strength of vertical and horizontal cleavages in Western Europe.

predominantly Protestant. In these countries, during the 1950s, the position of the individual in the social structure and the level of his income influenced voting more than did religious affiliation (Protestant or Catholic) or practice. Discussion of the American case would take us too far from the point: it would be sufficient to mention the Catholic vote in favour of the Democratic party, the moving frontiers of social stratification, the low electoral participation of the poor social strata, the ethnic vote in this multi-cultural society. One quotation will suffice. Writing at the same moment as Lipset and Rokkan, in 1967, Michael Parenti, following the distinction made by Talcott Parsons between cultural and social systems, insisted on the fact that "acculturation was most often not followed by social assimilation; the group became *Americanized* in much of its cultural practices, but this says little about its social relations with the host society... The minority still maintained a social sub-structure encompassing primary and secondary group relations composed essentially of fellow ethnics" (1967, 719). Such a description became adaptable two decades later to many large European suburbs.

Among two dozen pluralist democracies, the United States, Canada and Ireland are the countries for which one finds the lowest degree of class voting.

The case of Britain deserves special attention. Literature on the electoral behaviour of the British is extensive and includes some sophisticated research. Britain is regarded as a model of class vote. It is therefore a crucial case. One scholar went so far as to say: "Class is the basis of British party politics: all else is embellishment and detail" (Pulzer 1975). Let's see the results. R. Rogowski, who made a secondary analysis of the survey carried out by Butler and Stokes (1970), shows that the efforts to construct a better sociological indicator of electoral behaviour, by regression analysis, and taking into account occupation, education, father's social status, union membership, whether house-owner or tenant, etc., produced rather disappointing results. All these measures of social class could explain no more than 28 per cent of the variance in 1963, at a time when social class was still considered of great significance. If the vertical cleavages had been included in the regression analysis the results arrived at would have been more satisfactory. Vertical and horizontal cleavages are like interconnected vessels.

Richard Rose dethrones social class in Britain without pity: "The ideal-type classes do not fit the reality of British society. In 1964, only 14 per cent of the electorate conformed to the ideal-type of a manual worker; the proportion declined to 12 per cent in 1970 and 4 per cent in 1979" (Rose 1982, 150). However classes are identified, "most British voters do not have their vote determined by occupational class" (Rose and McAllister 1986, 50).

But whatever the explanation for these few countries may be, and even if we accept the hypothesis that during the 1950s, and the 1960s, social class was in these countries the most significant factor in voting, generalizations from these countries to Europe as a whole do not stand up to empirical test.

In fact, in ten European countries the vertical cleavages (religious affiliation, depth of religious belief, religious practice, ethnic or linguistic community, attachment to the region, etc.) which are called in sociological language "ascriptive characteristics" as opposed to "acquired attributes", have proved for decades, and particularly in the 1950s and 1960s, to be more discriminating than the horizontal cleavages that correspond to the socio-economic categories. The ten countries are: France, Italy, Germany, the Netherlands, Belgium, Austria, Switzerland and Ireland, followed by Spain and Portugal once they became democracies. Today, stretching Western Europe's boundaries somewhat, we could also include Slovenia, Croatia, the Czech Republic, Slovakia, Poland, Hungary, Romania, Lithuania, Latvia, Estonia, Bosnia and Cyprus. In almost all these Eastern European countries, linguistic, ethnic and religious identities are today much deeper than class identity.

Social class and religion, once paramount factors in explaining together voting behaviour lost their predictive value some time ago, whether considered singly or together. This weakening of the model may be interpreted by the profound changes that have taken place in society and by a three-fold decline: in social class, in religion and in the role of political parties.

Decline of the class vote

Class voting has declined for several reasons, three of which are particularly relevant: the reduction of the size of the industrial working class, the weakening of its cohesion as a conscious class, and the hostility of many autochthonous workers against non-European immigrants at the bottom of the "proletariat".

In the post-industrial society, although the number of blue-collar workers has declined, the socialist parties which are ubiquitous (except in Ireland) have continued to prosper, a feat possible because of the influx of the middle classes into the ranks of democratic socialism. In other words, the diversification in the socialist electorate can be better explained by the rise of the middle classes than by a reduction of the working class.

To demonstrate trends in class voting several authors (Lipset, Dalton and others) have updated the index first proposed by Robert Alford in 1963 and extended it to the 1980s. After enjoying much success, this index appears today of limited significance because, in the longitudinal analysis, it is assumed that the relative proportions of the middle and working classes do not change – which is clearly not the case. Simple statistics show that the different distributions of the electorate between the middle and working classes in 1960 and 1990 affect the proportion of each of the two classes voting for the left and the composition of the socialist vote.

Whatever reservations one may have about the class vote index in the updated form presented in the literature, the available empirical data show that the role of social class in explaining voting behaviour has weakened.

In *France* the proportion of the electorate accounted for by industrial workers fell from 51 per cent in 1951 to 41 per cent in 1965 and again to 30 per cent in 1988. Until recently, France showed a great variety in geographical distribution. Economic, religious and political data are available for the years 1950–70 for 3,000 administrative divisions, called cantons, which lend themselves to territorial analysis. Aggregate analysis and survey results indicate that in the 1950s there were significant correlations between socio-economic strata and voting, but they were far less significant than those between religious practice and voting.

The class voting fell considerably during the Gaullist decade. Actually, more than a third of the Gaullist tidal wave in the 1962, 1965 and 1968 elections consisted of voters from the working class, although at the time industrial workers made up between 38 per cent and 41 per cent of the working population (Dogan 1993). In the presidential elections of 1974 and the parliamentary elections of 1978 the class index, measured in left–right terms, changed very little because of the influx of votes from lower-middle-class wage-earners in the socialist electorate, and the reduction in the number of working-class people voting Communist (though in absolute terms the number of working-class voters had declined). The difference between the working-class vote (65 per cent) and that of primary school teachers, technicians and clerical employees narrowed in the 1978 elections with the left winning in these categories 65 per cent, 57 per cent and 54 per cent of the votes, respectively (Capdevielle *et al.* 1981, 312).

The election of a socialist as president in 1981 and his re-election in 1988, coupled with the parliamentary elections of the period, completed the conversion of the socialist party to middle-class and saw a steady decline of Communist influence among the working class. Class voting took another lurch: in 1988 the gap between the working-class and white-collar votes for the left faded away – 68 per cent and 64 per cent (SOFRES 1989).

An event rare in electoral history took place in the 1995 presidential elections when a substantial number of blue-collar workers voted for the extreme right (as happened during the Weimar Republic): an exit poll indicated that 31 per cent of industrial workers had voted in this way. The Communist candidate and another from the extreme left together polled no more than 22 per cent; the socialist candidate 21 per cent; and the centre-right candidates 25 per cent. In other words, more than half the working-class voters opted for one of the two extremes, showing their dissatisfaction after years under a socialist rule. The highest proportion of working-class votes for the extreme right has been noticed in towns or districts with large non-European immigrant populations. It was a contextual reaction. In certain social contexts an affinity was revealed between extreme left and extreme right. Already in 1993, the difference between the blue-collar and white-collar vote for Socialist and Communist candidates was very slight. In 1995, the class vote sign had turned negative: it was more than a decline, it was a collapse.

In *Italy* in the 1950s the poor agricultural population accounted for one-fifth of the electorate, voting Communist in some areas and Christian Democrat in others. The number of these farmhands gradually decreased as did that of tenant-farmers. At the same time the number of industrial workers concentrated in cities and suburbs in Northern and Central Italy has increased.

Italian territory presents a considerable regional variety from both the social and the political viewpoint, a fact which lends itself to sociological analysis of aggregate data, coupled with data gathered by sample surveys. Limiting the analysis to industrial workers, we find that in the 1950s about two-thirds voted Communist, Socialist or Social Democrat (in 1958 the figures were 37 per cent, 29 per cent and 5 per cent, respectively). The Christian Democrats attracted one-quarter of workers' votes (Dogan 1962). This class cleavage is impressive but it is nevertheless not as significant as the religious cleavage. From 1970 onwards, the balance of power between communists and socialists changed in favour of the former but, together, the two parties continued to win the majority of working-class votes. In the meantime the socialist party has increasingly attracted white-collar support. The rise of salaried middle classes also prompted increased heterogeneity in the communist electorate during the 1980s. The same has happened in the other parties.

In the early 1990s, in a climate of profound crisis and with the legitimacy of the regime under threat, the old parties were restructured, some of them split, many leaders were eliminated, doctrines changed, and new parties formed. The collapse of the *partitocrazia* led to a weakening of the links between social strata and parties. "Social class" lost its place in the system and even in political ideologies.

For *Germany*, on the basis of multiple correlation analysis covering social status, religion, region and rural–urban environment and spanning five parliamentary elections between 1953 and 1972, Baker, Dalton and Hildebrandt (1975) concluded: "Over the past two decades we find a marked decline in the total explanatory power of the four socio-structural dimensions". They explain this decline by economic prosperity. As indicators of social status they adopted occupation, income and educational level, which are all correlated. It is the change in social position far more than in the three other variables, religion in particular, that accounts for the decline in the working-class vote for the Socialist party. In a new study, this time covering the period 1953–83, R. Dalton updates the Alford index and shows a steep decline through nine parliamentary elections: 30, 37, 28, 26, 12, 17, 16, 16 and 10 (Dalton 1984, 127). As a primary explanatory factor "social class" falls to the ground.

Some authors have greatly exaggerated the importance of the class vote in *Britain*. The Conservative party has governed this country longer than the Labour party because of the "deferential" vote among the working class, estimated at over 30 per cent of the working class in the 1950s (Nordlinger 1967). Recent studies agree that there has been an erosion of the class vote from the 1970s onwards. The only disagreement is on the explanation of the decline and on its scale. The differences in interpretation stem from the inappropriate use of the Automatic Interaction Detector (A.I.D.) technique (Franklin and Mughan 1978). Some mistakes in electoral sociology are due to the naive use of sophisticated techniques. At the close of a critical analysis of various techniques the authors conclude that there has been "an unquestionable decline in the capacity of social class, measured by occupation, to explain electoral behaviour in Britain" (Franklin and Mughan 1978, 532).

In a detailed study, R. Rose points out that in 1964 only 57 per cent of blue-collar workers (unskilled, specialized and skilled altogether) voted for the party that claimed to represent them. In 1970, the figure was 54 per cent and in 1979, 45 per cent (Rose 1980, 19). This desertion of the Labour party continued throughout the sixteen years of Conservative rule. In 1994 the Labour party won new support from the middle classes, exceeding the number of working-class votes they won back.

Sweden is an ideal case for the longitudinal study of class voting. It is a model of neo-corporatist democracy, where the Social Democrats held power for 44 years up to 1976 and then won it back after a six-year interruption. In this country, in 1980 the public sector employed one-third of the national labour force; the growth of services such as health, pension, education, social housing, family welfare, etc., left only another third for industry, mining and construction. The share of GNP controlled (collected and redistributed) by the state and municipalities rose steeply from 30 per cent in 1960 to 70 per cent in 1983 (Särlvik and Holmberg 1985). The Alford index has been calculated by a group of Scandinavian specialists for the period 1956–82 and covering nine parliamentary elections. Its decline is clear in spite of some slight fluctuations due to the performance of the parties: 53, 55, 47, 42, 39, 44, 36, 38, 35 (Sundberg and Berglund 1984). The decline is largely due to the growth of the salaried middle classes attracted by the Social Democratic party. Even in Sweden, which is the country with the deeper cleavage between the working class and the other social strata, one in every four workers had voted in the 1960s and 1970s for the non-socialist parties (Särlvik 1969).

The class vote also declined in the other Scandinavian countries for the same main reason as in Sweden: the growth of the tertiary sector and the support for the Social Democratic party of a large share of white-collar voters in this sector. In *Denmark* the class vote index fell by half over nine elections between 1957 and 1984: 58, 56, 56, 53, 43, 27, 36, 43, 27. In

Finland there was a similar decline between 1948 and 1984: 46, 54, 40, 32; and in *Norway* just as steep a fall over seven elections between 1949 and 1979: 49, 44, 44, 40, 36, 37, 29 (Sundberg and Berglund 1984). These bald figures are the results of numerous analyses. The authors admit the reductionist nature of the two-fold dichotomy (left–right, manual workers–middle class) and the fact that the social structure changed during this period. However, in spite of the criticisms that may be levelled at this dichotomization, it must be admitted that in order to generalize it is necessary to simplify. There is no other way to reduce the mountains of electoral statistics to some kind of comparative quintessence.

R. Rose and D. Urwin (1969) suggest that a party that finds two-thirds of its voters in one and the same social category should be regarded as "cohesive"; if not, it should be qualified as "heterogeneous". In fact, what we have here is a statistical artefact. In the case of the Socialist parties, for example, if we consider a long period, from the beginning of the century, a kind of sociological law could be formulated: when the socialist parties were small they were predominantly working class; when they grew into large and sometimes government majority parties they became socially hetero-geneous parties. The phenomenon was already visible in the late 1950s: "the greater the strength of the socialist vote the smaller the working class component in the socialist electorate" (Dogan 1960, 41). In today's pluralist democracies there is no major party that is socially or religiously homogeneous. Only small parties can be homogeneous.

Decline of the religious vote

The influence of religion on voting behaviour has weakened in practically all European democracies because religious belief and practice have declined everywhere. There is no point in going over the history of this decline here; many recent surveys set out the evidence (Dogan 1995).

The best way to describe the weakening of religious cleavages is to study the phenomenon where it appears most plainly, as an ideal type, namely, in the *Netherlands*, because the religious history of this country from 1917 till today is of prime significance, full of lessons for Europe as a whole. Dutch society was long divided into watertight compartments: Catholics, Calvinists, Protestant-reformed, liberals and agnostics. Decentralized, with many large cities, none of which was dominant, this country took the form of a federation of communities and municipalities. In 1917, in the middle of World War I, the Netherlands institutionalized proportional represent-ation. "Consociative" democracy was established through the recognition of "blocs" or "pillars". Both masses and elites were vertically structured. In such a society the class vote was rudimentary.

This situation began to change in the mid-1960s at the very time when "consociative" democracy was reaching maturity. Secularization was causing the decline of the three religion-based parties, which were therefore forced to disband and merge into a single Christian Democratic party – which suffered a serious defeat in the 1994 elections.

The proportion of Dutch citizens who said they did not belong to any religion rose from 24 per cent in 1958 to 42 per cent in 1975, 54 per cent in 1987 and 57 per cent in 1992 (Dekker 1994, 6). Those acknowledging Catholic or Protestant affiliation fell from 75 per cent in 1958 to 38 per cent in 1992, whilst at the same time the other ideologies (Socialist, Liberal, Humanist, Communist and agnostic) climbed together from 25 per cent to 61 per cent (Dekker 1994, 5). The Netherlands was once the most structured and rigid country in Europe from the religious viewpoint, but today it is – with Sweden – the least-religious. Previously religion explained a considerable part of electoral variation. However, it is not social class that has replaced it. The factors that influence voting behaviour today are the current tangible problems and the political options available.

The fact that class cleavage is conditioned by the religious cleavage is particularly clear in *Germany*, where the class vote declined in part because of better relations between Protestants and Catholics and not only because of the narrowing gap between the classes. Detailed research shows that it is mainly the reluctance of Catholic voters to vote socialist that has diminished. For Germany there are two criteria to be considered: church affiliation and strength of religious practice. For a long time the Catholic population was massively behind the Christian Democratic party (61 per cent, against 18 per cent for the Social Democrats in 1953), whereas the Protestants were split between the two parties (Linz 1967b, 301). The German Institute of Statistics analysed the election results in terms of Catholic and Protestant voters from some 500 voting districts spread over the whole of Western Germany. These analyses show that the number of votes cast for one or other of the two major parties depended very much on the proportion of Protestants in the locality. In 1965, for example, votes for the CDU fell, by deciles of Protestants from 66 per cent to 40 per cent for men and from 76 per cent to 46 per cent for women, who had voted in separate polling stations (*Statistische Jahrbuch* 1966, 145). These figures leave no doubt about the predominant importance of religious faith in 1950 and 1960, but the link between Catholicism and the CDU gradually faded in parallel with the decline in attachment to religion. In 1957 the gap between the percentage of Catholics voting for the CDU and those voting for the SPD was 43 percentage points. In 1992, 35 years later, it was only 18 points: 47 per cent and 29 per cent, respectively (Noelle-Neumann and Kocher 1993, 716).

For Germany there is a wealth of documentation on variations in voting related to religious belief and practice spread over more than forty years. It shows a gradual disengagement from the church over these decades. Whereas thirty years ago the two religious criteria – religious affiliation and religious practice – jointly explained a significant part of voting behaviour, today they contribute very little to that explanation, and then only for the oldest voters.

In *Italy*, a number of surveys by the Doxa Institute between 1953 and 1963 indicated that two-thirds of Italians felt that a radical incompatibility existed between Catholicism and Communism. One could not, at one and the same time, be both a "good Catholic" and a "good Communist". According to the same surveys, nearly half all Italians felt there was also an incompatibility between Catholicism and a Socialism which, at the time, was still Marxist. In the 1960s the vast majority of Italians were hostile to any alliance between the Socialist and Christian-Democratic parties, on the grounds that there was a contradiction between Socialist doctrine and Catholic values. It was only later, during the debate on the legalization of divorce, that resistance to such an alliance weakened, far more among men than among women.

The most prevalent voting motivation was attachment to Catholic traditions (Dogan 1962). But gradually, the influence of the church diminished, partly because of the reticence of the church itself. In elections during the 1980s the religious factor in explaining electoral variation was reduced. Reasons for voting choice began to focus on specific problems: inflation, inefficiency of the public services, lack of confidence in the established political class, corruption, scandals, distrust of the traditional parties, etc. At the 1993 elections there was no religious platform. The majority of the Italian electorate is today politically "deconfessionalized".

In *France* in 1946 a referendum rejected the proposed new constitution because there was no "reference to God" in the preamble. A redraft including such a reference was adopted a few months later, again by referendum. Thirty-five years later, in 1981, nearly two-thirds of French people under 55 (and 42 per cent of those over 55) "found no comfort or support in religion".[1] The gap among practising Catholics between the proportion of those voting right and those voting left stayed about the same from 1968 to 1995, but in the meantime the number of non-practising Catholics doubled so that the impact of religion on voting fell considerably for the country as a whole. Significantly, religious issues have not appeared in electoral manifestos for the last twenty years, the only exception being the problem of government subsidies for private Catholic schools.

In the presidential elections of 1995, the religious indicators (regular and occasional churchgoers) were statistically three times more significant that the class-occupational indicators (for manual workers a 14 point difference between the percentages of the candidates furthest to the left and right, against 36 points difference, in the opposite direction, among churchgoers. Cf. survey SOFRES 1989).

In *Spain*, the proportion of practising Catholics fell from 56 per cent to 31 per cent between 1976 and 1983 (Orizo 1983, 177). Religious beliefs fell even more rapidly between 1969 and 1984 (Diaz 1991, 578). Traditionally, three cleavages have divided the Spanish public: regionalism, religion and class. Currently, the cleavages can be ranked in descending order of salience and controversiality, with regionalism first and class last. The massive vote for the socialist party shows how weak the religious influence has become (though this does not necessarily mean any strengthening of the class vote). Today regional identification seems to play a role at least as important as religion and social class.

In *Portugal* the predominance of the religious factor over the socio-economic factor comes out clearly in a sociological analysis of the ten northern provinces where religious practice varies from 24 per cent to 63 per cent of the population, and the ten southern provinces, where the variation is no more than from 2 per cent to 11 per cent (Nataf 1985). There was a close correlation between religious practice and voting at the 1976, 1979 and 1980 elections, and a complete absence of any significant link between the proportion of industrial workers and voting for the left (Socialist, Social Democrat and Communist). In rural areas, however, a notable difference in political behaviour is apparent between smallholders and agricultural workers, though in reality it reveals a difference in religious practice between the two categories of the agricultural population. The religious influence on voting has gradually declined.[2]

An indicator for the religious vote could be constructed, similar to that for the class vote, by deducting the non-practising (or non-believing) proportion of people voting for the right from the practising (or believing) proportion of voters voting the same way. The calculation would be possible for the recent period because the proportion of non-practising voters or non-believers is sufficiently large. But an international comparison would have limited significance because the practice of religion does not have the same meaning for Catholics and Protestants. What is more, longitudinal analysis is rarely possible because of the absence of statistics on religious practice among preceding generations. Since, moreover, religious belief is a question of degree and nuance, dichotomizing would be too reductionist. So the decline in the religious vote needs to be studied through various approaches tailored to suit each individual country. A convenient method has been suggested a long time ago by Seymour Martin Lipset when he found in the United States more variation within each religious group between the highest and lowest class than between Protestants and Catholics in the same class. This method, which avoids sophisticated and pretentious factor analysis, has been applied to several countries.

The only cleavage which has persisted throughout the entire period is the linguistic cleavage. The linguistic map of Europe in the 1990s reflects the map of 1900s, in spite of an increased geographical mobility (with a few exceptions where the population was displaced in Central-East Europe). But this persistence finds its main explanation not in historical roots, but rather in the neuropsychological limitations to the acquisition of a new language after puberty, because of the early lateralization of the brain. The process of socialization and the historical inheritance have here a genetic basis. Language and territory are the most intimate variables in electoral cleavages in Belgium, Switzerland, Spain, Canada, ex-Yugoslavia, most of Eastern Europe and the former Soviet Union.

Decline in the role of the parties

Political parties no longer play the same role in the functioning of democracy that they had in the 1950s and 1960s. After *The End of Ideology* (D. Bell 1960) came the "catch-all parties" (Kirchheimer 1966), "the waning of partisan identification" (Budge *et al*. 1976), the "volatility of the parties" (Pedersen 1979), their "depolarization" (Dalton *et al*. 1984; Alt 1984), the role of "rational voters" (Himmelveit *et al*. 1984), the "post-materialist values" (Inglehart 1984), the "instability of electoral behaviour" (Grunberg 1985), the "liberalization of socialism" (Lipset 1991), and the attention paid to issues to the detriment of party labels.

Empirical research has shown that there has been a significant reduction in ideological space over the last few decades. Assuming the distance between the extremes of right and left to have been one metre in 1960, it would today be no greater than a few decimetres, particularly in those countries that experienced extreme polarization in the 1950s. In Italy the Communist and Neo-fascist parties changed their doctrines and even their names. In France one can observe considerable reticence concerning the old ideologies, now replaced by substantive issues.

The majority of people in most European countries stand at the centre of the left–right scale. In detailed research on the period 1978–94, E. Noelle-Neumann showed dominance of the centre as compared to the extremes (Noelle-Neumann 1994). The same move to the centre and decline in polarization emerge in an analysis of nine other countries conducted in the 1960s (Sani and Sartori 1983). The attraction of the centre showed up clearly in the French elections. More recently the left has accepted economic liberalism, and the right, social solidarity.

The path followed by the socialist or labour parties is significant in this connection. In Germany the Social Democratic party had renounced the marxist ideology at the Bad Godesberg Congress in 1969. When the socialist party came to power in France in 1981, its programme included the nationalization of major sectors of the economy. But after two years of experience in government it veered towards liberalism and for ten years practised a policy contrary to its original programme. In 1995, the British Labour party in their turn have renounced their old ideology and curtailed the power of the unions within the party, which now also represents the values of the middle classes. Seymour Martin Lipset has traced the path of this move of socialism to the right and towards economic liberalism in a large number of countries (Lipset 1991).

Depolarization is only one aspect of the decline in identification with a party. Electoral volatility is another. In France, one month before the 1995 presidential election half of the electorate were still undecided. One citizen in three made a choice only fifteen days before the election (various surveys in March, April, May 1995). The same volatility has been found in the United Kingdom: at the 1980 election many voters waited till the very last minute to choose (Alt 1984, 302). This hesitation is evidence of availability and of the decline of doctrines, and of the priority that many voters gave to political issues rather than to party labels.

A survey following the presidential elections in France in 1995 showed that the majority of voters had firm opinions on a number of salient problems such as unemployment, education, corruption, institutional reform, etc., and that at least one-third of French people were indifferent to political doctrines and labels. One issue – non-European immigration – accounted for the success of the *National Front* in these elections. Voting for this party was an ideological gesture for only a minority of those who did so. For most it was a reaction to a practical problems of daily life in places greatly affected by immigration. In the European elections of 1989 the immigration problem was already the main reasons for the far right vote in the working-class areas.

The declining number of party militants, the difficulties encountered by the political parties' newspapers and the changes in the political vocabulary are symptoms of the waning role of the parties in political life. Another feature is the disappearance of the "parties of integration" as opposed to the "parties of representation" (except for the small extremist parties).

In the 1990s many workers who have voted over a long time for the socialist left, for the "party of the working class", have changed their mind, thinking that possibly the liberals and conservatives stand a better chance of getting the economy to prosper again.

Status inconsistency and the new cleavages

How can we explain that the role of the social class in electoral cleavages has diminished in spite of the fact that social inequalities persist, and why class identity weakens while the perception of inequalities is better diffused? One of the major reasons of this paradoxical situation could be found in the massive increase of cases of status incongruence. This concept was formulated in the 1950s by Gerhard Lenski (1970), but soon after was somehow neglected, overshadowed by the than dominant "social class".

Status incongruence can result from a gap between the level of income and the level of education, from vertical social mobility, from the loss of the hierarchical position, and from dozens of other inconsistencies between the social position in one domain and the relatively inferior status along other dimensions.

Status discrepancy in Western Europe can be observed today probably ten times more often than in the early 1950s. This increase appears in census results by simple cross-tabulation of various indicators like education, income, hierarchical position, qualification, social origin, ethnic origin, and so on. There is a logical relation between the spread of status incongruencies and weakening of social class consciousness. The neglect of status inconsistency in the study of electoral cleavages during the last two or three decades may be one of the reasons why often only a small part of the variance is explained. This neglect is astonishing when one remembers the pioneer study of Berelson, Lazarsfeld and McPhee (1954) in terms of cross-pressures.

Status inconsistency has become an essential aspect of the social stratification process in the complex post-industrial society. It is generated by the growth of the middle classes and the decline of the peasantry and the industrial working class. Vertical mobility is an important source of status discrepancy. Most studies on social mobility had focused on upward mobility, particularly during the post-war period of economic development: "the process of social mobility has become widespread as the twentieth century has advanced, largely as a result of the economic development that has produced occupational differentiation" (Turner 1992, 19). But in the more recent period, downward mobility has become equally important. Today, social mobility consists mostly in what, four decades ago, Lipset and Zetterberg called "the interchange of ranks" (1966, 565): for every move up there must be a move down. What was then a hypothesis is today empirically confirmed: "some proportion of the children of the middle class . . . fall in socio-economic status . . . some do not have the abilities to complete higher education or to get along in a bureaucratic hierarchy, and fall by the wayside. . . . Whatever the reason that some persons of middle class origin move downward, they leave room for others of lower-class background to rise" (1966, 570). Today, millions of Europeans born into middle classes are in this incongruent situation. The downward move can be intragenerational or intergenerational.

Another source of status incongruence is the freeing from primary social groups, particularly religious communities and family ties. As already noticed, religion intervenes less and less in electoral choices. Individual promotion through schooling predominates more and more over family background. Status inconsistency is a privileged ground for individualistic tendencies. Such an interpretation in terms of increasing individual freedom is not necessarily incompatible with the persistence of social inequalities.

The concept of strong or weak status crystallization also seems useful for understanding electoral cleavages. This concept refers to the degree of inconstancy or coherence of a person's ranking on different criteria. A strong status crystallization implies that a person is rated consistently by all important criteria whether the rating is high or low. In the 1990s, a large part of the population, including young people, appears to be in a situation of weak status crystallization. Solid social class can exist only if the majority of the population experiences a strong status crystallization.

Today, in Western Europe the most obvious case of status incongruence is the category of school teachers, who today are more numerous than were the workers in the heavy industrial plants of four decades ago. For many teachers there is a serious gap between the level of their education and role in the society and the level of their income. The leftist orientation of the majority of them can be better explained in terms of status rather than in terms of class.

Another case is the young people with a "diploma" in their pocket, but who do not find a job according to their aspirations. In most countries of Western Europe and in the United States there is, in the 1990s, an over-abundance of young people with a college degree for whom our highly technological society does not offer sufficient jobs – the existing ones being protected by the unions for the current occupants. In most countries, two-thirds of the people at the age of 18 are still in school. The advanced post-industrial society, in search of productivity, replaces people by machines, producing a new kind of educated proletariat, born into the middle class. In Western Europe in the last decade, except in Germany, one of every four or five young people under the age of 25 was unemployed. Those who accept a job beneath their abilities, a "degraded job", represent one of the most interesting varieties of status incongruence.

Frequent cases of status inconsistency can be found in the ethnic and racial minorities, particularly in Britain, France, Germany, Belgium, the Netherlands, Switzerland and Austria, as well as in the United States. Immigrants of European origin are integrated and assimilated in a single generation, the best example being the eight million French citizens of Italian, Spanish, Portuguese, Polish or Armenian origins. The children of these immigrants are not normally in a position of status inconsistency. When religion is combined with ethnicity and language, as with immigrants from the southern rim of the Mediterranean, the integration process takes two generations, and the younger generation often experiences a status incongruence. When color of the skin is added, the difficulties of integration are compounded. Many immigrants from South Asia or Black Africa feel excluded from the host society. Their main feeling is exclusion and not status inconsistency.

Sociologists and historians, among them W. Sombart and Seymour Martin Lipset, have asked why there is no socialist party in the United States. Among the factors stated are the continuous waves of immigrants who started at the bottom of social pyramid. Without being fully aware, American society had long been a supporter of slavery of the black population. In such a society of permanent immigration, with a voting system based on plurality, there was no room for "a party of the working class". Since the ethnic minorities obtained access to the political forum in the 1960s, and with new waves of immigrants, a major phenomenon is taking place transforming American society progressively and profoundly: multiculturalism. Already in 1971, Gary Marx wrote in the introduction to a reader on racial conflict: "Almost wherever one looks, race impinges itself upon the American conscience" (1971, 1). Multiculturalism is a new source of status incongruence. In such a society divided vertically in racial and ethnic cleavages, one of the two parties has become the party of all vertical minorities. Western Europe has not yet arrived at such a configuration of parties.

Multiculturalism, particularly in the United States, France, Britain, Germany and Belgium generates a society where status conflicts may predominate over conflicts between social classes. If this hypothesis is confirmed, the Western post-industrial society will remain for some time a society with deep vertical cleavages, which instead of being essentially religious, will be primarily ethnic. The change in the nature of vertical cleavages may be one of the most significant transformations since the publication of *Party Systems and Voter Alignments*.

Conclusion

In sociology, the concept of social class has maintained a central place for a long time. It has been highlighted in many theories and ideologies, to such an extent that religious, ethnic, linguistic and cultural stratifications have been somewhat neglected. However, if leftist movements, in particular socialism, have only lately succeeded in attracting an electoral majority, the main reason for this lateness is resistance from organized religion.

From this point of view, Karl Marx diagnosed correctly the "false consciousness" of "confessional voters", "manipulated" by "the ruling class". Several generations of Marxists have indeed perceived the "obstacle", but they have not analysed it sociologically. The task to demonstrate how during decades religion has played a role of barrier against "class", was left to electoral sociology, especially those sociologists who adopted the notion of criss-crossing cleavages.

Dozens of books and articles sustained the thesis of the predominance of social class in electoral behaviour, especially and curiously many non-Marxist American authors. How could such a fragile generalization be disseminated in manuals, how could it survive so long, and escape the critical eye of so many eminent sociologists, is a question that we shall make no attempt to answer here. It would seem that those of us sociologists who have not clearly perceived during the hot ideological debate in the years of the cold war, the countervailing factors to "class", have failed in our professional mission to bring a useful clarifying contribution to the debate.

One possible explanation is that most studies in electoral sociology in Europe were not published in English and therefore remained unknown to American specialists, who made generalizations from works published in English.

In reality, as demonstrated by empirical evidence, it was religion and everything which comes with it as ascriptive variables, that has predominated in electoral behaviour and not social class. Only in a few countries, out of twenty competitive democracies, social class appeared more influential than religion. But even in these few countries, social class has been counter-balanced by cultural or regional factors, such as the catholic minority status in Britain or the "periphery" in Norway. Even in these few countries social class has declined as an explanatory factor in electoral models during the last decades. The further back we go into the 1950s the more important religion, ethnicity and regional community become. Paradoxically, the vertical cultural cleavages were the strongest during the great ideological debate in Europe between 1945 and 1975.

The countries for which social class is still a major explanation today are also the countries where vertical cleavages are less important, and vice-versa.

Another possible explanation of the decline of class in voting behaviour, in spite of the persistence of social inequalities, can be found in the change of ethnic composition of the lowest strata of the working class, a pheno-menon already mentioned. Throughout Western Europe the lower strata of industry and services have been deserted by native workers, who have been replaced by non-European immigrants. Today a significant part of the working class is composed of immigrants who do not have the right to vote. In many countries class solidarity is being eroded. Some native workers, who think of themselves as "good stock" and who are surrounded by immigrants in the work place or in the immediate neighbourhood, protest against the parties perceived as responsible for immigration, by voting for extreme rightist parties. This phenomenon can appear at the electoral level only in multi-party systems, like in France or in Austria. It is not visible in a two-party system, like the British or the American. Here we see how electoral methods are conditioning contemporary electoral cleavages, as they did in the 1920s and in the 1930s.

The presence of non-European ethnic minorities weakens the solidarity of the working class. This ethnic cleavage is in Europe a new cleavage: it did not exist thirty years ago, and it is unlikely that will soon disappear.

The decline of class voting results also from the individualization of electoral behaviour. Everywhere in Europe the majority of voters have for a long time been influenced and sometimes conditioned by their attachment to a particular religion, by their socio-economic status or their perception of it, and by the ethnic, regional or linguistic community they belonged to. But today more than at any time in the past, with the development of education and the media, an increasing number of voters behave as free individuals rather than as members of a group or community. This individual emancipation as voters, reflects the general phenomenon of individualism seen by theoreticians such as Elias, Giddens, Luhmann, Inglehart or Therborn. The title of a recent book succinctly expresses this process of the liberalization of the individual: *The Individualizing Society* (Ester, Halman and de Moor 1993).

Electoral volatility and dealignment from parties, analysed by various authors, stem from individualization of voting, which in turn is a result of the parallel decline of religious influence, social diversification, the increase in cultural levels, the decline in size and changes in the composition of the working class, the decline of traditional rural populations, the homogenization of the national territory through the development of communications, and many other factors.

In short, the growing individualization of voting behaviour is the result of the parallel decline of the class vote and the religious vote and also of the decline in partisanship, with all the advantages and risks that this independence brings with it.

The decline of class voting has preceded in Western democracies the implosion of the Soviet Union. This decline was one of the greatest deceptions of Marxist ideologists. Electoral sociology must now build new concepts and more refined theories than concept of class, in order to understand the relationship between new inequalities and new behaviour.

Notes

1 Unpublished data from *European Value Study* 1981.
2 Unpublished data from *European Value Study* 1981 and *World Value Study* 1991.

7 Change and stability in the Finnish party system

Pertti Pesonen

Round years refresh old news. The year 1997 felt noteworthy because thirty years had passed since *Party Systems and Voter Alignments* was printed in 1967. For the Finns 1997 meant also the 80th year of independence from Russia, and March 1997 marked the 90th anniversary of Finland's (and the world's) first parliamentary election with universal suffrage and eligibility.

The Finnish party system became mass-based with many of its "frozen" features in 1907, and independence caused durable readjustments to it. Obviously the political parties and the party system as a whole have developed and have gone through many changes, but their stable features have also been remarkable. The same is true of the party systems of most liberal democracies. There has been no stability without change, nor have changes taken place without stability.

Profound changes have affected all European societies and also the political environments of their party systems. One can even identify and label distinct phases within the past thirty years. For instance, there were the years of the "rejection of political authority" (1965–80) and the "crisis of the welfare state and of communism" (1980–90), until it was time for "integration, unemployment and immigration" (Lane and Ersson 1994a).

Yet Alan Ware counted that of all the twenty-three established, independent liberal democracies in the late 1950s, only four (Belgium, France, India, and Israel) had a radically different party system thirty years later, at the end of the 1980s (Ware 1996, 213). In his comparison Finland belongs to the quiet majority, albeit with unique features, and it stands out, nevertheless, as one country whose economic development and social transformation took place exceptionally rapidly.

An update of Finland's party news since 1962

Table 7.1 is a reproduction of the table which in the 1967 volume illustrated the development of Finland's party system, first during the inter-war period from 1919 to 1939, and then during the post-war years from 1945 to 1962 (Allardt and Pesonen 1967, 330). Table 7.2 updates the information. It shows the composition of the Parliament (*Eduskunta*) and the

Table 7.1 Results of the Finnish general elections of 1919, 1939, 1945 and 1962

| Parties | Distribution of mandates | | | | Per cent distribution of popular vote | | | | | | | | | | | |
| | | | | | Total | | | | Urban | | | | Rural[a] | | | |
	1919	1939	1945	1962	1919	1939	1945	1962	1919	1939	1945	1962	1919	1939	1945	1962
Swedish People's party	22	18	14	14	12.1	9.6	7.9	6.4	24.6	14.4	11.9	8.2	9.7	8.2	7.2	5.6
Swedish Leftist	–	–	1	–	–	0.5	0.5	–	–	1.1	1.0	–	–	0.3	0.3	–
National Coalition (Conservatives)	28	25	28	32	15.7	13.6	15.0	15.0	21.7	18.4	20.4	21.9	14.0	11.4	11.9	10.5
National Progressive/Finnish People's party (1962)	26	6	9	13	12.8	4.8	5.2	6.3	14.2	8.9	10.1	11.1	17.3	3.5	3.3	3.6
Agrarian Union	42	56	49	53	19.7	22.9	21.3	23.0	1.3	1.7	2.1	3.3	20.6	29.7	26.8	34.0
Small Holders/Small Peasants (1962)	–	2	–	–	–	2.1	1.2	2.2	–	0.2	0.1	0.4	–	2.8	1.7	3.1
Social Democratic party	80	85	50	38	38.0	39.8	25.1	19.5	38.1	49.3	25.9	24.1	38.3	37.4	24.9	17.2
Christian Labor/Social Democratic Opposition (1962)	2	–	–	2	1.5	–	–	4.4	0.0[b]	–	–	5.2	0.1[b]	–	–	4.0
Democratic Union of the Finnish People (Communist)	–	–	49	47	–	–	23.5	22.0	–	–	28.2	24.0	–	–	23.8	21.2
Others[c]	–	8	–	1	0.2	6.7	0.3	1.2	0.1	6.0	0.3	1.8	0.0	6.7	0.1	0.8
Total	200	200	200	200	100.0	100.0	100.0	100.0	100.0	100.0	100.0	100.0	100.0	100.0	100.0	100.0
(Millions of votes)					(1.0)	(1.3)	(1.7)	(2.3)	(0.2)	(0.3)	(0.6)	(0.8)	(0.8)	(1.0)	(1.0)	(1.4)

Source: Official election statistics.
Notes: [a] Rural municipalities and townships.
[b] These votes are mainly included in the above figures for Agrarian Union.
[c] In 1939, all these mandates and most of the votes were given to the "Patriotic People's Movement" (extreme right); in 1962 the seat was gained by the Liberal Union.

Table 7.2 Results of the Finnish general elections of 1966, 1970, 1991 and 1995

Parties	Distribution of mandates				Distribution of popular vote											
					Total				Urban				Rural			
	1966	1970	1991	1995	1966	1970	1991	1995	1966	1970	1991	1995	1966	1970	1991	1995
Swedish People's party	12	12	12	12	6.0	5.7	5.5	5.4	6.8	6.1	5.7	5.3	5.3	5.2	5.0	4.7
Conservatives	26	37	40	39	13.8	18.0	24.6	19.5	17.9	23.6	23.1	21.2	9.5	12.3	14.5	13.9
Liberal People's	9	8	1	–	6.5	5.9	0.8	0.6	9.7	8.3	0.9	0.6	3.5	3.5	0.5	0.5
Center party	49	36	55	44	21.2	17.1	20.4	19.4	4.6	5.4	17.9	13.5	35.8	29.2	38.7	34.3
Rural party	1	18	7	1	1.0	10.5	4.8	1.3	0.2	6.4	4.5	1.0	1.8	14.8	5.5	2.1
Soc. Dem. party	55	52	48	63	27.2	23.4	22.1	28.1	34.3	28.9	24.7	31.1	21.4	17.7	18.7	24.2
SDP Opposition	7	–	–	–	2.6	1.4	–	–	3.2	1.6	–	–	2.1	1.1	–	–
Dem.Union/Left Wing Alliance	41	36	19	22	21.2	16.6	10.1	11.1	22.7	18.2	11.8	12.7	20.2	14.9	9.9	10.7
Christian People's	–	1	8	7	0.5	1.1	3.1	3.0	0.6	1.3	3.1	2.8	0.4	1.3	2.9	3.3
The Greens	–	–	10	9	–	–	6.8	6.5	–	–	9.3	8.2	–	–	4.3	4.3
Progressive Finnish party	–	–	–	2	–	–	–	2.8	–	–	–	3.3	–	–	–	1.8
Ecological party	–	–	–	1	–	–	–	0.3	–	–	–	0.3	–	–	–	0.2
Others	–	–	–	–	0.0	0.2	1.8	2.0	0.0	0.2	–	–	0.0	0.2	–	0.2
Total	200	200	200	200	100.0	100.0	100.0	100.0	100.0	100.0	100.0	100.0	100.0	100.0	100.0	100.0
(Millions of votes)					(2.4)	(2.5)	(2.8)	(2.8)	(1.1)	(1.3)	(1.7)	(1.8)	(1.3)	(1.3)	(1.0)	(1.0)

distribution of votes cast for the political parties during the late 1960s and in the early 1990s.

Among the political parties there have been both winners and losers, new appearances and disappearances, constants and flash movements. There has also been some fragmentation in the party system: the average number of parties receiving at least 1 percent of the votes rose from 8.0 in the 1960s to 9.5 in the 1980s, both means being about 2 percentage points higher than the European average (Gallagher, Laver and Mair 1995, 232). Yet the general picture of Finland's political parties and party system has been characterized by considerable stability.

The Conservative party belongs to the winners of the post-1960s "rejection years". Its vote shares began to grow during the 1970s, from only 13.8 percent in 1966 to the peak of 23.1 percent in 1987. Its support base was broadened by the rapid growth of the white collar groups, and it also began to receive new "sympathy votes" because of its 21-year long exclusion from government coalitions, from 1966 to 1987.

The Swedish People's party has been a survivor. Its share of the votes declined only 1 percentage point during the three decades from 1962 to 1995, while the percentage of Finland's Swedish-speaking minority decreased from 7.3 to 5.8 percent. In 1966 the party lost two seats in Parliament, but since then it has kept its 12 seats (one of the counted MPs being the representative from Åland).

The Finnish People's party, in turn, belongs to the losers. It changed its name to Liberal People's party in 1965. Unlike its "sister party" in Sweden it has suffered a gradual loss of voter support and parliamentary representation. It had no seat in Parliament between 1983 and 1991, and is out of it again since 1995.

A completely new non-socialist party, with some similarity to the Liberals, entered the political scene in 1994. It adopted the name of its distant relative from the beginning of the century, the Young Finnish party, but it translates its name into English as the "Progressive Finnish party". A strong supporter of the free market economy, this party is yet to make its breakthrough outside the capital city area, where it managed to turn two PhDs into MPs in 1995.

The largest non-socialist party, the Agrarian Union, had to adjust to the narrowing of its farmer base. It switched to the new name Center party in 1965. A corresponding move had been made by its sister parties in Sweden in 1957 and in Norway in 1959. In the election of 1970 the Center party suffered a humiliating defeat. Having often been more than twice the size of the Conservatives it elected the smaller Parliament group of the two, and it had a similar fate in three elections from 1979 to 1987. However, in 1991 it staged a mighty comeback after having spent four years in opposition.

The decline of the Center party in 1970 coincided with the astonishing victory of its former splinter group, the Small Farmers' party, which had changed its name to the Finnish Rural party after the 1966 election. Its parliamentary representation grew from one to eighteen seats. Then it had internal problems and a splinter party broke from it, but once again it came back with 17 MPs in 1983. However, new internal problems eroded its credibility and, after receiving only one MP, it also went bankrupt and was discontinued in the fall of 1995. What remains of its heritage functions under the new name True Finns.

One more non-socialist party has been in Parliament since 1970. The Christian People's party began to grow, although it never quite gained the relative significance of its Norwegian counterpart. Its parliamentary representation has slightly exceeded its relative vote share, because it has made good use of the "electoral alliance" option of the Finnish election system. Furthermore, there have been numerous short-lived miniparties, such as the Constitutional People's party which gained one MP in 1975 and one again in 1983.

The political left suffered a gradual decline in Finland. In the 1966 election the three leftist parties fared unusually well and rose to a majority of 103 seats in the 200-member Eduskunta; four years later two of them totaled 88 seats, and in 1991 the left was down to only 67 seats. However, the election victory of the Social Democrats halted the downward trend: the two leftist parties got 85 members elected to Parliament in 1995.

On the far left the Finnish Communists became a party with serious internal troubles. The party never electioneered under its own name; its front organization was the Finnish People's Democratic Union. Two wings of the Communists themselves presented separate candidate lists in the municipal elections of 1960, and the split within the party broke wide open in August 1968 as a consequence of conflicting attitudes toward the Soviet invasion of Czechoslovakia – only four days before the party had prepared to celebrate its 50th anniversary (founded in Moscow in 1918). Eventually the party went bankrupt. Since April 1990, the present Left Wing Alliance has continued the activity of the FPDU, but it does not want to have anything to do with the Communist tradition of the radical left; in May 1995 it expelled from its ranks all those members who wanted to remain in the Communist party as well.

The FPDU was for a long time an even-powered challenger of the Social Democratic party; twice (in 1958 and 1962) it gained the larger parliamentary group in the political left. But the SDP did not decline like the far left. It suffered a temporary setback in 1991, but between 1966 and 1987 its parliament group had varied only between 52 and 57 seats and its vote share between 23.4 percent (in 1970) and 27.2 percent (in 1966). In 1995 the SDP scored its best election result in all the fifteen post-war elections, receiving 63 seats. An opposition group had broken from it in 1958, but this Socialist League of Workers and Small Farmers was split and withered away by the 1970s.

The first new party of the 1980s was the Green movement. Still unorganized as a party, it gained two seats in Parliament in 1983, two weeks

after the German Greens had gained their first parliamentary representation. The party's support has been stabilized around 7 percent in elections
and 10 percent in opinion polls, which is fairly high in comparison with the
environmentalists and greens in other countries. In 1995 it also became a
partner in the government coalition of five parties.

The year 1969 marked a change in the formal status of Finland's political
parties. A Party Law was passed, requiring all political parties to be listed in
the party register which is kept by the Ministry of Justice. It had become
necessary to formalize the parties and make them clearly distinguishable
from other civic organizations, when parliamentary parties began to receive
financial support from the state in 1967 and when they were given a special
position by the renewed Election Law of 1969.

Any new party with national (not only local) political goals, a demo-
cratically functioning membership organization, and the signatures of at
least 5,000 enfranchised supporters, will be added to the register, but a
party which does not elect any member to Parliament in two successive
elections, will be removed from it. When the party register was cleaned of
those parties which had not won any seats in 1991 and 1995, fourteen
remained. In the election of 1995, eighteen parties nominated candidates,
and in 1997 the party register contained twenty political parties, including
the Communist party which was re-established in January 1997.

Party systems are dynamic, and there has been no lack of noteworthy
news about Finnish parties since the 1960s. During the 1980s scholars had
particular reasons to emphasize changes, including the birth of new parties.
In his summary of these developments, Onni Rantala reminded us that new
parties were typical of the non-socialist side only, while the parties of the
left coped internally with their tendency to splinter (Rantala 1982, 35).
Additional new parties appeared in Finland in the 1980s (the Greens) and
in the 1990s (Progressive Liberals), but very few accomplished a breakthrough. And unlike many West European countries, no radical political
group has entered the far right of the Finnish scene.

Thus, a review of the popular support and parliamentary representation
of Finland's political parties from the years of "rejection of political
authority" to the 1990s of "integration and unemployment", reveals more
stability than change; there really would be no reason to call the party system
"radically different" in the 1990s. Most of the time the Social Democratic
party has been the largest one but not large enough to be dominant, and
the Center party has been the second major party. Up to the 1980s the third
largest party was the FPDU. For a while there followed a system of four large
parties, but with the declining support of the Left Wing the Conservatives
have stood as one of the big three, while the tradition of having one party to
the left of the Social Democrats has also persisted.

In six of the fifteen parliamentary elections since 1945, the two largest
parties have totaled fewer than 100 members in the 200-member parliament, and they never had more than 110. That defines Finland quite

distinctly as one of Europe's "even party systems", a label given by Alan Ware for multi-party systems of at least three large parties where the largest two gain less than 65 percent of the seats (see Ware 1996, 162). When Klaus von Beyme listed in 1985 the ten "ideological groups" in Western democracies, he observed that Finland with eight parties was the only country that came close to having a party in each group (von Beyme 1985, 24).

The election of Finnish members to the European Parliament in October 1996 resulted in a well balanced illustration of the even party system: each of the three big parties won four seats, and the remaining four seats were divided among three other parties. Nine additional parties tried in vain to gain a seat. Inside the EP, Finland, like most EU countries, has members in five of the total of nine political groups. The Social Democrats and Conservatives fit well in the two big groups, the Party of European Socialists and the European People's Party, respectively. Likewise, the EP's Green group and the group of European United Left–Nordic Green Left provide natural contexts for Finland's Green MEP and two Left Wing MEPs. On the other hand, neither the Center party nor the Swedish People's party found an equally adequate counterpart in the rather artificial European party system. The MEPs from these two have joined the group closest to them, namely the EP's Liberal, Democratic and Reformist party.

The broadening social base of political parties

In the 1960s, Finland was an unusually rapidly industrializing country. Soon thereafter the tertiary sector began to dominate its economy. In the 1990s Finland was transforming to an advanced information society and had, according to some statistics, the world's highest number per capita of both mobile telephones and internet users.

The economic changes involved a variety of changes in social structure. The extent of internal migration is illustrated by the fact that the parliamentary representation of Helsinki and the surrounding Uusimaa (Nyland) constituency had grown from 31 seats in 1948 to 37 seats in 1962, then rose to 50 seats in 1991. In addition to internal migration, some 500,000 Finns emigrated to Sweden. The country also became more urbanized, the old age groups grew larger, and the young generations were educated more. The standard of living rose so rapidly that income per capita (controlled for inflation) tripled in thirty years, until the recession of the early 1990s halted that development. The worst of the recession was overcome in four years: one annual world survey of competitiveness ranked Finland 18th in 1995, but fourth (after the USA, Singapore and Hong Kong) in 1997 (*The Economist*, 29 March 1997, 27).

In the 1960s, as before, political parties based their role and voter support on the nation's class structure. For instance, in the well-known comparative analysis of survey data from the 1960s which reduced the party systems to the simple left/right dichotomy (Rose 1974, 17), occupation (class) explained 32 percent of the partisan variance in Finland as in Sweden, while religion and region explained nothing. But religion was the strong predictor of the left/right choice in Austria, France, Belgium, and Italy. In Ireland partisanship was not related to social structure, nor did it explain much in Great Britain either (Rose 1974, 17).

Since then, the Finnish parties have remained more stable than some social structures. Due to their declining numbers the farmers became an insufficient support base for a large party, and the industrial and construction workers, in turn, were pushed to second place when the service occupations became the major employer of the workforce. Among the economically active population, the share of agriculture and forestry went down from 35.5 percent in 1960 to 8.0 percent in 1994. The share of manufacturing and construction has declined less, from 31.5 percent in 1960 to 26.1 percent in 1994, while "trade and transport" went up from 18.0 percent to 32.8 percent, and services doubled from 14.8 percent to 30.5 percent (*Statistical Yearbook of Finland* 1997, 96).

When compared with other Western countries, Finland was industrialized relatively late and its social changes happened unusually rapidly. The social transformation had obvious consequences for the structure of party support. Table 7.3 shows the occupational profiles of the supporters of Finland's four largest parties in 1976, 1982 and 1991, and also dichoto-

Table 7.3 Occupations of younger and older supporters of the four largest parties in 1976, 1982 and 1991 (in percentages)

Occupation groups	Party and ages							
	FPDU/Left		SDP		Center		Conservative	
	18–40	41–75	18–40	41–75	18–40	41–75	18–40	41–75
1976								
Farmers	5	9	1	5	45	77	12	12
Workers	72	84	63	74	28	14	19	18
White collar	23	7	36	21	27	9	69	70
Total	100	100	100	100	100	100	100	100
(*n*)	(75)	(93)	(129)	(168)	(99)	(111)	(69)	(71)
1982								
Farmers	–	5	–	6	16	56	3	11
Workers	75	82	55	68	43	16	27	14
White collar	25	14	45	26	41	28	69	75
Total	100	101	100	100	100	100	99	100
(*n*)	(102)	(66)	(232)	(231)	(114)	(107)	(190)	(159)
1991								
Farmers	–	–	–	4	26	39	6	11
Workers	64	72	48	55	32	25	6	8
White collar	36	28	52	40	42	36	89	81
Total	100	100	100	99	100	100	101	100
(*n*)	(28)	(29)	(54)	(114)	(72)	(117)	(71)	(79)

Source: Adapted from Pesonen *et al.* 1993, 107.

mizes each measurement into two age groups, the younger (18–40 years) and the older (41–75 years) supporters of the parties.

Two parties have been consistently dominated by one of the three occupational classes, namely the FPDU on the far left and the Conservatives on the right. Each comparison also shows that the FPDU appeared to be a more homogeneous labor party for the older age group, while the younger supporters broadened the party's support base toward the white collar occupations. The 1982 measurement of Conservative party supporters shows interesting age differences: the party was supported by very few young farmers, but by relatively many young workers. Because of its traditional social roots, the Conservative party drew an obvious advantage from the rapid growth of the middle classes.

Farmers were in the majority among the older half of Center party's supporters up to 1982, but not any more among the party's younger supporters. Each comparison shows how the younger voters have broadened the social base of the party to include more workers and more people in the white collar occupations. Among the Center party's younger supporters, the farmers were the largest of the three groups only in 1976, and in 1982 they became the smallest group. The Social Democrats did not attract young farmers at all. The older SDP supporters have continued to have a clear, albeit decreasing worker majority, but the party's younger sympathizers became evenly divided between workers and white collar groups. All through this period the SDP was a less homogeneous labor party than the FPDU/Left Wing.

Table 7.4 turns the comparisons around; instead of party profiles its comparisons concern the distribution of votes cast by different social groups in the elections of 1983 and 1991. As the grouping of the electorate also takes into account people's life situation, the third largest group next to the white collar (middle class) occupations and the "blue collar" workers, are the retired "pensioners". Even the students outgrew the farmers. The sixth group, the "others", contains people who did not belong to the active labor force, such as the home-makers and the unemployed. In the electorate as a whole, the Social Democrats, the Left Wing, the Rural party and the Conservatives lost support from 1983 to 1991, while the Center party and the Greens were victorious in the 1991 election.

In both elections, a majority of Finnish workers voted for one of the two labor parties: about one-third chose the SDP and one-quarter chose the far left. In addition, in 1983 as many workers voted for either the Conservatives or the Rural party as for the FPDU, and in 1991 the Center party alone was almost as popular among the workers as the Left Wing alliance. Of the farmers, the majority has remained faithful to the Center party, while the Conservatives gained some farmer votes and the Rural party lost the tithes it still collected in 1983.

The far left did not appeal much to the white collar voters, about one-fifth of whom has supported the Social Democrats. As two-fifths of them

Table 7.4 Distribution of votes in 1983 and 1991 among six social groups in Finland (in percentages)

Parties	White collar		Workers		Farmers		Retired		Students		Others		Total	
	1983	1991	1983	1991	1983	1991	1983	1991	1983	1991	1983	1991	1983	1991
Swedish	7	8	3	1	4	4	5	5	11	7	–	5	5	5
Conservative	38	30	11	5	13	19	14	14	29	23	20	17	22	19
Center	14	17	9	21	69	74	15	28	14	26	44	26	18	25
Rural	7	6	12	3	9	–	14	5	7	5	9	6	10	5
Christ.	3	3	2	3	5	–	2	4	–	7	2	3	2	3
Soc. Dem.	21	18	37	34	–	–	32	28	19	10	15	25	27	23
FPDU/Left	6	6	24	24	–	–	17	12	3	4	10	7	13	10
Greens	3	9	2	5	–	3	1	1	9	15	–	7	2	7
Others	1	3	–	4	–	–	–	3	8	3	–	4	1	3
TOTAL	100	100	100	100	100	100	100	100	100	100	100	100	100	100
(n/1983)	(290)		(298)		(52)		(140)		(49)		(60)		(889)	
(n/1991)		(341)		(186)		(53)		(155)		(77)		(180)		(994)

Source: Adopted from Pesonen et al. 1993, 108.

chose the Conservatives, together the SDP and the Conservatives attracted the majority of the growing middle-class group in 1983. However, in the 1991 election these two losers of that year's election hardly got one-half of the white collar votes. Now the Center party and the Greens also harvested votes from this social group.

The rise of the Greens was largely based on their popularity among the students. On the other hand, the political left, very popular among the students in the 1970s, no longer attracted them in the 1980s and early 1990s. The left parties have found compensation for their lack of success among the students and the young in general, in an above-average reliance on the large group of pensioners.

One can conclude from Tables 7.3 and 7.4, that (1) the Center party has remained the farmers' main political representative, but its nation-wide success has become increasingly dependent on its ability to broaden the base towards the white collar groups, (2) the FPDU/Left Wing Alliance continues to be a fairly homogeneous labor party with difficulties in broadening its support into other social groups, (3) the Social Democratic party is also strongly based in the laboring population, but the SDP's strength also depends on its ability to attract middle class voters and to maintain the favors of the retired population, (4) the Conservatives are clearly a middle class party, but now a party that needs to compete for the middle class votes not only with the SDP, but also with the Center party and the Greens, and (5) the Greens have a youthful base: many students and very few retired people.

Thus, the class base of Finnish political parties, when the classes are defined through occupation, has become somewhat more diversified and the political socialization of new age cohorts seems to hasten the diversification, but the linkage between social classes and the party system remains quite relevant.

Region did not explain the distribution of the left/right choices in Finland, whereas a dichotomy in which the Center party and the FPDU/Left Wing would be combined against all the other parties, has been and remains associated with regional differences. Such political differences have depended, but not exclusively, on the economic and social differences between different parts of the country. Many regions in Finland, as in other countries, have preserved their special political traditions or "political climates", and some of those have shown remarkable continuity. The most obvious example of regionalism in Finland is the concentration of the Swedish people's party in those four districts where Swedish is spoken, whereas social structure does not offer such an evident explanation why the Center party wins one-half of all the seats in the two most Northern districts (in 1995: thirteen out of 26) but faces great difficulty in trying to attract voters in and near the capital city (two seats out of 50).

Differences in the occupational structures in southern and north-eastern Finland also explained to a large extent, but not entirely, why industrial and backwoods Communism emerged from the early socialist origins as two distinguishable political traditions. Both types, the traditional industrial and the traditional backwoods Communism, also continued since the 1970s even though their numbers declined. And in addition to these two, there emerged a third type, appropriately characterized as modern backwoods Communism (Zilliacus 1995, 162–85).

The shrinking red/white cleavage

It has been and still remains customary to group Finland's political parties into two blocs, the socialist and the non-socialist, which correspond to the left/right dichotomy. The former group of parties has included the Social Democrats, the Communists with their allies, and the other parties of the left, while the latter group included the rest of Finland's political parties. But the two Green representatives who were elected to Parliament in 1983 disliked both labels. They were seated in the middle of the party spectrum, but were unwilling to be related to the left/right dimension. In the election statistics for 1991, the group "others" included seven parties, namely, the Greens, the Finnish Pensioners' party, the Women's movement, the Independent Pensioners of Finland, the Ecological Party the Greens, the Humanity party, and the Party for Pensioners' and Green Mutual Responsibility. However, in addition to the 6.8 percent vote for the Greens, the six other "other parties" totaled no more than 1.6 percent of the votes in 1991.

The traditional cleavage in the Finnish society – not only politically, but also culturally, even in sports and some economic activity – into the "reds" and the "whites", has gradually lost its importance. During seven decades of Finland's independence it had its impact, very important also at the political elite level. The Social Democrats and non-socialist parties did not co-operate in the government before 1937. In that year the wide cleavage was bridged, enough to launch a fifty-year period of "red–green" government coalitions.

There were variations of the theme during that half-century, such as the war-time national coalitions of all parties, single-party minority governments, non-socialist coalitions, and "popular front" coalitions which included the Communists. There were also issues on the political agenda which got the Agrarian Union and the Communists to oppose jointly the Social Democrats and the Conservatives, but the co-operation between the Social Democratic party and the Agrarian Union/Center party remained the backbone of government coalitions. The red/white cleavage was thereby bridged, but without questioning the relevance of the ideological left/right dimension in Finnish politics.

In 1987 the era of "red–green" coalitions and the continuity of the left/right dimension in coalition formation, was brought to an end. After the election of 1987, Conservative party leader Harri Holkeri became prime minister of a cabinet which included Social Democrats and the Swedish People's party, but excluded the Center party. In 1991 a non-socialist coalition was formed with Center party's leader Esko Aho as prime minister, but again in 1995 an "unorthodox" coalition was formed. The SDP leader Paavo Lipponen is the prime minister and his "rainbow cabinet" includes the Conservatives and the Swedish people's party, but it also includes the Left Wing Alliance and the Greens. In other words, for the first time even the most distant parties of the left/right dimension co-operate in the government, while the ideological dimension's continuance is again broken so that the Center party is out and leads the opposition.

Thus the left/right dimension has lost its former rigidity. However, it is not gone. On the level of individual citizens, the ideological left/right dimension also continues to be relevant, although the party space has been shrinking along this basic dimension. Table 7.5 summarizes mean scores of the self-placements on the left/right scale by the supporters of different political parties. The distance on the ten-point scale between the mean location of the People's Democrats-Left Wing and the mean of the Conservative supporters was 5.9 points in 1975, but only 4.7 points in 1991. Both political groups had moved toward the center. So had the Social Democrats. The electorate as a whole had moved 0.6 points to the right.

The distributions of individual self-placements (Figure 7.1) show how difficult it still was for the Social Democratic voters in 1991 to cross the mid-point to the right-side of the cleavage. The supporter group of Center party, on the other hand, got a new profile in that year of the party's big election victory. Two peaks emerged among its supporters, one slightly to the left of the mid-point and the other one quite far towards the right end of the dimension, making the cohesive party of 1975 seem ideologically heterogeneous in 1991. When looking at the figure, one should keep in

Table 7.5 Self-placement of the supporters of different parties on the left/right scale in 1975 and 1991, mean scores and mean scores by age (left =1; right=10)

Parties	1975	1991	1975 18–40	1975 41–75	1991 18–40	1991 41–75
Swedish People party	7.1	7.2	–	–	7.3	7.1
Conservatives	8.2	7.7	7.6	8.3	7.6	7.9
Center party	6.3	6.4	6.5	6.3	6.2	6.6
Rural party	5.7	5.7	5.5	6.0	5.5	6.0
Christ. League	–	6.0	–	–	6.0	6.1
Soc. Dem. party	3.9	4.3	3.9	4.0	4.5	4.2
FPDU/Left	2.3	3.0	2.3	2.4	3.3	2.8
Greens	–	5.4	–	–	5.3	5.8
Others	5.3	5.3	5.2	5.6	5.7	5.2

Source: Adapted from Pesonen *et al.* 1993, 130.

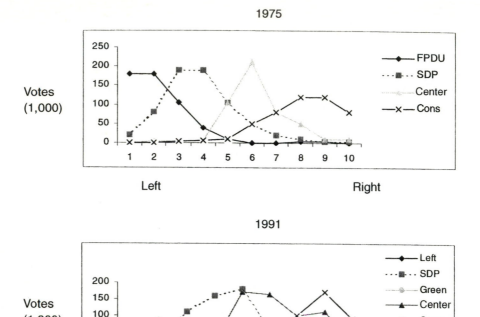

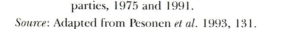

Figure 7.1 Distribution of the left/right dimension of the supporters of different parties, 1975 and 1991.

Source: Adapted from Pesonen *et al.* 1993, 131.

mind that on this scale all the survey respondents needed to "take sides", however mildly, because no one could choose the exact mid-point.

Several studies have revealed how those people who identify only weakly with their respective parties, are ideologically closer to each other than are the strong identifiers of the same parties. But beyond that, the ideological distances do not get any longer when one moves up from the strongly identifying supporters to the more pragmatic responsible level of party leadership. Accordingly, Figure 7.1 shows so little ideological overlap of the Conservative and Socialist party supporters, that one could not have predicted from their different ideological orientations how relatively easy it became for the highest elite level of the Conservatives and the so-called socialist parties to bridge the traditional red/white cleavage, without co-operation by their previous connector, the Center party.

The class base of the ideological and political left/right cleavage has rested even more on people's subjective class identification than on objective measures of their socio-economic situation. But people's willingness to identify with any social class has declined, both spontaneously and when asked to respond to a structured question which offers various classes to choose from. The same trend has been observed across nations.

As late as in 1975, 65 percent of a Finnish survey sample responded to an open question that they identified with some social class; so did almost equally many Germans and Austrians, while only 37 percent of British and American respondents said in those days that they belonged to a social class (Pesonen and Sänkiaho 1979, 111). By the year 1991 the percentage of spontaneous class-identifiers was reduced to 44 percent in Finland, and the decline had taken place primarily because subjective identification with the working class had gone down from 32 percent to only 11 percent.

As shown in Table 7.6, the Left Wing supporters were the only party group in 1991 whose clear majority identified spontaneously with a social class, although no more than 39 percent with the working class. The old ideological "class struggle" which still existed in people's minds and inspired the red/white political cleavage in the 1970s, has become more history than reality in the 1990s.

New political cleavages

In the 1990s most Finns did not perceive any strong conflicts between opposing groups in the society. For example, in the 1991 election study ten pairs of competing or hostile groups were listed, and for each pair the respondents indicated whether they thought that the conflict was strong or

Table 7.6 Spontaneous class identification related to party preference in 1991 (in percentages)

Social class	Political party								
	SPP	Cons	Center	FRP	Chr.	SDP	Left	Greens	Total
Working class	2	1	7	8	10	20	39	9	11
Middle class	32	26	16	17	21	17	6	21	18
Wage earners	–	2	–	3	–	3	3	1	1
Enterpreneur	–	1	1	3	3	–	–	–	1
Functionaires	–	1	–	–	3	1	1	2	1
Income class	5	6	4	8	3	5	8	5	5
Others	5	7	7	8	7	7	5	7	7
None/DK	56	56	65	53	52	47	38	55	56
Total	100	100	100	100	100	100	100	100	100
(*n*)	(62)	(252)	(310)	(40)	(38)	(302)	(93)	(130)	(1472)

Source: Pesonen *et al.* 1993, 116.

weak. The most obvious conflict was no longer the traditional one between the rich and the poor. More people thought that there is a conflict between the environmentalists and the business managers. The former conflict was considered very strong by 31 percent, but the latter by 36 percent of Finns. (Pesonen *et al.* 1993, 123–6).

When the "very" and "rather strong" answer-alternatives are combined, at least 67 percent were of the opinion in 1991 that the following conflicts existed in Finland:

- the environmentalists vs. business management
- the rich vs. the poor
- employers vs. employees
- the politicians vs. the people
- agricultural producers vs. consumers

Twenty years earlier both the conflict between the rich and poor and between the employers and employees had been perceived to be stronger than in 1991. But in a factor analysis of opinions on the perceived conflicts, the traditional class struggle dimension still came out as the strongest attitude dimension (explaining 27 percent of the variance). It was defined by the perceived conflicts between manual/white collar workers (considered important by 45 percent), employers/employees, the rich/the poor, and the socialists/the bourgeois (55 percent).

The second general conflict dimension can be called the "new conflicts", defined by juxtapositions between the unemployed/the employed (57 percent), men/women (32 percent), and the politicians/the people. The most generally felt and also typically new conflict between the environmentalists and business management defined the third dimension by itself, while the producers/consumers and the language cleavage Finnish-speakers/Swedish-speakers (44 percent) did not belong to any of the three general conflict dimensions.

Table 7.7 summarizes how party preferences were related to the three dimensions of perceived conflicts. The first dimension was measured by a sum scale adding together the four variables mentioned above, the second dimension by a sum scale combining the three "new conflict" variables, and

Table 7.7 The three conflict dimensions related to party preference (percent who emphasize the dimension)

Conflice dimensions	Political party								
	SPP	*Cons*	*Center*	*FRP*	*Chr.*	*SDP*	*Left*	*Greens*	*Total*
Class conflict	32	33	43	54	54	57	68	48	47
New conflict	35	38	36	38	51	43	42	45	42
Environment	26	31	35	21	48	47	46	55	40

Source: Pesonen *et al.* 1993, 126.

the third dimension by the "green" variable alone; in each case the scale values were dichotomized, and in the table the percentages of those persons are given who considered the dimension to be very or rather strong.

The Conservatives have a more harmonious image of society than do the supporters of the socialist parties. Clearly the idea of the traditional class struggle is strongest in the minds of the Left Wing sympathizers, and it is above average also among the Social Democrats and the two small parties near the center. The "new conflict" dimension did not differentiate the party groups to the same extent. It came out clearly only among the supporters of the Christian People's party. The third dimension, "the environment", seemed most often important to the Greens, and more than average also within the political left, while it was most irrelevant to the supporters of the Finnish Rural party.

Table 7.7 leads to the conclusion that Finland's party system does not reflect the perceived new social conflicts as much as it continues to reflect the traditional class conflict. However, the coverage of the analysis reported in Table 7.6 is obviously limited by the choice of conflicting groups that were listed in the questionnaire; nor does the table indicate distances between the different party groups in the system. The only distances that were reported in Table 7.5 and Figure 7.1 were those along the basic ideological dimension from left to right.

Of course the party space is not unidimensional, and neither are all cleavage lines of political competition based on social structure. Already in 1966, when survey respondents expressed their preference rankings of different political parties, the analysis suggested a party space of at least seven different political dimensions (Pesonen 1973). The left/right (socialist/ bourgeois) cleavage was the strongest, and two other familiar structure-based cleavages appeared, namely the ones between producers and agriculture versus consumers and urban industries, and between Finnish and Swedish speakers. A fourth social cleavage appeared between the recognized and noted centers and the "forgotten people", a new version of the center/periphery cleavage.

But, in addition, people's likes and dislikes of the parties structured the party system on the basis of strictly ideological and issue-based opinions which are not based on social cleavages. There was the separate political cleavage between Communism and anti-Communism, and the supporters of established parties appeared generally to resist the small and temporary parties. The last-mentioned antagonism also played a role in the actions of the elite level: in the beginning of the 1970s the established parties made some legislative attempts, e.g. in the renewed Election Law, to make it difficult for new parties to enter the system. The seventh cleavage that was suggested by the party rankings was even less structural and even more vague and time-bound: the victorious parties sailing "with the wind" and the losers sailing "against the wind".

Such a very general and fluid political conflict dimension has been increasingly apparent as the contrast between *government and opposition*. It would be self-evident in a two-party system, but because of the fragmented nature of Finland's even multi-party system and the resulting necessity of forming coalition governments, government responsibility has not always been easy to pinpoint in Finland. As in Italy, the country used to have short-lived governments which averaged only one year, until the pattern shifted during Mauno Koivisto's twelve years as president (1982–94) to more durable governments, formed after each parliamentary election and remaining in power during the full four-year term.

Opinion surveys and election results have shown that the government/opposition situation really matters: in general those voters appreciate the country's government more whose "own" party shares governmental power, while in elections the voters have had the tendency to punish rather than to reward the parties in government. Such was the background of the dramatic victory of the Center party, then in opposition, in the election of 1991. Again in 1995 followed a strong victory for the leading opposition party, which was this time the Social Democratic party. Another example of the dynamic is the observation that after each period of Communist participation in the government (1945–8, 1966–71, 1975–6, 1977–83), the party's electoral support declined, whereas the party gathered additional support during the periods when it was in the opposition (Zilliacus 1995, 187).

It is also possible that political parties consciously attempt to avoid taking clear stands on crucial but divisive issues. One useful but rare option which serves that purpose is to introduce direct democracy into the representative system of government. Finland's referendum in October 1994 on membership in the European Union contained such ingredients.

Table 7.8 shows first, how the electors' opinions on Finland's EU-membership were related to party preferences in September 1994, and second, how opinions on the Economic and Monetary Union were related to party preferences after Finland had been inside the EU for two years. The similarity of the opinion distributions is quite apparent. The Conservatives and the Swedish People's party voters were very much in favor of both the EU and the EMU, the Christian People's party voters were very much against both. On the political left, the Social Democrats tended to favor and the Left Wing voters tended to oppose both. The Center party was in a tricky position: in 1994 a majority of its supporters opposed EU membership although the party organization, including the party's chairman Esko Aho as prime minister, was for it. Later, however, the Center party's supporters did not seem to lean either for or against joining the third stage of the EMU in 1999.

The table suggests three general conclusions. First, the mass level of the party system reflected the important EU issue; but second, no party's supporters were unanimous and some party groups were badly divided or even

Table 7.8 Opinions on EU membership in September 1994 related to party vote in 1991; and opinions on the EMU in January 1997 related to party preference (percentages)

Party choice in 1991	The EU in 1994			
	Yes	No	Undecided	Total
Swedish People's party	71	12	17	100
Conservative party	68	12	20	100
Center party	20	52	28	100
Finnish Rural party	13	57	30	100
Christian League	10	60	30	100
Social Democratic party	42	18	40	100
Left Wing Alliance	20	50	30	100
The Greens	35	39	26	100
Other parties	33	33	33	99
Party choice in 1997	The EU in 1997			
	Yes	No	Undecided	Total
Swedish People's party	61	12	27	100
Conservative party	62	11	26	99
Center party	34	31	36	101
Christian League	12	69	20	101
Social Democratic party	51	18	31	100
Left Wing Alliance	31	42	28	101
The Greens	39	22	39	100
Other parties	52	22	26	100

Source: Pesonen 1994, 60; EVA 1997, 45.

against their leadership; and third, there seems to be considerable stability in party-related opinions on Finland's place in West European integration. Furthermore, it is obvious that this national decision has been handled outside the party system to such an extent that the parties have been able to accommodate their dissident members, preventing the EU opinions from causing new divisive splits in the system.

The relevance of political parties

One can also ask what has happened to the overall relevance of political parties among Finland's mass electorate. Obviously political parties and the party system continue to play a central role in representative democracy and in the functions of parliament. But in Finland, like in democracies in general, parties have lost a great deal of their relevance in the minds of the voters. This can be considered an aspect of political alienation, but it also involves the growing cleavage between *the masses and the political elite*. Such a development has become apparent in various ways.

While the perceived conflict between the politicians and the people appeared as one element in the general "new conflicts" dimension, the Finnish citizens have also revealed unusually little trust in their country's politicians. Furthermore, time series of the conventional measures of political alienation show that large and increasing numbers of Finnish citizens feel that they are neglected outsiders in the political process (Sänkiaho 1986).

One indication of the alienation of some young and not highly educated groups living in urban environments has been their exceptionally low voter turnout in elections (Martikainen and Yrjönen 1991, 41). National turnout in Finland's parliamentary elections has also declined, from the 81 percent level in the 1970s until 1983, down to only 72 percent in 1991 and 1995.

During the phase after 1960 which was named the "rejection of political authority", the citizens' political interest and political activity per se did not actually decline in Finland, but many active persons became willing to bypass the political parties when attempting to influence political decision making. Unconventional political acts became more acceptable alternative ways to influence politics: for the most efficacious citizens actual or at least potential protest behavior was not a substitute for party work and other conventional forms of political activity, but rather a channel to complement such activity (Pesonen and Sänkiaho 1979, 252–5).

Moreover, in the 1980s the desire to increase "people's power" and to bypass political parties in the process, created new pressures to institutionalize direct democracy. Therefore, the (advisory) referendum was added to Finland's Constitution Act in 1987, and a related reform was the replacement of the electoral college with direct elections of the president, first applied in 1994. At the time of the EU referendum in 1994, the strongest support for having more referenda in the future was found among those persons who were the most alienated from conventional politics (Pesonen 1994, 180). Quite a different channel of bypassing the parliament and the parties in it, has been the powerful role which national interest organizations have in making political decisions in Finland, in particular in connection with the comprehensive agreements on income policy.

Finland is by no means unique in that the traditional position of political parties has become weaker. This has been a general trend. Among the main reasons for such a tendency have been the growing volatility of the increasingly individualized and independent voters, and the personalized emphasis on political leaders rather than on party organizations and party identity.

The emphasis on individual persons rather than on the parties has been apparent in various ways in Finland. Even the turnouts in national elections show this. Turnout used to be regularly higher in parliamentary than presidential elections until Finland's highest turnout ever was recorded in the presidential election of 1982, and after that more people have voted in the presidential elections than in parliamentary elections. When the first direct election of the president was approaching in 1993, various so-called party primaries even prevented some parties from nominating their most obvious candidates for presidency, because many participants in the primaries disliked the strongly partisan backgrounds of the leading politicians. It is obvious that the parties are not going to repeat similar experimental primaries without first carefully reconsidering their procedures.

In parliamentary elections the list system of proportional representation is based on the assumption that the foremost purpose of voting in elections is to determine the relative strength of the parties and their rightful representation in the legislature. However, the Finnish system also obligates each voter to choose one individual candidate from the party list he or she is voting for. Although the choice of the party was originally the voters' primary choice, more and more voters say that actually they select first the individual candidate they vote for and pay only secondary attention to the party list that their ballot thereby supports.

Such general alienation from political parties has made it difficult for the parties to recruit new members into their organizations. Between the early 1960s and late 1980s the total number of party members increased slightly from 513,000 to 520,000 (Katz and Mair 1994, 5), but due to the enlarged electorate the percentage of electors who had joined a political party actually went down from 18.9 percent to 13.7 percent. Furthermore, before the parties cleaned and computerized their files and registers in the 1990s, there was also some tendency for the head-counts to become inflated.

Survey results have indicated that 11 percent of the young electors less than thirty years of age had joined a political party in the 1970s, but only 5 percent of the corresponding age group became party members in the 1990s (Borg 1996, 8). The numbers of members reported by the parties speak for themselves: the FPDU counted 70,000 members in 1964 but the Left Wing had 16,000 in 1995; the SDP reported 100,000 members in 1980 but 70,000 in 1995; the Conservatives went down from 92,000 in 1964 to 47,000 in 1995, and the Swedish People's party had 51,000 members in 1964 but only 37,000 in 1995. The most successful recruiter of its voters to members, the Center party, has also lost some but still reports 257,000 members. That is more than one-half of all the card-carrying party members in Finland (Sundberg 1996, 88–9).

Persisting identities

Political parties have been an essential element of Finland's legislature since early 1870s, and party organizations have faced the mass electorate since 1906 when universal suffrage was introduced. The parties were firmly based upon the social structure of the electorate and they, in turn, structured the electorate politically. Considerable stability remained a characteristic of the party system. Since the 1960s even the formally defined status and the public funding of political parties have helped to stabilize some aspects of the system.

Finland has a highly fragmented "even party system". In the Eduskunta there are ten political parties, or at least seven "relevant" parties, or more than five "effective" parties, and the party system is named "even" because there are three large parties, none of which is in the position to claim a dominant role. A few new parties have staged a breakthrough effectively enough to gain some real political power. Only two have lasted, the Christian League since the 1970s and the Greens since early 1980s. Both of them, like most Finnish parties, have counterparts in other countries. It remains to be seen whether the newborn of the 1990s, the Progressive Liberal party, will also succeed in securing a permanent place for itself. Comparable neo-liberal parties are not unknown in other countries either, some of them temporary, some likely to stay.

The emergence of new parties, the disappearance of the Liberals, and the short-time successes of the populist Rural party, as well as the decline of the far left, have brought about changes in the Finnish party system, enough to make the word "stability" sound like an overstatement. Perhaps continuity would be a more accurate expression. At least it is not an overstatement.

One outstanding example of continuity is the history of the Finnish Center Party, until 1965 the Agrarian Union. The party was founded to represent the farming population. But unlike the agrarian parties in several other European countries, it managed to keep its share of the voters and to maintain its role as one of the large parties despite the dramatic decrease of the agrarian population, still the majority of the work force in 1940, but down to 8 percent and declining in 1994. Votes from the workers helped somewhat, but the party's future is increasingly dependent upon its success among the middle classes.

Politics has become de-ideologized to such an extent that the Center party lost its favorable position as the connecting link in the middle of the party spectrum. Genuine Socialism and Communism belong to the past. A century ago the political left entered Finnish politics having a socialist society as the desired goal; in the 1970s the Social Democrats still wanted centralized political power and government-owned enterprises; whereas the catchwords of the 1990s have been the market forces and privatization (denationalization in earlier terminology). The left socialists who served as the partner and electoral veil of the Communist party, in their turn managed to pick up the heritage when Communism itself collapsed.

Social transformation occurred later and much faster in Finland than in most western countries. Nevertheless, the configuration of the party system has not changed much, it remains reminiscent of what is known as the Scandinavian party system. Familiar social determinants are still related to party choice, occupation is politically relevant. But each new generation of voters has broadened the parties' social bases, and subjective class identi-fication has lost its relevance.

While the party system does not change much, new kinds of problems and social conflicts need to be solved, unemployment became a major problem, and strained state budgets limit the availability of choices. There prevails a general feeling in Finland that the political parties, meaning primarily the political elites, have distanced themselves too far from the people. This is evident even in connection with Finland's current constitutional reform issue: the people seem more willing to protect the powers of the directly elected president than are the parties which, in their turn, want to emphasize more the role of parliament, the parliamentary prime minister, and the government.

Moreover, power and pragmatism are more important now than consistent ideology. Finland has ways of achieving a national consensus on divisive issues. The de-ideologization of politics and the complexity of the issues on the one hand, and the individualization of the voters on the other, provide some explanations why the role of political parties is not more widely appreciated. But even in the midst of belittling attitudes and the unwillingness to participate in party work, the parties have their significant role in responsibly governing the country.

Although the class-related ideological dimension from the left to the right has been shrinking, most Finns can point out what their own location is along this basic dimension of the party system. Thus the political frame of reference that has been cultivated by the parties, persists beyond people's identification with a social class. On the elite level the traditional left/right cleavage does not prevent any more the mutual co-operation of distant parties. The issues, goals, and approaches in Finnish politics have changed dramatically as a consequence of social transformation, economic problems, and changing international environment. By and large, the political parties have adapted themselves to new situations; resilience contributes to continuity in the party system.

Peter Mair concludes that in party systems "the structure of competition can persist even when the protagonists who are involved in its promotion may have changed beyond almost all recognition" (Mair 1997, 16).

In fact, Finland may have experienced even more change in "the structure of competition" than in the persisting identities of "the protagonists".

8   Japan – from emerging to stable party system?

Joji Watanuki

Introduction

Thirty years ago, I wrote a chapter on Japan in Lipset's and Rokkan's book (1967a, ch. 9). The chapter was placed in Part Four with the title "The Emerging Nations", together with chapters on Brazil and West Africa. In Japan, true democratic rule of the people and guaranteed basic human rights were introduced only after WWII, although elections for one House of the Imperial Diet had been held since 1890 and political parties had an even longer history dating back to the 1870s, when the Freedom and People's Rights Movement emerged, demanding the opening of parliament. As for political parties, the leftist parties were virtually excluded from the Diet with the exception of a few seats won by moderate social democrats after the introduction of universal suffrage for men in 1928. In these respects, Japanese democracy and party system could be regarded as "emerging" at that time. On the other hand, after 1955 when the Liberal Democratic Party and the Japan Socialist Party were created by the amalgamation of conservative parties and social democratic parties respectively, it was expected that these two parties might become mature in terms of ideology and consolidated in terms of organization as the years passed, and eventually a stable party system might emerge.

The development since then has betrayed this expectation. On the one hand, the Liberal Democratic Party has been successful in remaining the governing party for 38 years from 1955 to 1993, and, after a short exclusion from power in 1993, returned to power, though only in a coalition. However, its history is stained by scandals. On the other hand, the Japan Socialist Party has failed to consolidate its support, which reached one third of the total number of votes, i.e. about half of that for the LDP, in the late 1950s and early 1960s. That was the peak for the JSP. In the late 1960s, a new party based on a lay association of a Buddhist sect emerged and the Japan Communist Party gained some advances, both contributing to the shrinking of support and votes for the JSP. The final blow to the JSP came in the process of dealignment and realignment of the Japanese party system in the 1990s. Other new parties such as the Japan New Party,

Shinseito and Sakigake were formed in 1992–3, and fared fairly well in the 1993 general election.

The current situation of the Japanese party system

In the most recent general election of the House of Representatives, held on 20 October 1996, seven parties won seats in the House, but none succeeded in getting a majority (Table 8.1). Among the seven, there were three parties which kept the same name as used in the previous election of 1993, i.e. the Liberal Democratic Party, the Japan Communist Party, and the tiny Sakigake. In addition to these, the Social Democratic Party can be regarded as the renamed Japan Socialist Party, with a history of 51 years since 1945. The New Frontier Party was formed in December 1994, based on the amalgamation of four parties – Shinseito, the Japan New Party, Komeito and the Democratic Socialist Party. Shinseito was a product of the split from the Liberal Democratic Party in 1993, the Japan New Party was founded by Mr. Hosokawa in 1992, and the DSP originated from the division of the Japan Socialist Party in 1960. Komeito was formed originally as the political arm of Sokagakkai, which was the lay association of a Buddhist sect, in 1967. The Democratic Party, which appeared as the third largest party after the general election was a brand-new party formed only a month before the election, in September, 1997, by politicians from the Liberal Democratic Party, the Sakigake Party and the Social Democratic Party.

By European standards, with seven political parties gaining parliamentary representation, the degree of fractionalization is fairly average (Lane and Ersson 1994a). However, after the general election, splits from existing parties and the formation of new political parties persisted. Nine MPs who ran as independent candidates and won seats were solicited to join the LDP,

Table 8.1 Result of 1996 Japanese election

Seats	Single-member constituency		Proportional representation		Total
	Seats	Votes	Seats	Votes	
LDP	169	38.6	70	32.8	239
NFP	96	28.1	60	28.0	156
DPJ	17	11.6	35	16.1	52
JCP	2	12.6	24	13.1	26
SDP	4	2.9	11	6.4	15
SAKIGAKE	2	1.3	0	1.1	2
DRA	1	0.3	0	0.0	1
Independent candidates	9	4.6	–	–	9
Total	300	100%	200	100%	500

Note: LDP, Liberal Democratic Party; NFP, New Frontier Party; DPJ, Democratic Party; JCP, Japan Communist Party; SDP, Social Democratic Party; Sakigake means "harbinger"; DRA, Democratic Reform Alliance.

which wanted to increase its number of seats to approach, or even achieve, a majority. A group of politicians in the New Frontier Party headed by ex-Prime Minister Hata decided to form a new party with the name of Taiyo-to (the Sun Party) in December 1996, and another ex-Prime Minister Hosokawa seceded from the NFP in May 1997, with the intention of forming another new party in the near future.

Another feature of the 1996 general election was that it was held under a new electoral system combining 200 seats assigned through proportional representation (PR) and 300 seats from single-member constituencies. These two components are separated; the voters cast two ballots and the assignment of the seats to parties in proportional representation is not adjusted by the number of seats or votes won in single-member constituencies at all. This simple juxtaposition of single-member constituencies and proportional representation is used only in Japan, Russia and Taiwan (Blais and Louis Massicotte 1996, 55).

The effect of this electoral system to the distribution of seats is naturally a combined one. In single-member constituencies, the LDP got 56.3 percent of the seats with a total share of 38.6 percent of the votes. In proportional representation constituencies, however, the party could only get the proper proportional share of the seats in spite of the division of the nation into as many as eleven regions in calculating the assignment of the seats. Whether this electoral system will be maintained or not in the next general election is uncertain. Japanese politicians and the electorate had become used to the old electoral system of multi-member constituencies, which lasted from 1928 to 1993, i.e. for 65 years, except for one election in 1946. Some politicians in the LDP, and the SDP and the JCP as a whole, want the revival of the multi-member constituency system with some revision (such as the substitution of a single vote by a block vote). The proportional representation component is not liked – neither by Japanese voters nor by politicians, because they have been used to a style of election based on the choice of a candidate under multi-member constituencies for such a long time. However, further radical change of the electoral system would take a long time. The probability is that, at least in the next general election, which is due in 2000 at the latest, an electoral arrangement with a combination of single-member constituencies and proportional representation will be maintained, but the ratio of the seats assigned to each system might be changed in the direction of decreasing somewhat the number of seats assigned through proportional representation (from the current 200 to 150 or 100). Any decrease of the PR component will result in a seat distribution more favorable to the largest party (most probably the LDP).

Skipping the stage of mass and class parties

In the late 1950s and early 1960s, the LDP was in power, commanding the majority of the votes and getting slightly more seats than their share of the votes under the multi-member, single-ballot, plurality electoral system. But the Japan Socialist Party was doing well as the opposition party, getting roughly one-third of the votes and a corresponding number of seats in both Houses of the Diet. Organizationally, the JSP was supported by labor unions, which usually organized both blue-collar and white-collar workers in the same company under one organization. Since more white-collar workers were in big enterprises and unionized, and many blue-collar workers were employed in small companies without a union, the unions' influence as a whole was stronger among the former than the latter. Therefore, Alford's index of class voting, which treated white-collar workers as middle-class and compared the degrees of association of white-collar workers' support for the conservative party to that of blue-collar workers' support for left-wing parties (Alford 1963), was inapplicable to Japan. As to support and votes for the LDP, farmers and self-employed merchants and manufacturers were the stronghold. Organizational ties, such as village solidarity and trade associations were utilized. In short, the social cleavage between the "old" middle class of farmers and merchants versus unionized employees of white-collar and blue-collar workers was at the basis of the LDP vs. JSP confrontation augmented by a value cleavage of traditional values vs. modern values, and culminating in an ideological cleavage of capitalism vs. socialism and pro-US vs. anti-US. In my article in Lipset's and Rokkan's book, I used the label of "cultural politics" to express the nature of association between social cleavage and party system in Japan of that time, focusing on the influence of the value cleavage of traditional vs. modern values, as a contrast to European "class politics". On the ideological level, the Japan Socialist Party continued to cling to the ideology of socialism and anti-US diplomatic policy until as late as the late 1980s and, organizationally, it has repeatedly voiced the need to build up a European-type mass party throughout the 1960s and 1970s. However, the JSP failed to build such a party. Its membership never surpassed 100,000 or so. Its electoral strength depended organizationally on labor unions and on weak floating support from the electorate. Reorganization of the national federation of labor unions in the late 1980s deprived the party of its organizational leverage and the result was the devastating decline of the party. Unlike European social democratic parties, the JSP had no organizational or psychological assets to "freeze", and lacked the incentive and capability to correct ideological rigidity in order to defend its assets.

In contrast with the JSP, the LDP in the 1960s and 1970s behaved more cleverly. As a conservative party, it had nothing to do with the idea of being a "class party". But the LDP in the 1950s was more committed to backward conservatism, by which I mean the intention to cancel out post-war reforms introduced under the American occupation. At this point, ideology and traditional values were closely linked and this caused antipathy to the LDP among the younger and more highly educated sectors of the electorate. It compelled the young and the more highly educated to incline towards the

JSP. Since the 1960s, the LDP has attenuated this aspect, and an emphasis on economic growth and "fair" distribution of its fruits to every sector of society has become a kind of official ideology. As governmental revenues increased in a continuously growing economy throughout the 1960s, 1970s, and 1980s, in spite of the oil crises of 1973 and 1979, the LDP as the governing party has consolidated its image as a substantial catch-all party, in terms of its ideology, performance and vote-catching. Today, even among the white-collar and blue-collar workers, whose support and votes for the JSP alone surpassed those for the LDP, the LDP gets more support and votes than any other party (Table 8.2).

Organizationally, the LDP, when it was established in 1955, was a collection of MPs and their supporters. But this did not mean that LDP politicians were all local notables who could be elected without any organizational efforts on their side. Under the multi-member constituency electoral system, they had to compete not only with union-backed JSP candidates, but also with other LDP candidates. The practice of building up personal sponsoring associations (*koenkai*) by themselves had existed before the formation of the LDP and spread more extensively as the LDP developed. Officially, the LDP aimed to build up a mass party based on the concept of membership and collecting fees, and tried to incorporate personal sponsoring associations of its MPs into the party organization. Nominally, this was done and the LDP has been boasting millions of

Table 8.2 Voted party by occupation in 1996 general election

Single-member constituency

	LDP	NFP	DPJ	JCP	SDP	Others	Abstained	Total (N)
Farmers	65.5	20.9	0	3.6	2.7	1.8	5.5	100 (110)
Merchants and manufacturers	39.5	20.0	6.2	9.0	1.2	6.0	18.1	100 (420)
Managers	36.9	18.9	14.4	8.1	0.9	7.2	13.6	100 (111)
White-collars	28.2	19.1	12.4	9.8	3.3	5.4	21.8	100 (482)
Blue-collars	27.1	25.4	9.2	7.3	2.6	5.0	23.4	100 (303)
Housewives	35.0	18.3	10.2	10.6	1.9	4.6	19.4	100 (432)
Pensioners	40.7	19.1	10.2	7.7	4.1	5.8	12.4	100 (413)

Proportional representation

	LDP	NFP	DPJ	JCP	SDP	Others
Farmers	62.7	18.2	1.8	4.5	5.5	1.8
Merchants and manufacturers	38.3	17.9	9.5	10.5	2.7	1.8
Managers	35.1	18.0	22.5	6.3	2.7	1.8
White-collars	23.0	19.1	14.7	10.6	6.2	4.6
Blue-collars	24.1	25.1	9.6	7.6	5.0	5.3
Housewives	30.6	19.4	13.9	9.0	4.4	3.2
Pensioners	39.0	18.4	12.8	9.2	5.8	2.4

Source: JESII 1996 nationwide survey.

members (the most recent figure is 2.3 million as of December 1996). Substantially, those members have been and are primarily members of individual politicians' *koenkai*. Often the lists are provided and the membership fees are paid to the party by individual politicians.

One of the rationales for reforming the electoral system from a multi-member constituency system, under which LDP candidates competed with each other, to the combination of single-member constituencies and proportional representation was to discourage personal sponsoring associations and cut the costs of building and maintaining personal sponsoring associations. However, what happened in the small, single-member constituency system was the continuation of competition between personal organizations of individual candidates of different parties, especially between candidates of the LDP and the NFP (Table 8.3).

Table 8.3 deserves several comments: (1) Since the total number of eligible Japanese citizens is 97 million, the average affiliation ratio of 21.1 percent means that roughly 20 million are included in personal sponsoring associations by politicians. And, since the total number of candidates who ran for single-member constituencies in the 1996 general election was 1,561, simple calculation of the division of 20 million by this number is roughly 13,000. In fact, many politicians of the LDP and NFP are known to have several times more *koenkai* members than that. (2) Politicians who have strong *koenkai* can be successful without a party label. They can run as independents and win and, after the election, they have more freedom to move from one party to another. This facilitates and complicates party dealignment and realignment. (3) Even the JCP, which has the most solid party organization among Japanese political parties, has so far been adopting the policy of encouraging *koenkai* as additional support organizations. But it is reported that the JCP has decided not to do this any more, thus being loyal to the mass party principle. Whether it can successfully do without is quite doubtful. (4) On the side of new parties,

Table 8.3 Affiliation to *koenkai* by partisan vote in single-member constituencies (SM), 1996

Party of voted candidates in single-member constituencies	Affiliated	No. DK, NA.	Total (N)
LDP	29.2	70.8	100 (823)
NFP	23.1	76.9	100 (458)
DPJ	12.5	87.5	100 (222)
DSP	15.0	85.0	100 (60)
JCP	14.1	85.9	100 (198)
Others	26.8	73.2	100 (123)
Abstained	9.6	90.4	100 (415)
Total	21.1	78.9	100 (2299)

Source: JESII 1996 post-election nationwide sample survey.

such as the short-lived Japan New Party and the newly formed DPJ, the leaders talk about building a "network party" linking various citizens' groups and movements, opposing both a mass party based on membership and a party based on a collection of *koenkai*. However, the JNP failed to build such a party. The fate of the DPJ is still to be seen.

Weak and sporadic support for political parties

What Table 8.3 tells us is that, although an individual-centered political organization has been strong in Japan, it is not omnipotent. For the more than 70 percent of voters not involved in *koenkai*, evaluation of political parties plays an important role in guiding voting decisions (Richardson *et al.* 1991, 409–13). The equivalence to party identification in Japan has been regarded as party support measured by the question "which party do you support (in some polls, the adverb 'usually' or 'now' is added)?" The style of questioning is European, not American, indicating a weaker emotional attachment and a weaker effect of early socialization. In survey data, the correlation between party supported and party voted for has been high until now. However, there are two points to be noted: (1) The ratio of the respondents in the surveys who answer such questions with "I have no party to support", which slightly varies depending on whether the adverbs "usually" or "now" are included or not, and also on whether the survey is conducted at the election time or not, has been increasing since the 1970s and now surpasses 50 percent. Among people in their twenties, the ratio reaches as high as nearly 90 percent. (2) According to a study by Ichiro Miyake, based on data collected in 1983, when the party system was more stable than now, there existed a vast number of "sporadic supporters" and "sporadic voters", meaning more fluctuation between the positions of "no party to support" and "a particular party to support", and between non-voting and voting for a particular party, rather than transferring support or votes from one party to another. Miyake prepared Table 8.4, comparing Japan, Canada, the US and the UK (Miyake 1986).

Traditional values, modern values and post-materialist values

When we speak of value conflicts, we cannot avoid the issue of "post-materialist values". Did these values also emerge in the case of Japan, and, if so, what is the impact of these values on the Japanese conflict between traditional and modern values?

In 1972, when I used Inglehart's four items of "post-materialist" values in a nationwide survey, the proportion of pure "post-materialists" was only 4 percent, less than half the proportion found in European countries such as Italy, France, Germany and the UK as cited by Inglehart (Inglehart 1971, 995). However small, the correlation with age and education was clear. The more recent the birth cohort, and the higher the education, the more

Table 8.4 Turnover in party identification across three waves. Panel surveys: comparison of four nations

Turnover in party identification	Japan June1983– Dec. 1983– Dec. 1983	Canada 1974– 1979– 1980	US 1972– 1974– 1976	UK Feb. 1974– Oct. 1974– 1979
Same party across three-waves	54	59	68	73
Changing at least once	18	23	11	23
Non-identification at least once	33	22	24	6

Source: Miyake 1986, 33.

Notes: Dec. 1983 data for Japan are panel survey data of pre-election and post-election survey data.

Total percentages exceed 100 as "changing at least once" and "non-identification at least once" are not mutually exclusive.

Figures for Canada, US, UK are cited from LeDuc *et al.* (1984). Japanese figure is based on JES Survey.

persons were committed to this value. Therefore, I speculated that, with the continued trend of levelling up of educational level and accumulation of recent birth cohorts, this value would spread and might become a new basis of political cleavage (Crozier *et al.* 1975, 141–3). Moreover, commitment to this value correlated with support for leftist parties (the JSP and JCP). Thus, I also speculated that leftist parties might have the chance to utilize this value, and combine it with "modern values". In fact, Scott C. Flanagan, in a study based mainly on Japanese data, argued that post-materialist values should not be treated as different from modern values, but as more developed values in the direction of a more "libertarian" line (Flanagan, 1987).

However, according to our successive surveys in 1972, 1983 and 1993 (Table 8.5), post-materialist values have certainly increased steadily, but this increase has not come from younger birth cohorts. The increase appears to be the result of the spread of these values across all birth cohorts. This is a product of a period effect, not the generational effect. Older birth cohorts have increased their commitment to these values more than the younger ones, while younger birth cohorts show no outstanding commitment to these values. As for Flanagan's contention, factor analyses of both 1983 and 1993 data proved that those two value scales – the traditional vs. the modern and the materialist vs. the post-materialist – belong to different dimensions. Thus, Flanagan's argument does not seem to be sustainable. On the other hand, the correlation of materialist values with support and votes for the LDP has remained fairly clear. The number of pure materialists, however, has shrunk by two-thirds from 1972 to 1993. Leftist parties, the JSP and JCP, in the 1983 and 1993 elections, also continued to

Table 8.5 Distribution of the four-item values of Inglehart

A. *Distribution of choices of each item*

	Economy	Order	Participation	Free speech	Others DK, NA	Total (N)
1972	70.4	45.3	35.1	13.8	35.4	200% (2,468)
1983	63.9	38.2	54.3	17.0	26.6	200% (1,750)
1993	62.6	28.2	63.7	27.4	18.1	200% (2,320)

B. *Types of paired choices*

	Materialist	Mixed	Post-materialist	NA	Total (N)
1972	32.6	38.6	3.6	25.2	100% (2,468)
1983	20.9	54.8	7.6	16.7	100% (1,750)
1993	13.5	61.5	14.5	10.5	100% (2,320)

C. *Pure post-materialist type by age and sex*

		1976	1983	1993
Age	20–29	8.1	7.9	15.9
	30–39	3.4	9.2	15.5
	40–49	2.2	9.4	15.2
	50–59	2.6	7.1	17.4
	Over 60	1.3	11.7	16.7
Sex	Male	5.3	11.4	16.6
	Female	2.3	6.8	15.7

Source: *Akaruisenkyo Suishinkyokai* 1972 Survey; JES 1983 Survey; JESII 1993 Survey.
Cited from Watanuki 1995, 12.

benefit from post-materialist values to some degree. In 1993, when three new parties emerged and contested the election with considerable success, there was a slight sign that post-materialists were more attracted by those new parties than materialists were, but this similarity disappeared in the 1995 data on the House of Councillors Election, where those three parties were amalgamated into the New Frontier Party together with two other parties.

In any case, the majority of voters are "mixed" – half "materialist" and half "post-materialist".

Declining turnout but greater trust in institutions

The voting turnout of the 1996 general election was the lowest in the history of Japanese General Elections – 59.6 percent, dropping sharply from 73.3 percent in 1990 and 67.2 percent in 1993. The average of the three general elections is 66.7 percent, which is only a little bit low by European standards (Lane and Ersson 1996, 116). The sharp drop between 1993 and 1996 can be partly attributed to electoral reform. Electoral reform from multi-member constituencies to single-member constituencies necessitated the disappearance of familiar candidates from their constituencies and the reorganization of personal sponsoring associations. This has had the effect of lowering the turnout. On the other hand, the introduction of a proportional representation component has had no positive effect on the turnout rate. In addition to this low average rate of turnout, one should note the difference in turnout rates by age groups. Nearly two-thirds of voters in their twenties are estimated to have abstained (Table 8.6). On the other hand, compared to the 1960s, the turnout rate of the older electorate has increased. Lower turnout rates among the young, is a rather common phenomenon in other societies, but it seems that it is more extreme in Japan than in other countries. According to a study, the average differences of turnout by age in national parliamentary elections in twenty-two countries is about 30 percent (Franklin 1996, 220), but Japan's figure in the 1996 general election exceeds 40 percent. If so, the likely causes for that are: (1) lack of attractiveness of political parties and candidates to young people; (2) incongruency of personal sponsoring association type organizations with the life-style of young people; and (3) moderate post-industrial values diffused across age groups. This can be regarded as an ominous sign for the future stability of the Japanese party system.

In spite of the low rates of voting turnout, the institutions of parliamentary democracy such as elections, parties and parliament are highly supported by the Japanese electorate, including the younger generation. As Table 8.7 shows, the legitimacy of those three institutions is firmly

Table 8.6 Voting turnout by age groups in the 1996 general election (percentages)

Age	Male	Female	Total
20–29	33.6	39.5	36.5
30–39	54.6	60.2	57.4
40–49	64.0	66.9	65.4
50–59	70.4	70.9	70.6
60–69	79.2	75.6	77.3
over 70	75.8	61.3	66.9
Total sample	61.4	62.3	61.9
Election statistics	59.0	60.2	59.6

Source: Voting record check of 150 sampled voting districts, conducted by the Ministry of Autonomy.

Table 8.7 Legitimacy of institutions related to parliamentary democracy

1. Elections make it possible for people's voices to be heard in politics

	Agree	Disagree	DK, NA	Total (N)
1976	67.3	10.4	22.3	100% (1.796)
1983	77.9	6.7	15.4	100% (1.750)
1993	82.3	7.7	10.0	100% (2.255)
1995	82.3	2.1	15.6	100% (2.076)

2. The National Diet makes it possible for people's voices to be heard in politics

	Agree	Disagree	DK, NA
1976	58.3	11.7	30.0
1983	65.5	11.9	22.6
1993	65.9	17.2	16.9
1995	71.0	13.0	16.0

3. Political parties make it possible for people's voices to be heard in politics

	Agree	Disagree	DK, NA
1976	56.5	14.3	29.2
1983	70.1	9.4	20.5
1993	68.2	15.1	16.7
1995	71.3	12.1	16.6

consolidated. In all brackets of age groups or birth cohorts, there is an overwhelming majority support for those three institutions of parliamentary democracy.

High institutional support for elections, parties and parliament coexists with a rather low turnout with a sharp age difference, volatile party identification, and weak party organization reinforced by the prevalence of individual sponsoring associations.

Besides the introduction of the proportional representation component, which turned out to be so unpopular, the electoral reform included giving state subsidies to political parties, and extending the range of persons for whose violation of the election law the candidate will be regarded as responsible. The former was unquestionably intended to strengthen political parties and the latter to punish the corrupt activities of personal sponsoring activities. The effect of those measures are still to be seen.

Conclusion

Looking back on the past thirty years of rapid economic growth and social change in Japan, what is apparent is the lack of adaptive capability of the Japan Socialist Party. Its relative success in the late 1950s and early 1960s was not a genuine product of class politics, and was helped by the modern vs. traditional value cleavage. In the rapid social change of the subsequent years, the JSP failed to consolidate its supporters by mass-party type organization. In contrast with the JSP, the Liberal Democratic Party succeeded by bridging the agrarian and industrial cleavage through distribution of the fruits of high economic growth to rural areas, and by utilizing personal support organizations built and maintained by individual politicians. LDP's policy in recent years has been to amalgamate personal support organizations of individual politicians with the party organization. The change of the electoral system from a multi-member constituency system to a combination of proportional representation and a single-member constituency system has made LDP's task easier because, in the old system, LDP candidates competed with each other, through their own personal support organizations. Moreover, state subsidies to political parties starting from 1996 are causing the LDP to strengthen the position of party leaders. The LDP seems to be building a Japanese model of party organization based on newly introduced state subsidies and continued efforts on the part of individual politicians.

Other political parties are facing a number of problems. Organizationally, new parties are groping for a new form of party organization other than the mass party or LDP *koenkai* models, but no effective way has been found so far. As for their location in political space, too, they are struggling to find their proper position. It is difficult to find either new values or new issues which can be appealed to effectively. For instance, post-materialist values and the issue of environmental protection are widely endorsed but too attenuated to rely on in isolation.

The institutions of parliamentary democracy such as elections, the Diet and political parties are firmly endorsed. But the voting turnout has been going down, and the number of those who have no party to support have been increasing, especially among the younger generation.

The institutional bottle of parliamentary democracy is kept firmly in place, but the content – both the parties and the party system – is half-filled and has yet to be properly brewed.

9 The party systems of Spain

Old cleavages and new challenges[1]

Juan J. Linz
José Ramón Montero

The future that was not, or was it?

A re-reading of the pages in the Lipset and Rokkan volume devoted to the future development of the Spanish political system is a strange experience (Linz 1967a, 264–75). Although the discontinuities in party politics meant that some words of caution were included there, the changes that took place between the 1930s and 1960s were much greater than those anticipated by most political observers. Those pages presented not only a wide range of scenarios and open possibilities, but also a number of predictions, many of which were fulfilled while others, actually or apparently, were disproved. In 1967, it was impossible to know if a monarchy, and particularly a constitutional monarchy, would be consolidated, or whether the alternative monarchy versus republic would become a major issue. Nor to imagine that the mechanisms of consensus that characterized the transition from the authoritarian regime would allow the legitimation of the monarchy in a democratic referendum, or that the role played by the King would confirm and seal the absence of debate on the question monarchy–republic. Spain thus became the only country of the third wave of democratization in which the transition process opened with the instauration, or the restoration, of a monarchy (Powell 1991; Podolny 1993). Other points made in that chapter were more debatable. The prediction that none of the many bourgeois Republican parties that played such an important role between 1931 and 1936 would reappear was validated. It did not seem unreasonable to expect that an extreme right-wing party defending continuity with the Franco regime would hold on to some voters. However, this would not happen, initially because, before the first free election, Adolfo Suárez, the prime minister, dissolved the official party and transferred its assets to the state. Furthermore, the existing neo-fascist parties were definitively weakened by the characteristics of the transition to democracy. The mechanisms of the *reforma pactada–ruptura pactada* (negotiated reform–negotiated break) in general, and particularly the formation of the UCD and the presence of AP (Alianza Popular), a conservative party committed to the democratic constitution without fully rejecting the past, deprived those parties nostalgic for the authoritarian regime of their electoral space (Linz *et al.* 1981). In addition, the neo-fascist groups that did exist were both isolated and divided (Rodríguez Jiménez 1997, 444; Jabardo 1996): after receiving a minuscule 1 per cent of the popular vote in 1977, only in 1979 did a coalition of small extreme right-wing groups win a single seat (only to lose it definitely in the next elections). In this way, neo-fascism and the antidemocratic right were weaker than in Italy and even in Germany. As for the left, the analysis did not make precise predictions about the relative strength of the communists and socialists. The general impression existing at the time regarding the significance of the PCI (Partito Communista Italiano) and the prominence of the communists in the opposition to Franco in the workplace, universities and even among the liberal professions, meant that communist electoral support was over-estimated. Similarly, it was predicted that the PCE (Partido Comunista de España) would also have to compete with some small parties on the far left, and that the anarchist labour organization, the CNT (Confederación Nacional del Trabajo), as well as its political wing, the FAI (Federación Anarquista Ibérica), would be another victim of discontinuity and change.

The analysis was fundamentally the result of applying the patterns of political behaviour of Italians on the basis of the estimates of Mattei Dogan (1967) to the Spanish social structure of 1964: in other words, from analysing what the outcome in terms of the popular vote would be if the Spanish electorate were to vote like the Italians (bearing in mind the differences in the social structures of the two countries). As was noted at the time, this type of "intellectual experiment" (Linz 1967a, 268) had many obvious limitations, and could not take into account the changes in the social structure in subsequent years or in the global political climate in the mid-1970s. In the 1960s, comparison with Italy gave rise to the prediction that the major political force on the centre and centre-right would be a Christian democratic party. This was not to be the case, despite the prominent role played in the opposition to the Franco regime by leaders identified with Christian democracy (Tusell 1977). A combination of factors (the Second Vatican Council, the secularization of the Spanish population which strengthened the freedom of Catholics to make their own political choices, Cardinal Tarancón's opposition to the idea that the Church would be identified with a party even though the use of the word *Christian* in the name, and the disastrous election campaigns fought by some political leaders), thwarted the consolidation of Christian democratic political groupings (Huneeus 1985). However, the electorate that should, according to the prediction, have supported Christian democracy in fact gave its support to the UCD in 1977 and 1979. Indeed, the proportion of vote predicted almost exactly matched the combined vote of the UCD and the two nationalist parties that were ideologically closest to a Christian democratic party position. It could be argued, therefore, that the prediction was only half-wrong: there would be no Christian democratic party, but the UCD had a very similar electorate. In practice, the UCD served as a "functional alternative" (Linz 1993a, 35) to Christian democracy.

The analysis was correct in stressing the importance that the peripheral nationalisms would acquire in the Spanish party system. It did anticipate the increasingly key role that the nationalist centre-right parties would play over time, the institutionalization of the *Estado de las Autonomías*, and that some of these parties would become significant sources of support for minority governments of the statewide parties. The analysis also correctly predicted the larger share of the vote for the left in Spain than in Italy. But the predicted strength of the communists did not materialize, perhaps not surprisingly considering, among other factors, the crisis of communism after the Prague Spring. Instead, the PSOE received the largest share of the vote in the competition within the left. The Maoist communists and other far-left groups did also enjoy greater support than their counterparts in Italy, but ultimately this proved ephemeral (Laiz 1995).

The weakness of these extreme left-wing organizations contributed significantly to the strength of the socialist left, the left's commitment to democracy and, more generally, to the pragmatic and moderate character of Spanish politics after 1975, three features which contrasted sharply with the Second Republic. The PCE's espousal of Eurocommunism and the absence of an extreme right-wing force reduced but did not eliminate the possibility of a polarized multi-party system. The ideological distance between the PCE (whose leaders had taken part in the Civil War and whose members were later very active in the opposition to the authoritarian regime) and the rightist AP (whose leaders had served as ministers under Franco and were opposed to a radical break with Francoism) meant that it was impossible to rule out, a priori, polarizing tendencies in the multi-party system established in 1977. Despite this, the new democratic party system was radically different to that of the 1930s, considered to be a perfect example of Sartori's (1976, 155) category of an extreme, polarized pluralist system. In sharp contrast with these features, which played such a decisive role in the breakdown of democracy in the 1930s, a series of developments gave rise to a much less fractional, ideological and polarized multiparty system (Linz 1978; Montero 1988).

Spain is a case of general interest because of its history of *discontinuous democratic party politics*. How are old cleavages articulated in a system with relatively new parties? What factors determine voter alignments and structure interparty competition? Secondly, this chapter will focus on Spanish party *systems* rather than *a* party system: the multinational, multicultural and *asymmetric* federal state makes Spain quite unique in Western Europe.

Types of elections: founding, critical and realigning

On 15 June 1977, the Spaniards went to the polls for the first time since 1936. Most of them knew relatively little about parties legalized only a few months before. But survey data show that people had relatively clear ideas about the main ideological alternatives in the political market of Western

Europe, could identify with them, and place themselves on the left/right dimension. They also soon learnt which parties they would never vote for, a fact that narrowed down their choices considerably. The nationalists in Catalonia and the Basque country had developed their own distinctive identity some time before, and there was little question that they would not vote for statewide parties (Linz *et al*. 1981).

Two decades later, seven elections have been held for the Congress. The results define three different electoral periods in terms of the format of the party system and the character of interparty competition. The existence of such profound political changes in a relatively short time raises the question of the extent to which Spain has achieved a minimal level of electoral stabilization, that is, the establishment of stable relations between the parties and citizens, and among the parties themselves (Morlino 1998, 85). This process is of crucial importance for the institutionalization of the party system and the development of predictable patterns of electoral competition. It is true that, in terms of the parties, instability appears to be the norm. The main parties did experience a more or less traumatic period of mergers, coalitions, and splits. They all suffered crises which ended in the resignations of leaders, the redefinition of party images, and the development of re-equilibrating mechanisms with different outcomes. This party instability contrasts with the Spaniards' voting behaviour which has been closer to a model of stabilization than to one of recurring availability in an open electoral market subject to unpredictable variations. The evolution of the party system has therefore been marked by the continuity of the ideological preferences and the inability of political elites to sustain effective party organizations. In this sense, one could even suggest that Spain constitutes a case of "volatile parties" and "stable voters" (Linz 1986; Barnes *et al*. 1986).

The first period: founding elections and the making of a party system

The relative stability of the vote was already remarkable in the first electoral period (Table 9.1). In 1977, most voters opted for the UCD or the PSOE, which between them won 64 per cent of the votes and 81 per cent of the seats. Both were flanked by minority competitors on the extremes: AP on the right and the PCE and the PSP (Partido Socialista Popular, which would later merge with PSOE) on the left. And they all, in turn, faced competition from a variety of nationalist and regionalist parties, most importantly the PNV and PDC (Pacte Democràtic per Catalunya, a Catalan coalition which in 1979 would stabilize as CiU, formed by Convergència Democràtica de Catalunya [CDC] and Unió Democràtica de Catalunya [UCD]). The Christian democratic parties won less than 1 per cent of the vote: their potential electorate was attracted by the reformist democratic stance of Suárez and his success in managing the transition (Linz 1980). Almost two years later, the main novelty was a spectacular increase in

Table 9.1 First electoral period: votes and seats in the 1977 and 1979 general elections

Party	1977			1979		
	% Votes	Seats	% Seats[g]	% Votes	Seats	% Seats[g]
Left						
PCE[a]	9.3	20	6	10.8	23	7
PSOE[b]	29.4	118	34	30.5	121	35
PSP/US	4.5	6	2	–	–	–
Centre-right						
UCD	34.6	166	47	35.0	168	48
Right						
AP[c]	8.8	16	5	6.1	9	3
UN	0.4	–	–	2.1	1	0.3
Regional						
Basque Country						
HB	–	–	–	1.0	3	1
EE	0.3	1	0.3	0.5	1	0.3
PNV	1.7	8	2	1.5	7	2
Catalonia						
ERC[d]	0.8	1	0.3	0.7	1	0.3
CiU[e]	2.8	11	3	2.7	8	2
UCDCC	0.9	2	0.3	–	–	–
Andalusia						
PSA	–	–	–	1.8	5	1
Aragon						
PAR	–	–	–	0.2	1	0.3
Canary Islands						
UPC	–	–	–	0.3	1	0.3
CAIC	0.2	1	0.3	–	–	–
Navarre						
UPN	–	–	–	0.2	1	0.3
Others[f]	6.3	–	–	6.6	–	–
TOTAL	100	350	100	100	350	100
Eligible voters	23,543,414			26,836,500		
Voters	18,625,000			18,284,948		
	(79.1%)			(68.1%)		
Blank + void votes	317,030			326,544		
	(1.7%)			(1.8%)		

Source: Linz (1980, 112, and 120–1).

Notes: [a]Including its Catalan branch, PSUC.
  [b]Including in 1977 its Catalan branch, PSC.
  [c]In 1979 as the coalition CD.
  [d]In 1977 as EC.
  [e]In 1977 as PDC.
  [f]Without parliamentary representation (the most important of these being a number of extreme left-wing parties such as the PTE and ORT both in 1977 [1.2%] and in 1979 [1.8%]).
  [g]Percentages are rounded off.

abstention (Justel 1995). Although in most cases with only one deputy, the extreme right (in the shape of Unión Nacional [UN], a coalition of typically Francoist parties) and the radical Basque independence movement (through Herri Batasuna [HB], a coalition of different groups associated with the terrorist organization ETA) both won seats for the first time, as did a number of small regionalist parties. Nonetheless, neither the format of the party system nor the pattern of competition changed significantly (Gunther *et al.* 1986). The results shaped a moderate multiparty system characterized by intense competition between the two main parties, high levels of rejection of the two minor parties on the respective extremes, and the almost equal split between the left (an average of 42.2 per cent of the vote) and right (43.4 per cent). But far from reproducing the polarized confrontations of the 1930s, the UCD and PSOE shared a certain ideological proximity, neither the PCE nor AP defended regimes other than democracy, and all the parties were conscious of the fact that the Spaniards' striking ideological moderation only permitted a centripetal type of interparty competition.

In this period, both the UCD and PSOE suffered different problems of party institutionalization. The UCD had greater difficulty achieving this, not least because in 1977 it was not even a party. Rather, it was an electoral coalition made up of a younger generation of politicians who had begun their careers within the previous authoritarian regime and collaborated with Adolfo Suárez in the transition, as well as some opposition leaders identifying as Christian democrats, social democrats or liberals. The first steps towards institutionalization included converting the coalition into a party, choosing Suárez as its president, adopting a catch-all model which fused the different ideological tendencies, and constructing an efficient organizational infrastructure, with an extensive albeit passive membership, in the majority of the provinces (Caciagli 1986).[2] The UCD elites, reluctant to embark on organizational integration in a single party, were characterized by profound differences with respect to the type of party that they wished to build, its ideological priorities, and its strategies for electoral competition. These divisions intensified over the action of the government, began to undermine the position of Suárez, whose innovative leadership (Linz 1993b) had precisely constituted its principal political capital, and eventually ended in a serious process of factional infighting marked by public confrontations and desertions on all sides (Hopkin 1999; Gunther 1986a).

The PSOE's problems were rather different. Its images combined the moderation and responsibility shown by the main leaders with the ideological radicalism and revolutionary rhetoric of other leaders and party activists. The former tried to increase the party's appeal among moderate electors by toning down its programme and emphasizing its sense of responsibility. But these messages were undermined, particularly in the 1979 election campaign, by the maximalist rhetoric of many of the party's official statements, the unstable assemblyism of internal decision-making, and the clashes among different sectors over numerous issues. This duality was resolved in November 1979 during the Bad Godesberg of Spanish Socialism (Maravall 1991, 11), when an Extraordinary Congress reinforced the leadership of Felipe González and Alfonso Guerra, eliminated the definition of the party as Marxist, adopted a social democratic reformist programme, replaced the implicit threat of mass mobilization by the conventional mechanisms of catch-all parties, and re-established party discipline (Puhle 1986, 332–9). After a successful process of moderation, the PSOE was able to concentrate on its opposition to the UCD governments and, with the decomposition of the center party, present itself as a credible alternative.

The second period: critical elections and the remaking of the party system

The break-up of the UCD and the PSOE's success came in October 1982 (Linz and Montero 1986). The characteristics of the 1982 ballot appear to fit those of critical elections, that is, elections which produce a substantial and lasting change in the existing electoral alignments. Over 40 per cent of the voters changed their choice from the preceding elections of 1979. The parties underwent substantial changes, and the party system itself was radically transformed (Table 9.2). Spaniards massively supported an alternation in government, giving the PSOE a broad parliamentary majority, and erasing the UCD from the scene despite the party's two preceding victories. Due to internal crises, the PCE was left with a minimal share of the vote, whereas AP, which was on the verge of disappearing in 1979, emerged as the main party of the opposition. And the failure of the extreme right was total: Fuerza Nueva (the most important of the neo-fascist parties) disbanded after winning little more than one hundred thousand votes (some 0.5 per cent), and Solidaridad Española, led by Antonio Tejero, one of the protagonists of the 1981 coup attempt, obtained fewer than thirty thousand votes (0.1 per cent).

The PSOE's victory was extraordinary. The party doubled both its vote (topping ten million) and its parliamentary group. It was the most-voted party in 42 of Spain's 52 districts and in all of the autonomous communities except for the Basque Country and Galicia (Puhle 1986). The PSOE was able to govern alone for the first time since its foundation over a hundred years before; it was also the first time in Spanish history that a party had won an absolute majority of seats. The UCD was annihilated by an electorate that rejected the party's continual infighting and ineffective governments. No other European party had ever suffered a defeat of such magnitude: the party's more than six million voters in 1979 shrank to about one and a half million in 1982. Three out of four UCD voters opted for the AP or to a lesser extent the PSOE, and those who remained loyal to the party belonged to marginal socio-demographic groups (Gunther 1986a). The number of UCD deputies dropped from 168 in 1979 to just 12

Table 9.2 Second electoral period: votes and seats in the 1982, 1986 and 1989 general elections

	1982			1986			1989		
	% Votes	Seats	% Seats[e]	% Votes	Seats	% Seats[e]	% Votes	Seats	% Seats[e]
Left									
IU[a]	4.0	4	1	4.5	7	2	9.1	17	5
PSOE	48.4	202	58	44.6	184	53	39.9	175	50
Centre-right									
CDS	2.9	2	0.6	9.2	19	5	7.9	14	4
UCD	6.5	12	3	–	–	–	–	–	–
Right									
PP[b]	26.5	106	30	26.3	105	30	25.9	107	31
Regional									
Basque Country									
HB	1.0	2	0.6	1.1	5	1	1.1	4	1
EE	0.5	1	0.3	0.5	2	0.6	0.5	2	0.6
EA	–	–	–	–	–	–	0.7	2	0.6
PNV	1.9	8	2	1.6	6	2	1.2	5	1
Catalonia									
ERC	0.7	1	0.3	–	–	–	–	–	–
CiU	2.7	12	3	5.1	18	5	5.1	18	5
Galicia									
CG	–	–	–	0.4	1	0.3	–	–	–
Andalusia									
PA	–	–	–	–	–	–	1.0	2	0.6
Aragon									
Par[c]	–	–	–	0.4	1	0.3	0.3	1	0.3
Canary Islands									
AIC	–	–	–	0.3	1	0.3	0.3	1	0.3
Valencian community									
UV	–	–	–	0.3	1	0.3	0.7	2	0.6
Others[d]	3.9	–	–	5.7	–	–	6.3	–	–
TOTAL	100	350	100	100	350	100	100	350	100
Eligible voters	26,739,685			29,117,613			29,460,120		
Voters	21,440,552			20,487,812			20,599,629		
	(80.2%)			(70.4%)			(69.9%)		
Blank + void voters	504,536			443,125			280,150		
	(2.3%)			(2.2%)			(1.3%)		

Source: Data provided by the Spanish Ministry of the Interior.

Notes: [a]In 1982 as PCE; including its Catalan branch, PSUC in 1982 and IC in 1986 and 1989.
[b]AP in coalition with PDP in 1982; in 1986 as CP. In Navarre, in coalition with UPN.
[c]PAR in 1986.
[d]Without parliamentary representation (the most important of these being in 1982 the neo-fascist FN [0.5%] and the far-left PST [0.5%]; in 1986, MUC [1.1%, a split from the PCE], and the centrist PRD [0.9%]; and in 1989 the populist ARM [1.1%] and the greens LV-LV and LVE [0.7%]).
[e]Percentages are rounded off.

in 1982; and these did not even include Leopoldo Calvo Sotelo, the prime minister and the party's number two candidate for Madrid.

The PCE and AP also experienced contradictory fates. The protracted crisis in the PCE contributed to the loss of over one million voters, almost all of whom shifted to the PSOE. Reduced to a smaller electoral base and parliamentary representation than the Scandinavian communist parties, the PCE ended up splitting into three different parties (Gunther 1986b). AP embodied the other face of electoral fortune. The party's continued efforts to substitute a *natural* (i.e. conservative) majority for the *artificial* (i.e. centrist) majority of the UCD in order to compete directly with the PSOE in the framework of a two-party system appeared to bear fruit. This strategy seemed to have the support of some of the so-called *poderes fácticos*, especially business groups and the most conservative sectors of the UCD. The AP obtained five and a half million votes, a five-fold increase in the number of votes compared to 1979 and a twelve-fold increase in the number of seats. Like the scale of the UCD's failure, the AP's growth was equally remarkable in the European context. Even so, only some former UCD voters now gave their support to the conservative coalition. With almost one million votes less than the UCD in 1979, AP was still a long way behind the PSOE: contrary to the expectations of the conservative leaders, the *natural* majority lay for the moment at least with the PSOE (Montero 1986).

The 1986 and 1989 general elections showed more elements of continuity than change. The average vote for the parties on the left was greater (50.2 per cent) than that of the conservative parties (35.1 per cent). These elections gave rise to PSOE absolute parliamentary majorities, a smaller, but still considerable, gap between the PSOE and AP, the fragmentation of the opposition, and the stability of the nationalist parties. Although the PSOE saw its electoral support eroded over the course of the decade, opposition parties were unable to benefit from those losses. The processes of erosion had been set in motion, particularly in the late 1980s, with internal tensions the increasing conflict with the UGT (Unión General de Trabajadores, the allied trade union), the decreasing of its mobilization potential and the transformation of its electorate, which became older and less urban, more economically inactive and less educated. On the left, the competition between the PSOE and the PCE continued to be extremely unbalanced even after the PCE created in 1986 Izquierda Unida (IU), a coalition with other small and disparate groups which would attempt to channel the representation of a problematic new left.

The outcomes of the critical election of 1982 and its lasting consequences over the decade present three interesting puzzles about party competition in the centre and centre-right of the party system. The first is related to the crisis of the UCD, and the different explanations given for it. Many observers have mentioned the cost of governing during a difficult period, the economic crisis (with the accompanying effects of large-scale unemployment and high levels of inflation) and the rise of terrorism (Hopkin 1999). But the scale of its defeat and the ultimate dissolution of the party cannot be explained only by responses to its policies. The crisis was essentially an internal affair, reflected in the factional conflicts, the resignation of Suárez as prime minister in 1981 and the slow but continuous disintegration of the parliamentary group. Other observers, including the UCD prime minister Leopoldo Calvo Sotelo (1990), attribute the crises to the mistake of fusing into a single party the components of the heterogeneous coalition that won the 1977 election. However, there is evidence that leaders and deputies identified with, and coming from, the various different political groupings split among themselves, some staying in the party until the bitter end (Gunther 1986a). A related factor was the ambivalence of many of the faction leaders, the so-called *barons*, toward Suárez, who, on account of his social background, education, and career, did not fit their image of a leader, despite the fact that for the electorate he had been an undisputed and almost charismatic leader (Linz 1993b). But his successor as premier, Calvo Sotelo, was unable to hold the party together, despite his achievements in successfully bringing the military rebels to trial and his generally unpopular decision to take Spain into NATO (which would not be reversed by the Socialists when they came to power). Thus, there can be no doubt that although many voters would have turned their backs on the UCD because of the worsening economic situation and their opposition to particular policies, the unprecedented scale of its debacle cannot be explained without focusing on the elite fighting and the factional politics within the party. In the summer of 1982, the chronic internal tensions in the UCD gave rise to the desertion of some deputies to AP and above all to a series of splits that spawned three parties: the Partido de Acción Democrática (PAD) with a social democratic orientation and which would later be absorbed by the PSOE on the left; the Centro Democrático y Social (CDS), led by Suárez himself in the centre, and on the right the PDP (Partido Democrático Popular), with a Christian democratic orientation.

In the second place, AP's strategy to secure domination of the political spectrum to the right of the PSOE would only bear fruit ten years later. But in the early 1980s the conservative leaders overlooked the general leftward leanings of the electorate. There were also structural factors. One of those factors is that both in Catalonia and the Basque Country the middle class and the bourgeoisie were not ready to abandon the centre-right nationalist parties to support a party that appeared to represent Spanish nationalism and centralism. Whereas the PSOE and the communists could win the votes of both the immigrant working class and some lower white collar voters, a significant number of Catalan and, to a lesser extent, Basque workers, the statewide right could compete for only a small segment of the Catalan bourgeoisie and the Basque upper class. It is unlikely that the PP will ever overcome that obstacle. AP's failure to grasp this and other related factors partly explains its internal instability. The party experienced considerable organizational development (López Nieto 1997), but also engaged in constant soul-searching. The disappointment caused by its electoral stagnation in the 1980s provoked an intense process of conflicts, clashes and desertions which lasted until 1990, when Aznar became the leader of a party ideologically redefined as something akin to Christian democracy or liberal neoconservatism. AP had to change its name (from AP, after the *refoundation* in 1989, to the Partido Popular [PP]), and adopted very different and even contradictory political strategies.

Finally, the disappointment of the hopes raised by AP highlighted the importance of the statewide centre parties. In the 1980s, the vote of those to the right of the PSOE would remain divided between different parties. The CDS, a splinter of the UCD founded by Suárez, attempted to hold on to the progressive elements within the UCD and become a party playing a role comparable to the FDP (Freie Demokratische Partei) in Germany. Indeed, it was admitted into the international of liberal parties, but, and in spite of some local successes, it did not take off. A typical centre and middle party (Hazan 1997, 17), its strategy of also establishing itself as a pivotal party, able to participate in coalition governments led by the PSOE or AP, proved to be impossible during the 1980s: with parliamentary majorities in three consecutive elections, the PSOE government simply did not need it. The CDS's decline began as early as the 1989 general elections, and definitively culminated in the 1993 elections.

In 1986 yet another party, the PRD (Partido Reformista Democrático) tried to compete in the crowded space between the PSOE and AP. Its leader, Miquel Roca, a distinguished CiU parliamentarian and one of the drafters of the constitution, appealed to a small and select electorate. But voters were not ready to support a Catalan leader who not only was unwilling to give up his position within CiU and his identification with Catalan politics, but also stood in a highly confused partisan format. In the 1986 elections, the PRD won less than 1 per cent of the vote. It would be the crisis of these attempts to create parties at the centre of the spectrum – CDS, PRD and PDP – that would finally allow, as a result of the crisis in the PSOE in the 1990s, a victory of the PP in 1996. However, the structural limitations of the appeal of the right would deny this party an absolute majority.

The third period: realigning elections and new patterns of competition

After more than a decade of socialist ascendancy, a new period opened in the 1990s with evident signs of electoral realignment brought about by a number of factors: the incorporation of more than four million new voters into the electoral register, the impact of economic modernization and new educational levels, the social changes resulting from the welfare policies of the PSOE governments, the political resources generated by the consolidation of the *Estado de las Autonomías*. The political implications of these developments affected the main statewide parties, which experienced significant changes in the social profiles of their electorates; the party system was also altered as a consequence of the new conditions of competitiveness between the two major parties. In 1993, the PSOE lost its parliamentary majority and the PP saw a sharp rise in electoral support (Table 9.3). Voters for the parties on the left (48.3 per cent) still outnumbered those for the right (34.8 per cent), and the nationalists, above all CiU and the PNV, maintained their position in terms of both votes and seats. Nonetheless, the tighter competition between the PSOE and PP, on the one hand, and between the PSOE and the communist-dominated IU, on the other, spelt the return to a moderate multi-party system.

For the PSOE, its fourth consecutive victory combined the loss of sixteen seats with a significant increase in its vote. But the fatigue its electorate felt and the appearance of cracks in the party's internal cohesion already pointed to the end of its long period in power. For the PP this new defeat was offset by its 34 new seats, and the narrowing of the gap that separated it from the PSOE. The change of government finally came with the March 1996 elections. But the PSOE's defeat was less conclusive, and the PP's victory more modest, than expected: the socialists lost to the PP by a difference of only 340,000 out of a poll of over 25 million votes. Although the PP emerged as the party with the largest plurality, it took only 45 per cent of the seats in the Congress, while the PSOE retained 40 per cent. The PP's *bitter victory* and PSOE's *sweet defeat* did not, therefore, signal the end of the predominance of the left (with 48.1 per cent of the vote) over the right (with 38.8 per cent) – leaving aside the vote for nationalist and regionalist parties (Wert 1997). However, this third period has seen a major change in the way governments have been formed. Both the PSOE in 1993 and the PP in 1996 opted for single-party minority governments, maintained in power by the more or less formal parliamentary support provided by nationalist parties.

Following its defeat in 1996, the PSOE considered *volis nolis* launching a process of restructuring its leadership, democratizing its internal mechanisms, and updating its ideological appeals. To date, the PSOE has taken two main initiatives: González's substitution by Joaquín Almunia as secretary general of the party at the XXXIV party conference (June 1997), and the celebration of primaries to choose candidates for the most relevant institutional positions (Spring 1998).

The PP faced a different series of challenges. First, the party leadership passed through a process of generational replacement, with the arrival of large numbers of middle-ranking officials who had already worked with Fraga. Their experience and relative youth helped them transmit a message of continuity with the past, but also one of essential change. Second, the presence of this new elite favoured a new phase of the by now familiar strategy of *conquering the centre*. Third, the PP became the largest party in terms of membership: it has grown steadily since 1982, but above all since 1991, when the PP's electoral prospects began to look more solid.

Table 9.3 Third electoral period: votes and seats in the 1993 and 1996 general elections

	1993			1996		
	% Votes	Seats	% Seats[c]	% Votes	Seats	% Seats[c]
Left						
IU[a]	9.6	18	5	10.6	21	6
PSOE	38.8	159	45	37.5	141	40
Centre-right						
CDS	1.8	–	–	–	–	–
Right						
PP	34.8	141	40	38.8	156	45
Regional						
Basque Country						
HB	0.9	2	0.6	0.7	2	0.6
EA[a]	0.6	1	0.3	0.5	1	0.3
PNV	1.2	5	1	1.3	5	1
Catalonia						
ERC	0.8	1	0.3	0.7	1	0.3
CiU	4.9	17	5	4.6	16	5
Galicia						
BNG	–	–	–	0.9	2	0.6
Aragon						
Par	0.6	1	0.3	–	–	–
Canary Islands						
CC	0.9	4	1	0.9	4	1
Valencian community						
UV	0.5	1	0.3	0.4	1	0.3
Others[b]	4.6	–	–	3.1	–	–
TOTAL	100	350	100	100	350	100
Eligible voters		30,748,763			32,531,833	
Voters		23,718,083 (77.1%)			25,172,058 (77.4%)	
Blank + void votes		316,649 (1.3%)			369,127 (1.5%)	

Source: Data provided by the Spanish Ministry of the Interior.

Notes: [a]In 1993, in coalition with EUE.
[b]Without parliamentary representation (the most important of these being in 1993 the centrist CDS [1.8%] and the greens LV [0.6%], and in 1996 the regionalist PA [0.5%]).
[c]Percentages are rounded off.

Finally, IU has accumulated in this third electoral period many apparently intractable problems. After playing a constructive role during the transition (Linz 1981), the PCE suffered a series of internal crises that led to changes in leadership, organizational instability, and splits (Gunther 1986b). In 1986, communist leaders tried to take advantage of the almost seven million "no" votes in the referendum on Spanish membership of NATO by setting up the coalition Izquierda Unida (IU) (Alt and Boix 1991; Santamaría and Alcover 1987). This was based on an alliance among the PCE, small left-wing parties and some individuals who had stood out in the campaign against NATO. The new coalition provided voters dissatisfied with the PSOE an option that also represented the apparent modernization of the PCE. However, the dominant presence of the PCE gave rise to internal tensions as a result of the difficulties involved in harmonizing the limited electoral appeal of a communist party after the collapse of the Soviet Union with the crucial importance of the PCE in the coalition's daily activities (Bosco, forthcoming).

Party change and party system change: dimensions and features

Reduced electoral volatility

It might appear that Spain has seen considerable electoral volatility: the collapse of the UCD and the CDS, the oscillations in the PSOE's and PCE/IU's share of the vote, and the great leaps forward in AP/PP's electoral support would testify to the many changes that have taken place. This impression appears confirmed when the averages of the aggregate volatility index for Spain[3] is compared to similar indexes in other European countries since the mid-1970s: the Spanish figures are the highest, followed closely by those of the other new Southern European democracies (Gunther and Montero, forthcoming). But Table 9.4 reveals a rather different picture. After a scant volatility between the first and second elections, in 1982

Table 9.4 Electoral volatility in Spain, 1977–96

Elections	Volatility		
	Total	*Inter-bloc*	*Intra-bloc*
1979–77	9.9	1.9	8.0
1982–79	42.8	6.3	36.5
1986–82	12.1	1.7	10.4
1989–86	9.4	0.9	8.5
1993–89	9.9	2.1	7.8
1996–93	4.4	0.8	3.6
Mean	14.7	2.3	12.4
Deviation	13.9	2.0	11.9

electoral changes acquired an unusual intensity: if indexes higher than around 15 per cent have been interpreted as the consequence of earthquake elections (Ersson and Lane 1998, 31), the 42.8 per cent volatility in 1982 was truly extraordinary. In fact, figures of over 40 per cent are rare in Europe, and the elections in Spain in 1982 (and in Italy in 1994) are by far the most extreme cases of total aggregate volatility seen in Europe this century (Mair 1997, 67–8; Bartolini and Mair 1990, 70). It is true that after these critical elections volatility has remained below the European average (Lane and Ersson 1998, 196). But in both types of elections inter-bloc volatility has been relatively low. Electoral change is thus compatible with the fact that the Spaniards (and Italians) may give their support to a different party than in the previous election, but one within the same ideological space. This pattern highlights the importance that the barrier between the main parties on the left and right has for the stabilization of the electorate and the anchoring of inter-party competition: a barrier which very few voters cross, and hence limits transfers of votes between the two blocs of parties (Gunther and Montero, forthcoming; Morlino 1998, 88).[4]

Low party fragmentation

The stabilization of Spanish electoral behaviour is also reflected in the apparently scant variation in the number of relevant parties – although with some changes in the parties considered to be relevant and in the party system format. To date, electoral preferences have systematically converged on just a few parties. The level of party fragmentation is amongst the lowest in Europe. Despite the constant expansion of the electoral supply, it seems clear that the electoral market is relatively closed to new actors and that the electoral system operates against openness (as the differences between electoral and parliamentary indices confirm). Much of the low party fragmentation is due to the fact that the most voted party has managed to win at least 35 per cent of the vote and 45 per cent of the seats, and significantly higher figures during the socialist period. The concentration of the vote on the two major parties has also been high, oscillating between two-thirds and three-quarters of the vote, and between 80 and 88 per cent of the seats. Therefore, the combination of electoral preferences and the effects of the electoral system has facilitated throughout the three periods the formation of single-party governments, as well as the exceptional run of three consecutive majorities in Congress during the 1980s.

However, this distribution is also compatible with the presence in the Congress of Deputies of a relatively large number of parties and coalitions: 14 in the 1979 legislature, 13 in 1989, and 11 since 1996. In fact, in the mid-1990s, no Western European parliament had such a large number of political forces, except perhaps in Italy and Belgium; and leaving out the peculiar case of Belgium, because of the duplication of its parties, the Italian index of the effective number of parliamentary parties almost triples the Spanish one (Le Duc *et al*. 1996). The circumstance that most of these minor parties are *not* statewide parties emphasizes the importance of the regional cleavage as a second dimension of competition. Basque and Catalan nationalist voters have always had specific parliamentary representation, and by more than one party, while voters in the Canary Islands, Aragon, Andalusia, Navarre, Valencia and Galicia have been more sporadically represented by regionalist parties. This also highlights the distinctiveness of the Spanish party format among the countries in which a small number of large parties compete with different types of small parties.

A simple typology of party size and continuity over the seven legislatures makes it possible to distinguish from within the group of minor parties the *small, micro-* and *ephemeral* parties, in accordance with a number of elementary criteria (Table 9.5).[5] All the ephemeral parties appeared only in the first two legislatures, and most were regionalist. In turn, micro-parties also belong to the category of nationalist or regionalist parties, and have survived with different degrees of success throughout the period. But the most striking pattern is that the small parties are all, with the exception of PCE/IU, nationalist, and most of them have obtained parliamentary representation in every legislature. This pattern reinforces their significance within the Spanish party *systems*. The reasons are two-fold: first, because of their coalition potential with any large party at the statewide level; second, because of their governmental and/or leading roles within their own party systems at regional levels. The lack of a statewide centre party which could operate as a *hinge* with either the PSOE or the PP has allowed CiU, PNV and more recently Coalición Canaria (CC) to monopolize the coalition potential of the Spanish party system.

Closed competition for the government

The patterns of competition for government have shown a remarkable stability. As Mair (1997, 222–3) has recalled, the mechanisms of competition for government constrain the decisions of voters by converting their choices of a party into a simultaneous expression of their preferences for a potential government. A crucial dimension of the party system itself, in the Spanish case these patterns have crystallized into a *closed* structure of partisan competition. According to the criteria defined by Mair (1997, 206–14), this implies that the two changes of government (PSOE in 1982, and PP in 1996) have been complete (on both occasions one single-party government was replaced by another), the governmental formulae have been regular (on both occasions the alternation has simply applied the mechanisms which assign the government to the party that wins the elections), and the number of parties with a chance of forming a government has been limited.

Table 9.5 A summary of size and continuity: types of parties in the Congress of Deputies, 1977–96

Types	Parties statewide	Nationalist or regionalist	Legislatures						
			1977	1979	1982	1986	1989	1993	1996
Large[a]	PSOE		x	x	x	x	x	x	x
	AP/PP				x	x	x	x	x
	UCD		x	x					
Small[b]	PCE/IU		x	x	x	x	x	x	x
	AP		x	x					
	CDS					x	x	x	
	UCD					x			
		CiU	x	x	x	x	x	x	x
		PNV	x	x	x	x	x	x	x
		HB		x	x	x	x	x	x
		PSA/PA		x			x		
		CC							x
		BNG[c]						x	x
	Micro[d]	ERC	x	x	x			x	x
		EE	x	x	x	x	x		
		UV		x		x	x	x	x
		PAR/Par				x	x	x	
		EA					x	x	x
		AIC				x	x		
Ephemeral[e]	PSP/VS		x						
	UN			x					
		UCDCC	x						
		CAIC	x						
		UPC		x					
		UPN		x					
		CG				x			
Total of parties			11	14	10	12	13	11	11

Notes: [a]Large parties are those receiving 15% or more of the votes in at least two legislatures.
  [b]Small parties are those receiving between 1% and 15% of the vote in at least two legislatures (with the exception of the UCD, which disappeared after the 1982 election).
  [c]Obtained 2 seats for the first time in the 1996 legislature.
  [d]Micro parties are those receiving 1% of the vote *or* obtaining 2 or more seats in at least two legislatures.
  [e]Ephemeral parties are those obtaining seats in only one legislature (with the exception of the BNG).

In contrast with the patterns of competition for government in the Spanish Second Republic (Linz 1978), all the elections held since 1977 have produced a clear winning party, even if the distance separating it from the second party amounted to just the 340,000 votes between PP and PSOE in 1996; all the legislatures have had single-party absolute majorities or pluralities of variable proportions, in every case large enough to ensure daily parliamentary decision-making; and all governments have been homogenous and single-party (Table 9.6). The closed competition for the

Table 9.6 Governments by electoral periods in Spain, 1977–96

Government	Dates	Duration (in months)	Party	Parliamentary support (%)	External support	Type[a]
Suárez I	Jul. 77–Apr. 79	22	UCD	47	No	s–m
Suárez II	Apr. 79–Jan. 81	22	UCD	48	No	s–m
Calvo-Sotelo	Feb. 81–Oct. 82	21	UCD	48	No	s–m
González I	Dec. 82–Jun. 86	43	PSOE	58	No	S–M
González II	Jul. 86–Oct. 89	40	PSOE	53	No	S–M
González III	Dec. 89–Jun. 93	43	PSOE	50	No	S–M
González IV	Jul. 93–Mar. 96	33	PSOE	45	Yes (Ciu)	s–m
Aznar I	May 96–Na	Na	PP	45	Yes (CiU, PNV, CC)	s–m

Notes: [a]s–m indicates single-party minority government; S–M, single-party majority government.
Na, not applicable.

government has been accentuated even further by the bipolar competition between the PP and the PSOE, and, at another level, has been reinforced by the inclusion in the constitution of a series of provisions to give minority governments greater political stability. The combined result of these factors has been remarkable. Compared to the nineteen governments and eight prime ministers in the five years of the Second Republic, Spain has had four prime ministers during the last two decades. In fact, almost all the governments formed since 1977 have lasted as long as the parliaments that originally invested them, and the legislatures have usually run their full course.

Ideological moderation

The Spanish electorate has not only tended to vote for just a few parties, but also for moderate ones. Since the 1970s, most initially chose centre-right parties (such as the UCD), before switching to the centre-left (such as the PSOE), and more recently to a party like the PP, which hovers between the right and centre-right. Democratic parties have covered almost the entire parliamentary spectrum, whilst the extremist parties have obtained minimal support. This electoral moderation does fit with the pattern of ideological moderation. Many indicators show that it encompasses different social classes, age cohorts, and occupational groups, and has enjoyed an unusual degree of continuity since the 1970s (Maravall 1984, 32).

The positions voters assign to the parties have also remained relatively stable, although with some variations over time that might well reflect the shifting positions of the parties. The PCE and its successor, IU, is one of the least extreme communist parties at the European level (Montero 1994, 100). The PSOE's positions reflect the moderate policies of the socialist governments. Whereas the UCD was assigned to the centre-right, AP has been seen on the extreme right and remained in this range even in the 1980s, in spite of inheriting much of the electorate of the UCD and the efforts of its leadership to present it as a centre party. Even though in the 1990s its successor, the PP, was seen as moving slightly toward the centre-right, it is still perceived to be one of the most conservative parties in Europe. The short-lived CDS was perceived in the centre; its disappearance meant that there is no party of any significance between the PSOE and the PP, no party comparable to the Italian DC in a polarized multiparty system and no party playing the governmental role of the FDP in Germany. But despite the ideological distance between the PSOE and PP, it is possible to describe the Spanish party system as a bipolar, but not a polarized system (with the exception of the Basque case). But this depolarization in the electorate in the 1990s has been accompanied by some trends of increasing tension between the PP and the PSOE and personal animosity between their leaders José María Aznar and Felipe González. The generational change in the PP (with younger politicians who had not lived the search for consensus in the transition) and the more general centripetal catch-all politics (with the need for emphasizing the differences between parties which face little prospect for absolute parliamentary majorities) might have led to occasional outbursts of polarization which do not necessarily change the basic ideological moderation in the electorates.These patterns are similar to ones found in other southern European countries with significant communist parties, no strong centre parties, and relevant conservative parties. This configuration broadens the party space, widening the distance between its component parts, and therefore increasing the potential polarization of the party system. Spain stands out in terms of the ideological distance between the extreme parties (i.e. IU and PP) and shares with France the greatest ideological polarization between competing parties (i.e. the PSOE and PP) (Montero 1994, 101–3). But these comparatively high levels of polarization are not a cause for concern *per se*. Not least, because party elites have carefully avoided embarking on the type of polarizing strategies so common, for instance, among Greek parties since the 1980s (Kalivas 1996). Moreover, and reflecting the absence of a strong centre party and the predominant distribution of ideological preferences, since 1982 the bipolar configuration of the party system has encouraged centripetal competition, whereby the parties try to attract the voters in the centre of the continuum. The format of the party system means that this centripetal logic is compatible with the evenly balanced competition between IU and the PSOE on the left, the undisputed pre-eminence of the PSOE on the centre-left, and the PP's solid monopoly on the centre-right and right. However, the patterns of inter-party competition are more complex in some autonomous communities, where the regional cleavage has spawned nationalist parties across the ideological spectrum which compete amongst themselves and with other statewide parties on various dimensions.

A clear indicator of the diminishing polarization in the Spanish party system refers to the evolution of the images of the parties. The characterization of a party as *republican* became irrelevant after the left gave its support to the monarchical constitution of 1978. In the late 1970s and early 1980s, it made sense to ask if any of the major parties were or were not *democratic*, in the sense of abiding by the rules of the game. There was still some doubt about the democratic commitment of the PCE; we do not know if such scepticism exists with regard to IU, but it seems unlikely in terms of the evolution of the negative vote. Many voters had also doubts about the democratic commitment of AP; although we do not know either whether some still feel that way about the PP, the fact that in 1993 26 per cent considered the PP to be extremist suggest that only a minority is sceptical. The major change in the image of the parties on the left has been the weakening of their *Marxist* label. Voters clearly responded to the PSOE when it dropped its Marxist commitment in its extraordinary congress of October 1979. The communists, perceived as Marxist in 1978 by 62 percent, also successfully changed their image. Both the PCE and IU have retained their image as *defenders of the workers*, while the PSOE has to a large extent lost that image. Reflecting the neo-liberal policies adopted by socialist governments, a large number of voters see it as a party that *defends business* and the *middle class*. In fact, the PSOE is seen by two out of three Spaniards as defending simultaneously the interests of workers, business, and the middle class: there could not be a better image of a catch-all party compared to its initial image as a workers' party. Finally, AP was originally identified as a party that was most favourable to business. And although it is still perceived in that way, it also has become a party of the middle class with a smaller catch-all dimension amongst those who think that it defends workers. These data clearly show that voters hold images that portray the major parties as catch-all parties, above all in the case of the PSOE, and with profiles still defined as conservative and pro-business in the case of the PP. All parties have also strengthened the image that they are *able to avoid confrontations* in society and/or *able to govern*: another indication of the absence of polarization.

Changes in party systems: formats and layers

Over the last twenty years, the instability shown by the parties has been accompanied by modifications in the patterns of interparty competition in each of the three electoral periods: the frequent party changes have thus interacted with a rather unusual series of party system changes. The distinct electoral fortunes of the parties have given rise to party systems with different formats (as was the case between 1979 and 1982) and different mechanics (as between 1982 and 1996). The principal features of the party systems in each of the three electoral periods covering the last twenty years are outlined in Table 9.7. After the 1979 elections (which essentially confirmed the tendencies already seen in the 1977 founding

Table 9.7 Features of Spanish party systems in three electoral periods, 1977–96

	Periods		
Features	First (1979)	Second (1982)	Third (1996)
Volatility[a]	1.9	6.3	0.8
Interbloc	8.0	36.5	3.6
Intrabloc	9.9	42.8	4.4
Total	5914	5510	3811
Fragmentation			
Parties in parliament			
Statewide parties			
Nationalist and regionalist parties			
Total			
Party with largest plurality			
Votes (%)	3548	48,458	38,845
Seats (%)			
Two major parties			
Votes (%)	65,583	74,988	76,385
Seats (%)			
Number of parties (Molinar index)			
Electoral	3.04	1.81	2.63
Parliamentary	1.99	1.52	2.25
Competitiveness[b]			
Electoral	4.5	21.9	1.3
Parliamentary	13.4	27.1	1.3
Competition for government			
Party in government	UCD	PSOE	PP
Parliamentary support (%)	48	58	45
Number of governments[c]	3	3	1
Average duration (in months)	22	42	–
Type of government	Single-minority/ almost majority	Majority	Single minority with external support
Main opposition party	PSOE	AP/PP	PSOE
Polarization			
Votes for parties (%)			
Left	41.3	53.4	4.81
Right	43.2	35.9	38.8
Nationalist and regionalist	8.9	7.8	10.0
Index of ideological distance[d]			
Between most extreme parties			
PCE/IU-AP/PP	0.47	0.54	0.40
Between competing parties for government			
PSOE–UCD	0.22	0.20	–
PSOE–PP	0.34	0.37	0.31
Type of party system	Moderate pluralism	Predominant	Moderate pluralism

Notes: [a]Referred to the immediately preceeding election of 1977, 1979, and 1993, respectively; see text accompanying Table 9.4.
[b]See Sartori (1976, 218–19).
[c]The fourth PSOE government (July 1993–March 1996), which was part of the third period, has not been included.
[d]This index (which goes from 0 to 1) is measured by the absolute difference between the mean self-placements of their respective voters on the left-right scale divided by 9 (which is the theoretical maximum distance of the scale); see Sani and Sartori (1983, 321).

elections), the party system seemed to belong to the category of moderate pluralism (Santamaría 1981, 412–13). The number of parliamentary parties was very large, but the level of party fragmentation was much lower due to the major differences in their parliamentary sizes. The distance between the two principal competing parties (UCD and PSOE) was very small, and the dynamic of interparty competition was centripetal. In electoral terms, interparty competition was also characterized by the fact that both the PSOE and the UCD, as the two main parties, faced bilateral competition, respectively, from the PCE and AP, two minor parties situated in both cases on the extremes. The competitiveness between the UCD and the PSOE was accentuated by the low level of partisan identification, the division of the spaces of left and right for the statewide parties, and the increasing consolidation of the regional cleavage for the statewide and nationalist parties in certain key communities, notably the Basque Country and Catalonia (Maravall and Santamaría 1986, 224). At the governmental level, in turn, the small electoral gap between the two main competing parties suggested that the centre-left opposition stood a good chance of winning power in the future (Di Palma 1980, 137).

The party system was radically transformed in the third general elections in 1982. The new party system had a different format in terms of both the number and above all the parliamentary size of statewide parties. Although the continued strength of the two main parties led many observers to define the new system as a more or less "imperfect" two-party system, the distance between them displayed the typical mechanics of a predominant-party system, in which, obviously, the PSOE was the dominant party (Sartori 1976, 195–9): the PSOE won three clear successive electoral victories, in which it obtained absolute parliamentary majorities, and managed to maintain a lead in terms of seats of a maximum of 27 per cent in 1982 and a minimum of 19 per cent in 1989, over AP-PP, the second party. The ideological distance between the two main parties increased considerably following the disappearance of the UCD. However, the continuity of the distribution of preferences among the voters ensured also the persistence of the centripetal competition between the PSOE and AP/PP.

In the 1990s, the predominant party system of the 1980s developed into a new variant of moderate pluralism. As is well known, Sartori (1976, 199–200) has argued that the former is a *type* rather than a class of party systems: it can easily develop a variant of multi-partyism. Equally, party system change may easily occur through relatively slight modifications in the strength of the principal components of the system (Mair 1997, 53). This is precisely what happened in the 1993 and 1996 elections.[6] The levels of competitiveness between the PSOE and PP increased enough to take the PP to power after more than a decade of socialist governments, and to be reflected in the extremely small differences in both parliamentary and electoral terms. Rather than permitting the entry of green or some type of new right parties, as in many other European parliaments (Donovan and Broughton 1999), the format of the party system continued to reduce the number of statewide parties and to increase that of nationalist and regionalist parties. In electoral terms, the system is still marked by the bipolar configuration around the PP and the PSOE. At the parliamentary level, the PSOE majorities of the 1980s gave way in 1993 to a PSOE minority government with the external support from CiU, and then in 1996 to a PP minority government also with external support from CiU, the PNV, and CC. In these circumstances, the roles of the nationalist and regionalist parties would obviously be strengthened. Although minority governments are generally associated with moderate pluralist party systems (Strom 1990, 241), cases of formal external support are unusual, and cases in which support comes exclusively from non-statewide parties rarer still. In fact, Spain in the 1990s is unique due to the dual circumstances that the only parties with coalition potential were the nationalists and regionalists, *and* that practically all the relevant parties with coalition potential actually had governmental relevance (Sartori 1976, 300–1).

These peculiarities have been accentuated by the coexistence of the statewide party system with distinct regional party systems in some autonomous communities. In federal states, the dominant pattern is that of a federation-wide party system, in which there may be occasional regional variations in the electoral strength of one of the statewide parties and perhaps occasional third, minor parties. However, some complex multi-national states (closer to being state-nations rather than nation states) have different party systems at the state and sub-state level (Linz 1997a, 34). This has been the case in Belgium over the last twenty years. And this is also the case in Spain, but with significant differences in the complex interaction existing between (i) the statewide party system, (ii) some regional party systems, and (iii) a number of specific statewide party sub-systems. In the 1990s, the interaction between the different party systems and the new roles played by the nationalist parties supporting the PP government has endowed party competition at the statewide level with a number of distinctive characteristics. The fact that these parties control governmental resources in their communities gives electors an additional incentive to vote for them in general elections. Moreover, their parliamentary representatives perform wider roles than normal: they could see themselves as representatives of their voters, of their party leaders (who control the government in their communities) and of their regions as a whole. In a sense, they are likely to become *ambassadors* of the regional government at the center (Linz 1997a, 36). And their parties might best be seen as *pressure parties*, in the sense that their principal function in the state parliament is to put pressure on the government in order to obtain as many particularistic policy concessions as possible for their regions (Molas 1977, 189).

These roles have became particularly significant when in May 1996 the nationalist parties decided to exercise governmental relevance as external supporters of the PP minority government; CiU, PNV and CC, on the one hand, and the PP, on the other, signed a so-called "Pact of Investiture and Governability" through which the former committed themselves to giving external support to the PP government during the legislature in return for a large number of policy concessions.The refusal of both CiU and PNV to participate in the *Spanish*, central government allows them to avoid the dilemmas nationalist parties have to resolve when faced by the choice between office-holding, policies and electoral success (De Winter 1998, 238–9). Their decision to provide external support without commitment enables them to appear at one at the same time to be promoting the adoption of moderate policies at statewide level *and* maintaining their principled challenge to the unity of the state, when not the ultimate utopia of independence. More particularly, the nationalist parties can easily avoid charges of irresponsible behaviour by refusing to participate in a coalition government which could give them portfolios and high-level offices, and hence votes: they already occupy the regional government in their respective communities, and it is there that they develop their basic activities as office- and vote-seeking parties. This position also means that these parties can reject or even veto policies that they consider unacceptable. Moreover, these exchanges in the policy arena are usually followed by *logrolling* agreements, by which the government *buys*, or rather the nationalist parties *sell*, legislative support on one issue for concessions in a totally different area (Strom 1990, 98).

Consequently, CiU and the PNV play at the same time two contradictory roles (Colomer 1999, 49). While on the left–right dimension both parties (but especially CiU) play a moderate, pragmatic, pluralist, and committed role, on the regional dimension both parties (but particularly the PNV) have tended to provoke an escalation of demands based on unilateral, conflictive and untrustworthy, when not actually semi-loyal, strategies. Thanks to their governmental relevance, the nationalist parties have facilitated the so-called *governability* in most socio-economic policy arenas. At the same time, however, they have also contributed to the widening gap that separates them from statewide parties on the regional policy, as well as to a confrontational style of policy-making in this terrain. There is cooperation at the central level in spite of their differences on regional policies. Yet, on the other hand, the bargaining processes and willingness to reach agreement seen in the Congress of Deputies have not been reciprocated at the regional parliaments: either the regional governments have not needed the statewide parties, or they have denied the legitimacy of these *Spanish* parties to develop truly nationalist policies. In this way, the cooperation seen at the central level is replaced by harsh, principled and sometimes semi-loyal competition at the regional level. The different institutional venues for party relationships give rise to totally distinct patterns of party interaction. Many of the policies for which the nationalist parties have given their support to the central government have been pragmatic and favoured moderation in the policy-making process. But the need to compete for votes at the regional level has encouraged the nationalist parties governing their communities to develop both policies based on cultural and/or linguistic identities, as well as strategies of directly challenging the existing federal-type arrangements and/or the unity of the state

These centrifugal drives have facilitated nationalist polarization (at times, with discriminatory and primordialist contents [Linz 1985a]) of the political institutions at the regional level, while intensifying the conflictive intergovernmental relations at the statewide level (Moreno 1997, 73–5). These drives have also inspired the strategies of supraregional and extra-parliamentary agreements that the nationalist parties (particularly, CiU and PNV) have implemented since 1998, demanding the replacement of the *Estado de las Autonomías* by some still imprecise confederal formulae, questioning those articles of the 1978 constitution that define the most important elements of the state–regions relation, and proclaiming the goal of independence in the medium to long term. It is true that there are significant differences in the political styles and features of the nationalist parties that have signed these agreements. Nonetheless, it seems that the centrifugal dynamics which inspires them all will prove scarcely compatible with the so-called *Bundestreue*, or the basic loyalty to the federal constitution and to the state, which works as a kind of the *soul* of an intergovernmental relationship and without which multinational federalism might not be a stable solution (Linz 1997a, 52). In this respect too the structural conditions of the Spanish party systems can be seen to be relatively exceptional in European terms.

Structuring voting choices: parties and cleavages

Party identification and social partisanship

Scholars using different empirical criteria to measure party identification in Spain have all agreed that it is particularly weak (McDonough *et al.* 1998, 133 ff.; Schmitt and Holmberg 1995). According to the Eurobarometer surveys, since 1985 Spain has systematically shown the lowest levels of partisanship of all the European Union countries.

If party identification cannot explain the stabilization of Spaniards' electoral behaviour, to what extent might this be due to the existence of organizations (such as the parties themselves, trade unions or lay religious groups) which mediate between their members or sympathizers and the candidates? In this respect too, Spain constitutes a rather peculiar case. Since the mid-1970s Spain has had lower levels of party membership than Portugal or Greece, let alone most other European countries (Morlino 1998, 169 ff.). The union affiliation rate among salaried workers is also low. The net density rate rose to 24.7 per cent in the late 1970s, only to drop to 13.2 per cent in the early 1980s, before rising again to 22.7 per cent in

1994, thereby putting Spain along with France towards the bottom of the European league table in this respect (Jordana 1996). Moreover, organizational ties between the unions and the (respective) parties have become increasingly tenuous, and cooperation ever looser. This has been further undermined in the case of the PSOE, whose relations with the Unión General de Trabajadores (UGT) deteriorated during the late 1980s, leading to a situation of chronic conflict and the breakdown of party–union relations (Astudillo 1998). The panorama of the religious associations has been even worse. Claiming over one million members throughout Spain in the 1960s, Catholic Action organizations dropped to 100,000 members by 1972 (Hermet 1985, 224 ff.) and continued to lose members and influence after the return to democracy; in the early 1990s, only 3 per cent of Spaniards stated that they belonged to a religious organization.[7] The low levels of party-, trade union- and religious organization-affiliation rates are components of a long-standing syndrome of a poorly developed civil society. Despite an upsurge in associational life during the transition, since the early 1980s the proportion of Spaniards declaring that they do *not* belong to any voluntary association has remained relatively stable at around 70 per cent.

The structure of cleavages: class and religion

As in other European, and above all Catholic countries, the basic cleavages with roots in the nineteenth century were social conflicts derived from class differences and religious conflicts between clericals and secularizers. The more limited economic development and relatively slow industrialization in Southern Europe meant that class conflict spread to rural society, nourished by the existence in much of Spain of *latifundia*, absentee landowners, and a large and growing landless rural proletariat. In the centre and north of the country, smallholders with conservative values and traditional religious allegiances supported the centre and even the extreme right. Moreover, both the urban and the rural proletariat were largely secularized and, in contrast to the situation in Belgium, the Netherlands and Germany, social reform tendencies in the Church came too late to attract a significant part of the working class to Christian trade unions and parties. In many parts of Spain, class and religious cleavages were cumulative rather than cross-cutting. Besides, leaders of the working class organizations rejected reformism, and anarcho-syndicalism acquired an influence without parallel in other European countries. Bourgeois anti-clericalism further fuelled polarization on the religious axis, particularly after the 1931 constitution. Thus, the Second Republic was confronted by an extremely divisive cleavage structure of social and religious conflicts, as well as by a marked regional cleavage and the fierce confrontation between republicans and monarchists. The cumulative character of these cleavages and the extreme, polarized party system decisively contributed to the democratic breakdown of 1936 and Civil War (Linz 1978).

However, this cleavage structure had changed dramatically by the 1970s. The traditional polarization along class and religious lines was engraved in the minds of the elites as a sort of *contramodelo* when it came to reestablishing democracy. The left, and particularly the communists, adopted the position of the "outstretched hand" toward Catholics. Moreover, from the late 1960s onwards the Spaniards underwent an increasingly intense secularization process. As a result of this fundamental shift, the 1978 constitution included a compromise on religious issues and, with the exception of some clashes and disagreements on education, divorce and abortion, religion did not constitute a divisive cleavage at the mass level. Politicians, who were well aware of voters' attitudes, including those of practicing Catholics on some of these issues, were prepared to not exacerbate conflicts on the religious–secular divide. This does not mean that religion, or more specifically, religious practice and identification are not associated with party preferences. The cleavage is there, but it does not have the saliency it had had since the nineteenth century and particularly during the Second Republic.

Class conflict evolved in a similar way. Revolutionary options disappeared, and maximalist positions were abandoned over the course of the transition (Fishman 1990). The development of an incipient welfare state under Franco contributed to this development. But the most important factors were the extraordinary decline in the number of landless peasants and, more generally, the decreasing importance of rural society: in 1930, agriculture accounted for 46.5 per cent of the Spanish active population, yet by 1981 this figure had dropped to just 15 per cent (Linz 1995, 156). Industrialization, migration to the cities or to other European countries, upward social mobility and the fall in the birth rate had reduced the ranks of the radicalized, rural proletarians who had contributed so much to the intensity of social conflict during the Second Republic. A new industrial working class with few links to the organizations and the ideologies of the past had emerged in the cities and, in the latter years of the Franco regime, began to share in the fruits of economic development. In the late 1970s, the electorate did align along class lines, but without the intensity and bitterness of the 1930s. Appeals by an exclusively working class movement and party made no sense in light of these changes in the social structure. The timing of the return to democracy also contributed to reduce the impact of the social cleavage: the fact that parties (re-)emerged in a relatively modern, well-educated society, in which the television was the principal mass media, meant that the social cleavage was very different to that which had existed when most European parties were founded. The old cleavage lines, therefore, had not completely disappeared, but their significance in the new democracy was very different.

How have Spanish parties articulated these cleavages? To what extent has the cleavage structure been reflected in patterns of voting behaviour during the three electoral periods? Table 9.8 offers an initial answer with

Table 9.8 Social profiles of party voters in Spain, 1979–96 (in percentages)

Profile	PCE/IU 1979	1982	1996	PSOE 1979	1982	1996	UCD 1979	AP/PP 1979	1982	1996
Gender										
Male	62	67	55	55	50	48	42	49	48	48
Female	38	33	45	45	50	52	58	52	52	52
Age										
18–24	25	18	23	15	17	12	7	10	12	15
25–34	26	32	30	21	23	18	11	9	14	19
35–44	17	18	23	21	18	18	21	20	18	15
45–54	14	13	12	18	17	14	21	28	23	17
55–64	12	10	8	11	11	15	17	21	16	17
65 and more	6	10	4	15	13	23	23	12	16	18
Class and occupation										
Service	7	10	14	6	5	6	7	21	12	11
Intermediate	20	16	14	23	18	13	24	31	29	18
Working	28	27	15	21	20	14	8	3	7	11
Unemployed	11	15	19	5	8	12	2	1	2	9
Retired	6	11	9	11	10	27	13	7	11	20
Housewife	18	12	14	30	33	21	43	29	31	21
Student	11	9	15	5	6	6	3	8	9	10
Subjective class[a]										
Upper and upper-middle	8	3	14	7	5	8	16	42	31	25
Middle and lower-middle	13	11	24	19	24	31	24	30	30	36
Working	79	83	62	73	67	61	60	29	34	39
Education										
Primary (and less)	54	44	23	60	61	53	65	30	45	41
Secondary	31	46	57	31	27	38	19	40	33	41
University	15	10	19	9	12	8	16	30	23	17
Size of community[b]										
Less than 10,000	24	26	17	31	30	28	46	24	31	29
20,000–50,000	10	13	19	15	16	24	18	17	12	19
50,000–100,000	5	3	11	4	7	8	3	10	4	8
100,000–200,000	4	4	37	4	4	30	5	4	9	29
More than 200,000	57	54	16	45	43	11	29	45	44	14
(N)	(360)	(152)	(422)	(1,142)	(2,060)	(1,379)	(1,569)	(155)	(882)	(1,272)

Sources: Primary data from 1979, 1982 and 1993 DATA surveys, and Banco de Datos, CIS, for 1996.

Notes: [a]Data for subjective class come from the 1993 post-electoral CNEP survey; number of cases are 112 for IU, 484 for PSOE, and 327 for PP.

[b]In the 1996 survey, the two most populated strata are from 100,000 to 400,000, and more than 400,000.

respect to the social cleavage: it shows selected data on the social profiles of the voters for the statewide parties in three characteristic elections. The most significant aspects of the data consist, first, in the explicit refusal of the parties to search for more or less homogeneous *reservés* or for a *classe gardée* as a consequence of the extraordinary changes in the social structure. Second, in the relatively successful way in which, from the very beginning of the transition, the main parties have developed catch-all strategies, albeit with systematic differences between them. And third, in the significant changes in the social bases of the parties in each of the three electoral periods.

During the successive elections in the 1980s, and despite some erosion of the socialist vote, the support for the PSOE was sufficient to maintain its dominant position, the PCE gained little from adopting the new format of Izquierda Unida (IU), and AP retained the same (low) level of electoral support despite a succession of organizational and leadership changes. But this relative continuity in the vote of the main parties masked, above all in the late 1980s, a number of extraordinarily important changes in their social bases, changes which would crystallize in the elections in the third period. As seen in Table 9.8, there are remarkable differences in the social profiles of the respective parties between 1982 and 1996, as well as among the three parties in 1996. In the case of the PP, its presence has declined among the higher social and occupational categories, but increased among workers, the inactive population, and the young (data not shown). This has enabled the PP to replace the PSOE as the party which most closely fits the social profiles of the electorate as a whole (Wert 1997). Moreover, this process has also contributed to further blur the class cleavage through the articulation of parties that, whilst obviously drawing votes from specific social and occupational profiles, have developed typically catch-all strategies and receive typically catch-all electoral support. The same is also true, albeit not entirely, of IU, even though it is an electoral coalition dominated by the PCE. Its social bases have changed significantly: the weight of workers, male and older voters has decreased, whilst that of higher social and occupational categories, women, and the more educated has increased (Bosco, forthcoming). Finally, the PSOE has combined high levels of electoral support with a substantial change in the profile of its voters, now distinguished by the greater weight of older voters, the inactive, the least educated and those living in rural areas (González 1996).

The religious cleavage has also significantly changed during the last two decades. In the mid-1970s, the Spaniards' progressive estrangement from the Church and the Church's own reappraisal of its relations with the authoritarian regime failed to calm the fear of a strong resurgence of the religious cleavage. It soon became clear that Spanish voters were divided over religious issues, with some polarization in attitudes towards the Church, and a strong correlation between religious identification and party choice (Linz *et al.* 1981). However, the disruptive potential of the religious cleavage was not realized. Political elites resorted to consensual procedures in drafting the constitution, adopted a pragmatic attitude in negotiations over their differences with the Church, and refrained from mobilizing voters around religious issues (Gunther, Sani and Shabad 1986). For their part, Church elites clearly supported the democratization process, showed similar restraint in their handling of their differences with the new political elites, and explicitly refused to support the parties which presented themselves under the Christian democratic label in 1977.

At the mass level, Spain could be described as a society which combines a Catholic cultural identity with significant estrangement from the Catholic Church, and in which expressions of religiosity are kept usually out of the public realm of politics.

Trends in vote anchoring

To what extent have the parties been able to *encapsulate* political conflicts (as Bartolini and Mair [1990, 1–2] put it) as a crucial means of structuring the vote and, consequently, stabilizing their electorates? What factors have served to *anchor* the vote, thereby contributing to the institutionalization of the patterns of party competition? Table 9.9 offers a tentative answer to these questions: it shows the results of a multivariate analysis that attempts to explain voters' electoral choices through basic indicators of class, religiosity and ideology.[8] A number of trends can be highlighted. In the first place, the indicators relating to social class appear to have a limited capacity to explain voting choices: the Spanish case, therefore, fits the general tendency towards the decline of class voting in Western countries (Nieuwbeerta 1995). In the second place, the relevance of religiosity has declined even more strongly. In 1993, religion played a minimal role in anchoring the socialist vote (2 per cent), and relatively little in distinguishing between PP voters (8 per cent) and those of the left-wing parties; the

Table 9.9 Factors of electoral behaviour in Spain, 1979–93: a multivariate analysis of the influence of class, religiosity and ideology

Variables	Elections		
	1979	1982	1993
Objective social class	0.064	0.170	0.127
Subjective social class	0.054	0.044	0.024
Union membership	0.113	0.056	0.023
Religiosity	0.145	0.206	0.058
Ideology	0.206	0.226	0.405
Total[a]	0.548	0.808	0.781

Source: Gunther and Montero (1994, 516–30).

Note: [a]The figures refer to the weighted average R^2, and represent the cumulative impact of the preceding variables.

only exception was the much higher figure for the IU voters (21 per cent). In the third place, the impact of union membership on anchoring the vote has followed a similar downward tendency.

Finally, the ideological factor (that is, the extent to which voters see themselves and parties in terms of left versus right) seems to have greater importance than the social-structural anchoring of the vote, which has been declining, or party identification, which is very low, or social partisanship through secondary organizations, which is minimal. Assuming that ideological perceptions tend to be widespread, salient and stable in terms of party choice, then voters' identification with the left or right might serve as a substitute and/or complementary mechanism when socio-structural or psychological factors are weak, or are losing force over time. According to the data in Table 9.9, the ideological factor has the highest weighted average R^2 in every election; moreover, it has been increasing to the point that this variable alone explains 40.5 per cent of the variance in the vote. It is true that, in contrast to the other factors, this ideological anchor does not tie voters to a specific party, but rather to the generic spaces of left, centre and right, in each of which there might be various competing parties. Hence, it does not rule out electoral changes between parties competing within a given ideological space. However, it does stop voters from leaping over the barrier separating the two opposing ideological camps – that is, it hinders inter-bloc volatility. In this way, the cleavage which currently divides the party system for many voters does not accurately reflect class positions and much less so religious orientations, but essentially expresses a vision of politics associated with the spatial terms of left–right through the voter's identities, loyalties and/or sympathies.

Party systems in the *Estado de las Autonomías*: nationalism and regionalism

The 1978 constitution provided for the division of Spain into regions with their own elected parliaments, governments, public administrations, and resources. A complex process involving negotiations between the parties and four referenda to approve the autonomy statutes, ended with the creation of the seventeen autonomous communities. While some responded to nationalist aspirations existing on the periphery, others, with less historical basis, essentially reflected the interests of politicians. All of these autonomies are now important political realities in what has become a *de facto*, asymmetric federal state. The party systems and sub-systems in the autonomies reflect this situation, and are an essential component of the Spanish polity. In this final section of our chapter we will discuss just three aspects of this new *Estado de las Autonomías*, namely some electoral dimensions of the regional cleavage, the interplay between national identities and politics in the Basque Country and Catalonia, and the problem of violence in the Basque Country. Although our analysis is essentially limited to the Basque and Catalan cases, there are relevant non-statewide parties in most of the other fifteen communities (Pallarès *et al.* 1997).

Communities, parties, and the regional cleavage

The cleavage structure is complicated by the existence of the regional cleavage. Spain is a multicultural, multinational, and multilingual society that in some respects is even more complex than other linguistically or nationally heterogeneous countries such as Switzerland or Belgium. This complexity, which has a long history but dates particularly from the nineteenth century and the birth of the first nationalist parties, contributed to the crises of the Second Republic in the 1930s and resurfaced during the transition (Linz 1973; Linz *et al.* 1981). In the new democracy, the electoral rendering of the regional cleavage has crystallized, firstly, in the existence of so-called *regional voting*, or major variations in the distribution of the vote across most communities; secondly, in the presence of strong nationalist parties in a few communities and a wide variety of regionalist parties in nearly all the rest; and thirdly, in the multilayered character of the Spanish party systems, articulated through the coexistence of a statewide party system, some regional party systems, and a number of specific statewide party sub-systems (Pallarès *et al.* 1997). The resulting mosaic has been labelled the *electoral Spains* (Vallès 1991), in reference to the great diversity of patterns of party competition in the different communities. Table 9.10 shows aggregate data for these phenomena in each community. The index is calculated by adding the absolute difference between the percentage vote received by each party within each community and the average vote received by it across the seventeen communities, divided by two (see Hearl and Budge 1996, 169).

Naturally, the level of regional voting is particularly high in those communities with nationalist or regionalist parties, whose electoral strength is also shown in Table 9.10: no European region (except the quite exceptional case of Northern Ireland) surpasses the percentages found in the Basque Country or Catalonia, and no European country has as many regions in which the non-statewide parties are as significant as Spain. The vote of the nationalist and regionalist parties has increased with the stabilization of electoral behaviour (the mean for all the communities was 9.7 in the 1977 elections, 12.7 in 1993, and 10.9 in 1996) and, as could be expected, has always been higher in the elections for the communities' regional parliaments (Alcántara and Martínez 1998). The regional cleavage is particularly intense in the Basque Country, Catalonia, and Navarre, where a number of nationalist parties ranging from the extreme left to the centre-right compete among themselves and with the statewide parties within the format of distinct regional party systems. In these communities, the cleavage derives from historical, cultural and political features that have generated conflictive perceptions of national identities, and is structured by governments

Table 9.10 The *Electoral Spains:* index of regional voting and vote for nationalist and regionalist parties by autonomous communities and electoral periods, 1977–96 (in percentages)

Community[a]	Index of regional voting electoral periods[b]				Vote for nationalist and regionalist parties: electoral periods[b]			
	First	Second	Third	Average	First	Second	Third	Average
Basque Country	46.7	51.9	45.7	48.7	49.3	56.4	48.9	52.2
Catalonia	36.8	33.5	35.1	34.9	26.1	37.4	43.8	36.0
Navarre	34.9	18.6	15.6	22.4	34.7	19.8	16.9	23.2
Canary Islands	29.8	22.7	25.5	25.5	9.4	14.1	26.9	16.4
Galicia	26.3	22.1	19.2	22.4	7.9	9.1	15.1	10.5
Valencia	16.7	11.9	12.7	13.5	4.3	5.2	11.3	6.7
Andalusia	18.7	21.9	19.1	20.2	6.7	3.9	3.5	4.6
Aragon	14.4	11.4	16.2	13.6	9.4	7.8	13.3	3.8
Balearic Islands	17.1	16.2	14.6	16.0	4.0	2.6	5.2	3.8
Cantabria	12.5	11.7	12.5	12.2	1.2	0.2	7.1	2.4
Rioja	16.4	13.3	12.4	13.9	4.2	0.0	3.9	2.4
Extremadura	15.4	16.2	13.9	15.4	0.3	2.9	1.3	1.7
Asturias	18.0	13.1	11.8	14.1	1.5	0.5	1.8	1.2
Castile-León	17.0	14.6	12.9	14.8	1.9	0.4	1.5	1.1
Murcia	12.7	11.6	11.5	12.5	1.7	0.1	0.1	0.6
Madrid	16.2	13.7	15.1	14.8	0.9	0.1	0.1	0.3
Castile-La Mancha	13.3	11.5	12.5	12.3	0.7	0.0	0.3	0.3

Source: Oñate and Ocaña (1999).

Notes: [a]Communities are ranked by the average share of the vote for nationalist and regionalist parties.
[b]Figures for each period are averaged.

equipped with extraordinarily wide-ranging institutions, policies and resources. In other communities, regionalist parties have benefited from the opportunities offered by the decentralization process and the institutional consolidation of the *Estado de las Autonomías*. Both developments have given nationalist parties and regionalist entrepreneurs the possibility to compete profitably with the statewide parties, to use the political resources generated by the new bureaucracies, and to foster national and regional identities, not the least through their ability to make more or less demagogic resort to claims of relative deprivation with respect to other communities and against the central government. In all these cases, the electoral strength of the various competing nationalist parties in the Basque Country and Catalonia, and the relevance of regionalist parties in many other communities, sketch an exceptional map in western European terms.

Thus, Spanish parties display patterns of cooperation and competition at different levels. Table 9.11 illustrates the multilayered character of the

Table 9.11 Party systems and party sub-systems in Spain, 1996[a]

	Statewide parties				Nationalist parties				Regionalist parties			
	Party	Vote	Ideology	Nationalism/ regionalism	Party	Vote	Ideology	Nationalism/ regionalism	Party	Vote	Ideology	Nationalism/ regionalism
Party systems												
Spain	IU	10.6	2.9	5.5								
	PSOE	37.5	3.7	6.1								
	PP	38.8	6.5	7.2								
Basque Country	IU	9.2	2.7	4.1	HB	12.3	2.5	8.4				
	PSOE	23.6	4.0	5.7	EA	8.2	4.5	7.6				
	PP	18.3	6.2	4.5	PNV	25.0	5.1	7.2				
Catalonia	PSOE	39.3	3.8	5.6	ERC	4.2	2.9	9.0				
	PP	18.0	6.5	5.5	IC–EV	7.7	3.1	7.1				
					CiU	29.6	5.2	8.1				
Navarre	IU	12.5	3.2	7.6	HB	8.2	2.3	7.1	CDN	5.3	5.9	6.7
	PSOE	30.2	3.5	6.8	EA	3.8	4.7	9.4				
	PP-UPN	36.8	7.4	7.8								
Party sub-systems												
Galicia	IU	3.7	2.5	5.8	BNG	10.1	2.9	7.0				
	PSOE	33.0	3.7	5.8								
	PP	48.5	6.6	5.9								
Andalusia	IU	13.5	2.7	7.0					PA	3.1	4.5	7.4
	PSOE	46.5	3.6	7.1								
	PP	35.5	6.2	6.4								
Canary Islands	IU	5.5	2.5	7.4					CC	25.2	5.0	7.4
	PSOE	29.8	3.9	7.8								
	PP	37.7	7.1	7.5								
Valencian community	IU	11.1	2.9	5.7					UV	3.5	5.2	6.1
	PSOE	38.2	3.7	5.4								
	PP	43.8	6.2	5.7								
Madrid	IU	16.5	2.9	4.0								
	PSOE	31.3	3.7	4.9								
	PP	49.3	6.8	5.6								

Source: Primary data from Banco de Datos, CIS.

Notes: [a]*Vote* refer to the percentage of valid votes in the general election of 1996; *ideology* refers to the means for voters of each party on ten-point Left–Right scales; and *nationalism/regionalism* refers also to the means for voters of each party on eleven-point scales in which 0 is minimum and 10 is maximum nationalism (for voters of nationalist parties) or regionalism (for voters of statewide and regionalist parties). For *Spain* only the statewide parties have been included despite the representation enjoyed by both nationalist (i.e. HB, BNG, ERC, EA, PNV and CiU) and regionalist (i.e. CC and UV) parties. For the latter parties, percentage of the vote and ideological and nationalism/regionalism means have been calculated at the level of their respective autonomous communities.

Spanish party systems, which is evident from the number and electoral support of the most important parties, as well as from the ideological self-placements and the nationalist or regionalist positions of their voters in 1996.[9] In the Basque Country, Catalonia and perhaps Navarre, both the number of parties and their patterns of interaction clearly diverge from the general pattern of the statewide party system (in which, moreover, they nearly all have parliamentary representation). In these communities the relevance of the regional cleavage is reflected in the relative weakness of the statewide parties, the presence of several electorally strong nationalist parties and their complex competition along the ideological and regional dimensions. In the Basque Country and Catalonia, the importance of their distinct party systems is confirmed by the separate celebration of regional elections and the existence of a large number of institutions with significant resources, including governments controlled by the nationalist parties since the early 1980s. In contrast, the other communities selected in Table 9.11 are characteristic examples of statewide party *sub*-systems, in which the absence of the regional cleavage simplifies electoral competition, ideological distances are weakened by the low level of party fractionalization, and all the competing parties essentially adopt similar regionalist positions.

These different patterns of party competition crystallize at the institutional sphere in the regional parliaments (Table 9.12). As we have already emphasized, the fact that minor nationalist parties in Congress are at the same time the governing parties in their respective communities strengthens their role in the formation of central government. In contrast to the FDP or the Greens in the German system (which are both statewide parties that are rewarded or punished by voters for their role in the coalition politics at the center), the nationalist parties in Catalonia and the Basque Country are only responsive to their own electorates.

Most regional party sub-systems can, therefore, be classified as *imperfect* two-party systems (Llera 1998): the indexes of the effective number of parties are very low, electoral preferences are basically concentrated in the PP and the PSOE, and third parties are either marginal or increasingly becoming irrelevant. Again, the exception consists of the distinct Basque and Catalan party systems; whereas the Basque case belongs to the category of polarized pluralism (Linz *et al.* 1986; Llera 1994), the Catalan case approaches that of a predominant-party system (Marcet and Argelaguet 1998). Moreover, in both cases, nationalist parties enjoy a greater and more influential presence than the statewide parties in institutional arenas other than the parliament in their respective communities. It is interesting to compare the Basque Country and Catalonia with Galicia and Andalusia, the other two communities which share the possibility of holding separate elections and are entitled to the greatest powers, competences and resources in the new *Estado de las Autonomías*. In the Basque case, the profound fractionalization existing among nationalist and statewide parties in both the central and the Basque parliaments disappears at the local level:

Table 9.12 Regional parliaments: distribution of seats, number of parties and type of government, 1995–99[a]

	Parties			Nationalist or regionalist	Total of seats	Number of parties[b]	Type of government[c]
	Statewide						
Community	IU	PSOE	PP				
Basque Country	2	14	16	43[d]	75	x.x	PNV+EA
Catalonia	11	34	17	73[e]	135	3.4	CiU
Navarre	3	11	–	36[f]	50	x.x	UPN
Canary Islands	–	19	14	27[g]	60	x.x	**CC+PP**
Balearic Islands	3	13	28	15[h]	59	x.x	PSOE+UM+?
Galicia	–	15	42	18[i]	75	2,4	**PP**
Aragon	1	23	28	15[j]	67	x.x	**PP+Par**
Cantabria	–	14	19	6[k]	39	x.x	**PP+PRC**
Asturias	3	24	15	3[l]	45	x.x	PSOE
Rioja	–	13	18	2[m]	33	x.x	**PP**
Castile–Leon	1	30	48	4[n]	83	x.x	**PP**
Andalusia	13	52	40	4[o]	109	2.6	**PSOE+PA**
Valencia	5	35	49	–	89	x.x	**PP**
Extremadura	3	34	28	–	65	x.x	**PSOE**
Castile–Mancha	–	26	21	–	47	x.x	**PSOE**
Madrid	8	39	55	–	103	x.x	**PP**
Murcia	1	17	27	–	45	x.x	**PP**

Notes: [a]Communities are ranked by the percentage of seats obtained by nationalist and regionalist parties. Regional elections were held in 1995 in Catalonia, 1996 in Andalusia, 1997 in Galicia, 1998 in the Basque Country and 1999 in the other 13 communities.

[b]Index of effective number of parliamentary parties according to the criteria of Taagepera and Shugart (1989).

[c]Bold letters denote majority governments; otherwise they are minority governments.

[d]Euskal Herritarrok (formerly Herri Batasunna) (14 seats), Eusko Alkartasuna (6), Partido Nacionalista Vasco (21) and Unidad Alavesa (2).

[e]Esquerra Republicana de Catalunya (13 seats) and Convergència i Unió (60).

[f]Unión del Pueblo Navarro (in coalition with PP, 22 seats), Centro Democrático de Navarra (3), Euskal Herritarrok (8) and Partido Nacionalista Vasco–Eusko Alkartasuna (3).

[g]Coalición Canaria (25 seats) and Insularists (2).

[h]Partido Socialista de Mallorca (5 seats), Unió Mallorquina (3), Agrupación de Formentera (1) and Pacte de Progrés (6).

[i]Bloque Nacionalista Galego.

[j]Partido Aragonés (10 seats) and Chunta Aragonesista (5).

[k]Partido Regionalista de Cantabria (6 seats).

[l]Unión Renovadora Asturiana.

[m]Partido Riojano Progresista.

[n]Unión del Pueblo Leonés.

[o]Partido Andaluz.

due to the small size of many of the municipalities in the region and the strong nationalist sentiments found in rural areas and many small towns, the nationalist parties enjoy overwhelming superiority. This reflects the very different level of support for the statewide parties in the large urban, highly industrialized cities with large Spanish immigrant populations, and in the periphery, where nationalism, and even extreme nationalism, holds sway.[10] The Catalan case differs at the parliamentary level because of the duality between the PSOE's strong presence in the central parliament and the CiU's dominance of the regional parliament. But at the local level CiU also enjoys a disproportionate presence: once again, the strength of nationalist parties lies in the enormous number of small towns, whereas the PSOE is particularly well-established in the larger towns and cities, with their major immigrant populations and where the larger part of the population lives. The contrast with Galicia (another region with a distinctive language and some nationalist sentiments) and Andalusia could hardly be greater: in both cases statewide parties dominate representation at every institutional level.

Attitudes toward the state and national identities

After more than twenty years of extensive and intensive decentralization, what are Spaniards' attitudes toward the current institutional configuration of the *Estado de las Autonomías*? To what extent have national identities evolved towards exclusive identification with either Spain or a specific region? Answers to these questions vary enormously in different autonomous communities and parties (Linz 1985a; Montero and Torcal 1990; Moral 1998). As Table 9.13 shows, a certain consensus seems to have emerged around somewhere in between the two opposing poles of a unitary, centralist state with a long history, and the demands for self-determination and secession defended by minorities at the state level but which can actually become decisive pluralities in certain regions.[11] In the case of the latter, nationalist parties diverge among themselves in the Basque Country and Catalonia, at the same time as both communities diverge from others with relevant nationalist (like Galicia) or regionalist parties (like Andalusia). It is clear that even in Spain as whole only a minority favour a centralized state, and that the new state enjoys the support of a large majority of Spaniards. In the Basque Country, the three nationalist parties maintain very different positions with respect to independence, and even the largest party, the PNV, is divided into two pluralities, one of which favours supreme autonomy and the other the ultimate goal of independence. The differences are not as great in Catalonia, although the majority of the ERC's small electorate inversely mirrors the preferences of the majority of voters for the largest party, CiU. In the other two regions selected, respondents favouring independence account for an insignificant minority of the voters of both nationalist and regionalist parties: they only

Table 9.13 Preferences for different forms of state in the Basque Country, Catalonia, Galicia and Andalusia, 1996[a] (in horizontal percentages)

Community/ party	Preferences				(N)	Vote (%) in last regional elections[b]
	Centralized	Autonomy as at present	More autonomy	Independence		
Basque Country	3	25	33	31	(280)	00
IU	–	27	46	18	(11)	5.6
PSOE	5	45	40	5	(20)	17.3
PP	14	43	29	–	(7)	19.9
HB	–	–	5	91	(21)	17.7
EA	–	6	28	61	(18)	8.6
PNV	2	14	41	39	(44)	27.6
Catalonia	10	36	29	21	(779)	
IC	11	40	31	16	(45)	9.7
PSOE	15	39	23	17	(208)	24.8
PP	33	43	20	4	(76)	13.1
ERC	–	–	23	74	(39)	9.5
CiU	–	23	40	34	(184)	40.9
Galicia	16	52	16	5	(361)	
IU	23	53	18	6	(17)	0.9
PSOE	6	52	21	2	(58)	19.5
PP	19	51	16	2	(108)	52.2
BNG	14	45	18	16	(58)	24.8
Andalusia	17	48	20	3	(832)	
IU	6	56	31	6	(68)	6.7
PSOE	17	46	21	3	(290)	44.4
PP	29	47	22	1	(167)	34.2
PA	20	40	27	13	(15)	6.7
Spain	16	44	21	8	(4,910)	

Source: Primary data from Banco de Datos, CIS
Notes: [a]Rows may not add up one hundred because non-answers have not been included. Party is party voted in the general election of 1996.
[b]In 1995 in Catalonia, 1996 in Andalusia, 1997 in Galicia, and 1998 in the Basque Country.

differ in the extent to which they are satisfied with the present level of devolution or aspire to greater autonomy.

These data point to the fact that parties – even nationalist parties – have a very different position on centralism, autonomy and independence, and therefore cannot be lumped together in any analysis. The same is true of the much more critical question of voters' national identities. In the literature on nationalism, there is often an implicit assumption that people are members of a nationality group on account of primordial characteristics, such as language, religion, descent or identification with one nationality or another.

Nationalism is thus based on a distinction between *us* and *them*, the *in group* and the *out group* which are essentially mutually exclusive. The reality of multinational societies is very different. People who have lived together for centuries have dual identities. Sometimes they may identify more strongly with one nationality, at other times with another. Another misleading notion is that all those who have distinctive primordial characteristics will identify themselves with the relevant nationalist political programme, and further- more that national identity necessarily leads to demands for self-determination and independence. In fact, the more we move away from demands for cultural, autonomic, linguistic and cultural rights to territorially based nationalism, nationalist leaders are likely to claim and demand identification with the nation from all those living in the territory, irrespective of their primordial characteristics (Linz 1985b, and Linz *et al.* 1986).

Many case studies show that there is a large gap between sharing certain primordial characteristics and the demands of political nationalism. Hence, any attempt to understand politics and the party systems in the multi- national Basque and Catalan autonomies must take into account a wide range of factors, both those relating to allegedly primordial characteristics, and those involving subjective identity which, as we have already noted, are by no means perfectly correlated.

Data from the period 1979 (that is, after the constitution recognized the multinational character of Spain and the enactment of the autonomy statutes) to the mid-1990s clearly reveal the importance of multinational identities in the Basque Country and Catalonia: in both communities, significant minorities clearly choose one identity, Spanish or Basque or Catalan, but large numbers choose dual identities, putting greater or lesser emphasis on one or the other. The data also show that exclusive identities have in fact diminished over time, and that with the recognition of the distinctiveness of the autonomous communities, dual identities may actually be gaining ground. In the Basque Country in 1996, 9 per cent identified themselves as exclusively Spanish or as more Spanish than Basque (versus 28 per cent in 1979), 50 per cent stated they felt just Basque or more Basque than Spanish (versus 48 per cent in 1979), and 36 per cent opted for "as Spanish as Basque" (versus 24 per cent in 1979). In Catalonia we find a similar trend. Whilst in 1996 24 per cent identified themselves as Spanish or as more Spanish than Catalan, 37 per cent as Catalan or as more Catalan than Spanish, and 36 per cent as having dual identities, in 1979 the percentages were respectively 38, 27 and 36 (Linz 1985a; Shabad 1986; Montero and Torcal 1990; and Moral 1998, 40). It makes no sense, therefore, to speak of two exclusive and conflicting communities – Spanish versus Basque or Catalan.

Since national identities are closely related to party choice, both dimen- sions must necessarily be considered in order to understand the party systems in the Basque Country and Catalonia. To this end we have again compared these two communities with Galicia and Andalusia. In Table 9.14,

Table 9.14 Subjective national identification by party in the Basque Country, Catalonia, Galicia and Andalusia, 1996[a] (in horizontal percentages)

Community/ Party	Identification					(N)
	Spanish	More Spanish than regional	As Spanish as regional	More regional than Spanish	Regional	
Basque Country	5	4	36	29	21	(281)
IU	–	9	55	27	9	(11)
PSOE	5	5	76	9	5	(21)
PP	14	14	57	14	–	(7)
HB	–	–	–	25	75	(20)
EA	6	–	–	56	39	(18)
PNV	2	2	25	48	23	(44)
Catalonia	13	11	37	26	11	(783)
IC	16	13	38	27	2	(45)
PSOE	21	15	37	20	6	(208)
PP	24	18	49	9	–	(76)
ERC	–	–	7	33	60	(40)
CiU	1	4	25	48	20	(185)
Galicia	5	8	43	35	7	(362)
IU	6	6	41	41	6	(17)
PSOE	2	11	47	35	4	(57)
PP	6	11	47	29	6	(110)
BNG	2	–	27	57	14	(44)
Andalusia	5	10	68	13	3	(834)
IU	6	4	68	17	3	(69)
PSOE	4	10	68	15	3	(288)
PP	6	22	65	6	2	(164)
PA	1	–	75	13	6	(16)
Spain	16	11	50	16	15	(4,915)

Source: Primary data from Banco de Datos, CIS.
Notes: [a]Rows may not add up one hundred because non-answers have not been included.
Party refers to party voted in the 1996 general election.

data on the national identification of the voters of different parties clearly show, firstly, that in Andalusia and Galicia, with the sole exception of the BNG, the absence of the regional cleavage produces similar distributions of identity among parties belonging to different ideological spaces. And that, secondly, in Catalonia and the Basque Country none of the parties relies exclusively on support from voters with one or another national identity, although in both cases the statewide parties have fewer supporters among those feeling, respectively, predominantly or only Catalan or Basque. In

Catalonia, as is to be expected, one third of PP voters feel Spanish, and half have a dual identity. The PSC–PSOE, which draws most of its support from the industrial working class in the metropolitan area of Barcelona (still largely formed by immigrants and the sons and daughters of immigrants) has a quite similar distribution. Although this similarity might appear surprising in the light of the two parties' positions with respect to Spanish nationalism, it is easily explained by the facts that the PSOE has the support of the immigrant working class, while the PP voters are more likely to belong to that part of the Catalan bourgeoisie that has long been identified with Spain. The ERC, the minority nationalist party, draws its supporters from those who express an exclusively Catalan identity or feel more Catalan than Spanish. However, in the case of CiU, the dominant Catalanist party, a large proportion of its voters identify themselves as Catalan or more Catalan than Spanish, but a substantial 25 per cent feel they have a dual identity. Clearly, parties in the Catalan party system cannot adopt an either exclusively Catalan or Spanish position without risk of losing some of their voters with dual identities.

Positions are more polarized in the Basque Country. Two-thirds of PP voters have a dual identity, while the other third feels basically Spanish. The PSOE, which mainly represents the industrial working class (particularly in the outlying towns of the great metropolitan area of Bilbao and some other industrial enclaves), also fundamentally depends on those with dual identities, a pattern which makes it very different from the Catalan branch of the PSOE, many of whose voters have a Catalan identity. On the nationalist side, we find very significant differences between the parties. Not surprisingly, three out of four voters for HB (and EH [Euskal Herritarrok], its successor after the regional election of 1998) claim an exclusive Basque identity, whereas EA (Eusko Alkartasuna, which, led by the former prime minister of the Basque government, split from the PNV in 1986) voters are divided between those who feel only Basque and more Basque than Spanish. And finally the PNV, as the dominant party on the nationalist spectrum, has a minuscule proportion of voters who feel themselves to be Spanish, but depends largely on those with a balanced dual identity, on those who feel more Basque than Spanish, and to a lesser extent on those with an exclusive Basque identity.

Parties and violence in the Basque Country

Our analysis of the evolution of the party system from a potentially polarized format in the late 1970s to a moderate multiparty system shortly after is congruent with the virtual disappearance of political violence that still made sporadic appearances during the course of the transition. The only notable and tragic exception is, of course, the Basque terrorist organization ETA, which has been responsible for over three thousand violent acts, including over 50 kidnappings, almost 800 murders, and many more cases of extortion, blackmail and intimidation both in the Basque Country and in other parts of Spain (Reinares 1988; Domínguez 1998). For a number of reasons that space does not permit us to discuss here, ETA has successfully managed to create both a complex social movement and a political subculture within which violence has been justified, supported and even practised at a mass level (Llera 1994, 99). The movement's main purpose has been to mobilize popular support in order to channel sympathy towards the terrorists and recruit new members willing to participate in different types of criminal activity (Mata 1993; Reinares 1996). In other words, violence has been a key feature of the Basque polity for over three decades, continuing even after ETA declared a "truce" in September 1998.

An ambivalence characterizes the positions of many moderate social and cultural nationalist leaders over the last 20 years and the strategies still being followed by most leaders of the PNV and EA, but this is not the case of the Spanish electorate as a whole, which rejects violence of whatever origin. And while in the Basque country significant segments of the population fully supported ETA's criminal activities for many years, one of the most encouraging recent trends in this respect is that large sectors of Basques have now redefined their attitudes toward ETA terrorism. In 1978 about half of the Basque electorate saw ETA activists as *patriots* and *idealists*, and only 7 per cent as *criminals*. These proportions began to change dramatically in the 1980s, and by 1996 had fallen by half. In 1989, a larger proportion was still undecided between the favourable and the more negative answers. While in the past few people were ready to use expressions like *terrorists* or *madmen* to refer to ETA, opting instead for the ambiguous term of *manipulated*, by 1996 this ambiguity seems to have disappeared and one third of the Basque electorate does not shrink from describing the members of the organization as *terrorists*.

In the 1990s, the attitudes of the voters of the different parties toward ETA have followed predictable patterns, albeit with some relevant changes (Table 9.15). Of course greatest support for ETA comes from HB voters, most of whom express critical justification of the organization's criminal actions. Among the other parties of the nationalist spectrum, EA voters express a combination of rejection with that element of semi-loyalty which is agreement with the organization's goals, but not the means, whereas the majority of PNV voters do express total rejection This rejection is obviously still stronger among voters of the statewide parties. Although there is a cleavage between nationalist and statewide party voters, it has been substantially reduced due to the change of attitude on the part of the PNV's electorate. Only the voters of HB have steadfastly continued to give full support to the group's terrorist activities, allowing us to define the organization as an extremist anti-system, disloyal party. It is the only party in which a 75 per cent majority saw the ETA terrorists as *patriots* and *idealists* in 1993; in the PNV, these perceptions were held by 21 per cent. The fact that a majority of the Basque electorate, irrespective of their

Table 9.15 Attitudes toward ETA by party voted in the Basque Country, 1993 (in percentages)

Attitude	Party voted						Electorate
	IU	PSE–PSOE	PP	HB	EA	PNV	
Total support	–	–	–	8	–	–	1
Basic agreement, but acknowledging errors	-	-	-	42	5	1	5
Agreement with goals, not means	6	2	-	36	23	7	11
Before yes, not now	22	13	4	6	33	27	18
Indifference	2	1	1	1	1	2	2
Fearful	4	7	7	1	2	6	7
Total rejection	65	74	87	1	34	56	51
No answer	1	3	1	5	2	1	5
(N)	(110)	(183)	(88)	(152)	(102)	(313)	(1,800)

Source: Data kindly provided by Francisco J. Llera.

commitment to nationalism, sees ETA as a criminal rather than idealistic organization has led to the political isolation of HB. But this isolation has been softened by the existence of some ambivalence among one-fifth of PNV voters and one-third of those for EA, who see ETA activists as idealists. More importantly, it has been undermined by the ambiguous statements made by some moderate Basque nationalist leaders calling on the Spanish state to negotiate with ETA to resolve the so-called "Basque problem", a semi-loyal stance which is complemented by their claims to the right to self-determination, their aspirations to independence for the Basque Country, and their ambivalence toward, when not outright rejection of, the Spanish democratic institutions, and particularly the constitution.

In September and October 1998, after the massive popular reaction all over Spain to the assassination of a number of PP local councillors and a wave of intimidation and attacks against members of the statewide parties in the Basque Country, the ETA leadership made a virtue of its growing political isolation and organizational weakness by declaring a suspension of terrorist activities. This initiative was preceded by a new phase in the strategies of *all* the nationalist parties (HB under its new label of EH, EA and the PNV, all of which were also joined for the occasion by IU), which signed in Estella a radicalized programme aiming at independence and the integration of Navarre and the French Basque provinces into the existing Basque territory: in more practical terms, the new strategy meant that, in exchange for the interruption of terrorist violence, the moderate nationalist parties abandoned their moderation to embrace the goals defended by the anti-system organization. This outcome has radically transformed the previous political atmosphere of cooperation between moderate nationalist and statewide parties in a number of coalition regional governments (a

PNV–PSOE coalition governed the Basque Country from 1986 until 1998) and antiterrorist policies (agreed in the so-called Ajuria Enea Pact, signed in 1989 by all representative parties opposed to violence and, logically, without the participation of HB). Instead, after the regional elections of 1998, EH signed an agreement committing it to provide external support to the minority coalition PNV–EA government, and the divisions between nationalists and non-nationalists seem to be now much deeper than before. The "truce" declared by ETA and HB's adoption of the new face of EH have helped bring it electoral gains in the regional elections of October 1998 and in the local elections of June 1999. And the institutional co-operation in the Basque parliament between the PNV–EA government and a still disloyal EH has given birth to politics of confrontation along the lines of the regional cleavage defined in predominantly primordial terms, and consequently to increasing polarization between nationalist parties and statewide parties both in the Basque Country and in the central parliament. The impact of ETA declaring the "truce" ended, and the renewal of terrorist activities remains to be seen.

Conclusions

Over forty years after the last free elections, a three-year civil war, and almost forty years of authoritarian rule, in 1977 the Spaniards embarked on a new democratic era with new parties and political elites. Within the new institutions derived from the *reforma pactada-ruptura pactada* and the consensual 1978 constitution, we have seen how elites and voters have competed freely for power in elections that have avoided polarization and given rise to stable governments. The attempted coup on 23 February 1981, in which there were no casualties, was opposed by all the relevant political and social organizations, and totally failed to undermine the consensus support for the democratic institutions and parties. Since then, this consensus has become consistently stronger. The new features of the cleavage structure, the electoral outcomes, and the party systems have contributed to Spain's well-established membership of the select category of democratic, stable and efficient polities. Despite the extraordinary volatility caused by the critical elections of 1982, the Spaniards' electoral behaviour has become increasingly stable. The changes in the party system during these electoral periods have been matched by the persistence of a number of dimensions: limited electoral, and above all parliamentary fragmentation, voters' ideological moderation, centripetal competition among parties, and the existence of stable single-party governments with at least sufficient parliamentary support. And just as the party system currently appears to have relatively stabilized at the statewide level, the cleavage structure shows similar signs of consolidation in terms of the definitive weakening of the religious factor and the continued decline in class voting. In contrast, the regional cleavage has intensified under the protective shadow of the constraints of the democratic transition and particularly the construction of the *Estado de las Autonomías*, a development that has led to the emergence of seventeen regional political systems with new representative institutions, distinct electoral processes, and endowed with significant resources for the emerging regional elites. In many communities, the new political opportunity structure has given rise to regionalist parties with some influence at the regional level and occasional presence in the Congress of Deputies. In others, however, the crystallization of distinct regional party systems, with nationalist parties ranging from extreme Left to Right and competing with the statewide parties along class and religion cleavages as well as over divisive conflicts related to linguistic policies and sometimes incompatible perceptions of national identities, constitutes a serious challenge to the inclusive capabilities of political integration of the new Spanish democracy.

The nationalist and regional party systems in the autonomies represent a unique experiment in the context of a federalized Spain. After Franco's death, Spain did not only have to complete a transition to democracy, but also a transition from a unitary, centralized state to a federal-type state; that is, from a state conceived by most Spaniards as a nation-state with a dominant language, Spanish, to a multinational and multilingual state-nation founded on the constitution. It is important to stress that Switzerland, the oldest multilingual democracy in Europe, is not truly multinational, since the German, French, Italian and Romansch speakers have not developed national identities or a party system based on such an identity. Belgium has some similarities with Spain. But we should not forget two major differences, namely that there has been relatively little migration between the two parts of the country, and that the main parties share ideological perspectives (whether liberal, Christian democratic or social democratic) in spite of the linguistic divide, although they have to compete with linguistic nationalist parties.

In any case, it is also important to emphasize that this radical change in the form of the Spanish state was supported by all the parties, including the main Catalan party, and overwhelmingly approved in a popular referendum by the Spanish electorate, including in Catalonia. Only the Basque nationalists departed from this consensus. However, the PNV as the main Basque party subsequently supported the autonomy statute derived directly from the constitution, and since then, with the exception of HB, Basque nationalists have participated in Spanish and Basque politics. HB (and now EH) has challenged these institutions, although it has freely participated in elections and held office in local government in the Basque Country; its subordinate links with ETA, of which HB is only a part within the larger network of terrorist activities, allow us to define it as a disloyal opposition. The ambivalence of other Basque voters and the PNV leadership towards Spain's democratic institutions and the party's relations with HB–EH could lead us to see considerable semi-loyalty. We would therefore argue that the existence of nationalists in the periphery that question the state as well as the democratic institutions and processes in that state is the most serious problem, and potentially an element of instability, in the otherwise successfully consolidated Spanish democracy.

Notes

1 We would like to thank Justin Byrne, Pablo Oñate, Rocío de Terán and Mariano Torcal for their assistance, the Comité Interministerial de Ciencia y Tecnología (CICYT [SEC95–1007]) for its financial support, and the Center for Advanced Study in the Social Sciences, Instituto Juan March, for the use of its excellent facilities.

2 In February 1981, UCD claimed a membership of 152,104, its highest since the foundation. The ratio between its members and voters (in 1979) was 2.4, and the ratio between its members and the Spanish electorate was 0.6; see Montero (1981, 44), Caciagli (1986, 255–6), Hopkin (1999, 103) for similar data for other parties.

3 Expressed as a percentage, the volatility index measures the net difference between the results obtained by the main parties in two successive elections; see Bartolini and Mair (1990, 20 ff).

4 Data for aggregate volatility in Spain are also similar to those for individual volatility, which are based on estimates made from post-electoral surveys measuring individual voting shifts in two successive elections; see Montero (1992, 289–95).

5 These criteria have been adapted from those discussed by Mair (1991, 44).

6 In Table 9.7 we have used the data on the 1996 elections, as it was these that produced the change in government with the PP's coming to power.

7 These figures are based on data taken from the 1993 CNEP survey archive.

8 This section rests on arguments which are developed more extensively in Gunther and Montero (1994, and forthcoming). The pseudo-R^2 indicates the extent to which each independent variable or group of variables contribute to an overall explanation of the vote for each party. In order to take the strength of the cleavage anchoring explicitly into account, and to create a meaningful figure for the entire statewide party system, weighted average R^2 figures were calculated for each selected election.

9 In Table 9.11, in the case of the Spanish statewide parties, we only show data for those parties with representation in the Congress of Deputies. For the autonomous communities we give all the parties winning at least 3 per cent of the vote in at least one district; in these cases, the parties' electoral strength refers to their respective communities. The ideological and nationalist/regionalist positions refer to the self-placement of their respective voters (either at the statewide or the regional levels) on the appropriate scales.

10 In the Basque Country, the superiority of nationalist parties is additionally reinforced by the elections to the so-called "Historical Territories", equivalent to the provinces, whose importance is reflected in the fact that representation in the Basque parliament is the same (25 seats) for each of the provinces in spite of their very different population.

11 In Table 9.13, the indicator, which has repeatedly been included in numerous surveys, refers to the extent to which respondents prefer different forms of state. Four alternatives are generally offered: "a state with a central government without regions"; "a state with autonomous communities like the existing ones"; "a state with communities with greater autonomy"; and "a state in which communities can become independent".

Glossary of Spanish Parties and Coalitions

AP	Alianza Popular
ARM	Agrupación Ruiz Mateos
BNG	Bloque Nacionalista Galego
CAIC	Candidatura Aragonesa Independiente de Centro
CC	Coalición Canaria
CDC	Convergència Democràtica de Catalunya
CDS	Centro Democrático y Social
CiU	Convergència i Unió
CG	Coalición Galega
CP	Coalición Popular
EA	Eusko Alkartasuna
EC	Esquerra de Catalunya
EE	Euskadiko Ezquerra
EH	Euskal Herritarrok
ERC	Esquerra Republicana de Catalunya
EUE	Euskal Esquerra
FN	Fuerza Nueva
HB	Herri Batasuna
IC	Iniciativa per Catalunya
IU	Izquierda Unida
LV	Los Verdes
LV-LV	Los Verdes-Lista Verde
LVE	Los Verdes Ecologistas
MUC	Mesa para la Unidad de los Comunistas
ORT	Organización Revolucionaria de Trabajadores
PA	Partido Andalucista
PAR	Partido Aragonés Regionalista
Par	Partido Aragonés
PCE	Partido Comunista de España
PDC	Pacte Democràtic per Catalunya
PDP	Partido Demócrata Popular
PNV	Partido Nacionalista Vasco
PP	Partido Popular
PRD	Partido Reformista Democrático
PRP	Partido Riojano Progresista
PSA	Partido Socialista de Andalucía
PSC	Partit dels Socialistes de Catalunya
PSE–PSOE	Partido Socialista de Eustradi–Partido Socialista Oberero Español
PSOE	Partido Socialista Obrero Español
PSP/US	Partido Socialista Popular/Unidad Socialista
PST	Partido Socialista de los Trabajadores
PSUC	Partit Socialista Unificat de Catalunya
PTE	Partido del Trabajo de España
UCD	Unión de Centro Democrático
UCDCC	Unió del Centre i la Democràcia Cristiana de Catalunya
UN	Unión Nacional
UPN	Unión del Pueblo Navarro
UV	Unió Valenciana

New perspectives
and areas

10 Freezing pillars and frozen cleavages

Party systems and voter alignments in the consociational democracies

Kris Deschouwer

Introduction

There is at first sight no reason at all to discuss in one chapter the fate of the consociational democracies, at least not when party systems and voter alignments are on the agenda. The four "classical" cases – Austria, Belgium, the Netherlands and Switzerland – do not belong to one category because of common characteristics according to the classifications presented by Lipset and Rokkan. Each of the consociational countries is discussed in the introductory chapter of the 1967 volume – the Netherlands even quite extensively – but there is no common treatment. And furthermore, none of the country chapters in the 1967 volume deals with one of the consociational democracies, let alone with the four of them as a single type of democracy.

The most obvious reason – and most perfect excuse – for the absence of our four countries is of course the fact that the very concept of consociational democracy had not been fully developed at that time. Lehmbruch's book on "Proporzdemokratie" in Austria and Switzerland is published in 1967, while Lijphart's first systematic presentation of the concept of consociationalism is published in 1968. In Lipset and Rokkan (1967a) there is no reference to the concept, and there is no reference to Lipset and Rokkan in the early consociational literature. But both the Lipset and Rokkan classifications and the consociational theory deal explicitly and extensively with societal divisions, with subcultural segmentation, i.e. with cleavages. Lipset and Rokkan also discuss the very special way in which some of the cleavages in some countries are institutionalized: through the organizational closure of subcultures. The concept of "verzuiling" or pillarization, which is so central in consociational theory, is prominently present in Lipset and Rokkan. Reference is also made to the country chapters in Dahl's *Political Oppositions in Western Democracies* (1966), where scholars like Daalder (the Netherlands, 1966), Engelmann (Austria, 1966) and Lorwin (Belgium, 1966) discuss the nature and the form of the political conflicts, and of course deal with concepts like segmentation and pillarization.

Looking back today we should therefore definitely be able to find some relevant and insightful links between the work of Lipset and Rokkan and the origin, development and eventual decline of consociational patterns of decision-making. This link is the pillarization of cleavages. The central idea then of this chapter is that the consociational theory allows us to say something about the development of the four classical countries after the period of full electoral mobilization. The common features of consociational democracies are not to be found in the way in which the cleavages originally developed, but in the way in which they have been institutionalized. The consociational theory might then give us some ideas on how to account for the survival of cleavages, on how to explain the subsequent freezing of them. And maybe – but this will be much more tentative – there is some common road to be found along which highly institutionalized cleavages in consociational countries unfreeze.

Cleavage structures in the consociational democracies

In this first section we go back to the origins. We use the critical junctures of Lipset and Rokkan to see which kind of cleavage structure came about in Austria, Belgium, the Netherlands and Switzerland. We simply assert that these four countries are the classical consociational countries. Other countries could be added to the list and have indeed sometimes been added to the list (like Lebanon, Uruguay or Colombia) (Lijphart 1969), but their non-European nature makes it a bit problematic to keep them on board, while the collapse of their democracies also excludes them from the family of (successful) consociational democracies. Maybe it is exactly their non-European nature, i.e. their belonging to another tradition of cultural mobilization and decision-making which explains their failure to remain in the category of consociational democracies.

The presence of Switzerland has been debated extensively (e.g. Barry 1975; Church 1989; Sciarini and Hug 1999), and it would lead us quite far if we tried to produce here the convincing arguments to keep Switzerland in the group. We will simply assume that this group of four belongs together according to the consociational theory, and then see to what extent the confrontation with the cleavage theory allows us to keep them together. Switzerland will then indeed prove (like for many other political features) to be slightly different here and there.

It should be very clear from the beginning that according to the typology of alliance–opposition structures proposed by Lipset and Rokkan (1967a, 38), the four consociational countries do not fall into the same category. The Netherlands and Switzerland belong to the mixed religious area. The line of demarcation between Reformation and Contra-Reformation cuts right across these countries. The Netherlands and Switzerland then seem to be close to each other at the starting point, and follow the same line of evolution towards Lipset and Rokkan's "type IV", which means that the main driving forces in the national revolution were the urban elites. "In each of these countries the clash between the nation-builders and the strong Roman Catholic minorities produced lasting divisions of the bodies politic and determined the structure of their party systems" (p. 39). But the way in which these divisions led to the formation of a modern political system differs sharply between the Netherlands and Switzerland. Dutch politics became to an increasing extent national(ized) politics, and the divisions produced national movements and parties (Daalder 1971; Kriesi 1990). In Switzerland the debate on the national revolution was "solved" by not solving it, was settled by allowing for the institutionalization of the confederal legacy into a federal state, by combining cantonal conservatism with national liberalism (Kriesi 1990).

Belgium and Austria are clearly different. They are both homogeneously Catholic countries. The secession of Belgium from the Low Countries in 1830 was a deliberate attempt to produce a homogenous country (forgetting however at that time the linguistic heterogeneity). But at the same time it was an attempt by liberal elites to set up a modern and secular state. The confrontation of these two state-building elites lead to a copybook example of the Church–State cleavage. The labor–capital cleavage came cutting right across it a few decades after the formation of the state. And the linguistic tensions between Dutch and French cut across the two other from the early twentieth century on.

The history of Austria is again fairly different. The religious predisposition is the same, but the further processes of state formation, nation-building and industrialization are different. In Austria this finally produces the deep separation between the Socialist–urban group and the Christian–conservative camp. German nationalism comes about as a cultural resistance against the Austrian nation-building.

There is much more to be said about the way in which the four consociational countries developed, and about the type of cleavage structure that emerged from these developments. But we only want to make the point here that these cleavage structures are different. Even without going into the details and by simply sticking to the very general categories suggested by Lipset and Rokkan, we have no empirical evidence that would allow us to classify the four consociational cases into one single category. And this should be no surprise.

Modernization and segmentation

The distinguishing features of the consociational countries are to be found in the patterns of democratic decision-making. These patterns can be explained as a response to the potential instability of the system. The potential instability is produced by the intensity of the societal divisions. The consociational countries are different (or at least supposed to be different), not because of the type of their cleavage structure, but because of the depth and strength of the cleavages. Their societies can be labeled as "segmented" (Lorwin 1971).

These subcultural segments are stable and solid. That is exactly the problem. The stability and solidity is the result of the way in which the conflicts have been institutionalized. Several organizations defending in one way or another the interests of the subcultures, form clusters, encapsulate their members into a closed network. This network is called a "pillar", a term that seems to have been coined in the 1940 in the Netherlands (Stuurman 1983, 89)

But this does still not solve our problem. If the common feature of the consociational countries is not the type of cleavage structure, but the way in which the cleavages were institutionalized, we only have a new question. How can one explain this peculiar development of the cleavages in a number of countries? Lipset and Rokkan do mention and discuss "pillarization" or institutionalized segmentation (1967b, 15–18). Their starting point is the parties of religious defense in the religiously mixed countries. These parties "tended to isolate their supporters from outside influence through the development of a wide variety of parallel organizations and agencies" (p. 15). They go on to say that the best example is the Dutch one, but also that this type of conflict does not always need to lead to pillarization. They suggest a Dutch–Swiss comparison to learn more about the "conditions for the development of pluralist insulation". For Socialist parties though they claim that parties in opposition will tend to be more pillarized, while victorious (governing) parties will become depillarized and more open. This labor party strategy is also to be explained by the degree of openness of the society in which it emerges. In countries where the emerging labor movement was strongly repressed, "the working-class organizations consequently tended to isolate themselves from the natural culture and to develop Soziale Ghettoparteien" (1967a, 22). The countries where this happened are: Germany, Austria, France, Italy and Spain.

The suggested comparison of Switzerland and the Netherlands would lead us again to the differences in the process of nation-building. We can basically assert that subcultural isolation as a strategy of protection against secular (or liberal-Protestant) nation-building is less relevant when there is hardly such a thing as nation-building (Kriesi 1990). The centralized Netherlands contrasts sharply with the confederal Swiss logic. But this comparison with Switzerland does not lead us very far in our search for the conditions for pillarization in the religiously homogeneous Belgium and Austria. The idea of "winning" and "losing" working-class parties is also interesting, but again does not provide a clear view on the specific conditions that would be unique or almost unique to consociational countries.

Lipset and Rokkan point at a number of useful insights, but do not provide a systematic account of the conditions we are looking for. Therefore 1967 was clearly too early. But is there something to be found at a later date? The answer is negative. Consociational theory itself did not explicitly deal with the conditions for pillarization. Segmentation and pillarization form the starting point of consociational theory, which has been dealing extensively with the consequences, but not with the conditions of consociationalism. If conditions are taken into consideration, these are conditions for the functioning of consociational decision-making itself (very explicitly in Lijphart 1977, 1985), not the societal conditions that account for the subcultural insulation. Causal explanations are not the strongest characteristic of consociational theory (see e.g. Barry 1975).

An interesting idea is put forward by Ellemers (1984). He wants to look at pillarization as "a specific process during a specific period of time in a specific kind of society" (p. 130). He links pillarization to modernization (see also Hellemans 1990) in an explicit attempt to find out why the concept is mainly used for Belgium, the Netherlands, Austria and Switzerland. These four countries have in the very first place their scale in common: they are small countries. To a certain extent this is the consequence of the fact that they did not want to become part of a larger national or political entity, or seceded from such an entity. The reason for that is "their cultural, religious, linguistic or ethnic diversity, which in some way formed part of their national identity" (p. 130). These countries were divided, but none of the subgroups could dominate. Even if there was something like a national center, the degree of particularism remained high. Small size and particularism based on cultural diversity are their common characteristics on the eve of modernization. And therefore modernization required special institutional arrangements. Centralized decision-making had to be developed, since the small scale did not allow for the development or use of more than one center or of more diversified arrangements. One of these arrangements is then pillarization. And Ellemers goes on to describe the development in pillars in the Netherlands, and in the Netherlands alone.

Stein Rokkan (1977) has suggested a more general comparative way to deal with pillarization. This brings him to a more detailed description of what pillarization exactly means, and to the construction of a multi-dimensional approach to study variations in types of mobilization. This is useful indeed, but does again not deal with the reasons for pillarization, or – in the case of the consociational countries – with the reasons or conditions for extreme pillarization.

And this all leads us to a very simple conclusion. As far as the conditions for pillarization as a special way of institutionalizing cleavages are concerned, we have merely and mainly discovered an interesting research agenda. There are bits and pieces around, but no systematic account of the matter. We will therefore leave it, and turn to more familiar grounds: the political consequences of pillarization.

Pillarization as a response or response to pillarization?

The mainstream consociational theory considers consociational decision-making in the first place as a response to pillarization. Because the societal subcultures are solidly institutionalized, majoritarian decision-making is out of the question, at least if the political elites agree not to destroy the system as such. The potential "centrifugal democracy" becomes then a "pacification" or consociational democracy (Lijphart 1968). Pillarization is the problem for which consociationalism is the solution.

Yet this very simple view can be and has been criticized. There is a problem of historic timing. What came first? The sequence can easily be changed. One can say that pillarization only came about after and as a result of consociational practices. Pillarization appears then as a deliberate construction by political and social elites that helps them to keep control over the masses. By insulating them in subcultures and by keeping communication limited to the top-down communication inside the pillar, a long-lasting loyalty of the masses can be secured. Especially Marxist authors (e.g. Stuurman 1983) have used this argument to explain why the elites chose in the first place for the institutionalization of cultural and religious tensions. But even without this ideological predisposition, there is a point to make about the sequence of events (Andeweg and Irwin 1993; Andeweg 1999).

Lijphart acknowledges the problem: "I could have prevented a great deal of confusion about my interpretation of Dutch politics and consociational theory as a whole, if I had spelled out more clearly the *three different roles* (my italics – KD) that verzuiling or segmentation plays in the theory" (1984b, 11). Indeed, he states that the pillarization of society is in the first place a basic given of a potentially unstable plural society. In the second place, pillarization or further reinforced pillarization is the consequence of consociational democracy. And in the third place it is a favorable condition to continue the consociational practices. Pillarization then is both a dependent and an independent variable.

We will leave the historical and methodological debates behind, and move further with the interesting idea that there is a dynamic mechanism of reinforcement at work. It is not really important for us here to know how fully fledged the pillars were at the time (if this time can indeed be identified) when political decision-making started taking the subcultural divisions into account. Even if they were only poorly developed, the consociational practices themselves will have strengthened them, after which the pillars became to a greater extent the cause of further consociational arrangements as well as the tools for these arrangements. Consociationalism is a form of "dynamic conservatism" (Ellemers 1984), because it is able to deal with many new problems, but most of the time deals with them in a similar way.

All the techniques of consociational decision-making take into account the existence of societal subcultures, but two of these techniques clearly reinforce their existence: granting autonomy and proportionality (Lijphart 1984b, 11). Granting autonomy is the most obvious solution when different subcultures produce incompatible political demands. When it is not possible (or problematic for the legitimacy of the decision) to answer only one of these demands – eventually the majoritarian one – the solution is agreeing to disagree. Every subgroup accepts the fact that the other is different, and tries to live with that. That is not too difficult if the groups do not have to live together, but can organize each its (sub)society according to its cultural norms. An existing subgroup, even when it is not (yet) completely organized and pillarized, receives the means to become organized. It becomes more than a set of organizations, it becomes an organized subculture. Pillarization has thus been strengthened.

Proportionality, this other device that avoids majoritarian decision-making, fulfills exactly the same function. If means are divided in a proportional way, the entities are first recognized as such, and then reinforced and legitimized. Pillarization through consociational decision-making produces more pillarization.

So far we have concluded that we were not able to see any common cleavage structure in the consociational countries. We have also not been able to identify clearly the reasons why the cleavages in some countries seem to be deeper and stronger, therefore giving birth to procedures of decision-making that can be recognized as consociational. But we have concluded that once the cleavages are very deep, the consociational practices surely help in keeping them where they are. Pillarization might not be an easy thing to explain, it is certainly something for which we can clearly and easily assess the consequences. Pillars seem to be freezing devices.

Freezing pillars

Lipset and Rokkan have asserted that "the party systems of the 1960s reflect, with few but significant exceptions, the cleavage structure the 1920s" (1967, 50). This idea travelled as the freezing hypothesis, although it was not really presented as a hypothesis. It was given as the reason to stop the story of emerging cleavages and parties in the 1920s. The support market was then closed. There were no more large groups to be mobilized and incorporated into the system.

This freezing (hypo)thesis received quite some attention. There has been a lot of scholarly research on electoral continuity and change, on electoral volatility and stability, on the search for the relevant new cleavages that could eventually mobilize new generations. Whether the party systems remain frozen or are definitely unfrozen, is still a matter of interesting debates (see e.g. Bartolini and Mair 1990). But one aspect of the freezing idea remained in the shade, or at least was not systematically dealt with: how and why did the cleavages freeze? Lipset and Rokkan give but very few ideas (yet they do consider the topic as "an intriguing set of problems for comparative sociological research" (p. 50)). They mainly stick to the "closure" concept. They look at the period of mass mobilization, describe the conditions in which it came about, and then explain the outcome of this mobilization. And when the wave is over, the political landscape is shaped and its shape does not seem to change anymore until the 1960s.

Our attempt to link consociational theory to the analysis of emerging cleavages, brought us to a point where we might produce some insights on the mechanics of freezing, at least for highly pillarized and consociational countries. Therefore a closer look is needed at the role of political parties in consociational democracies. This role is obviously important, and has been treated as such, but in a rather implicit way. There has been little systematic account of the role and place of parties in consociational systems. Yet such a more explicit analysis sheds light on the way in which parties and party systems reproduce themselves (Luther 1992; Deschouwer 1994; Luther and Deschouwer 1999).

In a book assessing the current consociational status of Austria (Luther and Müller 1992), Richard Luther stresses this central role of the political parties: "Political parties play a crucial role both in the political sociology and the 'overarching' elite behavior of consociational political systems. First, it is primarily the parties who mobilize their respective subcultures and it is through party structures that subcultural interests are aggregated and the subcultural political elite recruited. Second, it is above all between the elite of the political parties that the overarching accommodation occurs" (Luther 1992, 46).

This suggests a double effect of consociationalism. The first is a vertical one, and refers to the internal institutionalization of the parties as the central actor of the pillar. Consociationalism freezes the parties. The second is a horizontal one, and refers to the way in which political debates and interactions are conducted. The parties are the core competitors and the crucial problem-solvers, even if this occurs in other that the purely party-political arena. Consociationalism freezes the party system. The "partyness" of both the vertical segments and the horizontal relations at elite level, is very important. The parties penetrate deeply into society. Many aspects of the social life are in one way or another linked to the parties. They are omnipresent. And the parties also penetrate deeply into the structures of decision-making. They are the major actors in the electoral arena, in the parliament, in the government, in the bureaucracy, in the corporate circuits of decision-making.

Consociational decision-making always involves the parties and their respective subcultures. Grand coalition, oversized coalitions, power-sharing, log-rolling, mutual veto, proportionality, segmental autonomy: this is always the language of the parties. This rigid and very fixed set of rules introduces and institutionalizes a certain "language of politics" (Mair 1997, 13). Any new problem will be defined, discussed and pacified by molding it into the forms of the frozen structure of competition. Consociational democracy tends very much to close the structure of competition (Mair 1997, 211). This is dynamic conservatism indeed.

These mechanisms are of course not typical or unique of consociational democracies. But we can certainly say that they are much more pronounced in consociational democracies. The formal and informal fixed procedures of consociational systems are more numerous, more widespread, more inflexible. Does this then mean that the consociational parties and party systems are more deeply frozen than the others? Do consociational parties and party systems keep their old forms longer? Are they more difficult to challenge (Deschouwer 1994)? That is not sure, but it is at least an interesting and theoretically plausible proposition. The only way to test it, is to expand the comparative perspective and to compare consociational systems with other systems. Yet this would already assume that in this respect the consociational countries have enough in common to classify them into one single category. Before we can embark then for this broader comparative exercise, we do need to explore first the extent to which consociational countries have indeed a common pattern of "freezing". This chapter is only devoted to the latter goal.

If consociationalism and its pillars freeze better, there are two different and contradictory possible outcomes. The first one is prolonged stability. The system is then so deeply frozen that it takes more time to unfreeze. The second – also plausible – outcome is rapid and radical change. The freezing of the system by the inflexible language of politics, can make the system and the parties unable for many years to take into account societal changes and/or new political demands. The very fact that the system is so rigidly cartelized, with always these same party elites defining the game, its rules, its players and its outcomes, might then make the system extremely vulnerable for anti-establishment protest. The latter scenario is the one described and predicted by Lijphart. It is the scenario of the so-called cartel democracy.

From consociational to cartel democracy: thirty years after

When Lijphart published his first book on the Dutch consociational model in 1968, he already stated that consociationalism was coming to an end. Many changes were occurring in Dutch society, the most important of which was the introduction of more adversarial politics. The language of politics was changing. The frozen consociational structures were melting down.

The second edition of the book in 1975 made this even more explicit. Here he presents a type of democracy called "depoliticized" democracy (which in the original Dutch version was labelled "cartel democracy"). This type of democracy is to be seen when the elites still play the closed classical consociational game, while society has become much more homogeneous, i.e. has gone through a process of depillarization. Or to put it differently, the pillarized logic is still present (and maybe stronger than ever) at the elite level and in the official language of politics, while its societal or cultural aspect has been eroded (Huyse 1984, 1987).

Consociational democracy can then become the victim of its own success, by raising its own challengers. The coming of age of the welfare state in a pillarized context, makes the pillars organizationally stronger than ever. Many new state tasks are performed by the pillar organizations. And at the same time these pillar organizations become more professionalized than ever. They perform tasks for which highly educated personnel are needed. This opens the door for new and secondary elites, whose professional loyalty can rapidly replace or become more important than their sub-cultural loyalty (Ellemers 1984). That means a great challenge for the system. New parties can eventually be created, proposing to do away with the consociational language and structure of politics, asking for a more participatory and open form of democracy. And the proportional electoral logic of the consociational democracy will certainly not stop them from reaching representation.

Is this what really happened in the consociational countries? Is the second outcome, the one predicted by Lijphart, also the one supported by empirical evidence? That seems to be more or less the case indeed, but it is not so easy to discover one clear single pattern. The four consociational countries are of course only similar as far as consociationalism is concerned, while several other variables do play a role as possible predictors of party change and party system change. A broader comparative analysis is needed to single out the effects of consociationalism as such.

In the remaining part of this chapter, we will for each of the four countries give a general overview of the political developments since the invention of the concepts of freezing and consociationalism. We will obviously focus on continuity and change.

In the Netherlands we expect to see quite some change and a drift away from consociational democracy. That was at least the picture presented by Lijphart in 1968. Yet in 1989 he is rather critical about this assumption. Using the mainly institutional indicators of consensus democracy which he developed in *Democracies* (1984a) to compare the Netherlands before and after 1967, he finds hardly any change at all. The main difference is that in the latter period the governmental coalitions tend to be more often minimal winning. Dutch society might have gone through changes, the mechanics of the system did not really follow. Lijphart admits that he has overestimated the importance of the societal changes, and underestimated the conservatism of the institutions. He refers to the freezing hypothesis of Lipset and Rokkan as an instructive example of this conservatism (Lijphart 1989, 141).

There is however a methodological and conceptual problem here. By measuring the amount of change in terms of institutional variables, the chances of finding substantial change are fairly low. Lijphart's original description of consociational democracy however, is not the same as what he calls later "consensus" democracy. The latter is institutionally defined indeed, while the original consociationalism refers to procedures, to techniques, to mechanics of the system. Some of these might be part of the formal institutions, but they do not need to be entrenched there. And then this one change depicted by Lijphart – more minimal winning coalitions after 1967 – is of course also simply an artifact of the fusion of the three denominational parties into the one CDA in 1977.

How then can we assess the changes, if change there is? We want to see whether and how long the cleavages have remained frozen, and whether the unfreezing comes suddenly in the form of radical anti-establishment challenges of the system. A good start is taking a few classical party system measures. If the cleavages are frozen, we expect elections with low volatility. We also expect the old and traditional parties not to be challenged by newcomers, which means that we expect the total score of the traditional parties to be fairly stable. And we also do not expect changes in the degree of fractionalization. Whatever that degree is (the varying cleavage types can account for variations in the starting point), it should not go up or down as long as the system is frozen.

Austria seems to be the typical case of our expected way out of consociationalism. The stability of the system is extremely high until the early 1980s (see Table 10.1). The two major parties, the Christian-conservative ÖVP and the socialist SPÖ control more than 90 percent of the votes. Except for the election of 1949, the volatility is as low as can be. In 1975 it does not even reach 1 percent. The degree of fractionalization of the party system hardly changes. It settles at 0.60 after the full independence of the Staatsvertrag and is still 0.58 in 1983.

Table 10.1 Indicators of party system change in Austria

	Total score[a]	Volatility	Fractionalization
1945	94.4		0.55
1949	82.7	12.0	0.64
1953	83.4	3.6	0.64
1956	89.0	5.7	0.60
1959	89.0	2.9	0.60
1962	89.4	1.7	0.59
1966	90.9	4.8	0.58
1970	93.1	6.5	0.56
1971	93.1	2.0	0.56
1975	93.4	0.4	0.56
1979	92.9	1.3	0.56
1983	90.8	4.8	0.58
1986	84.4	9.7	0.63
1990	75.1	9.9	0.68
1994	62.2	14.7	0.74
1995	66.4	3.8	0.72

Note: [a]Parties included are: ÖVP and SPÖ.

Yet the 1986 election is the beginning of the end. The period of classical consociational seems to be over. The SPÖ had formed a coalition with the liberal FPÖ, the successor of the former German Nationalists. This party had always been an outsider. It did not participate in the consociational logic, in the Proporz agreements between the black ÖVP and the red SPÖ. The coalition was short-lived, especially when the FPÖ moved clearly in an anti-system and anti-establishment direction under its new leader Jürg Haider. The 1986 elections saw the classical consociational parties lose 6 percent, and in 1990 they went even further down. The fractionalization of the party system reaches 0.68, with the Greens entering the scene and the FPÖ starting its way up. Since 1994 – an election with a volatility of 15 percent – Austria has a new party system. The old two-party system is gone and has been replaced by a three-party system, in which the third party, Haider's FPÖ, challenges the old system and its representatives ÖVP and SPÖ. These two traditional consociational parties have so far no other option than form and reform the good old grand coalition – a consociational-like device – which gives then new ammunition to the challenger. The Austrian "cartel democracy" behaves exactly like Lijphart predicted it in 1968, although he was looking at the Netherlands.

The changes in the Netherlands came earlier indeed. The figures in Table 10.2 show much more change than Lijphart found by measuring only institutional characteristics. The traditional consociational parties – the three religious parties, the socialists and the liberals – controlled 90 percent of the votes in the early 1960s, but were down at 72 percent in 1971. After this second high volatility election, the fractionalization of the system had moved up from 0.77 in 1956 to 0.86. The major challenger was D'66, but several other parties (the Farmer's Party, DS'70, the Pacifist Socialist Party . . .)

Table 10.2 Indicators of party system change in the Netherlands

	Total score[a]	Volatility	Fractionalization
1946	86.2		0.79
1948	86.9	5.6	0.80
1952	86.7	6.3	0.80
1956	91.5	4.1	0.77
1959	91.7	5.9	0.78
1963	87.5	5.0	0.79
1967	78.8	10.8	0.84
1971	71.6	12.0	0.86
1972	73.0	12.6	0.85
1977	83.6	14.3	0.75
1981	76.4	9.6	0.78
1982	82.9	9.3	0.76
1986	85.3	10.2	0.73
1989	81.8	8.4	0.74
1994	66.2	22.2	0.82

Notes: [a]Parties included are: CDA (until 1977: KVP, ARP, CHU), PvdA and VVD.

came to question the old parties and the old rules of behavior. The challenge of D'66 was most obviously oriented against the consociational nature of the system. Its proposal to have the prime minister elected directly – to cite only this very striking example – was clearly meant to be a majoritarian alternative to the consociational logic. Yet D'66 was rather easily incorporated in the system. It joined the government for the first time in 1973, after which it was confronted with severe losses. It is difficult to classify D'66 later on. Is this still a new and challenging party, or can it be considered as a new participant in the old game? It surely went back to opposition, but became a governing party again in 1981 and since 1994. And that is maybe the best evidence to support the idea of unfreezing, because this new partner can not be considered as a political movement that has emerged out of the early mobilization and pillarization phase.

The other indicator for the end of classical consociationalism is un-doubtedly the fusion of the three religious parties. It marks the end of one of the main lines of opposition in the Netherlands's modern history. The fusion made the fractionalization index drop in 1977 from 0.85 to 0.75, but in 1994 it is again at a solid 0.82. After 1994 the Christian Democrats even end up on the opposition benches, which marks in a very symbolic way the end of the old system.

The Dutch pattern is thus fairly "normal". It comes close to the Austrian one, but with a time-lag. The pattern as such is the same: stability followed by rapid change for which one of the indicators is the successful mobiliz-ation of anti-establishment (i.e. anti-cartel or anti-consociational) sentiments. The Dutch critical election was 1967. The Austrian one came in 1986.

The Belgian story is quite complicated, but does fit into the general pattern. The first critical election was 1965, with an electoral volatility of 16 percent (Table 10.3). It marked the entry of three new parties: a Flemish Nationalist in the north, a Walloon Nationalist in the south and a Francophone Nationalist party in Brussels. They are in the first place and at first sight "old" parties, in the sense that they mobilize on one of the classical cleavages. The differences between north and south had thus far been contained and controlled by the three national parties (Christian Democrats, Socialists and Liberals). From the early 1960s on, these tradi-tional parties are increasingly unable to find internal compromises on the linguistic and regionalist issues, and are therefore challenged by pure and radical defenders of these issues. But the new parties also mobilize the criticism of the old system in general. They blame the traditional parties for their cartel-type decision-making, for their control over the pillars, for the general "partyness" of politics and society. One can say to a certain extent that the three new nationalist parties are three D'66 type of parties.

Yet the effect of their successful mobilization of both the anti-establish-ment sentiments and the ethno-linguistic demands, will have the perverse effect of strengthening the consociational logic of the Belgian political system (see for more details, Deschouwer 1996, 1997). The traditional

Table 10.3 Indicators of party system change in Belgium

	Total score[a]	Volatility	Fractionalization[b]	
1946	83.0		0.69	
1949	88.4	10.9	0.69	
1950	93.5	10.8	0.64	
1954	90.5	7.7	0.67	
1958	93.4	5.4	0.63	
1961	90.5	4.8	0.67	
1965	84.4	16.1	0.75	
1968	80.6	7.1	0.81	0.76
1971	72.4	6.5	0.82	0.79
1974	74.3	3.5	0.84	0.78
1977	77.4	6.1	0.82	0.76
1978	77.2	6.0	0.87	0.77
1981	73.1	14.4	0.89	0.81
1985	78.1	10.0	0.88	0.78
1987	79.1	4.5	0.88	0.78
1991	70.1	12.2	0.90	0.82
1995	72.7	7.7	0.89	0.81

Notes: [a]Parties included are CVP, PSC, SP, PS, VLD and PRL.
[b]Second column is the fractionalization score counting the two Christian Democratic,
Socialist and Liberal parties each as one single party.

parties did not survive the tensions, and fell apart into linguistically homogeneous regional parties. The national party system disappeared and was replaced by two regional party systems, in which the parties of only one language group compete. Only at the governmental level the two systems come together. The split of the party system reinforced the importance of especially the two largest political families: Christian Democrats and Socialists. The first is by far the largest party of the Dutch-speaking part of the country, the latter dominates in the Francophone part. A national government does not only require constitutionally a coalition of parties of both language groups, it requires in an almost natural way the involvement of the two major families. Political decision-making at the Belgian level demands more than ever the subtle agreements, the mutual vetos, the consensus-seeking and the proportionality of consociationalism. The reform of the state into a federal logic, followed neatly the consociational lines. Regional autonomy was granted to the ethno-linguistic subgroups.

By responding to the demands of the regionalist parties, the Belgian political system introduced consociationalism in the pacification of the new cleavage. And by doing so it certainly did not take away the basic reasons to criticize the consociational logic. The nationalist parties of the sixties slowly lost their electoral support, but new challengers like first the Greens and later the Vlaams Blok easily gained momentum. And the two Liberal parties (especially the Flemish VLD), who are clearly the losers of the federal reform (Liberalism is not a leading force in one of the two language groups), join the challengers in their demands for radical changes. They support the idea of referenda, of direct election of the prime minister, i.e. of much more majoritarianism. The three traditional political families control now (since the early seventies) some 70 percent in stead of 90 percent of the votes. But one of the traditional families does not see itself as part of the classical game any more, which means that the "total consociational score" is even less. Looking back, one can surely say that 1965 marked the end of consociationalism (a major agreement had settled the religious "school war" already in 1958), but parts of consociationalism came back through the back door. So Belgium does fit into the pattern of stability followed by rapid decline. The search for responses to the challengers however produced a very peculiar story. And therefore both a number of consociational devices and the challenging of them can still be witnessed today.

Switzerland is – not surprisingly – less easy to fit into the model. The "total score" indicator shows clearly a decline of the votes in the 1960s (Table 10.4). Between 1963 and 1971 the four parties of the "magic formula" – Social Democrats, Radicals, Catholic Conservatists and Swiss People's Party – lose together some 10 percentage points. But nothing really spectacular is to be seen. All four parties simply lose a few points. They recover slightly during the seventies, but do go further down in the eighties. 1991 is an absolute minimum, with only 69 percent of the votes. The fractionalization of the party system does not show any spectacular changes either, but it is very slowly going up.

We see a change from 1967 on, but it does not look like the kind of change we could witness in the other three countries. If change there is, it is gradual and slow. Furthermore it is not possible to identify exactly the challengers. Just like the country itself, the alternatives to the traditional four parties present themselves in a rather scattered way. There is a bit of

Table 10.4 Indicators of party system change in Switzerland

	Total score[a]	Volatility	Fractionalization
1947	82.5		0.81
1951	85.1	3.9	0.80
1955	85.6	2.2	0.80
1959	85.4	1.7	0.80
1963	85.6	1.7	0.80
1967	79.8	6.0	0.82
1971	75.3	7.2	0.83
1975	78.1	2.7	0.82
1979	81.6	6.5	0.82
1983	77.8	5.4	0.83
1987	71.6	6.3	0.85
1991	68.7	8.8	0.86
1995	73.9	5.0	0.85

Note: [a]Parties included are SPS/PSS (Socialist Party), FDP/PRD/PLR (Liberal Democrats), CVP/PDCS/PDCPS (Christian Democrats) and SVP/UDC (Swiss Peoples' Party).

Green success, a bit of right-wing populism, and many other smaller old and new parties. Can we consider these parties to be challengers of the consociational logic? There is certainly not one major movement, similar to the Dutch D'66, the Austrian FPÖ or the Belgian regionalists. Our little comparative exercise raises two questions with respect to Swiss politics: why is there no real, visible and united challenge of the consociational logic, and why are the eventually scattered challengers not able to grow more rapidly? The answer to both question is probably the same, and is the general easy way out to explain the Swiss exceptionalism: Switzerland is different because it is Switzerland.

We can eventually assume that Switzerland is a full member of the consociational club, but then we do have to take into account the very fact that its political institutions are different. Since Switzerland is so highly federal, it can be part of any club without this making too much of a difference. Even if Switzerland is consociational, the governmental level at which it is consociational is not the most important or the most relevant level to understand political mobilization is Swiss politics. Can one – for instance – imagine a united anti-European party in Europe, scoring high at elections for the European Parliament? The Swiss "cantonalism" (Hughes 1993) seems to be an effective brake on the mobilization of any national movement. Even the traditional parties can hardly be considered as genuinely federal. Swiss stability seems to be safe, because Switzerland does not really exist (Steinberg 1996), because of its extreme federal or even confederal institutional logic.

There is one intriguing indicator however that might well be a "functional equivalent" for the party-political mobilization of the anti-establishment and anti-cartel feelings: the dramatically declining voter turnout in Swiss federal elections (and referenda). The turnout was 73 percent in 1947 and dropped below 50 percent ever since 1983. Is this the Swiss way to turn one's back to the system? Is the extreme federal organization of the country making it impossible to turn this exit option into a anti-establishment voice? It would mean that behind the very gradual and slow decline of the traditional parties, there it at least a potential for mobilization. It remains to be seen whether some societal developments – like the expansion of mass communications – can turn this potential into a real political movement. The chances are not that high, because even mass communication is not federal. It is divided along the linguistic lines. And these division lines, contrary to Belgium, are also not a matter of federal mobilization. If we assume that Switzerland is or was consociational, we have to add immediately that it was and is different.

Conclusion

We have in this chapter tried to deal with the four classical cases of consociational democracy in the light of Lipset and Rokkan's concepts of cleavages and voter alignments. The starting point was that these four countries have indeed something quite relevant in common: their cleavage structure has been institutionalized in a number of closed networks of organizations or "pillars". The exact origin or explanation of this pillarization as a way to institutionalize conflict lines remains fairly open. The consequences, so we argued, are on the contrary very clear. The pillarization did not only provide for a clear system of voter alignments, but also for a fixed language of politics. This has in the consociational countries produced a deeply frozen cleavage structure.

If then pillars can be considered to function as "freezing devices", we should be able to see and to measure stability in the party systems of the consociational countries. This is indeed the case. Following Lijphart's assumptions about the way in which the Netherlands was moving out of the consociational logic, we extrapolated this to the other countries. We were then looking for a period of stability, followed by a rapid decline. We did find this in the Netherlands, Belgium and Austria, but with a different timing. For Switzerland we did not find this pattern. This means at least that further research is needed on the relation between cleavages, pillars, parties and party systems. Lipset and Rokkan presented their so-called "freezing hypothesis" as an intriguing set of problems for comparative sociological research. The work remains to be done.

11 From post-communism to neo-communism?

The reconstitution of the party systems of East-Central Europe

Ulf Lindström

Instant Rokkan

Perhaps superficially in more senses than one, Eastern Europe is reentering the realm of Stein Rokkan's "Conceptual map of Europe".

The fall of the Berlin Wall jolted political sociology. East-Central Europe flourishing with parties, scholars rushed to classify them across the revolutionary East, across orthodox typologies from the West. A few demummified from the previous period of democracy, some adopted by sister-parties in the West, most parties, however, were new creatures. Who would vote for whom and why?

For cues on voter alignments, Figure 11.1 offers "instant Rokkan". Taking precautions not to distort his original typology too much (entries in bold type are to be discussed below), the transmutation reveals the unique nature of transition from communism.

The economic agenda has been dominated by privatization (E IV). How fast, with what exceptions, are companies to be privatized? This conflict, unresolved since privatization has stopped short of capitalization, is merging with that of the state's overall influence over the economy, including market-liberal proactivism. As for the labor market, the opposing part of the working class is still the state, the latter to be replaced by the capital owners (including the red barons who impounded old combinates) (E III). The economic conflicts have a global backdrop. Deindustrialization is paving the way for the knowledge industry and an international market in which the European Union (EU), World Trade Organization (WTO) and the International Monetary Fund (IMF) have a larger say than before.

Conflicts embedded in the rural sector concern the state handing over land to peasants; to the original owners, co-operatives, or letting the green barons who impounded government land keep their booty. This pits peasants against peasants, including those who were denied becoming peasants, as well as peasants against hired hands at the farms (E II). The rural sector has rekindled the conflict of interests between the producers and consumers. The saliency of this conflict will be affected by public subsidies to agriculture, ultimately reflecting East-Central Europe's relationship to the EU.

Interactive nodes
Center

E IV *Conflicts over boundaries of economic system:*

Privatization →
State control over private enterprise

Meritocracy in and vs. the state

E III *Industrial class conflicts:*
Workers vs. state →

Non owners vs. the state

E II *Rural class conflicts:*

Workers vs. state →
farmers vs. farmers →
workers vs. owners/ management

Non owners vs. the state

E I *Rural–urban conflicts:*

Primary producers vs. consumers
Farmers vs. creditors →
Farmers vs. EU/WTO

Communitarianism in and vs. the state

C IV *Conflicts over boundaries of cultural system:*

Nationalism vs. internationalism.
Value conservatism vs. intellectual radicalism

Neo-modernism vs. neo-communism

C III *Conflicts over religious identity:*
State vs. Church. Fundamentalism v. Latitudinarism/secularism

Agnosticism vs. sectarianism

C II *Conflicts over lifestyles:*

Egalitarianism vs. conspicuous consumption

Universalism vs. tribalism

C I *Conflicts over linguistic identity and resources:*

Subject vs. dominant language.
Dialect vs. standard script.
Diglot proficiency. Computer literacy

Authenticism vs. professionalism

(Left vertical axis: TAX BASE / ECONOMY)
(Right vertical axis: CULTURE / WELTSCHMERTZ)

Periphery
Stationary arenas

Figure 11.1 Reemerging and **new** configurations of conflicts in East-Central Europe.

Source: From Rokkan; conflicts in **bold type** refer to the transition between the industrial and the knowledge society common throughout Europe (Rokkan 1981, 64).
Note: Arrows (→) indicate likely sequence of confrontations.

Conflicts of cultural origins that divide electorates relate primarily to the many facets of nationalism, of which border adjustments and the acquiring of property by foreign owners (and returned expatriots) immediately surged after 1989. Nationalism is also reflecting the near past as a question of loyalty to the nation or the USSR before the transition. Nationalism will remain dormant as a conflict between the dominant ethnic group and minorities (C IV).

The religious revival gives the churches the options of exit, voice and loyalty vis-à-vis the state, none of which will steer clear of conflicts among the clergies, congregations and secular leaders (C III).

As the effect of the market economy becomes visible in public places conflicts over lifestyle will feed other cleavages. States in which the egalitarian way of life was sanctioned, making extravagant display of lifestyle a sign also of political opposition, the citizens are now expected to tackle multifaceted expressions of lifestyles in public places (C II). Reacting along a register of acceptance and disapproval, the community is rarely convinced that the system rewards the virtuous. Instead, it is likely to associate wealth with greed on part of the old *nomenklatura*, criminals, and the precommunist bourgeoisie and nobility.

Conflicts that used to pit the dominant language against minority languages and dialects now also include foreign languages. Language is power, a means of individual positioning in the knowledge society, an issue of collective distribution of proficiency in foreign tongues, including that of computer languages (C I).

The first two or three free elections in Estonia, Latvia, Lithuania, Poland, the Czech Republic, Slovakia, Hungary, Slovenia, Rumania, Bulgaria, and Albania have left an abundance of variance unexplained.[1] Turnout varies between 40 and 90 percent. Parties quadruple their gains and losses. Parties disappear. Parties that outlawed others are back in cabinet positions. Parties that are fundamentally opposed to each other form coalition cabinets.

The volatility of the electoral arena raises the question what it is about East-Central Europe after the transition to democracy that is inadequately accommodated by Rokkan's conceptual map. In view of this – and the quest for new approaches in accounting for recent change in *West* European politics – what are the theoretical implications for the Lipset–Rokkan thesis on the freezing of party systems and voter alignments? (Lipset and Rokkan 1967a).

These questions invite anachronism and ethno-centrism. East-Central Europe cannot return to the time when it last knew its own democratic institutions those that, by proxy, were covered by Rokkan's conceptual map and proceed from there as if 44 years of communist rule had left no imprints. East-Central Europe cannot rebuild its infrastructure, reform its economy and remodel its social security net using the technology, methods of production and class structure that were starting to become obsolete in the West as *PSVA* came out. Whether part of the "global village" or not, East-Central Europe cannot emulate the contemporary agenda of Western Europe and expect it to bring stable alignments to the electoral arena (Lane and Ersson 1997).

East-Central Europe plays havoc with Rokkan's understanding of political development. Violating the trajectory he proposed, East-Central Europe confronts critical junctures in awkward sequences. Penetrated by a defunct state, still waiting to be remobilized by the citizenry, society is put under critical depositioning by a new state supposed to disown more and more of its power in the process. And to what avail? Evenhandedly scaling down government to make room for novel thoughts in a pastoral landscape is futile. East-Central Europe is Europe, not a habitat of disinterested institutions.

Which horizontally self-supporting contexts are to structure the parameters of representative politics in East-Central European politics? Will the contexts reinforce each other so as to mitigate electoral turbulence, preclude mindboggling cabinet coalitions and restore mutual trust among the citizens and elected representatives?

Identifying the all-European contribution of Rokkan, this chapter juxtaposes – as implied by Rokkan – the nonvariable conditions at work as Western Europe rebuilt its democracy after World War II and the dynamic ones that confront East-Central Europe today. Employing "controlled anachronism", this is a prologue to the analysis of party systems and voter alignments throughout Europe after 1989.

Time-specific Europe, time-less Rokkan, or vice versa?

"Instant Rokkan" is lost in distorted perspectives. His original typology of voter alignments offers a modernist perspective of the transition from the agrarian to the industrial economy. Figure 11.1 sets the typology in an economy which is partly post-communist, partly pre-communist but most of all acommunist and amodernist. Renounce of vertical institutions, the typology is insensitive to the consequences of the dismantling of the state.

East-Central Europe is facing a neo-modernist challenge: the concurrent revival of the citizen and the reclaiming of the democratic nation-state. A modernist state formation requires a sustainable middle class. Without a middle class whose virtue cues the bulk of the citizenry on its road ahead to a life in a better world – never in the best of one world – the political sphere is ruled in and by a state of exceptionalism.

Indirectly confirming the nodal status of the middle class, Rokkan accounted for the cleavage structure and voter alignments of nation-states through the variation in mobilization around, not among, the middle class. Significantly, he used the term "defence" whenever the working class, peasants and ethnic minorities distorted the process by organizing socialist, agrarian and ethno-territorial parties. Repeated questioning of the nodality of the middle class makes his insight span time and space. *This suggests that East-Central Europe reentering Rokkan's conceptual map is conditioned by the reconstitution of a middle class.*

Zeitgeist coupled with parsimony, the refinery of variance across Europe, made Rokkan omit the middle class. What does that mean to the validity of his *Nachlass* in East-Central Europe?

Superimposing the horizontal mobilization of cleavages – left vs right, center vs periphery – on the vertical reconstruction of postwar Europe, Rokkan implied the rebuilding of the infrastructure to be constant. He took a communicative rather than institutional interest in infrastructure. Like consumerism in America, infrastructure bridged gaps, opened for the dissemination of ideas that brought standardization to the nations of Europe. Subservient in the unfolding of the modernization drama, the local pillars, the local middle class, were indistinguishable across nation-states.

Rokkan too was living in a Europe under siege. After 1945 Western Europe, working-class youth as well as junior scholars, adhered to an American outlook that saw society as socially uniformly mobile despite all cleavages. In 1967, *PSVA* represented a political sociology as European as it could get. In 1989, Europe finally returned to its own mosaic, to address *la différence* with the support of neither a bipolar world demonology nor, arguably, Rokkan's conceptual map.

Post-Rokkan: adding insult to injury

Besides his emphasis on distances Rokkan offers one hint to the contemporary analyst of the numeric prominence and politico-cultural dispersion of the middle class: "Votes count, but resources decide" (Rokkan 1970) What sets the politics of the early post-war decades apart from that of today is the fragmentation of one sustainable middle class upholding one inclusive virtue into an army of middle classes nursing a plethora of virtues and vices associated with resources engendered chiefly by occupational position.

The agrarian society sired human beings *cum* manpower, another mouth to feed, another hand to till the soil. The industrial society sired human beings whom employers used as manpower. Nevertheless, through the numeric and corporate channels of democracy, they strove to be reborn as human beings. The knowledge society sires those who, found "competent" rather than hirable, realize themselves as human beings *as* manpower: "owners of employment". Are they as keen as the masses and the pillars of the industrial society to use the vote and fill the ranks of corporate interests? Or, to elaborate on Rokkan's twin-channel democracy, does ownership of employment mean indifference to whether votes count and resources decide as long as professional competence provides access to political influence?

Cultivating networks of the communist era, public employees are likely to substitute the class struggle for the interest of professional and localistic causes warming to historicist coalitions. Agonized by the failure of modernist parties to offer alternatives, private employees tend to the nontransparent networks of a market perverted by an informal economy and arbitrary political interference. Disrespectful of community values as well as the received wisdom of the business community, entrepreneurs, whose diligence and modesty in lifestyle are to serve as role models of the virtue of the market economy, are held in suspicion as representatives of the middle class of shamelessness.

In the vacuum left behind as the proletariat disappeared as the subject of power, in the space modernism allots the middle class, microcosms are appointing themselves to do new works of wonder. Once again the agenda is vulnerable to falling prey to historicism. Only this time East-Central Europe is exposed to a cacophony of causes, not a unison one extolling the ethnos (1848–1918), fighting a race (1939–45) and glorifying a class (–1989).

East-Central Europe too is emulating Asian-American knowledge fetishism. Knowledge bytes instead of watts, computers instead of machinery, competence instead of skills, college graduates instead of workers, MBAs instead of entrepreneurs gives the economy competitive thrust. Knowledge is to inoculate the citizens against new historicisms peddled by antimodernist microcosms. Carpet-bombing society with education and training (ignoring parallels to earlier investment fetish) is trusted to foment economic growth, a responsive polity and a view of mankind that honors citizenship.

Knowledge is not the same in Europe as in Asia and America.[2] For all its praise of *la différence*, Europe legitimately questions distinctions (Seidman 1983). Replacing the division of labor and ownership of land as social differentia, "competence" will still covary with the societal organization of knowledge.

Knowledge is offered, acquired and put to use in subtle correspondence with Rokkan's socio-cultural conflicts. True, the density (coverage and penetration) of old cleavage systems is reduced. But in emphasizing competence as a panacea to all ills, elected diets distance themselves from classes whose skills and ways of life are represented in the institutional make-up of the industrial society. A similar sense of alienation by representative and one of patronizing by administrative bodies is felt among low-skilled labor, unemployable, immigrant labor, single-mother households, and their offspring. Self-made men and women, streetsmart rather than educated, owners of versatile capital rather than employment, are deprived of political representation in the knowledge society.

Serving professional hubris, knowledge adds insult to injury to Rokkan's cleavages. Disallowing conflicts as discursive malfunction, professional abuse of knowledge makes the powerless turned ignorant resort to exit or one-dimensional unreason defending themselves as one-dimensional subjects. The discourse of power is met with the ascriptive face of power-lessness, mute or raging, seldom exchanging viewpoints. Post-communist (unlike post-fascist) transition is predisposed to foster one-dimensional opposition. Instantaneously and contagiously, neo-communism cultivates the victimization and exclusion that accompany the fall of a project that, as a hybrid of modernism and historicism heralding the liberation of the wretched and downtrodden, can never be anything but incomplete.

Abolished by the outgoing regime, subject to depositioning policies by the incoming, the embryonic middle class is to mantle a mission as huge as that of raising a new nation-state. Anachronistic, it is an assignment that brings back *Vormärz Europa*, images of a sustainable bourgeoisie leading a life in between the bourse and the cathedral; suave, civic-minded and decently patriotic. Paying homage to Biedermeier (1815–48), this way of life has since incurred Germanic scientific contempt for political projects that stop short of historicist commitment (Seidman 1983, ch. 10).

Life down the road, inside or outside the EU, is in a knowledge society. It recognizes vertically acquired competence, professionalism or *vita activa*. Patronizing communitarianism (horizontal bonds of loyalty), profession-alism feeds a public agenda of tribalism. Distinguishing citizenship from its lesser species, the renaissance way of life, *vita contemplativa*, is dilettantism. Yet, known to have surrendered to many kinds of *raison d'état*, tribalism is no excuse for anyone not to recall that the imperative of the state is to exercise or abdicate constitutional power.[3]

Reversed Rokkan

Rokkan attributed political development to cleavages that grew as a result of contexts reinforcing in each other's proximity. Contextualism in its purest form, this is horizontal ecological analysis set in a landscape unspoiled by vertical institutions. The sources of the process of cleavage formation were retrospectively accounted for (Berntzen and Selle 1990). Rarely did Rokkan consider political development as progress emanating out of deliberations set *in* the vertical space in between these cleavages. As the polity overcame critical junctures, as bipolar confrontations lost their momentum, he added a new pair to the trajectory. The outcome of the confrontation between the first pair, the institutional impact on the vertical space in between the cleavages that makes for an ever more complex citizenry, was recast as contextual backdrop for the next stage in the unfolding of the polity. Seemingly without talking to each other, voters and representatives are genetically coded by the past in their responses to the performance of contemporary institutions.

However, if no one else, the family sees to that overlapping generations of citizens come of political age governed by the memory of which pair of parties advanced and resisted reforms. Whenever voters and representatives let themselves be agitated by the contemporary performance of public institutions, new life is blown into individual and collective perceptions of the width and depth of the original cleavage that divided the arch antagonists. With pleasure and displeasure voters and representatives recognize each other as friends and foes, upholding the demonology central to the Lipset–Rokkan thesis, "Parties do not simply present themselves *de novo* to the citizen at each election" (1967a, 2).

At *Stunde Null*, "How quickly were the parties [of East-Central Europe] able to recruit support among the new masses of enfranchised citizens, and what were the core characteristics of the groups of voters mobilized by each party?" (ibid). It was *quickly* alright, but support was recruited neither among *new* voters nor *masses* or, for that matter, groups with *core* characteristics.

Second-guessing the grass-roots for emerging cleavages, a self-selected elite announced itself as leaders of a runaway multi-party market. "De-mummified" political families lent parties claim to pre-communist times. Most founders were turncoat nomenklatura and aborted entrepreneurs. Elsewhere the latter would have gone into business. Located in the center of events, parliament, unlike the elusive market, attracted enterprisers. Parliament "offered greater incentive to fragmented articulation of single interests [and] narrowly defined causes[.]" (Lipset and Rokkan 1967a, 1). Parties that clear the threshold of representation are eligible for public finance. Parliamentary representation equally grants party leaderships democratic patina and platforms into the future, dear resources in a seemingly endless time of retreat.

In the first free elections the parties competed for votes in a *t-minus-one* landscape. Devoid of political rights, it was a setting in which "core" characteristics of the citizenry had been supplanted by social rights defined in life-span terms. The electorate, as individuals and members of communities, had no experience of parties taking turns at offering the voters better deals, taking the heat for not delivering as incumbents. In the *t+1* landscape, offering real choices among contending parties, eight out of ten voters found themselves in the vertical landscape beget by the communist regime. Duties that the citizens had been obliged to observe under the old regime, such as work, were suddenly turned around to become rights. Eight out of ten voters in East-Central Europe hold that it is the responsibility of the government to provide every citizen with a job (Evans and Whitefield 1995, 568). At first impression, "The voters do not simply present themselves *de novo* to the parties, not even at free elections".

Rokkan gave actors a voice, in the form of mass psychological extra-polations. The rebuilding of western Europe eventually met with "the revolution of rising expectations". Yet, political disbelief never caught up with him or the citizenries of western Europe. Instead, he was to witness the return, even strengthening, of party identity, whereas "Five-sixths of people in central and eastern Europe [in 1993–4] showed no trust in political parties". (Rose 1995, 552ff.). While 65 percent of the Hungarian electorate take a reflective attitude to trust, the extremes split dismally:

* vote,	have party identity,	trust parties	2%,
* don't vote,	don't have party identity,	don't trust parties	33%.

Officially granting one another pardon for 44 years of wrongdoings is one thing. Electing oneself new voters with ready-made party identities, let alone 44 different ones, is something else. Not even enjoying 44 months of confidence, parties now expect the electorate to forget the transition, not to memorize what they inflict on the community as they push ahead. Posed as prospective platforms, the parties among themselves do not control a critical mass of the electorate. To identify with a party, especially when it is serving as incumbent, is to be surrounded by those who at best pity party loyalists.

Not cued to expect much of a future from parties competing to de-frost entitlements, voters split on trust in a way that makes sense. Discontent is not continuously exchanged into the kind of demonology mobilized and reinforced by Rokkan's horizontal contexts. Until regulated horizontally, distrust is directed vertically against the top.

Low turnout is a mute reaction based on expectations. Grandmother's pension, father's unemployment benefits, the unwed daughter's aid and her child's allowance produce a four-fold one-dimensionality, a stigma across generations. Families do not simply present themselves *de novo* to their members at each Sunday dinner. In some, litanies hover in the air over the unfairness of an estranged political system: "we are not communists, but the benefits . . .".[4]

Collective, selective and postponed memory

Eastern Europe was flung open to bold theorizing in 1989, such as the communist era having elapsed parallel to a societal permafrost. Whatever the regime imposed, civil society wintered out. Alas, society did not freeze. It was decaying (Clark and Wildavsky 1990).

Absolved from public status, the people turned to nonpublic webs of short distances. Absolute powerlessness tends to corrupt. Networking encourages "amoral familism", ties between those living in town and the cousins in the country. Confirming anthropologist Banfield's findings on primitive cultures, life under communism means to "Maximize the material, shortrun advantage of the nuclear family; assume that all others will do likewise" (1958, 85).

Pacified as one-dimensional men, the people entered the stage as pioneers and were forever destined to exit as senior anti-fascist fighters. Not convinced that the nation was still on a war footing, the civil sphere was vulgarized. Communitarian deliberation among citizens – "politics" – is not to be distinguished from petty bartering among family and friends. Indeed, getting by in the transition from communism means resisting the return of the future. Dichotomized at three levels of society, at times the resistance and its rewards are multiplicatively distributed:

- Macro: is the economy/infrastructure privatized by openly, fully and irrevocably transferring the activity of the state to the shareholding public? If not, which are the branchwise, geographic and "strategic" exceptions?
- Meso: does local/infrastructural vulnerability of having the source of livelihood wiped out excuse the state to postpone privatization? If so, what principles and which exceptions apply for the state to exempt local governments and old infrastructures?
- Micro: are nonpay benefits from combinates transferable to state funds? If exceptions apply, households not affected by the first wave of privatization – and those employed in companies owned by the management/employees – will appreciate the privatization of their work-place being postponed for another year.

How long will exceptions be the rule, furthering pockets of resistance amid the transition?[5] At the intermediate stage of transition, the Balkan nations have most of the privatization process ahead of them. Those at the advanced stage of transition are to be split, though. Deep privatization has been pursued only in Estonia and Hungary. Not even Klaus' government of the Czech Republic was up to the expectation of the European Bank for Reconstruction and Development (EBRD). It had "yet to announce its decision on the privatisation of other 'strategic' entities, including the railways and the utilities". (1996, 146). Half of the countries at the advanced stage, among them Poland and Slovenia, have resorted to half-measures of privatization. Management/employee buy-outs, instead of market capitalization, are making the economy even more vulnerable to political interference than state ownership. Come hard times, companies owned by the management/employees will be looking for communitarian support to help them stay afloat, not least among the 18,946 mayors of East-Central Europe's local governments (Lidström 1996).

In themselves and in vulnerable variants exposed to continuous reforms, pockets of resistance comprise households with no or narrow professional profiles, local governments with one-source economies and utilities with unsafe mandates. Living close to fellow households, local governments and utilities, they exchange experience of how to survive and reposition themselves for the years ahead. Not randomly distributed, this is a cumulative resource. It brings empowerment to some institutions, dependency to others. Households that keep their employment may be offered a company-supported mortgage to buy the former combinate's apartment.

Some local governments get no help to keep their old combinate while, inspiring resistance, the neighboring town is raking in state subsidies for an even rustier combinate and technically expendable utility office.

The communist legacy cannot be severed by fiat as if it had been alien to European civilization. In a post-communist (unlike post-fascist) landscape all institutions are tainted by the past. The family and civil service do not easily forget the past. Meanwhile, parties – with which the Lipset–Rokkan thesis deposits the collective memory of the community – are advised not to stimulate the accumulation of communitarian memory during the transition. Tiptoeing around the family and the civil service means that these two institutions retain the upper hand to define the past, present and future. Those born into powerlessness rest their fate with the state; to others the state is a means of ascent as well.

Victims of and victimized by the incomplete fall of communism, worrying whether "everybody else is doing it", households, managements, mayors and director generals do not put everything into the perspective of the "prisoner's dilemma". They also do things on their own. It is out of accumulated trust in their own capacities that a growing economic and cultural capital is to return trust in government. Trust is no exception, however, commodified by the advancing knowledge society, trust comes late to some institutions.

Apocalypse once, apocalypse twice

Western Europe's apocalypse of 1945 lasted for 15 years. Eastern Europe's apocalypse of 1989 was followed by another: the globalization of infrastructure. East-Central Europe, unlike Western Europe after 1945, cannot remain with one foot planted in old technology, the other in a national market, and its mind in America.

After 1945, for 15 years of implementing a *planned* economy condoned by American foreign policy (Marshall aid), accompanied by American popular culture, Western Europe not only drew on technology and capital from the US, American individualism was embraced as a way of life. Disrespectful of *la différence*, of the values (not the institutions) of the labor movement, even the working-class indulged in consumerism and social mobility. The accompanying inequalities did not cause alarm. For policies of redistribution the state eyed stationary sources of revenues. The assets of the emerging middle class – its skills, places of work and purchasing power – were going nowhere. Behind trade barriers and national manufacturing standards, West European industry produced supplies for the domestic infra-structure and goods for the domestic consumers.

Coupled with the dismantling of the state, East-Central Europe faces interactive technology, capital and markets. Where the boundaries of technology, capital and market begin and end and where politics interfere for, i.a., revenue collecting is not obvious.[6]

Transportation by land, sea, rail and air, distribution of manpower, gas, water, electricity, mail, telecommunication, airwaves, liquor, tobacco and pharmaceuticals – run as national monopolies or oligopoly operations in Western Europe after 1945 and well beyond – are to be deregulated in East-Central Europe too. In addition, liberalization of public procurement and capital flow in the securities market will make the economy less governable by national means. In technological self-confidence and political disbelief, the infrastructure of the EU states is adapting to the challenge of high technology. Utilities are to be governed by market mechanisms. East-Central Europe is under similar pressure. As EBRD (1996, 5) notes, "The sheltering of infrastructure from excessive political intervention is necessary both to achieve cost-reflective tariffs and to unlock access to private finance for needed investments".

Providing half the non-farming labor force with its livelihood, the reconstruction and expansion of the West European infrastructure after 1945 empowered the legislatures and the state bureaucracies with tools of national standardization. Employment with the utilities, and private firms contracted by the utilities, offered the population in the periphery safe jobs and uniform dreams of leaving for advancement in the center. Opening for social mobility, the lower rungs of the utilities were still worlds below and apart from the higher levels. Common, however, to the infrastructure and the spirit it fostered was a solid belief in progress based on observable facts. This was the era of the techno-patriotic middle class.

National infrastructure in Western Europe distinguished itself for the symbiotic relationship between the public operator of the service and the private producer/retailer of hardware. Backed by domestic telecommunications industries, radio and television stations became state operations, enjoyed with national marks of radio cabinets and TV sets. Responding to consumer demands for this and similar new services, both the operators and the retailers set up regional branches. For each technical innovation the arena of the regional middle class expanded.

East-Central Europe would be served by the rise of an equivalent to the techno-patriotic middle class, not least in the provincial towns. Communism having wasted resources copying technology already available, ideology and anticipated disapproval from international financial regimes discourage the state from heavy-handed meddling with high technology. Approached by global market leaders, the East-Central European state is under pressure to opt for leap-frogging. Outdated switchboards are to go the same way as the Tupolevs.

Leap-frogging rules out a repeat of the process that after 1945 created the techno-patriotic middle class of Western Europe. State-of-the-art hardware and cost-efficient management cause redundancies. Soon enough only 20 percent of the manpower it once took to operate the utilities will be needed.

In the unfolding of the transition, the civil servant of East-Central Europe is unlikely to enjoy the benign attitude of society at large that the civil servant in the West experienced after 1945. Fearing the worst, not sharing the naïvety of the Marshall Plan, EBRD suggests that (1996, 6, italics mine):

> IFIs [international financial institutions] can play a very important role in generating the conditions for a more commercial infrastructure . . . (in many cases restructuring of infrastructure *is an on-off exercise for a country . . .*). IFIs can provide guidance and covenants on the right kind of pricing so that resources are allocated efficiently and *drains on the public purse are avoided*.

From post-communism to neo-communism?

Devoid of meaning in the East, "post-communism" marks the end of *socialism* in the West. Neo-communism is what remains of European historicism, of which there is still plenty enough. Carrying the torch of the Judaeo-Christian heritage that leads the chosen back to paradise, neo-communism is pan-European. Unlike its grandscale predecessor, neo-communism not only recognizes individuals as subjects. It is stoking the victimization of an ever growing number of laggards among an ever more complex flock of chosen.

Neo-communism is not monolithic. It renounces the idea of one single class as the avantgarde. Unabatedly historicist, unbending in its view that evil forces keep the people from knowing what is in their real interest, neo-communism is committed to repatriating them to the best of all worlds, only one world at a time. Neo-communism is multifaceted, far from exclusively propagated by the ex-communists of the East and left socialists of the West.

Reserved for the oppressed working class, democratic socialism/social democracy in the West drew on "scientific" recognition of its liberation project. Neo-communism subordinates *Weltanschauung* to *Weltschmertz* and drapes it in legitimate science. Socialism was the extrovert project of the proletariat. Neo-communism prods the introvert empathy of a middle class reconciled with the tax-and-spend approach of government. Issues are to be addressed by the appropriate assignment of professions, not correct class analysis.

Neo-communism is cultivated by a middle class who refers to the public sphere as a "discourse democracy". Indeed, problems "that are more common than one thinks" are introspectively discursive. They are discussed and accidentally dealt with since, unlike political parties, "one" is neither a public, acting or accountable entity.

Under the hegemony of the open society, or the mood of progress after 1945 in the West, *Weltschmertz* was steamrolled either way, by the right as well as the left. Commanding potent institutions to put the entrepreneurship of the middle class of shamelessness on to constructive paths, social engineering did not impede economic growth. Social engineering gave households, firms and governments the incentive and confidence to, on their own, in pace and in peace, take one and one step only beyond their present position.

Legal regulation of public assistance overdue, public policies are needed to address social problems. A complex issue, the parliaments of East-Central Europe, unlike those in the West during the hectic years of reconstruction, cannot count on anti-communism to check political disorder and socialist parties to close ranks to defend progrowth legislation in return for improved social provisions to the working class (Sassoon 1996, ch. 6). In the industrial society the working class and its party took a socio-economic view of opportunity hampered by inequality. In the knowledge society, the middle class and its representatives take a therapeutic view of risk and inequality. Stirred by social alarmism, of all people the one-dimensionally represented – cohorts such as pensioners and nonowners of employment depending on entitlements – are expected not to lose their nerve and fall out of pace with the rest.

East-Central Europe presents neo-communism with a unique setting. Parliament substituting the old social security net for a new charter of rights, such a charter cannot be defined in the proximity of the virtue of an average middle class, or as a charter acknowledging one oppressed and chosen working class. Having failed to liberate the wretched and down-trodden, societies in transition from communism cannot form a consensus on one community being more oppressed than any other. Faced with victimization the distribution of social provisions will reflect deliberations conditioned by input from professional experts.

Parliaments backtracking to postpone reforms, ". . . the pace of structural change is now slower than it was in the first half of the 1990s" (EBRD 1996, 2). Misallocating, housing and household tariffs on utilities and transportation are still subsidized beyond cost-recovering. Mass unemployment, to shock therapy a sign of cleansing for the coming of knowledge-based production, has not afflicted the region. Stalled by mobilization of the residuals of class-based representation, this is a gender-biased ideology that pushes female labor force participation down. The fate of working women says something about who and what causes neo-communism is apt at defending.

Neo-communism will bring the plight of the rising middle class to bear on parliament. In its rapport with professional interests, neo-communism, East and West alike, is in its element when put to verbalize and visualize non-average middle class issues. "The misuse of public opinion research and focus groups to find out what the people think or wish and the justification of platforms, electoral promises and policies by such a simpleminded notion of responsiveness, ignores the fundamental role and duty of political leaders to influence, shape and sometimes oppose ill-conceived ideas that may well be dominant in the public" (Linz 1997b, 122).

East-Central Europe is to develop an American or European style of responding to social conflicts. Anonymous to the general public as a virtue-carrying class, the middle class of the US and EU is depositioning itself into amoral professional microcosms. Gazing at each other across gulfs of mutual incomprehension, the middle class self-generates conflicts. America resolves them by litigation invoking professional depositions. Europe addresses the conflicts through discourse among a bloated class of public employees. Chasing not only ambulances, lawyers make the American middle class see each other in court, sometimes through the full length of the judiciary system. Both sides represented to have their testimonies out in the open, professional interests, even scholarship, clash to do damage to each other too.[7] Appropriation-chasing counsellors make the European middle class fraternize with its national civil service. A sequential discourse on unequal footing, focusing on one issue/group at the time with no verdict at the end of the day, professional prestige is not put on the line. Court rulings on the inconclusive causality between context and acts of individuals are of consequence to American, not European, public policy and its professions.

Juxtaposing national mandates with those across the EU, peer-politicking among professions – "In our country, too", "Not in our trade, either" – reaps excuses to ask parliament for upgraded national standards. Mutual prejudice, publicly insinuating that European colleagues neglect their duties, serves the same purpose. If national positions are threatened – like the manning of customs and air traffic controls, deregistration of health personnel, deauthorization of brokerage firms, deidentification of cattle – each trade will court its lay public with evidence of "our" domain being unique. Going to EU summits, council and party caucus meetings, elected representatives are advised not to finger their own national trade when considering ideas of how to offset amoral professionalism. Returning home, it is not their priority to be the first to implement vague commitments to deregulate professional idiosyncrasies.

The state incapable of reconstituting a techno-patriotic middle class, the citizens of East-Central Europe may either wait for knowledge fetishism to make them owners of employment or elevate themselves to a nondescript middle class position. For inspiration on self-help they may recall the making of the American middle class. Each year as Sears mailorder catalogue reached backwoods America, families gathered around the kitchen-table to dream of prosperity, deal out the workload ahead and forget about the failure of the neighboring family. As it sits down to browse the opportunities, the embryonic middle class of East-Central Europe is rubbing shoulders with an ever more elaborate system-blame that blurs the transparency of modernism in European social thought.

True, ". . . the deterioration of the [East-Central European] economy does not necessarily translate rapidly into erosion of support for the political system" (Linz and Stepan 1996, 442). Asking if this can last in the long run is meaningless. Worse, the effect on support for democracy of the inverted correlation as it originates among the grassroots is theoretical at best. For what about families who have already respected and confirmed the relationship between public policy and the acquiring of material assets? Unless willing to share in the cynicism levelled against parties, they get no access to a public forum from which to mount gratitude to the state. For where is the arena from where the *moderately* successful families, like those in western newsreels of the 1950s, can serve as representative examples to their families, neighbors and acquaintances?

Virtual Rokkan

Adding verticality, the bold entries in Figure 11.1 emphasize the contextual settings in which parties and voters confront conflicts in the post-1989 European polity, East and West alike. The Economy–Culture and Center–Periphery axes of Rokkan's typology have been specified in, respectively, the Tax Base–*Weltschmertz* and Interactive nodes–Stationary arenas axes. Distances informing Rokkan's theory, this solution acknowledges the diffuse and elusive rather than specific and correctible permeability of the nation-state.

The economy

Served by an infrastructure that brought national standardization, the economy is less than ever before regulated by accountable domestic actors in control of specific sectors or general spendings, whether through legislation or corporatist bargaining among big interests. A knowledge-based economy differs from a class-structured one: today governments not only must ask what is taxable but what is taxable at the counterproductive risk of flight of tax base. Few tied to the territory, a growing number of sources of wealth and tax revenues can react to national legislation by threatening to relocate. To discourage actors from calculating cost-benefits of physical and fiscal border crossings, to eliminate uncertainty and retain sovereignty, European tax and fiscal policies are harmonized. However, focus groups unsettling domestic harmony by demands for more government intervention, harmonization of means causes extra distress. Invariably armed with professional affidavits to argue their cases, focus groups – amorphous successors to organized interests – are variably met with political responsiveness.

Culture

Never a domain closed to outside influence, each nation-state had its share of cultural conflicts adopted from what inspired the first grand project of the continental middle class, the revolution of 1848. The educated middle class is gone, turned into owners of employment responsible for the health, education and welfare of people. With the globalization of a middle-class culture of sorts, *Weltschmertz* screens the cultural conflicts that are all-owed to influence national electorates.

Center and periphery

Elusive in spatial as well as mental connotations, center and periphery will be even more indistinct in the knowledge society. Once seats of financial transactions, national capitals are now subject to securities exchanges and other interactive nodes. Consequently, the nation's periphery is no longer as exposed to one center. As "wired outbacks" some may transcend consecutive borders and layers of administration through the use of interactive telecommunication services. Others, which may encompass entire nations beyond the capital, even form cross-national areas of depression, decline to become stationary settings exposed to nondescript consumer culture, now and then mobilizing authentic communitarian protests against the meritocracy.

Returning to Lipset and Rokkan (1967a, 3), "We shall consider the possibility that the *parties themselves* might establish themselves as significant poles of attraction and produce their own alignments independently of the geographical, the social, and the cultural underpinnings of [contemporary] movements."

The four corner cells of the typology are pivotal. For purposes of maintaining cohesion, winning elections and forming coalitions with other parties, parties of a historicist and modernist bent are likely to move about the typology in ways that leave distinct footprints behind. Modernist parties, or the dominant faction of these parties, will maintain the idea of there being a curable authenticism that should be addressed from a worldview that banks on intersubjective data supplied by extra-professional meritocracies. Historicist parties, or the dominant faction(s) of these parties, will tend to neo-communist projects as professionally defined of and for the national middle class, conveyed as competing authenticisms that draw equally on the popular legitimacy of communitarianism.

The mid-left cells in Figure 11.1 are marginal also in the sense that they are decontextualizing. Unidimensionalized by the discourse of knowledge, nonowners of employment are losing their attraction among the parties as sources of stable electoral support. Weakened by depleting numbers and exit on part of its adversary, organized labor is marginalized as a partner to corporate coalitions. Across negotiation tables set by government labor faces corporate representation of national branches that are weakened by global conglomerates signing local deals in return for local perks. Labor's representation on the boards of utilities and public authorities is about rearguard protection in face of technological change. Labor, like other nonowners of employment, is increasingly referred to taxes and transfers as its source of livelihood. Politicized in much the same way as the peasantry was after World War II, labor will be seen fighting the state, staging confrontations wherever the discourse of power, in flesh and blood, is passing through communicative nodes.

Among contemporary institutions two will be the last to abandon the European nation-state: mass media and political parties. Compared to households, firms, organizations and authorities, they have few incentives to scout for resources outside their own country. In the final analysis, mass media and parties have no international public. In the perfectly borderless world in which citizens float around arenas only, households cross borders to enrich themselves, firms do business, organizations adopt problems and public authorities share routines how to address problems. Doing that they also get themselves into trouble. Trusting only familiar institutions to come to the rescue, if need be by engaging the media to victimize themselves, the nation-state is where to return the buck. For their part, parties ridicule themselves and embarrass their sister parties if they ask to run in the elections of foreign countries to fight credit card scams, late payments, embezzlement and bribes.

After 1945, for the elite and masses alike, Sputnik and Telstar were to expand distances. Today satellites mean different things to different people. For the nondiglot masses new technology is put to use to *implode* distances. One eye to 24-hour global TV news, national news desks are renationalizing middle-class *Weltschmertz*, "how *you* will be affected, what *we* can do to protect our . . .". No longer basking in unreflected praise, technology is serving the aesthetics also of anti-modernism, the neo-luddites as much as the neo-taylorists, the neolysenkos as much as the neo-mendelites.

No longer dwarfed by a United Nations preoccupied as mediator between the West and East, IGOs and INGOs (international government/non-government organizations) know how to find an attentive market for global issues among professional interests in Europe. Meanwhile, the OECD and similar regimes are putting out standardized guidelines for how public administration is to meet the challenges, emphasizing focus on result, value for money, devolution, flexibility, client and service orientation, etc. (Olsen 1997, 7).

As workers and entrepreneurs across Europe know, the state allows import of commodities in order to push inefficient domestic wares out of business. In contrast, ruining the OECD's analogy between politics and markets, *Weltschmertz* is an import substitute and the tax-financed market is insatiable.

Director generals pride themselves for the unique and unexpendable competence of their authority. Eager to do what the OECD recommends them to do, director generals are responding to an attentive public.

Western Europe overhauling its civil service, the middle class now relates to authorities that are less confident about what kind of civil service commends appropriations from parliament. Utilities and public authorities are to be governed by the market mechanism, some as fully privatized, some as quasi-nongovernmental institutions. For a start, all are pushed to adopt make-believe market mechanisms for internal auditing. In return, they are trusted with a mandate to define their own regulatory reach and to spot new opportunities and unknown hazards. The aggregate mass, radius and, invariably, decibel and echo of their regulatory operations increase.

What the OECD sees as a panacea against public authorities living in a world of their own, guzzling tax money, is counterproductive. Market mechanisms excuse active rent-offering on the part of the authorities. Flattened hierarchies encourage staff of lower levels to spot new tasks for the authority. Trying to find new clients to substantiate the authority's need for additional funding, to forestall criticism from politicians for not being on top of new challenges, is a drain on gross national income and, less correctible, a menace to a public agenda structured by horizontal demonology.

Implementing the OEC's public administration within the format of its member states is futile. It takes fiscal-territorial change to alter the political economy of *Weltschmertz*.

The implosion of distances leaves representative thoughts in limbo. Self-discipline alone restrains elected representatives from letting themselves be abused by opportunities to show compassion with victims of hazards that are hypercommunicative rather than worthy of public attention. Uncertain what empathy pays off into, MPs reach out to one too many rather than one too few of the focus groups asking for understanding. Representatives take risks not to hear out the director general behind the alleged hazard, the clients and the growing community of fellow-suffering near and dear.

In a context stripped of its demonology, with a state apparatus inherited from the epoch of social engineering/communist planning, contempt of politicians is conditional. Confronted with consecutive disclosure of focus groups rather than – like elections are meant to be, like collegiate director generals are meant to observe – a line-up for the offering of graded grace based on what the community can afford, they become accessory to political implosion. Extending empathy to victims of hazards disclosed by professions and the mass media, the more "unknown human sides" MPs are showing, the more they dissociate themselves from what supposedly got them elected, the platform of the party as meant to represent the context of the party's position in the horizontal demonology.

This is not necessarily contempt for democracy. To represent, to acknowledge one face at a time and offer it compassion, is legitimate. To represent two faces at the same time, however, is tantamount to ideology and will eventually force a vote. MPs honoring the party's *Weltanschauung* sink into oblivion. Forgetting the platform, ignoring economics, abandoning the floor of parliament, MPs who roam the foyer dealing in cases make it difficult for their parties to "produce their own alignments independently of the . . . underpinnings of [contemporary] movements".

Conclusion

Distance, spatial as well as mental, is central to Rokkan's understanding of things political. Hence, "proximity" is a keyword to the transmutation of his conceptual map to East-Central Europe.

Rokkan introduced his conceptual map in the proximity of American hegemony. Social science, political leadership, and the West European middle class itself subscribed to the rebuilding of democracy near American ideals. The USSR and Eastern Europe serving as the proxy for the "worker state", even the West European labor movement remobilized the working-class in proximity to the way of life represented by the American middle class. Also the reception of Rokkan's conceptual map, how his peers came to recognize *PSVA* as a seminal work, was influenced by proximity. Ideologically, the conceptual map was a relief to scholars not willing to equate their interest in structuralism with Marxism. Culturally, the map allowed European scholarship, battered by American supremacy, to reclaim its own territory without relapsing into accounts of European politics that drew on murky notions about "national characters".

In whose proximity is East-Central Europe to evolve the horizontally selfsupporting contexts that reinforce each other so as to mitigate turbulence in the numeric channel of democracy? East-Central Europe has no post-war America against which to model its middle class. The working class is dispersed. So is the USSR. Historicism, however, is still alive and well in Europe. Yet, the political left has no project. Victimization, left at the mercy of middle-class professionalism, serves as a proxy for mobilization.

Figure 11.1 is about Europe's most recent search of boundaries in time and space out of which, referring exceptions to "any other business", an agora opens for averages to become common wisdom, debated as common concern, and ultimately put to the vote by citizens. In contrast to the agro-industrial society's intersubjective facts of social engineering and percentages of political representation, a cacophony of public and not so public variance is allowed to be orchestrated to the tune of quasi-scientific professionalism. The statistical records behind Rokkan's conceptual map of Europe are blurred. Consequently, the public status of the citizenry is depreciated into the flashing of one-dimensional individuals, disenfranchizing rather than enfranchizing the objects of public policy, debasing rather than empowering the acting subjects of public policy.

Free to share commitments in the knowledge society, for each time political parties compromise to let themselves and their representatives be presented *de novo* to an audience afflicted by selective amnesia, little is added to and a bit taken away from the community's reserves of accumulated memory. In the multi-party Social/Christian Democracy, classes and congregations were selfsufficient with visions of tomorrow. In a knowledge democracy, however, professions take more than an academic interest in scholarship. Interfoiling their catches with national and other bias, sharing them with national media, political parties battle professions instead of themselves for the agenda-setting momentum. Responding as collective institutions, parties resort to what, by definition, appears to be hasty, unpredictable and ineffective answers. It remains for other institutions, the household in general and some households in particular, to join in the bashing of parties as not to be recognized any more or, as in East-Central Europe, recognize them *de novo* time after time.

It is the voter who either does not recognize herself in her new outfit as owner or non-owner of employment or recognizes her fellow numbers too well. It is these resources that decide if votes, other than for the redrawing of boundaries by accession, secession, devolution and currency reforms, again are to count.

After 1989, European party systems and voter alignments are to be distinguished by the viability of horizontal and *vertical* demonology (cf., Figure 11.1) as conditioned by the configuration of variance in the emerging knowledge society:

(1) Of nodal status, unmaking the post-war standardization that Rokkan saw as a nonvariable effect of infrastructural expansion, new technology is opening for mergers and acquisitions of operations heretofore off limits on a transnational scale. Met with political downscaling, this allows the market mechanism to govern what remains of national utilities too. Supervisory public authorities exempt from a brush of the market invent internal ones for themselves.

(2) Nursing a harmonized tax base, states are marginalized as national forums and channels for the exercise of social engineering, responsiveness in accordance with fair distribution of scarce assets and the incorporation of new modernist representation. The public agora as once regulated by a techno-patriotic middle class is compartmentalized into insular forums of transnational professionalism.

(3) In the Manichean void after 1989, as the suspended illusion of the West waits to merge with the suspended present of the East, democracy is discoursive at the premise of a professionalism supposedly based on pure science. However, as inseparable from the national sentiments embedded in the existing institutions as once pure ideologies were, this professionalism is intermittently reinforced and split by drawing on horizontal bonds of loyalty.

(4) The agenda imploding, neo-modernism is referred to find its way about the political economy of *Weltschmertz*.

Notes

1 For theoretical and empirical contributions on the party systems of East-Central Europe, see Kitschelt and Rose, respectively, in *Party Politics*, vol. 1., no. 4, 1995. For a macro- level account of the elections, see Berglund and Aarebrot 1997, ch. 5.

2 Evidence of how "European authenticism" interferes with knowledge-based rationalism is provided by the European business community. Put to rank Europe's 20 best companies in 1995, the list contained: 9 companies whose stock had underperformed the stock exchange index of their respective home country; 7 of the 17 nonfinance companies included were worth less than the capital invested in the companies. *The Economist*, Nov. 23, 1996.

3 Holding the notion of the citizen and nation-state for barren, individuals and communities are said to be free to pursue their objectives in a world whose distances, if not altogether dead, are to be observed only "until further notice". Indeed, states have been known to serve their subjects, and those of other states, with very short and cruel notices. See Cairncross, 1997 and Heelas *et al.* 1996.

4 This family is not likely to take part in representative democracy, let alone enrich discourse democracy. Instead the family is soon targeted for empowerment programs with an ambivalent view of the power of electoral politics. If only for the record, this family serves as a case in point for the introduction of compulsory voting (cf., Lijphart 1997, 10). Compulsory voting prevents the causality of participation to become absurdly reversed by the so-called "common wisdom" of ordinary people. Compulsory voting severs the links of exclusion excused by the community as a mark of incurable underclass. But grandma's vote for the Communist party does not "explain" why the son is unemployed. Compulsory voting also dismisses popularly held myths that abstention "explains" entrepreneurship.

5 "The Fund's [IMF] economists estimate that Poland could grow by 5.7% a year if it maintained its current educational levels *and halved the share of government consumption* [italics mine] as a percentage of its GDP; it would then reach the poorer EU countries' average income level in 18 years' time." *The Economist*, Oct. 26, 1996.

6 Of no explanatory value, a counterfactual note puts this into perspective. If the 1989 revolution of Eastern Europe had occurred in the wake of the Hungarian uprising in 1956, communism would have gone down as an episode. If the Prague Spring of 1968 had ended in the fall of communism, East-Central Europe would have gone about pragmatically privatizing handicraft, retail and the service sector. If Solidarity (John Paul II and President Reagan) had accomplished its goal in 1980, East-Central Europe would not have felt the pressure to commercialize the infrastructure on top of privatizing everything else.

7 This format of eyeball to eyeball confrontation between two and only two parties has a legislative counterpart in the Westminster parliamentary system. Consequently, a well entrenched two-party system – drawing attention to parliament, stemming notions that the alternative to the cabinet's policy will bring in the best of one world – is only superficially occupied with questions of whether voters have confidence and trust in the parties.

12 Party systems and voter alignments in the new democracies of the Third World

Vicky Randall

The question this chapter addresses is the relevance and utility of the Lipset/Rokkan party-cleavage thesis for the analysis of party politics in the Third World. Given the vast potential scope of this subject, I have had to limit discussion to some central issues, inevitably thereby failing to do justice to the theoretical complexity of the party/cleavage model or to the intricacies of specific Third World cases. I begin by briefly addressing some significant definitional problems and conceptual ambiguities within the question as posed. I then consider some of the other difficulties in the way of an answer. The third and longest section examines some of the more obvious respects in which the experience of Third World countries would seem to depart from the pattern of party system formation described by Lipset and Rokkan, and suggests that underlying these differences have been more fundamental differences in terms of the pattern of national economic and political development and of system autonomy. In conclusion, however, I indicate ways in which the model may nonetheless have something valuable to contribute to our understanding of party politics in the Third World.

Examining the question

While a substantial literature has amassed over the years concerned with political parties in the Third World, rarely has this directly engaged with the Lipset–Rokkan paradigm (for exceptions, see Cammack 1994; Dix 1989; Chibber and Petrocik 1990; Scully 1995; Jaung 1995). This seems, moreover, to be almost as true of the more recent "democratization" literature as of the earlier generation. There are, of course, inferences to be drawn for the Third World from applications of the model to other "marginal" cases (on Eastern Europe, see for instance Evans and Whitefield 1993; Budge and Newton 1997). But in the main, attempting to answer the question under discussion requires some fairly elementary path-clearing before more sophisticated analysis is possible.

Neither element of the relationship to be analysed here is free from ambiguity. Taking first the subject or region to which the Lipset–Rokkan model is to be applied, an initial eyebrow has to be raised at any term like "new democracies". This begs too many questions about the nature of the democratization process that has been observed from the late 1970s: is it really about democracy, will it endure? Rather than drawing a line round some hypothetical set of newly democratic countries, it seems preferable to consider all Third World countries, and not limit discussion to the last twenty or so years, while recognizing that the Lipset–Rokkan argument is likely to have most relevance for those which have come closest to liberal-democratic ground rules for party competition. I shall however consider the case of the "new democracies" as part of this wider field.

But that brings us to the next thorny issue, which is the meaning and indeed the plausibility of the concept of a Third World. While in the first two to three decades following World War II, this concept was useful and did correspond to a meaningful sub-category of societies as demarcated on a number of important criteria (post-colonial, predominantly agricultural, to varying degrees economically dependent and so forth), it has become increasingly difficult to defend. Embracing by convention well over a hundred states, which are enormously divergent in terms of culture, history and economic indicators, its coherence has been further undermined by the emergence of the NICs, ending of the Cold War and break up of much of the Second World and by economic and cultural processes of globalization. I shall not then claim that the Third World is, or remains, a coherent entity, although, in seeking to explain features of its party politics, I shall refer to aspects of their "structural" context which though not unique to the Third World, nor evenly spread amongst its constituent societies, have in recent history tended to be concentrated there. These concern the timing and sequence of "development" and the comparative lack of system autonomy. Otherwise I shall simply take Third World to be shorthand for Central and Latin America, the Caribbean, the Middle East, Africa and Asia, those vast regions that have been so peripheral to the Western viewpoint and to Western political science.

The other element in the question is, of course, the Lipset–Rokkan model itself. Issues arise here first about the character and scope of the model's claims, and second, partly related to these, about the relevant direction of empirical inquiry and appropriate forms of empirical evidence or confirmation. The Lipset–Rokkan thesis, as originally set out in the Introduction to the 1967 volume, provides a model of party formation based on the experience of western European democracies. It presents party systems as the precipitate of three intertwined processes of national integration, industrialization and democratization. It is concerned firstly with the nature of the internal social cleavages which emerged as a consequence of the processes of national unification and integration, and of industrialization. It is secondly concerned with the way in which these cleavages were politically incorporated during the process of political liberalization and democratization and became "frozen" or institutionalized in the resultant party system.

Lipset and Rokkan identify a range of social cleavages which have been salient. More tentatively, and while recognizing also the extent of variation within individual countries, they suggest a tendency for these cleavages to emerge not simultaneously but in a sequence related to the processes of political and economic development. There are first those cleavages associated with the process of nation-building or what the authors term the "National Revolution". A cleavage strongly evident in the initial phase of nation-building may be territorially based, reflecting primarily opposition of individual local rulers to central authority. However Lipset and Rokkan suggest that "Purely territorial oppositions rarely survive extension of the suffrage" (1967a, 12). Their place tends to be taken by broader social divisions that are at the same time territorial and cultural: the cleavages between centre and periphery and between church and state. This first set of cleavages interacts with a second which reflects the processes of industrialization: that is, the two "functional" cleavages: land–industry and employer–worker. Though noting many exceptions, the authors suggest that polarization on these functional or economic lines tends to occur later and is of course constrained and shaped by persistent cultural cleavages, but that in the long run it comes to predominate. Moreover, while cleavages associated with territorial and cultural conflict helped to differentiate European party systems, the employer–worker cleavage has tended to bring them close together.

In accounting for the emergence of party systems, Lipset and Rokkan invoke the notion of successive "thresholds" or stages in the lowering of barriers to political participation. These are presented as hurdles facing an emerging political movement, but also serve to indicate types of party system. The legitimation threshold refers to the point where the movement is accepted as a legitimate political actor, while the incorporation threshold concerns the extent to which movement supporters are enfranchised. The representation threshold refers to the strategies a movement must pursue in order to gain political representation, in particular whether they need to enter an alliance or can effectively compete alone; this is strongly related to the electoral system. The threshold of majority power describes the extent to which numerical dominance brings systemic advantage or is constrained by checks and balances and thus links the party system to wider constitutional questions. Lipset and Rokkan argue that, in Europe, the translation of social cleavages into an (embryonic) party system tended to occur while the barriers to participation were still relatively high, that is when the principle of legitimate opposition had been conceded and limited voting rights introduced, but before the era of mass suffrage. The crucial sentence is "The decisive sequence of party formation took place at the early stage of competitive politics, in some cases well before the extension of the franchise, in other cases on the very eve of the rush to mobilization of the finally enfranchised masses" (1967a, 34).

In what is, to some extent, the third step of their argument, Lipset and Rokkan maintain that the parties formed in this crucible period were able to persist despite subsequent social change, basically because they got in first. Though the precise reasons for this persistence are difficult to know, they note that it was those parties which were able to establish mass organizations and entrench themselves in local government before the final push to mass mobilization, which tended to survive, by structuring and narrowing the "mobilization market" and making it difficult for newcomers to break in. The corollary of this, incidentally and of potential relevance to the Third World, is that "'post-democratic' party systems proved markedly more fragile and open to newcomers in the countries where the privileged strata had relied on their local power resources rather than on nationwide mass organizations in their efforts of mobilization" (1967a, 51). There is perhaps implied a fourth step in the argument – or certainly some of those who have sought to apply the model seem to have assumed so. This is that not only will "pre-democratic" mass parties survive and pre-empt the structuring of the mobilization market, but that these parties, whatever their original social constituency and as socio-economic class grows in importance as a basis of social cleavage, will increasingly come to represent broad sets of interests ranged on a Left–Right continuum.

This is a highly specified model that refers to a particular historical and cultural conjuncture. At the level of general approach, then, we have to ask, how is it to be extended to other contexts? Certainly in the case of the Third World, it may often not be either legitimate or useful to transfer specific categories of cleavage and threshold from one context to another – Sartori's famous travelling problem. At what level of specification should the model be applied? Related to this what exactly is the core or kernel of the model? Which elements are most essential? How can we judge whether it is confirmed by experience in the Third World or not?

A further, more specific, issue concerns the nature of the relationship between a given cleavage and the parties it is associated with. There are a number of points here. The first has to do with what counts as a cleavage. Are we concerned primarily with social divisions, or differences, which are "real" in so far as they are associated with conflicts of interests implied by the structuring of society, but which need not be consciously recognized or explicitly or politically articulated? Much of the time Lipset and Rokkan talk about cleavages in this sense. Then the implication is that such cleavages in some manner produce political parties. But this is a very inadequate conceptualization of a complex process, involving for instance mediation by politicians with their own agenda. Or in the words of one critic, the notion of social groups "giving birth" to parties "is as implausible empirically as it is metaphorically unnatural" (cited by Ozbudun 1987, 398).

At other times, however, Lipset and Rokkan talk about "oppositions" that have been to an extent constructed by parties. They consider the possibility that the *parties themselves* [authors' emphasis] might establish themselves as significant poles of attraction and produce their own alignments independently of the geographical, the social and the cultural underpinnings of the movements.

(1967a, 3)

It may well be that this second conception of cleavage has much relevance for political parties in the Third World. But from the point of view of the overall logic and operationalization of the Lipset–Rokkan model it is also much more problematic than the simple social cleavage notion. It is easy enough to deduce social cleavages within a society from an analysis of its structure, so that the existence of these cleavages can be established independently from the nature of political parties, and the relationship between cleavages and parties subsequently explored. But where cleavages are defined as those oppositions set up by parties themselves, then the thesis that parties are based upon cleavages is in danger of becoming a self-confirming tautology.

Second, even supposing we stick with the simple social cleavage conception, in what sense do parties "represent" the groups delineated by the cleavage? In terms of historical origins, mobilization is likely to entail some element of elite instigation and organization. Need this elite be "of" the social category in question or simply appeal to it? In the longer term, when seeking to identify parties with particular social groups, are we primarily concerned with patterns of support, and if so what proportion of a putative constituency would we expect to support its "natural" party? Or is it more a question of how parties and their leaders project themselves, their image, their pledges, their policies? Related to this conceptual issue is the question of *how* one would set about determining whether a party system reflected social cleavages, past or present. Supposing it were readily available, what kind(s) of information should we be looking for: measures of the strength of party identification, analysis of voting behaviour, public perceptions of party identity, social characteristics of active supporters or of party elites, party platforms?

Putting the question in a Third World context

The model as originally elaborated was explicitly based upon western European experience. No claim was made that it would be directly relevant to the Third World. But if we do seek to apply it two immediate and obvious practical problems present themselves. The first is the number and heterogeneity of Third World countries. Related to this, experience of party politics, of parties and party systems have varied enormously both between and within Third World regions. It might appear that parts of Latin America come closest to the sequence of party development specified by Lipset and Rokkan (Lipset 1964) with Chile the prime candidate (Scully 1995), but that continent also includes Mexico's ruling PRI and the traditionally weak, state-based political parties of Brazil. The Middle East and tropical Africa seem to stand at the greatest remove, but how does the Lipset–Rokkan trajectory encompass the party history of Pakistan, Thailand or Indonesia?

The second problem is that generally, and in comparison with western societies, not only have there been few applications attempted of the Lipset–Rokkan model as already noted, but collection and analysis of relevant data are much less advanced. This is not true everywhere. In India ecological analysis has a long and distinguished pedigree (see Brass 1985), while sample survey techniques have enormously improved in sophistication and reliability in recent years. Mainwaring and Scully in the introduction to their recent edited volume on party systems in Latin America (1995), cite a range of survey data while noting that its availability varies between countries and that it is insufficiently standardized in form to allow cross-national comparison. Other countries where relevant survey data are available include Jamaica (Payne 1988) and South Korea (Shin 1995). A valuable indicator of the social constituency political parties seek to appeal to might be party programmes and manifestos. By no means all Third World parties produce such documents. For instance when the Democrat Party released a 32-page booklet outlining its policies in the Thai General Election of 1995 it was the "first time in Thai political history" that a party had given details of its programme (Murray 1996, 366). But in so far as such programmes are produced it would be valuable to have some equivalent of the Manifesto Research Group (Budge 1994) to collect and systematically compare them. Going back to the point raised earlier about what constitutes evidence, we must conclude that not only is it unclear what kinds of data would best indicate a party-cleavage relationship but it is unlikely that the data, without further primary research, will be readily available.

Exporting Lipset–Rokkan: problems of comparability

Following these preliminary remarks, I shall examine some of the more obvious reasons that might be put forward for querying the relevance or usefulness of the Lipset–Rokkan model for understanding the emergence of party systems in the Third World. I shall begin by considering some immediate points of contrast between European party systems and cleavages on the one hand and those in the Third World on the other, together with possible ways in which these might be reconciled with the Lipset–Rokkan model. But I shall then suggest that these contrasts are symptomatic of more basic underlying differences in the context of cleavage and party formation. These differences are in the first instance to do with the timing and sequencing of the development process but more fundamentally concern system autonomy, the extent to which developments within individual Third World states have been determined by external influences.

Cleavages and party formation

An initial objection to the application of the cleavage/party system model to the Third World might be the lack of equivalence between the social cleavages identified in the model and the bases of cleavage in many Third World societies. Setting aside problems of the cultural variability of the content of these categories, it is true that the principal axes of cleavage identified in the model – regionalism, ethnicity, religion, urban versus rural interests and class, whether in terms of landlords and peasants or employers and workers – can all be discovered at work in differing Third World contexts. There are doubtless arguments that could be made about the uniqueness of *caste* as a unit of social differentiation in India and Sri Lanka. Perhaps the most difficult of these concepts to translate is religion. In the original model, this is intimately identified with Christianity, with its distinctive role both in the early history of European cultural integration and in later processes of nation-building. The question is whether other religions, such as Islam, Hinduism and Buddhism can be regarded as filling the same logical space, within the emerging political system.

But to the extent that the model's cleavages do apply, their relative importance and sequencing, and implications for party formation, do not necessarily conform to the model's expectations, in at least two ways. In many regions, the "functional" cleavages around economic interests, still appear to play a minor role as a basis of party formation or identification, many decades on from the original transition to political "mass mobilization". Thus in Africa, Bienen and Herbst argue that "class still is not a salient cleavage in most African countries, the ideological organisation of parties and associations is highly fluid, and the major issues are still not well-defined"(1996, 26). Rather ethnicity and regionalism have persisted as the most fundamental cleavages within African societies, despite the supposed attempts of single-party rule (discussed further below) to overcome them: "recent political developments have revealed that almost three decades of single-party autocratic rule had failed to engender a real sense of nationhood that transcended ethnic and regional identities" (Takougang 1996, 52–3; see also Fox 1996; Kaspin 1995; van Cranenburgh 1996).

This is one respect in which differences within the Third World are most noticeable, with the countries of Latin America most closely approximating the European model. To varying degrees within that continent, the enormous reduction of the indigenous Indian population and installation of Catholicism as the official and near-universal religion over three centuries ago helped to marginalize ethnic and religiously based conflict, while industrialization from the late nineteenth century contributed to the increasing salience of functional or economically based divisions. In this context, the country which is sometimes cited as best conforming to the Lipset–Rokkan specification is Chile (Scully 1995). The party system originally crystallized in the nineteenth century around the conflict between clerical and secular forces, forming liberal and conservative tendencies; then in the early twentieth century and with the emergence of urban class conflict the system incorporated parties based on the working class and finally in the 1950s, political mobilization of the peasantry was associated with the formation of a new centre party. Not only did the character and ordering of basic social cleavages resemble those of many European countries, but, Scully argues, at each of these three critical junctures, fundamental social cleavages were translated into concrete party alternatives.

This last observation relates to the second point of difference. Even if the cleavages to be found in western Europe can also be found in the Third World, they have not necessarily or usually had the same relationship to party formation. For instance, South Korea, like a number of Latin American countries, is ethnically and culturally relatively homogenous and it is more industrialized than most of them. The beginnings of a process of democratic transition can be dated back to 1987 and yet the emergence of a sizeable industrial labour force – nonfarm wage workers numbered 4.1 million by 1975 and 7.7 million by 1985 – has had minimal impact to date on the party system. One important contributory factor here has been nationalism, which with North Korea on its border has taken the form of virulent anti-communism. Labour-based politics has been suspect and independent trade unions only began to assert themselves at the end of the 1980s. Consequently no significant labour-based party has been able to emerge (Berry and Kiely 1993; Jaung 1995).

A different kind of example of apparent lack of correspondence between patterns of social cleavage and party formation is provided by Jamaica's party system. Jamaica's two party system has its roots in the period preceding mass suffrage in 1944. Manley's PNP (People's National Party) was founded in 1938 and Bustamente's JLP (Jamaica Labour Party) in 1942. These two parties have persisted and alternated in power ever since. Yet during that time, as Payne (1988) describes, their respective ideologies and bases of support, have changed significantly more than once. In the early years the PNP was Left-tending and appealed in particular to the brown middle-class while the JLP was more populist and appealed simultaneously to blacks and to a section of the white upper class. These differences diminished over the 1950s and 1960s, to the point where the leadership of the JLP came itself increasingly to be dominated by brown middle-class professionals. In the 1970s increased ideological polarization, associated with conflicting diagnoses of Jamaica's economic crisis, accompanied a further shift; the PNP becoming "very much the party of the lower social classes", following an explicit appeal to the black vote, while the JLP emerged as "the party of the upper end of the social system" (Payne 1988, 146). Seeking to explain this combination of party persistence and seeming rootlessness, Payne suggests that the very cross-cutting nature of social cleavages could furnish part of the answer: "Jamaicans generally possess a number of politically relevant affiliations (class, race, generation, party) which pull them in conflicting directions and reduce the zero-sum character of political conflict" (1988, 153). But for him the main explanatory weight must be carried by more purely political factors, and most notably the legacy of British colonial rule. While, then, Jamaica's party system may seem to satisfy the Lipset–Rokkan specifications to the extent that it has, relatively, mass parties, which were established before mass suffrage, and which, very roughly speaking, have tended to divide consistently on a Left–Right wing axis, there has been no corresponding consistency in the parties' *social* base. Rather than being the product of social cleavages, then, it might be more accurate to say that the party system has created and institutionalized political cleavages in society. This, of course, is compatible with the alternative possibility that Lipset and Rokkan contemplate (see above) that political parties may themselves construct "their own alignments".

The most striking departure from the Lipset–Rokkan pattern of party–social cleavage alignment can be found in India and a succession of African states, where at the critical period of party formation, prior to and at the point of gaining political independence, social cleavages were subordinated or incorporated within a single "national" basis of mobilization. Nationalist movements did not necessarily repress or deny sub-national cleavages, in fact they might well appeal to them as a means of drawing groups in. In time, moreover, many "national" parties were perceived to be less national in character than claimed: parties like the CPDM (Cameroon People's Democratic Movement) and Banda's MCP (Malawi Congress Party) were seen to favour specific regions and linguistic groups in for instance language policy, the elaboration of national symbols and the location of development projects, which is one reason why such divisions have resurfaced with democratization (Takougang 1996; Kaspin 1995). Nonetheless, to the extent that parties were national in the scope of their appeal, they were premised upon the primacy of a very different and transcending kind of cleavage, between that society and the colonial power. This form of cleavage really does not feature directly in the Lipset–Rokkan conspectus (though, for instance, Lipset (1964) sees national independence as one of the mobilizing causes of the Finnish Social Democratic Party at the end of the nineteenth century).

One possible way of reconciling nationalism with the Lipset–Rokkan model is offered by Sinnott's discussion (1984) of the Irish case. He suggests that Irish nationalism, which so crucially marked the formation of the party system in the Irish Republic, could be understood as part of a centre–periphery conflict relating to the original United Kingdom, that comprised both Britain and Ireland. The 1918 Irish election followed the single largest extension of the franchise in Irish history. The overriding issue was secession, and as the party urging it, Sinn Fein won a dramatic victory. But the impetus of nationalist sentiment did not die away immediately following secession in 1922. "Certainly secession had an impact. Far from signalling an entirely new beginning for the party system and electoral alignments, however, its implications for the parties and the electorate can only be understood in the light of the prior mobilization of the periphery into a consensus against the centre" (Sinnott 1984, 302). That is, the centre–periphery cleavage within a former larger political unit, by constituting the basis of political mobilization in the peripheral region, carried over into the process of initial party formation in the newly sovereign state formed in that region. While such an argument is possible, is it helpful? Sinnott's motivation in making this claim for Ireland is to resist suggestions that Ireland deviates from a common European pattern. In the case of the Third World it would make more sense to relate the salience of this national cleavage to the observations about system autonomy made below.

What kind of parties?

The Lipset–Rokkan model tends to assume that the parties that emerge with universal suffrage will be or will soon become "mass" parties. If they do not become mass parties they stand much less chance of long-term survival. This assumption is implicit in the model's account of the way in which parties formed just before or during the first phase of mass mobilization have been able to structure the electorate over the longer term. This raises the question of what is meant by a mass party. Duverger's original typology, which distinguished between mass and elite (caucus or cadres) parties, turned above all on the question of membership. Moreover what mattered most was not the size of party membership but the importance of the members to the functioning of the party and of their contributions to its finances. Duverger's conceptualization has been criticized and to an extent superseded, although it should in fairness be noted that he acknowledged himself that the distinction between cadres and mass party "though clear in theory, is not always easy to make in practice" (1956, 64), citing the cases of indirect party membership, through for instance trade unions, and of the limited demands made on members in the American political parties. For these he even coined the term "semi-mass parties". It is also increasingly recognized that in Western democracies, there are and have been "no fully-fledged mass parties" (Katz and Mair 1996, 532). Even so it is likely that our commonsense understanding of what constitutes a mass party – involving centralized organization effectively linking leadership to branches or localities, mass membership and extensive, cohesive and stable party support – bears little relation to most Third World parties of any era. The nationalist movement/party that emerged in many Third World countries on the eve of political independence often had "mass" dimensions. Yet Chodak (1964) who incidentally maintained that the elite–mass distinction was less than illuminating when applied to tropical Africa, suggested that in that region the mass party was more like a "congress", or movement including families, tribal unions, literary societies, trade unions and even smaller regional parties. After independence, in such countries as Ghana, Mali and Ivory Coast, the dominant party became increasingly powerful, giving rise to analogies drawn with the "totalitarian" communist parties of the Soviet world. But subsequent events and political analysis revealed that the power of this dominant party had been to a large extent a function of the weakness of other political contenders and institutions. The limitations both of its organizational capacity and of its popular support became apparent (Bienen 1970; Zolberg 1966).

In so far as individual Third World parties have approximated mass parties, it is still necessary to ask on what basis mass allegiance has been secured. In many, if not most, Third World countries, clientelism pervades party relationships, whether between party leaders and the state, between leaders and followers or between the party and the people at large. It is arguable that party politics could not have developed at all in post-colonial societies without such patronage-based linkages, and indeed they have also featured prominently in the gestation of modern political parties in the Western world. Elements of clientelism are recognized to persist in the United States, Japan and Italy, and no party system is likely to be entirely free of them. But if a party relies heavily for support on clientelistic chains and the distribution of patronage, what does this imply for its ability to articulate the perceptions or interests of a given social constituency?

It is not just that access to sources of patronage gives the victor party an enormous if not insuperable advantage and by the same token diminishes the possibility of fair competition between parties. Mobilization through clientelistic chains reaching out from centre to periphery often serves to cut across cleavages, especially "horizontal" cleavages of class or caste. This has been illustrated for instance in Jayanntha's study (1992) of electoral behaviour in Sri Lanka, in general elections from 1947 to 1982. He examines three constituencies, two rural and one urban and shows how in the rural constituencies, clientelism persisted, that is, dominant families continued to mobilize voters, though their bases of patronage changed over time from private means to privileged access to state resources. In one constituency, both patrons and voters came from the same predominant Goigama caste, in the other the patrons came from a numerically minor upper caste, but in both cases, Jayanntha shows, the actual basis of mobilization was not caste but clientelism. To the extent that clientelism operates in this way, it would seem to undermine the kind of party–cleavage relationship that Lipset and Rokkan have highlighted.

Amongst the European country studies included in Lipset and Rokkan's pioneering volume (1967), Dogan's discussion of Italy and, more briefly, Linz's discussion of Spain, touch on the question of clientelism but in neither case is it really made clear how this might affect the relevance of the party–cleavage model, although there is an implicit recognition that it is problematic. Thus to his typology of workers and their voting patterns,

Dogan appends "the *clientele* worker", still to be found in parts of the Mezziogiorno, observing

> Unemployment being chronic, the worker without skills considers himself rather privileged compared to the unemployed, when after a long wait and thanks to recommendations, he finally finds a job. On election day, he will give his support quite naturally to his protector, who is himself only a link in a *clientele* chain.

(1967, 177–8)

Perhaps the main, and largely justifiable assumption in both these case studies is that clientelism is declining to the point where it will no longer have a substantial bearing on overall voting behaviour.

Clearly Third World party systems have themselves varied as regards both the scale of clientelistic practices and the degree to which they operate unmodified by other bases of party identification and support. In India, the persistence of (relatively) competitive party politics may itself have been a factor in the increasing "democratization" of caste, or as the Rudolphs (1967) have expressed it the transition from *vertical* caste mobilization to *horizontal* mobilization of lower castes on their own behalf. In so far as clientelism has been associated with social and economic inequality, it might also be anticipated that in more "developed" countries its importance would diminish (a point I return to in the following section). Further recent developments, the trend towards economic and political liberalization in combination, might be expected to place additional constraints on the opportunity and, in some respects, the demand for patronage-based party politics. This is for instance argued by Ferdinand (1994), with particular reference to recent changes in Mexico and Taiwan. One of the factors precipitating the collapse of authoritarian rule in some tropical African countries – Benin would be an extreme example – has been exhaustion of government coffers. The resources for patronage were simply running out. At the same time policies associated with structural adjustment, and economic liberalization more generally, involving cutbacks in public employment and expenditure, removal of subsidies, dismantling of state-run marketing boards and so forth, have further reduced the resources for newly elected governments to deploy.

To what extent have clientelistic patterns persisted through the democratizing wave of the last two decades? While it is difficult to give any kind of authoritative and final answer at this stage, clearly clientelism has not disappeared and in many countries continues to be a salient feature of party politics. In the Middle East, democratizing moves are still in their infancy. Pool (1994) however comments that many authoritarian governments in that region have responded cautiously to international pressures for economic liberalization measures, such as reductions in food subsidies and privatization, because their social consequences could spark political unrest. In some of these states, at least,

> the state still remains responsible for a considerable amount of
> economic activity and while economic liberalisation remains partial,
> government institutions, particularly local government in the rural
> areas, are able to 'manage' elections . . .
>
> (1994, 211)

In tropical Africa, similar accounts of the resurgence or persistence of
clientelism can be found. In October 1991 Chiluba's MMD (Movement for
Multi-Party Democracy) successfully challenged the ruling UNIP (United
National Independence Party) in Zambia's first freely contested general
election for at least twenty years. But while the MMD has subsequently
promoted many measures of economic liberalization, it has also exploited
its remaining powers of patronage to reward its supporters and attract
others away from competing parties (Mphaisha 1996). In Asia, clientelism
plays a significant role in party politics in Pakistan (Taylor 1992) and in
South Korea (Jaung 1995) and is rampant in Thai party politics (Murray
1996); all three of these countries have been described as undergoing some
limited process of democratization. It even continues to be significant in
many parts of Latin America, where the process of (re-)democratization
began much earlier. For instance, in at least three states, Argentina, Peru
and Mexico, "poverty alleviation programmes" (PAPs) have been used to
foster electoral support. Thus in Mexico, a succession of electoral reforms
and the relatively poor showing of the PRI (Partido Nacional Revolucion-
ario), which, under different names, has dominated Mexican politics since
the 1930s, in the 1988 national elections, encouraged expectations that
"the door had been opened to a much more competitive, multi-party
system". But in practice, opposition parties had great difficulty in building
on these electoral gains. Most relevantly,

> the Salinas' administration's innovative public works and anti-poverty
> program, called National Solidarity, has reminded low-income Mexicans
> that it is only the PRI-government apparatus that has significant
> material resources to distribute – not the opposition parties.
>
> (Craig and Cornelius 1995, 250)

(We should, however, note that since then, the dominance of the PRI has
been more effectively challenged by the Party of the Democratic Revolution
(PRD). Following elections held in July 1997, its leader, Cardenas became
Mayor of Mexico City while the PRI lost its majority in the lower house of
Congress.) Clientelist practices have also continued to characterize the
party politics of Brazil. Even though, from party leaders' point of view,
reliance on party-directed patronage might be considered ill-advised in the
context of reduced government resources and when faced with a mass
urban electorate, "leaders of catchall parties have been slow to recognize
the fact" (Mainwaring 1995, 397).

A third frequent characteristic of political parties, and even party systems,
in the Third World has been that they lacked autonomy from the state.

Generally here we are referring to the state as a whole, although in the case of the Ba'ath Party in Iraq, for instance, there has more specifically been insufficient institutional autonomy from the military. This lack of autonomy is closely related to the prevalence of authoritarian forms of rule discussed below. In some cases authoritarian regimes established political parties for a range of related motives – to institutionalize the regime, to increase its legitimacy – but such parties, entirely fashioned from above, lacked all possibility of authentically articulating social cleavages or interests. Examples would be the ARENA Party, established by Brazil's military rulers in the 1960s (but for the more ambiguous case of the official opposition MDB see below) and Indonesia's Golkar Party which persists to this day. In other cases parties that captured power became indissolubly fused with the state, while the party as an autonomous organization largely "withered away" (Clapham 1985), a process that could be identified in a number of tropical African one-party states. This kind of dependence on the state is not to be confused with the frequent voluntary, as it were, support of conservative parties for those in positions of political authority. It is clearly incompatible with the Lipset–Rokkan model to the extent that it denies political parties freedom of manoeuvre in shaping their relationship with the electorate and other parties.

Party system persistence

But perhaps still more problematic for the application of the Lipset–Rokkan thesis to the Third World have been the infrequency and discontinuity of competitive party systems. The party-cleavage model looks at the way political parties, both those with institutional roots in society and newcomers, interact in the struggle to win the mass electorate's vote. To that extent it is premised upon competition. Moreover, the model tends to imply the persistence of competition. Lipset and Rokkan are careful not to suggest a single linear progression through participation "thresholds". Though beginning from a baseline in which all thresholds are high, they envisage four possible end states in which legitimation and incorporation thresholds are both low, but thresholds of representation and majority vary between high, medium and low. Even so, there is an assumption that the first two thresholds will fall, and once down will remain so.

But the great majority of Third World countries have not enjoyed anything approaching persistent competitive party politics. In 1993, Pinkney cited eight exceptions, where, at least on a generous definition, competitive party politics had survived since Independence: India, Jamaica, Trinidad, Tobago, The Gambia, Botswana, Mauritius and Papua New Guinea. Since then The Gambia has succumbed to military rule. In Latin America, Costa Rica's competitive party system has endured since 1948 and those of Colombia and Venezuela since the late 1950s. At the other extreme a very few Third World countries, including Libya and Saudi Arabia, have never known competitive party elections. Much more commonly an initial phase of competitive party politics has more or less rapidly given way either to one-party rule, *de iure* or *de facto*, or to military rule. One consequence of this pattern of alternating competitive party and authoritarian regimes is that one of the central cleavages characterizing party systems in the wake of a period of authoritarian rule often consists of forces aligned with the old regime facing a combination of forces opposing it (although following the new order's "founding" elections, and especially if it is defeated, the opposition may rapidly splinter, as for instance in Burkina Faso 1991–2 and Kenya 1992–3).

Although these may seem like major departures from the implied Lipset–Rokkan scenario, they do not, of course, mean that party politics in the Third World is completely *sui generis* and contains no tendencies comparable to those observed in western Europe. In their original analysis, Lipset and Rokkan noted (1967a, 52–3) the effects of such interruption by authoritarian rule in France, Germany, Italy and Spain. In Spain and to a lesser extent Italy, experience of competitive party politics before the installation of Fascist regimes had been so brief that the party system had had little chance to take root. Nonetheless, the authors comment "in the cases of France, Germany and Italy the continuities in the alternatives are as striking as the disruptions in their organisational expressions" (ibid).

Similarly it has been widely noted that, despite authoritarian interludes, Third World party systems once established often show surprising resilience. This can result from two rather contradictory processes: where an incoming regime suppresses all forms of party politics, it stifles the possibility of "spontaneous" party system development, tending to freeze the existing system so that it remains all there is to build on, when the new political "opening" presents itself. Examples include Ghana 1969 and 1979, Argentina 1973 and 1983 and Chile 1988. A good recent example is the experience of Mali (Vengroff 1993). Following the fall of Moussa Traore's military regime in 1991, a range of legislative measures widened the scope for political participation. In the first instance no less than forty-seven different political parties were fielded, but Vengroff argues that only three of these have been of real significance, competitively speaking. Moreover of the two most serious contenders, the US–RDA (Union Soudanaise–Rassemblement Democratique Africaine), was founded in 1946 and came to power in 1957. The second, Adema (Alliance pour la Democratie au Mali), had its origins in several parties that went underground after Traore seized power in 1968. Vengroff concludes, "The roots and ongoing bases of support for today's competitive parties are closely linked to Mali's historical development, especially in the period following World War 2" (1993, 544).

On the other hand, some one- or dominant-party regimes (Malaysia, Mexico, Singapore, South Korea, Taiwan) have tolerated multi-party activity, while reinforcing the dominant party's advantage through some combination of constitutional procedures, coercion and electoral malpractice.

Although this means such parties can persist into an era of more genuine party competition, however, they are inevitably "weak" and their credibility may be damaged by their longstanding cooperation with a discarded regime. Brazil, under the 1964–86 military regime, presents an interesting half-way case, there was neither outright suppression of parties nor co-existence. The military virtually banned all existing parties but then formed two new parties, ARENA to represent the regime and the MDB (Brazilian Democratic Movement) as the "official" opposition. Since the members of these parties were drawn from sitting members of Congress and since the parties were also allowed to accommodate factions through the mechanism of the intra-party list, old party groupings survived under the umbrellas of the new.

Not only have parties, and even party systems, regularly survived periods of authoritarian rule but one-party systems themselves can in some cases be seen as representing the culmination of a process of party form-ation along Lipset–Rokkan lines. Thus Collier (1978) sought to distinguish between types of one-party regime in post-independence tropical Africa. She suggested that the type of one-party regime varied according to the circumstances of its formation, and specifically the degree to which party dominance had already emerged in the pre-independence period. One-party systems could originate in three ways; through the total electoral success of the leading party, through the merger of two or more parties or through repression or outright banning of opposition parties. She con-cluded that "Where a one-party regime was formed by election or merger, these regimes were based on parties that had fared well under the competitive elections introduced during the period of decolonisation" and that these regimes had greater legitimacy and were less susceptible to military overthrow; examples are Ivory Coast, Kenya, Malawi, Tanzania, and Zambia. (Collier does not deal very satisfactorily with the case that would seem to contradict this argument – that of Ghana, where Nkrumah's Convention People's Party won a decisive victory in the first General Elections in 1954 and became the governing party on Independence in 1957 but was ousted by a military-cum-police coup in 1966. It could however be argued that the turnout for the 1954 election was very low – at 30 per cent – and that the CPP's victory almost immediately triggered the formation of a range of opposition parties, including the powerful National Liberation Movement, with an important base in the Ashanti region, suggesting that the CPP's competitive position was never as secure as it may have looked.)

Sequence of development

So far, I have been examining some of the specific ways in which parties and party systems in the Third World might appear incompatible with the Lipset–Rokkan model. But underlying these contrasts are more basic differences of context. It is fair to say that Lipset and Rokkan assume a certain sequence of historical development. In so doing, not only are they drawing upon European history but they invoke the modernization perspective of Talcott Parsons "for purposes of *distinctly developmental* analysis" (1967a, 26, their emphasis). This is not the place to engage in lengthy critique of the assumptions of modernization theory (but see Randall and Theobald 1985, ch. 1). Despite its shortcomings it is true that it would be difficult to manage entirely without some such notion (Roxborough 1988), and it has enjoyed a new lease of intellectual life with renewed attempts to correlate measures of democratic performance with indices of economic and social development (Lipset *et al.* 1993; Moore 1995). Nonetheless the extent to which it can illuminate the process of party system formation in the Third World must be strictly limited.

Granted Lipset and Rokkan (1967a, 34–5) emphasize the importance of differences in the timing and character of the National Revolution, of the timing and character of the Industrial Revolution and of the interaction between them – "How far had the National Revolution proceeded at the point of the industrial 'take-off'?" – in accounting for party system variation amongst European countries. The assumption still is that there *will* be a national revolution and there *will* be an industrial revolution, that these twin developments will unravel over a considerable span of years and will occur either before or during but certainly not after the arrival of mass suffrage. By contrast, they briefly refer to "current strains of nation-building in the new states of Africa and Asia" (1967a, 13). As Rokkan recognized in a later discussion (1975),

> the great mass of the systems that rose to sovereign status through the break-up of the Iberian, Eastern European, Asian and African empires have had to cope with issues of national-cultural identity, issues of participation, and issues of economic inequality all in one: developments left them with little or no time to reach even temporary institutional solutions to one set of challenges before they were forced to cope with the next set.
>
> (574)

Party systems themselves both reflected and had to deal with this situation. In many regions, boundaries inherited at independence were shaped more by the convenience of colonial administrators than by indigenous ethnic and cultural solidarities. Thus Chodak (1964, 267) noted that whereas in Europe parties had developed within well-established state frameworks, in Africa, "parties constitute a premise for the formation of national structures, they are to a great extent the originators of these structures". This is one respect in which it might be argued Latin American countries were at an advantage; ethnic conflicts were mainly (if brutally) resolved and national boundaries established well before extension of the franchise.

Nor is it simply that, in the way recognized by Rokkan above, a number of Third World countries have had to cope with national integration, industrialization and political mobilization all at once. The problem has often been that they have faced the social disruption associated with aspects of modernization such as the rapid, unplanned growth of cities and raised economic expectations but not necessarily either substantial industrialization or even significant economic growth. Moreover, it has tended to be where nation-building problems are at their most acute, notably in Africa, that economic difficulties have also been most severe.

Nor finally, and to some extent anticipating the argument of the next section, can it be assumed that at some future stage, all Third World countries will have accomplished national and economic revolutions along western European lines. While such a developmentalist perspective is more plausible in relation to Latin America and the NICs, than elsewhere, even in these regions the *forms* of economic development that are occurring, whether characterized as "dependent capitalist development" or export-led growth within an increasingly global international economy, are giving rise to different class structures and alignments, and specifically to situations in which the possibilities of labour-oriented mobilization and party formation are constrained. The experience of western Europe and the model of party formation that goes with it do not necessarily hold a mirror to the future of the Third World. Third World nation-states have come late to a game that is rapidly and unpredictably changing.

We have seen some of the consequences of these perhaps rather obvious observations for party politics in the Third World. For instance, they help to explain the frequent interruption of competitive party systems. Thus in Latin America, Nun (1967) in seeking to explain the prevalence of the "middle-class coup" in Latin America pointed to an important contrast with western Europe, which reflects the different sequencing of industrialization and political mobilization. Whereas in Europe on the eve of the First World War, only 10–15 per cent of the population were enfranchised, in Latin America, at a roughly comparable level of economic development, the rate of electoral participation was 44 per cent in Argentina (1963), 36 per cent in Uruguay (1958) and 31 per cent in Chile (1964). With mass mobilization, the middle classes in these states, who had themselves only recently and often with but limited success challenged the old landed oligarchies, faced intense and destabilizing redistributive pressures while still at a relatively early stage of industrialization or economic development. Accordingly, they turned to the increasingly middle-class-led military to protect their interests.

The temporal proximity if not simultaneity of National Revolution, economic change – if not industrialization or growth – and the institution of mass suffrage in many other regions of the Third World likewise helps to explain such features of post-independence party politics as the predominance of non-class cleavages, the prevalence of cadres parties and the pervasiveness of clientelism.

Lack of system autonomy

But we cannot leave the story there. For this syndrome of concurrent developmental crises is related, though of course not entirely reducible to, another crucial feature of the context of Third World politics, its striking if also variable, lack of autonomy. It is not necessary to embrace whole-heartedly the more extreme versions either of dependency theory or of globalization theory to recognize that Third World polities in the past and in new ways presently have been enormously constrained and shaped by external forces, cultural, economic and political.

To begin with, party politics has been shaped by the legacy of colonial rule. Colonial policies may well have helped to fashion the social cleavages that provided some of the social content of party politics, and of course it was the reaction against colonial rule that formed the basis of nationalist movements that tended to subsume other social divisions. But, in the Caribbean, tropical Africa and South Asia, the institutional legacy of colonial rule should also be recognized. To a large extent, multi-party politics in the immediate post-independence period, was a legacy *imposed* on Third World societies. It did not constitute a prize struggled for by a democratic movement, though the extent to which nationalist movements or their leaders had acquired a commitment to democratic institutions was certainly a factor in determining the longevity of competitive party politics following independence. The persistence of competitive party politics in India and Jamaica for instance owes much to the way in which democratic values were able to strike root in the new national middle class during a relatively protracted transition period.

The arrival of competitive party politics, it could be said, was at a time not of the people's choosing and coincided with the problems of nation-building, themselves again in large part, a legacy of colonial rule. We have seen some of the consequences of this history in the breakdown of fragile competitive party systems and the emergence of a succession of one-party or military regimes.

But as dependency theorists have emphasized, the impact of external forces hardly ceased at independence. They continued importantly to shape options for economic development, as was most dramatically evidenced in the "debt crisis" of the 1980s (partly triggered, it must be conceded, by the actions of supposedly Third World oil-producers) and the structural adjust-ment requirements largely imposed on a succession of indebted Third World states by the IMF and World Bank. Associated severe economic difficulties have formed an important part of the background to recent trends away from authoritarian rule. In addition, and without applying equal pressure in each case, Western donors have in the 1990s advocated steps towards democratization, usually meaning specifically competitive party politics. Judgements differ as to how far democratizing moves reflect pressures from within, and especially the growth of "civil society" and how far they are a response to external pressures. The role of social change, as manifest in urbanization, a growing middle class, in many cases the growth of organized labour, should not be underestimated. Nonetheless and especially in parts of Africa and the Middle East there is a sense in which once more the *timing* of democratization has been imposed from outside the polity, rather than emerging from an internal power struggle. That is, to go back to Lipset and Rokkan, in these countries, the political revolution to an extent has simply been arbitrarily inserted into situations of economic stagnation or crisis and of precarious national integration.

Further, economic crisis and the terms of structural adjustment conditionality but above all the collapse from 1989 of the former Soviet bloc have greatly weakened the credibility and appeal of socialist arguments and parties. The implications for party systems in the Third World are not necessarily straightforward. In the Lipset–Rokkan model, parties based on the labour movement are seen as frequently being in the van of the turn to mass politics with more conservative parties following reluctantly in their wake if they are successfully to compete in an era of mass suffrage. This might suggest that in emerging party systems, it will be more difficult for new left-wing parties to establish themselves and that the impetus to mass party politics will be correspondingly reduced. However, in Latin America, where socialist parties are already well-established in a number of countries, Mainwaring and Scully (1995) suggest that the electoral appeal of *moderate* left-wing parties may actually have increased, because they are no longer perceived as such a threat to the existing social order.

There is one final point to make, under system autonomy. This concerns the telecommunications "revolution" which has occurred from the 1970s. In relation to the Lipset–Rokkan model this could perhaps be called a *fifth* revolution (fifth because Lipset and Rokkan (1967, 47) already tentatively identified a fourth, the Russian Revolution of 1917 and its sequel). Although it has been incorporated and experienced differently amongst different Third World states it has its origins to an extent in *global* technological change. There are still many parts of the Third World where television does not feature prominently as a medium of political communication. Nonetheless, and where it does prevail, it can affect the relationships between party and society which are at the core of the Lipset–Rokkan model. Skilful use of the media can reduce parties' dependence on their original social base. Specifically where this is combined with some form of Presidential rule, it is regularly observed that it can make it easier for party leaders to appeal directly to voters, rather than being dependent on effective party organization. As Mainwaring and Scully report for Latin America, "Party politics in the 1980s were reshaped decisively by the expansion of the modern media and modern campaign techniques" (1995, 471). The most spectacular instances of election by TV have been the "catapulting" into power of relative unknowns, with minimalist supporting party organizations, namely Collor in Brazil (1989) and Fujimori in Peru (1990). Shin's survey (1995) of attitudes towards political parties in South Korea suggests a further possible effect. He finds that the extent to which respondents are exposed to media coverage of party politics is inversely correlated with the degree of their psychological attachment to individual parties but not with support for a democratic party system as such. At any rate, the overall implication of this consideration of the impact of global developments in telecommunications is that they may be one additional factor undermining processes of party institutionalization, which in some cases have begun or resumed only very recently, and thus simultaneously undermining the possibility for parties to articulate meaningfully with bases of social cleavage in Lipset–Rokkan style.

Conclusion

The preceding discussion has highlighted the ways in which the experience of party system formation in the Third World differs from that described in the Lipset–Rokkan model. Salient social cleavages have differed in significant respects and have been differently reflected in the process of party formation. Political parties could rarely be described as "mass" parties, they have generally been clientelistic, a characteristic that appears to have persisted well into the new era of democratization, and in many cases they have lacked autonomy from the state. Finally the development of competitive party systems has been regularly interrupted and disrupted by periods of authoritarian rule. Underlying these differences have been broader contrasts in the *context* of party systems. Processes of national unification and integration, and of industrial development have not necessarily preceded political mobilization nor indeed have they necessarily been realized subsequently. This in turn is partly a consequence of these systems' lack of autonomy in relation to external economic and political forces, as epitomized in the legacy of colonization itself, the nature of subsequent economic change and the kinds of external pressures that contributed to the more recent "wave" of democratization.

None of this means that the Lipset–Rokkan model has nothing to say about party politics in the Third World, but it does suggest limits to the model's possible application. Lipset and Rokkan abstract from a highly particular historical experience of party formation in western Europe. As such they refer to a process that is most unlikely to be repeated in these precise terms in most of what has come to be termed the Third World. That is to say that the model's capacity to *predict* party system development in the Third World is very limited. Parts of Latin America may offer partial exceptions to this generalization. It is possible too that the current industrial unrest in South Korea presages the emergence of a more effective party of the labour movement. But in general, it seems unlikely that for the foreseeable future, most of the Third World will witness the kinds of party development presently being traced in a number of central and eastern

European countries. There the first free elections, held around 1990, were dominated by parties developing out of the pro-democracy movement and the former ruling communist parties were roundly defeated. However the communist parties retained important organizational assets with branches country-wide and, revamped and renamed, enjoyed a fresh surge of support as the new governments embarked on policies of economic restructuring that hit the working class particularly hard. Thus Budge and Newton (1997) suggest that as the party system settles down, something akin to the Lipset–Rokkan model may be occurring, with parties increasingly arrayed upon a left–right axis and consolidating mass organizational bases, driven by the logic of "contagion from the left", or the need to compete with mass working-class-based parties. The crucial factor here is of course the prior existence of highly organized communist parties, for which there is no real counterpart in the Third World's "new democracies".

The preceding discussion has also suggested the limitations of too exclusive a focus on social cleavages as a basis for party formation in the Third World. Admittedly the Lipset–Rokkan model does distinguish successive thresholds in which institutional considerations such as the nature of the electoral system play a central part. However, part of their argument is precisely to criticize the tendency of earlier authors to overstate the importance of such factors (see 29–30). In the Third World, however, the institutional legacy of colonial rule has often played a crucial role. Thus it could well be argued that in India and Jamaica the timing and character of the colonial bequest of mechanisms of political representation contributed decisively both to the survival and to the form of party systems. Application of the Lipset–Rokkan model to the Third World underlines the need to supplement its insights with other kinds of perspective.

It might be argued that a further limitation of the Lipset–Rokkan model – one that I have not yet touched on directly – is its failure to pay sufficient attention to the role of political culture in the shaping of party systems. Their model takes for granted the increasing hegemony of liberal-democratic assumptions and norms, whereas other cultural traditions such as Islam or Confucianism both resist these norms and show little sign of withering away. I cannot pursue this complex question here beyond saying that the wisest position to adopt seems to me an agnostic one – we do not really know what difference culture can make in the long run – but that one should also be aware of the way in which such "clash of civilization" arguments can be deployed by those with a vested interest in the preservation of difference. For that reason, I suggest that one of the positive contributions the Lipset–Rokkan model can make is to provide an *analytic framework* that, up to a point, can travel. The questions posed about the nature of cleavages, about thresholds of participation and the relationship of both of these to party formation and persistence get us away from the view that much of the Third World is impenetrably alien and beyond the scope of conventional political science.

As to what the model can illuminate in the Third World context, one contribution is in helping to explain why party systems on the western European pattern have *not* emerged. It is useful, up to a point, to recognize what has been absent from the process of party system formation in so many Third World countries. The model, secondly, can illuminate, though it cannot on its own explain, the differences *between* Third World regions and countries, indicating the importance of such factors as patterns of social cleavage and levels of party institutionalization on the eve of mass mobilization. Finally though the model offers what seems to me one of its most valuable perceptions – though such a view would not be universally endorsed even by the contributors to this book – about the way in which party systems have tended to "freeze" around the organizational patterns of initial mass mobilization. As we have seen this has relevance for a range of party systems in the Third World, not simply those in which competitive party politics has persisted but those in which competitive and authoritarian regimes have alternated and indeed for many one-party systems.

Acknowledgement

I should like to thank Ian Budge for his constructive comments on an earlier draft of this chapter.

13 Party systems and voter alignments in small island states

Dag Anckar

"Parties are the core institution of democratic politics", Seymour Martin Lipset writes in a recent review article (1996, 169). In the same article, he makes reference to a statement by E.E. Schattschneider: "democracy is unthinkable save in terms of parties" (1996, 169). The work by John H. Aldrich which is the subject of Lipset's review, repeats this statement: the saying is here that "democracy is unworkable save in terms of parties" (1996, 170). This belief in the essentiality of parties for democratic life is of course wide-spread. The opening sentence in Richard S. Katz' volume on *A Theory of Parties and Electoral Systems* reads, "Modern democracy is party democracy; the political institutions and practices that are the essence of democratic government in the Western view were the creations of political parties and would be unthinkable without them" (1980, 1). "If asked to define Western democracy", Katz explains, "one could do little better than to say that it is the selection of major political decision makers through free elections among candidates of competing political parties" (1980, 1). To this definition Katz adds a statement in firm conviction, "Every country that generally would be considered democratic is governed in this way" (1980, 1).

This belief, however, may be questioned. Some years ago Axel Hadenius published a book on democracy in Third World countries, establishing, for a sample of 132 countries, a scale to measure the level of democracy in each and every country; this scale running from 0 to 10. The results indicate that a group of seven countries achieves the highest possible rank and score, i.e. a full 10 points. Very close to this group is an eighth country, scoring 9.9 points (1992, 61–2). In the universe of Third World countries at least, these eight countries undoubtedly form a democratic elite; more than other nations, they subscribe to democratic values, standards and institutions. The eight countries are, in alphabetical order: Barbados, Cyprus, Dominica, Federated States of Micronesia, Kiribati, Marshall Islands, St Vincent and the Grenadines and Tuvalu. The list is intriguing, indeed. Out of the eight countries, no less than four, namely Micronesia, Kiribati, Marshall Islands and Tuvalu, manage without political parties! They are governed in accordance with democratic ideals, and for this no parties are needed. Let me also add to the list the case of Belau. This tiny island state gained independence as recently as in 1994, and was therefore not included in Hadenius' study. There is little doubt, however, that Belau deserves close to a full 10 points, would Hadenius' criteria be applied to this nation (Anckar *et al.* 1998). What makes Belau interesting, is that this country also lacks a party system.

It is the aim of this chapter to relate central thoughts in the classical work by Seymour Martin Lipset and Stein Rokkan on party formation and democratization (1967a) to the political life of those political entities that may be labelled "small island states". On the basis of what has been already said, this task is anything but easy. It is, in fact, almost insuperable, the Lipset–Rokkan framework being adopted for and derived from Western European democracies and this chapter dealing, in part, with very different systems, traditions and environments. To simplify enormously, whereas Lipset and Rokkan expect to find democratization and parties where there are nations and a degree of industrialization, in the world of small island states there are often parties and notable democratization but neither nations nor industrialization. This being the case, only occasional references to the thoughts of Lipset–Rokkan are inserted in the presentation that follows. At the most general of levels, the framework may of course be applicable. For instance, an absence of political parties in democracies does not imply an absence of politics or an absence of a subsystem for the task of goal attainment, to use Parsonian terminology. An absence implies, however, that the tasks of the subsystem are performed in a manner which differs from what is to be expected, and that the differences are about party systems as well as voter alignments. It may be illuminating to insert already at this point two observations on small island political life.

In an interesting travel-book in Swedish, laconically called *Öar* (Islands), Anders Källgård describes one evening in the Nanumea island, one of the nine atolls that make up the micro-state of Tuvalu. This is one evening when the fishing canoes are left lying in the sand. It is election day, votes are counted, voters eager to know how Naama Latasi, a woman candidate, has performed in the election. News is that Naama has indeed been elected to the Tuvaluan Parliament, which, by the way, has 12 members, and Källgård is not surprised by the outcome, since Naama is known for her goodness and wisdom, and her family is fairly rich and she has been studying abroad (1994, 47–9). Two points in this observation merit attention. First, the emphasis on personal qualifications rather than affiliation to a particular group is a rather frequent occurrence in the world of small islands. Personal attributes and even family ties outweigh in many countries and places party platforms and party ideas, parties being regarded as systems of discordant politics, aiming at winning at all costs. Also, it is still in many places the case that parties are "transient, unstable and identified with personalities more than policies" (Crocombe 1992, 14). Second, the islandness of islands is an important factor. Rather than focusing on national issues, island voters are occupied with local things, with issues defined within the island as an electorate. Island nations are often consortiums of mini-nations, they are entities but they are not always systems.

The second observation is about elections and electoral behaviour in Pentecost, Vanuatu, and draws upon a report by Mark Bebe and Leo Clement. After explaining the chiefly system operating throughout Pentecost, which includes lesser chiefs who inherit their positions as well as higher chiefs who earn titles through a system involving "killing pigs in increasing numbers through a series of stages, each of which is linked to a particular title" (1995, 267), the authors describe the context of elections in that island:

> Chiefs in general are highly respected and listened to, a fact which is important for understanding modern politics on Pentecost. People tend to follow the direction of their chiefs in their areas when it comes time to vote in an election. Moreover, the chiefs regulate the access of outsiders to their particular areas. Representatives of a political party, for example, would need to request permission from the chief in a particular area before campaigning. A negative response would make it difficult to hold any meetings, not because they would be physically prevented from doing so, but due to the fact that people in the village would respect the position taken by their chief and probably not attend.
>
> (1995, 267)

Indeed, in small island states issues relating to party systems and voter alignments may be quite confusing and different. However, the universe of small island states is not a homogeneous one. It comprises very different elements, which are shaped by a variety of circumstances, some of which will be discussed in the following. The plan of my presentation is as follows. First, the small island states of the world are identified. This exercise, then, delimits the group of states which provides the pool of observations, illustrations and impressions that will be used in the analysis. Second, the bulk of the chapter is about four different factors, that have created or contributed to the shaping of party systems and voter alignments. Under this heading will be discussed, in this order, the smallness factor, the geographic factor, the colonial factor, and the custom and tradition factor. The first two factors emanate from the focus on small island states, smallness and islandness being defining characteristics of the entities at hand. The third and the fourth factor emanate as empirical connotations of small island states: almost all these states have been colonies and many represent cultural heritages that are alien to the Lipset–Rokkan conception of political life. Since the four factors are interlinked and intertwined in a variety of ways, to discuss them separately may, admittedly, seem a less than well-considered strategy. For matters of convenience and also perspicuity, this strategy will, however, be used.

The small island states

The method for identifying small island states having been described at some length elsewhere (Anckar 1993), a few comments may suffice here. Let it be said, then, that in order to delimit a population of small island states one needs, first, to identify the island states of the world, and, second, to decide which of these states are small and which are not. Concerning the matter of island states, use is made, first, of a conventional definition, stating that islands are subcontinental land areas surrounded on all sides by water (Glassner 1990, 47). In this view, then, island states are states that are surrounded by water. The spatial shaping of such states may, however, differ. Some island states consist of one island, some are archipelagic, some, like Brunei, are parts of an island, some, like Papua New Guinea, consist of parts of an island as well as adjacent islands. Modifying the definition to include such spatial variation, an island state may be defined as a state which is an island or a part of an island or consists of islands and parts of islands. When these definitions are applied to the universe of the independent states of the world, a group of forty-six island states emerges. The task now remains to single out from this group those island states which are small.

It is stated in the literature that no wholly agreed definition of a small state exists, and that any definition is to some degree arbitrary (Sutton and Payne 1993, 581). This is certainly true, and the fact that ceiling points differ among scientific disciplines adds to the confusion: whereas economists and strategists often make use of a cut-off point of 10–20 million people, political scientists accept much lower points and often add a further distinction between small states and microstates (Sutton and Payne 1993, 581). Furthermore, the usefulness of this very distinction is often contested, and little consensus exists about the ceiling population of microstates (e.g. Ogashiwa 1991, ix). Here, to determine the size of states, average figures are used: those states are considered small which are below average for area as well as population and satisfy some further quantitative as well as qualitative criteria. By this method, out of the total of 46 island states, 32 are considered small. The states are listed in Table 13.1, which also, for each state, presents data on area and population. An appendix to this chapter lists some important regime characteristics of the states.

The smallness factor

The first question to be addressed here is whether or not the smallness of small island states carries implications in itself for the party systems of these units. Indeed, the thought that the size of units makes a difference for political life is well represented in the history of political thought and political science: for instance, Montesquieu, in his *The Spirit of Laws*, argued that it is a natural property of small states to be governed as republics, of middling ones to be governed by monarchs, and of large empires to be

Table 13.1 The small island states of the world: size in terms of area and population

State	Area, sq km	Population
Antigua-Barbuda	442	66,000
Bahamas	13,865	262,000
Bahrain	661	533,000
Barbados	430	259,000
Belau	458	15,000
Brunei	5,765	270,000
Cape Verde	4,035	384,000
Comoros	1,860	585,000
Cyprus	9,250	725,000
Dominica	751	72,000
Federated States of Micronesia	702	109,000
Fiji	18,330	747,000
Grenada	378	91,000
Iceland	102,820	260,000
Kiribati	717	66,000
Maldives	298	231,000
Malta	316	359,000
Marshall Islands	605	46,000
Mauritius	1,865	1,084,000
Nauru	21	10,000
St Kitts–Nevis	261	44,000
St Lucia	616	153,000
St Vincent and the Grenadines	389	108,000
Sao Tome and Principe	964	124,000
Seychelles	404	72,000
Singapore	616	2,812,000
Solomon Islands	29,790	321,000
Tonga	699	103,000
Trinidad and Tobago	5,130	1,265,000
Tuvalu	25	10,000
Vanuatu	14,765	154,000
Western Samoa	2,840	170,000

Source: The Times Guide to the Nations of the World, 1994.

ruled by despots (1989). Among modern authors Robert Dahl and Edward Tufte have in their by now classical treatise on *Size and Democracy* (1973) developed at some length a paradigm that explicates the differences that are likely to exist between small and larger democratic political units. These differences include observations on party systems, most notably the number of parties which can be expected to be very low in small units and clearly higher in larger units. This is for several reasons: conflict resolution in larger systems requires the existence of formal and impersonal organizations, i.e. parties; small units are homogeneous, dissenters from the majority view therefore form a small proportion of the total and have difficulties in finding a sufficient number of allies; homogeneity also reduces the number of available nodes around which group life can form (1973,

92–3). "Indeed", the authors claim, "in the politics of homogeneity parties scarcely exist" (1973, 97). And they go on by asserting that as parties begin to appear in the small community, "homogeneity initially tends to insure the dominance of a single party" (1973, 97). On the other hand, as heterogeneity increases one-party dominance declines, other parties gaining a following among those who dissent from the majority perspective and parties becoming more nearly equal competitors: "Within a given democracy, the larger the political unit, the greater the relative size of the minority party or parties" (1973, 97).

These propositions, then, it would seem, suggest theoretical explanations for an absence or very low frequency of parties in small systems, like the partyless democracies we have mentioned. However, the propositions do not seem able to survive empirical testing. For one thing, small units are not by far so homogeneous as one would perhaps expect (Anckar, D. 1997e). And furthermore, the outlook of the party systems of small island states is anything but uniform in terms of number of parties. In fact, if one slightly modifies Giovanni Sartori's scheme for the classification of party systems (1976, 125), now distinguishing between (a) systems with no parties or one party only; (b) two-party systems; (c) fragmented systems, counting three to five parties; and (d) atomized systems, counting more than five parties, an application of this categorization on the small island states population will show that each category is indeed well represented. To the number of nations with no parties should be added the Maldives and the Republic of Nauru, as well as the authoritarian regimes of Bahrain and Brunei. Two-party systems may be found in, for instance, Bahamas, Cape Verde and Malta, whereas, for instance, Barbados, Dominica and St Vincent and the Grenadines represent fragmented systems. Finally, atomized systems can be found in, for instance, the Comoros, where 16 parties are active, Iceland with nine parties, Mauritius, likewise with nine parties, and the Solomon Islands, representing eight parties (Anckar, D. 1997a). Small island states do not represent an uniform pattern; size, apparently, makes no difference.

Similar results are reported by Hadenius, who in his study of democracy and development finds that large states are less democratic than small states, the association between size and democracy being, however, strong only at a low level of size. Furthermore, the association becomes weaker, when other factors are introduced in the analysis. Above all, whether or not the state is an island appears important: smallness counts, because small nations are often islands (1992, 126). In the end, however, even the island factor becomes insignificant. Hadenius concludes that the connection between size and democracy has proved to be spurious to a substantial extent (1992, 127). In like manner, in a recent study of the relation between size and democracy, Carsten Anckar (1997) concludes that size makes a difference only when and if associated with two other factors: whether or not the unit in question is an island and whether or not the unit in question is a former English or American colony.

And yet, smallness may indeed make a difference. In their volume Dahl and Tufte put forward the thought that their paradigm is perhaps less suited for inter-nation comparisons, nations being, however small, still too big in size. It may be the case, the authors write, that their reasoning applies only to very small systems, like towns, say, having a population of under 10,000 (1973, 94). "Whatever this threshold may be", the authors go on, "it is, most likely, lower than the population of even a very small country like Iceland" (1973, 94). The fact that the world is today clearly more atomized and miniaturized in terms of nations offers, however, a possibility to test this idea by Dahl and Tufte on inter-nation data as well, and it seems, indeed, that the idea has some validity. Within the category of smallness, thresholds of size seem to be operative. When and if of the democracies of the world, only the smallest ones are observed, an impact of size on party fragmentation, which is otherwise not to be detected, suddenly appears (Anckar, C. 1995, 188–9). In like manner, among the small island states of the world, when the smallest are singled out to form a single category, patterns of partylessness or dominance by one party begin to appear. Eight cases out of the ten smallest of the small islands confirm the rule that small nations have no parties or are dominated by one party, ten out of fourteen of the larger of the small islands disconfirm this rule (Anckar, D. 1997a).

In the context of this chapter, similar observations can be made. Of the altogether three democratic island states with populations less than 20,000, none has parties, of the altogether five democratic island states with populations less than 50,000, four have no parties, of the altogether ten democratic island states with populations less than 100,000, the same four have no parties. Of course, other factors than size alone determine whether or not there are parties in a democracy. However, one should take care not to dispose easily of the impact of size, as the patterns are suggestive enough. To possess explanatory power, diminutive size may, however, not be diminishingly diminutive. Thresholds probably operate downwards also, not only upwards. An effort to apply the reasoning of Dahl and Tufte on really small units, namely electoral constituencies in the tiny Republic of Belau, indicates an impact of size in elections to the House of Senate but not in elections to the House of Delegates, where the constituencies are extremely small (Anckar *et al.* 1998).

The geographical factor

Besides being surrounded by water, island states have other geographical characteristics as well. Many of them consist of several islands, meaning that they are archipelagoes, and, thereby, that they have noncontiguous territories (Merrit 1969). In some instances, island states stretch over huge areas, the foremost example being Kiribati, "a nation of water" (Teiwaki 1988), which has about 70,000 inhabitants and covers a territory as far east to west as from England to Russia. Of the 32 small island states of the world, according to my count, twelve, like Cyprus or Iceland, are one-island states, whereas of the remaining twenty, a number of six, like Antigua-Barbuda or Trinidad and Tobago, are two-island states, and fourteen, like the Seychelles or the Maldives, are archipelagoes in a more strict sense of the word (Anckar, D. 1996, 701). There is indeed a lot of noncontiguity in the island world.

Does, then, this island peculiarity count for very much in terms of party systems or voter alignments? Probably not. There are some features of the political architectures of small island states that are related systematically to noncontiguity (Anckar, D. 1996), but these features do not include the shaping of party systems nor patterns of voting behaviour. Admittedly, from a strictly theoretical point of view, one would expect the geographical feature of noncontiguity to count. Noncontiguous units consist of parts that are at distance from each other; distance again, because it creates enstrange-ments and sometimes even hostility works against the emergence of national ideologies and the origin of political structures and loyalties that derive from or promote a national ideology. Voter alignments can be expected to be with the parts of the whole rather than with the whole in itself, with islands rather than with the island state.

The Federated States of Micronesia offers a good example of the mech-anisms that could be expected to work. The country, the four principal islands of which are Chuuk, Yap, Pohnpei and Kosrae, which are also the constituent states of the federation, was said in the process of becoming an independent nation to face an immensely difficult task, the task of accommodating "the needs of six widely dispersed districts having distinct languages and cultural traditions, and disparate levels of acculturation, while establishing a national government with sovereign powers" (Burdick 1988, 253). Indeed, the list of imminent undertakings was impressive: "Questions about long-term political affiliation with the United States, relations with Japan and other Pacific countries, threats to national unity, the development of a viable economy, the establishment of an effective national government, and the coordination of powers between national and state administrative agencies all clouded the dawn of the fledging country" (Hanlon and Eperiam 1988, 85). And indeed, the tasks have not been fully accomplished. Micronesia is still grappling with problems concerning unity and the management of distance. Regionally defined clashes of interest have emerged from time to time, involving, for instance, efforts from the island group of Faichuk to obtain an independent statehood status from the rest of Cuuk and much complaints among Pohnpeians over alleged dis-criminations, manifested also in doubts whether Pohnpei should continue in the Federation (Petersen 1989, Hanlon and Eperiam 1988, 96–7). Indeed, about the Pohnpei case it has been said that it represents "nation-destroying" rather than "nation-building" (Petersen 1989, 284). A national party system has not evolved, and in elections candidates are usually chosen on the basis of regional and kinship ties rather than political issues (Burdick 1988, 266). A small episode, vividly accounted for in one of the best travel-books there are about Micronesia, tells the story in a nutshell:

> In a session of FSM Senate . . . Kalisto Refolopei, a Truk senator with a tough-guy reputation, hurled a coffee cup across the room and stamped out of the session. It wasn't clear what was bothering him that day; some people say he was upset at his failure to obtain government jobs for a couple of constituents. The Ponapeans – all but one who was subsequently unseated – walked out and the Kosraens followed. The Yapese flew home. All the old questions about unity arose. And remain. Sometimes, the very idea of an islands nation seems oxymoronic, internally contradictory, like jumbo shrimp.
>
> (Kluge 1991, 76–77)

However, to repeat, geography does not generally speaking seem to relate to an absence or a low frequency of parties neither to an inability of voters to identify with national goals and aspirations. True, comparisons of the extent to which island states are noncontiguous and the extent to which they maintain organized party systems indeed seem to suggest that the more noncontiguity there is, the less of a structure characterizes party life and the ties between parties and voters. The analytical problem here, however, is that extended noncontiguities are to be found in the Pacific region, which happens to be the very region which is unique also in another sense, that of accommodating in politics to a high extent cultural heritages and traditional customs. A recent paper by Lars Nilsson (1997) provides dispersion measures for a large set of archipelagic island states; these measures, which are unfortunately influenced to some extent by the population figures of the respective countries, report the value of 41 for Belau, 62 for Kiribati, 33 for the Marshall Islands, 28 for Micronesia, and no less than 76 for Tuvalu. These figures should be compared to the corresponding values of, for instance, some Caribbean archipelagoes like Bahamas (3), St Kitts-Nevis (1), St Vincent and the Grenadines (1) and Trinidad and Tobago (0), or some African archipelagoes like Cape Verde (1), Comoros (1), Sao Tome and Principe (2) or the Seychelles (18). It is intriguing, indeed, that the five democracies without parties that were mentioned in the introduction of this chapter are exactly the five most wide-spread archipelagoes (Anckar and Anckar 2000), but the picture is blurred by the fact that these countries, as is evident from the last section of this chapter, are also among those who cherish cultures and customs that are alien to party life.

Another topic in the field of geography needs to be touched upon. In cases which display a specific archipelagic feature, a corresponding very specific cleavage tends to appear. In two-island nations, i.e. states which consist in the main of two separate parts, both of which are islands (Anckar, D. 1996, 699), a clear-cut center–periphery relation often emerges. This is true, for instance, of the Caribbean island state of Antigua and Barbuda, the smaller part of which, namely Barbuda, continuously complaining that it is treated like a colony and does therefore not feel itself to be an integrated part of the nation (Goutier 1997). The tension between the two parts of the state is fueled by a still unresolved conflict concerning the issue of landownership on Barbuda, specifically whether Barbudan land is owned by Barbudans themselves or by the larger state (Richardson 1992, 187–8). Another Caribbean state, St Kitts and Nevis, provides a still more evident example. The alliance between St Kitts and Nevis came about in 1882 as a consequence of events in colonial history and has prevailed because the two parts are by conventional standards too small to form separate political units. Several historical, political and economic circumstances have, however, worked to create and maintain a tension between the two parts, and the marriage between the two islands has been described as "an uneasy alliance" (Magida 1985). To a historical rivalry between the islands must be added a structural economic imbalance of Nevis as well as a Nevisian history of discrimination. "Many Nevisians still feel that their island does not get its share of the national cake while there is a view among Kittians that Nevis is suffering, without any real cause, from a kind of battered child syndrome", Roger de Backer writes in a presentation of the islands (1993, 8). Accordingly, there have been suspicions and fears of Nevisians against St Kitts, manifested even in sentiments about secession. The fact that this microstate has adopted a federal structure may in itself seem odd; indeed, a miniature has resorted to the methods of a giant. The unifying factors being weak, mental distances prevailing, and a widespread scepticism still remaining in Nevis over the current alliance, one can, however, well understand the rationality of a federalist arrangement (Anckar, D. 1997b).

The colonial factor

Almost all small island states are former colonies, and this has shaped, to a large extent indeed, the political destinies, architectures and institutions of these countries. For one thing, it made a difference who the metropolitan power was. In the context of small island states at least, England deserves credit: island states emanating from British rule became democracies. True, Tonga is an exception (Lawson 1996, 79–115), although it needs to be remembered that this country was never fully colonized (e.g. Campbell 1992). Fiji, since independence in 1970 "the shining example of democracy, multicultural harmony and development in the Pacific, and indeed a standard for the entire Third World" (Kay 1993, 28), is following two *coups* in 1987, intended to thwart the political consequences of the electoral defeat that year of the Fijian-dominated Alliance Party, another exception (Lawson 1991; 1996, 37–76). So are the Arab island of Bahrain, and, for an extended period of time, the Seychelles. Exceptions, however, do not constitute a rule. The American legacy also deserves credit for democratic achievement, perhaps more so in terms of results than in terms of methods. The achievements of France and Portugal are less impressive. The Comoros (France), Cape Verde (Portugal) and Sao Tome and Principe (Portugal) all turned into authoritarian one-party states, and it was only in the wake of the transition-to-democracy movement in the late 1980s and the early 1990s that these former colonies embarked upon radical democratization programs, abandoning their single-party positions and adopting free elections and multi-party systems (Anckar and Anckar 1995). Neither should, in the case of the Condominium of the New Hebrides, France be commended for her contributions to Vanuatu's progress towards independence, the British supporting an orderly transition and the French initially trying to block it (van Trease 1995a).

Colonial boundaries seldom corresponding with pre-colonial ethnic entities, the decolonization processes, in the creation in a very concrete sense of new states, had to come to terms with a variety of problems relating to wider identities and national sentiments (Ghai 1988a, 28–30). Sometimes the methods that were chosen were clearly to the benefit of nation-building and national integration, as in the case of the former British Gilbert and Ellice Islands colony, which was separated into two parts following a referendum in Ellice in 1974, Ellice becoming in 1978 the independent state of Tuvalu and Gilbert becoming in 1979 the independent state of Kiribati. The separation came about as a consequence of a Gilbert–Ellice rivalry in the wake of the evolution of centralized government; the rivalry being between two distinctly different people (van Trease 1993, 7–9). It is something of a paradox, clearly incompatible with the Lipset–Rokkan idea of party systems developing in the wake of national revolutions, that the two nations emerging from the Gilbert and Ellice misalliance are democracies without parties. The thought is by no means exorbitant that the alliance would have given birth to territorially based parties, had it continued into an era of independence, marked by national disunity.

In other cases, the emerging new nations were artificial constructions, manifestations of mixed varieties in terms of race, language and religion. The problems that colonizers sometimes faced are well illustrated in a statement by one observer, emphasizing that the early efforts to construct an entity out of Micronesia in fact implied the integration of an area with nine languages and a number of distinct cultures as well as four colonial masters within living memory (Quigg 1969). Quite so: according to another initiated and more recent observation, "nowhere is the complexity of cross-cutting cultural, geographic, linguistic, and political ties more evident than in the Federated States of Micronesia" (Petersen 1989, 285). Also, in some cases decolonization was really "upside-down decolonisation", resembling the present Netherlands dilemma in the Caribbean (Hoefte and Oostindie 1991), the metropolis rather than the colonies pressing for independence.

The relations between Britain and her Caribbean dependencies after the 1967 West Indies Act developed in this direction: whereas prior to the Act the general view was that the colonies were simply too small to support independence, this view for various reasons was soon turned into a British wish to simply get rid of the burdens (e.g. Thorndike 1991, 123–4). Writing about Dominica, Irving Andre notes that independence was rather a question of when control should be accepted from a colonizer which appeared only too willing to relinquish its constitutional ties to the island (Andre and Christian 1992, 78). The result was in several cases an emergence of new and small states, the capability of which to achieve and maintain nationhood may be questioned.

Decolonization processes formally transfer authority from a metropolitan government to its successor. This does not automatically mean that the structures, devices and designs of authority are transferred as well; in practice, however, for a variety of reasons, departing colonizers often leave owner's marks. About the South-Eastern Caribbean island states it has been said that their political culture "can be summed up as one characterized by mimicry", as the history and extent of their economic and psychological dependence "dictated a degree of servility and a concern to reflect in their institutions the values and assumptions of their mentors" (Thorndike 1991, 128). Also, of the eleven small Pacific island states, the Marshall Islands being the most obvious exception, almost all have adopted the governmental system of the metropolitan power (e.g. Ghai 1988a, 32–5; Anckar, D. 1997c). This is not to say that the colonies were forced to adopt certain systems and devices. In fact, in the Pacific at least, the process of making constitutions for the new states was almost everywhere democratic, involving in numerous cases extensive discussions among the leaders of the countries as well as broad consultations with the people (Ghai 1988a, 6–24). On the other hand, one can of course argue that the colonized people were in fact not given much option in deciding the system of government, the independence process often involving mental and other preparations for a transfer of metropolitan models to the colonized people (Neemia 1992, 7). Be this as it may, the end result was in the vast majority of small island cases a correspondence between the system of the metropole and the system of the new nation. Most small island states being former British colonies, this end result was the Westminster model.

Like all models, the Westminster model is more a tool of analysis than an empirical description (Lane and Ersson 1994b, 70–3). In applications of this model, therefore, various modifications can be used and invented, without the essentials of the model being lost. In fact, a model transfer which accepts impositions uncritically may be counter-productive, as it does not take into account the specifics that may prevail in the new environment. Discussing requirements for the creation in Caribbean of cohesive societies, Lloyd Searwar presents an important point of view:

It cannot seriously be disputed that a cohesive society, especially in the case of a small state, is the best safeguard against pressure or destabilisation. At present our divided societies lend themselves too readily to the internalisation of external conflicts, not of their own making. The chief instrument for the promotion of cohesiveness must continue to be the operation of parliamentary democracy after the Westminster model. However, that "model" is defective in several respects. In the absence of the restraining conventions and customary rules which obtain in the country of its genesis, the Westminster Model can lend itself all too readily to dictatorial rule. It provides a Prime Minister with enormous residual power without the customary restraints.

(1991, 235)

The islands have, on the whole, been very conscious of this type of danger, and the Westminster model has in many places and in many respects been adopted to suit the actual conditions: "Although the current political systems in Western Samoa, Fiji, Kiribati, Tuvalu, Vanuatu, Solomon Islands, Papua New Guinea, the Cook Islands and others all incorporate various aspects of the Westminster system, each of them is very different from the other" (Crocombe 1992, 10). The many varieties cannot be dealt with here and now; in fact, one issue only will be briefly discussed, which relates directly to party systems and voter alignments. This issue is about electoral systems and the impact of such systems, notably about the distinction between proportional systems and majoritarian systems. Proportional systems aim at making the elected body as similar as possible to the electorate at large, whereas majoritarian systems are motivated by different views of representation (e.g. Nurmi 1987, 178–90). Proportional systems then, according to conventional wisdom, for several reasons force the formation of parties. For one thing, even small parties have under these systems prospects of seats, as the support among the electorate reflects in the number of seats. Furthermore, as the number of parties in the legislature increases, the prospects for small parties to gain influence improve correspondingly. Under majoritarian systems, the effects on party formation are different. The expectation is that only few parties emerge; to the extent that party systems are outcomes of electoral systems, majoritarian systems impose restrictions.

In the small island states, in elections to national parliaments, plurality systems with one-member constituencies are widely used, this being in full accordance with the Westminster model. Out of 32 small island states, according to my count, 15 adhere to this system, another 10 making use of plurality systems with multi-member constituencies. This means, it would seem, that the possibilities of testing the validity of conventional assumptions of the link between electoral systems and party systems are slim indeed. There is simply not enough variation in the independent variable; since the proportional systems are very few, the impact of proportionality is difficult to assess. However, the sterility of the independent variable notwithstanding, there is a lot of variation in the dependent variable: earlier in this chapter observations have been reported which indicate a diversity of party system patterns. Since dissimilarities can hardly be consequences of similarities, it follows that conventional wisdoms fail: between electoral systems and party systems no link appears to exist.

One reason for this somewhat disturbing finding is perhaps that the distinction between proportional and majoritarian systems becomes less distinct in the context of small island states. This is because these states have specific characteristics in terms of voter alignments. As noted above, majoritarian systems are no ideal solutions from the point of view of political representation. Taking this notion as a point of departure and drawing on Arend Lijphart's thesis that majority rule is unfit for plural societies (1984a, 22–3), Tatu Vanhanen has argued that several of the small Caribbean island states, like Bahamas, Barbados and Trinidad and Tobago, because of the ethnic fragmentation of these countries, would be better off using a proportional system (1990, 187–8). This may well be a valid observation as far as these individual cases are concerned; it is, however, unclear to what extent the observation can be applied to the universe of small island states. Hannu Nurmi has suggested that the virtues of majoritarian systems are more obvious when the geographic representation is deemed important and when the parties do not feature as the main foci of the ideological identification of voters (1987, 180); this remark is, no doubt, highly relevant in the context of small island states, many of which are at the one and the same time archipelagic and sceptic towards the virtues of party life and party organization. To state this differently, because of specific patterns of voter alignments in small island states, the independent variable becomes blurred, majoritarian systems taking over much of the functions of proportional systems. The diversity of the dependent variable is thereby matched by a diversity of the independent variable.

The customs and tradition factor

In her recent work on *Tradition Versus Democracy in the South Pacific*, Stephanie Lawson argues that the concept of tradition is one of the most important components of an ideological arsenal which has been used to counter the development in the Pacific region of more democratic norms of political conduct and organization (1996, 5). In Lawson's view, the idea of tradition has been deployed not so much in defence of highly prized aspects of unique cultural identities, "but in defence of elite power and privilege against growing demands for accountability in government as well as more extensive opportunities for participation by those without traditionally derived political or social status" (1996, 5). There is no doubt much to Lawson's analysis, which focuses on the Pacific cases of Fiji, Tonga and Western Samoa, Fiji representing a traditionalist emphasis on chiefly rule,

Tonga subscribing to values relating to monarchy and aristocracy, and Western Samoa still maintaining, although now to a lesser degree, the *matai* system. (Earlier, from independence up to 1990, the franchise was in Western Samoa restricted to bearers of traditional *matai* chiefly titles. Today universal suffrage is introduced, eligibility for candidature, however, still being confined to the *matai*.)

However, Lawson also warns against the construction of the two components of tradition and modernity as absolute categories occupying opposing poles of a rigid dichotomy (1996, 5). Again, she is right. There is no doubt in the world of small island politics plenty of room for an agreement between tradition and modernity on the leading principles for political life. This is certainly true for regions outside the Pacific: democracy in Iceland, for instance, has a long tradition embedded in cultural heritages (e.g. Petersson 1994). But it is true also for Pacific regions. For instance, about the marriage between culture and democracy in political life in Papua New Guinea, it has been said that the fact that many vital democratic values have equivalents inherent in indigenous cultures contributes to explanations of the absence of fundamental political rifts in that country (Deklin 1992, 47). Also, conscious efforts have been made and are made in many places to integrate culture and democracy. About the Kiribati constitution it has been said that it is "a marriage of Westminster principles and local values and concerns" and that it is "a workable compromise between local values and standard constitutional forms" (Macdonald 1996, 41 and 45). According to Uentabo Neemia, "In varying degrees, Pacific countries have made many efforts to adopt the Westminster model and representative democracy inherent in it, to suit local conditions and cultural values. They do this both structurally, in modifications to the constitution and to law, and functionally, in the complementation of the existing constitution" (1992, 8). To mention just one more example, writing about the Pohnpei Island in the Federated States of Micronesia, Resio Moses and Gene Ashby note:

> The democratic system introduced by the Americans under the United Nations Trusteeship did not supplant the traditional government. Rather, the responsibilities of administration came to be divided between traditional leaders and those directly related to civic administration. Traditional authority has been reduced, but Pohnpeians have adjusted to this change. Conflict has been avoided by accommodation. The elected leaders show great deference in language and behaviour to traditional leaders, who in turn often award high honorific titles to those democratically elected in the municipal governments. The traditional leaders support the elected executives in their municipalities and advise people how to adapt democratic forms to traditional customs. The executives and councilmen refrain from actions or activities that might infringe on the role of traditional leaders.
>
> (1992, 215)

Still, one cannot deny that tradition and democracy often come into collision. For one thing, to integrate culture and democracy is anything but easy, as the diffusion of Western democratic values and institutions to small island contexts confronts various problems of scale, thresholds of size, and incompatibility of levels. A British colonizer is reported to have asked in the early 1970s an apposite question about the Solomon Islands: "Can a system of democracy suitable for a country of 58 million be photographed down to suit a population of 152,000 with about 80 spoken languages and no written literature . . . with the habit of agreeing by consensus rather than by majority vote and with a suspicion bred from a history of foreigners, foreign ideas and foreign motives" (Alasia 1989, 144). Second, it is not always the case that democratic values and democratic institutions have equivalents in indigenous cultures. Rather, as a rule the reverse is true, this of course creating all sorts of difficulties and imbalances. Above all, cultural inclinations towards communalism and hierarchical social structures, both these factors in fact promoting a consensual system of decision-making, have proved in many places to be stumbling-blocks.

The resistance is in part ideological in nature. The Constitution of Tuvalu is in its preamble quite outspoken, as it is stated that the guiding principles of Tuvalu in government and social affairs generally are "agreement, courtesy and the search for consensus, in accordance with traditional Tuvaluan procedures, rather than alien ideas of confrontation and divisiveness". In other constitutions, like those of, for instance, Kiribati and Vanuatu, the same ideals are expressed; sometimes other devices are used to signal the same conviction. It is no coincidence that the name of the Belau Parliament, *Olbiil Era Kelulau,* means "The Place of Whispers", this referring to a tradition of making decisions in local and other councils within a consensus system by quiet consultation and often secret negotiations between leaders, supporters and fractions (Quimby 1988, 116). In this traditional process the decision-makers, assembled in the *Abai,* exchanged opinions and thoughts through appointed messengers, discussion being conducted by this quiet method until a decision was reached and unanimously accepted before made public. By this fashion, everyone's support of the decision was ensured and credit was shared by all (Fourth Olbiil Era Kelulau, 19). It is, no doubt, difficult to think of any method that would be more distant from the open divisiveness of modern party politics.

This is not to say that party politics has no future in the Pacific. It is certainly an important observation that the trend in some Pacific countries has been towards the organization and strengthening of parties, and that this trend can be expected to continue (Ghai 1988b, 360). Discussing the political culture of Kiribati, the former President of that country is able to identify this same trend; however, he adds some qualifications and reservations:

Traditionally, *I-Kiribati* made decisions in the *maneaba* by consensus, rather than voting. Things have, however, begun to change in the outer islands. . . . Furthermore, a clear party system is beginning to appear in the *Maneaba ni Mangatabu,* which many people regard as irrelevant to the process of electing their members. At present, the average person in the village does not fully understand what political parties are or how a party system works. In the general election, people vote on a personal basis; there is little knowledge of or concern for a candidate's political affiliation. It is the members of Parliament who then organise themselves for the purpose of forming the Government.

(Tabai 1993, 318)

As is evident from this quotation, a resistance against the idea of party politics appears not only on ideological levels but in terms of behaviour as well. Among the people, political parties have a bad reputation. For instance, reporting impressions from fieldwork in Vanuatu, Ellen Facey has noticed that modern party politics are condemned by many in that country, who regard politics as a destructive enterprise characterized by heated argument and even incitement to violence of members of one party against those of another, the preference, therefore, being for a one-party government rather than one with two parties or more (1995, 214). For students of modern politics, such sentiments may be hard to understand. The sentiments need, however, to be placed in context. The voters in many small island states are no Lipset–Rokkan voters, whose identity is formed through processes of nation-building and industrialization. They are people who live in villages and similar small communities and who are socialized into clans and subclans, the values and interests of which are difficult to relate to party platforms and party ideologies. "The Nation" and all it stands for are something "out there" which only become reality on specific occasions, like national elections (Jacobsen 1995, 240). One implication of this attitude is that politicians are expected to take care of local matters; they are elected because they have as local "bigmen" proved their capability and because of expectations that they can provide for the local community. These expectations, in turn, motivate politicians to give local affairs their best attention; a circle is thereby created which fosters close ties between politicians and constituencies and distances politicians as well as voters from the sphere of non-local party politics. Another circle is also created. Since politicians are not attached strongly to parties, parties lack stability, and in some places, "members of the major parties criss crossing the floor frequently", coalition governments have been formed to avoid periods of chronic confusion (Ghai 1988b, 360). These poor party performances are not likely to inspire popular confidence in parties as institutions.

In conclusion, there is little doubt that factors relating to tradition and culture have had and still have an impact on the proliferation of party systems and voter alignments. More than elsewhere, this is the case in the

Pacific islands, where the assimilation of western democratic institutions and principles by the traditional society has encountered the largest difficulties and faced the most serious challenges. In these traditionally stratified societies, in many places, the final breakthrough of democratic politics is long in coming, and there is little reason to doubt the accuracy of an adventure guide to the South Pacific, which suggests that there are areas in Vanuatu where independence makes not a whit of difference: "Most of the Big Namba tribesmen in north Malekula could care less who runs the country" (Booth 1990, 289). Earlier in this section a rather optimistic view was presented on the integration of aspects of democracy into traditional culture in Papua New Guinea; to balance this view, a different interpretation of the same situation is quoted here, which in fact suggests that two parallel systems are working, one modern which does not count for much, and one traditional, which counts:

> Free media, democratic electoral politics, representative government, an independent judiciary, flourishing universities – they exist, but the inherited Australian-style political and legal system simply does not prevail in setting standards to curb the willfulness and wantonness of the ruling bigmen. Somehow, grass-roots social movements – of women, workers, students, farmers, the regionally aggrieved – and effective political parties must develop to compensate for the deficiences of leaders and bureaucracies, and to generate popular support for reform which the party system at present seems incapable of doing.
>
> (King 1991, 60–1)

Conclusion

In defence of the relevance of island studies to the field of academic geography, some authors have argued that social and economic processes on islands are not distinctively different and that islands offer an exceptional opportunity to study, under relatively controlled conditions, the entire spectrum of ecological, demographic, economic and social factors that influence population–environment relationships. This is because systems on islands are small and easily modelled, yet at the same time representative of larger systems. Islands, it is said, "are not essentially different, but merely more extreme, and conveniently replicated versions, of what is found in the more familiar continental world of conventional geographical study" (Bayliss-Smith *et al.* 1988, 283–4).

What is true of geography, however, is not necessarily true of politics. Island social science, David Lowenthal maintains, has not matched natural science; few sociological or psychological insights have been developed to account for the special character of insular human life and culture (1992, 19). Still, Lowenthal advocates the view that islands are very different. He sees islands as "special and different, unlike continental areas in their societal, cultural, and psychological makeup" (1992, 19). In fact, a case can be made for both views. Islands are replications, and they are not. It all depends, on perspectives, questions asked, levels of analysis and generality. It is one central observation in the work by Lipset and Rokkan that cleavages are frozen and that this reflects in the party systems of Europe which are similarly frozen (1967a, 50–1). Leaving aside here the various suggestions, hypotheses and ideas forwarded by the authors to link social cleavages and party politics, the observation by Lipset and Rokkan really boils down to the idea that politics reflects social structure. This is certainly true for small island states as well as other states; one needs to consider, however, that the social frameworks often are fundamentally different.

Island frameworks are shaped by factors like smallness, remoteness and territorial fragmentation; these factors interact in a variety of ways, which influence the shaping of party systems and the nature of voter alignment. Smallness may not affect systematically the number of parties in island nations, but may, because of an uniform problem setting and an economic monoculture, which are almost inevitable consequences of smallness, decrease the ideological and attitudinal distances between parties. "With only minor differences, all parties agree that the momentum of development should continue, inflation should be kept under control, unemployment reduced and regional imbalances eliminated", A. R. Mannick writes in his presentation of politics in Mauritius (1989, 95). Remoteness implies isolation, isolation fosters the survival of tradition and custom, it thereby works against the adoption of modern and western views of political conduct and political method. Geography, in its archipelagic forms, implies remoteness, especially in regards to outer islands; geography thereby creates and maintains internal centre–periphery relations which undermine the emergence of a national identity and strengthen separate island identities. To the constraints of insularity and smallness one should in many cases add the historical legacy of the colonial period, as well as the fact that many small island states have established political orders in a distinct cultural environment which must shape the solutions to problems just as it has shaped the problems (Macdonald 1996, 4).

Quite often the solutions imply a peculiar dualism. Although achievement does not count for everything in industrial societies, and although there are differences between traditional societies in terms of the importance of ascription, it is still quite common to believe that power discrepancies in non-industrial societies follow tradition and ascribed statuses, whereas achievement is more important in industrial societies (Eriksen 1995, 147). The dichotomy is well and alive in small island places in a very specific sense: the two systems operate side by side, in parallel. Writing in the mid-1980s about Fiji leadership, Rusiate Nayaeakalou, a Fijian social scientist, criticized the idea that change was possible within the framework of traditional culture. The idea contained, he stated, a basic contradiction in that one cannot change and preserve the same thing at the same time; the belief that one can simultaneously preserve and change a way of life was a "monstrous nonsense" (quoted from Lal 1992, 112). Still, this is exactly what is done in many places. Many islands adhere to democracy Westminster style, but also to democracy Vanuatu style; politics is election-guided but also chiefly-guided. In fact, the co-existence is encouraged even on doctrinaire levels, as, for instance, in the prescription of "The Pacific Way" as an appropriate development strategy for the Pacific small island societies, this strategy comprising efforts to decrease urbanization, to replace imports with locally produced substitutes and to discourage consumption of other imports as culturally undesirable, to reduce government activity by reconstructing local community support, and, in the sphere of politics, to utilize customary political structures which are seen as based upon consensus (Cameron 1992, 151). Very little is known in terms of systematic research about the premises, forms, methods and consequences of this dualism. It goes almost without saying, however, that the dualism carries implications for the formation of party systems and voter alignments.

Finally, one needs to consider that islands do not form an uniform category: "small islands, like small continental states, are diverse in character" (Newitt 1992, 2). The distinction between mainland countries and islands may therefore in some instances become blurred: whereas some islands are in some respects and aspects similar to mainland countries, others are not. Some island states and island regions even constitute in some respects and aspects distinct island subcategories. Discussing the case of the insular Caribbean, Justin Daniel emphasizes that political life in this region is double-faced: on the one hand people as well as elites place a strong value on the electoral process and have a firm belief in the legitimacy of their political institutions, on the other hand, because of a clientelism, historically modelled on the paternalistic system of plantation, this framework accommodates authoritarian tendencies and mechanisms which may lead to the supplanting of democratic norms and procedures (1994, 13). Daniel's discussion of this somewhat strange dualism is illustrative of the complexity of factors operating in island contexts, and a lengthy quotation from his study is therefore a proper endnote to this chapter:

> These two faces distinguish political systems of the Eastern Caribbean from others in the region or in the world and make them unique. Variables such as size and insularity, history of enslavement and the legacy of the British political model have played a determinant role in the emergence of this specific type of state. But no single variable can provide an exclusive explanation. . . . The explanation lies in the specific articulation of different variables: the combination of size and insularity, of small populations in small territories, fosters the kind of cohesion that facilitates both the persistence of democratic values and institutions and personalized relationships rooted in the tradition of the plantation. Moreover, the political stability of these states is cemented by insular identities which have a dynamic effect on internal political structures while preventing the development of any form of Caribbean nationalism.
> (1994, 13)

Appendix 1

The small island states. some regime characteristics.

A. *Year of Independence.* 1944: Iceland; 1959: Singapore; 1960: Cyprus; 1962: Trinidad and Tobago, Western Samoa; 1964: Malta; 1966: Barbados; 1968: Maldives, Mauritius, Nauru; 1970: Fiji, Tonga (1875); 1971: Bahrain; 1973: Bahamas; 1974: Grenada; 1975: Cape Verde, Comoros, Sao Tome and Principe; 1976: Seychelles; 1978: Dominica, Solomon Islands, Tuvalu; 1979: Kiribati, St Lucia, St Vincent and the Grenadines; 1980: Vanuatu; 1981: Antigua and Barbuda; 1983: St Kitts and Nevis; 1984: Brunei; 1991: Federated States of Micronesia, Marshall Islands; 1994: Belau.

B. *Colonial Background.* Independent from the UK: Antigua and Barbuda, Bahamas, Bahrain (British protected status), Barbados, Brunei (British protected status), Cyprus, Dominica, Fiji, Grenada, Kiribati, Maldives (British protected status), Malta, Mauritius, St Kitts and Nevis, St Lucia, St Vincent and the Grenadines, Seychelles, Singapore, Solomon Islands (British protected status), Trinidad and Tobago, Tuvalu. Independent from France: Comoros. Independent from Portugal: Cape Verde, Sao Tome and Principe. Independent from Denmark: Iceland. Independent from status as Anglo-French Condominium: Vanuatu. Independent from UN Trusteeship (USA): Belau, Federated States of Micronesia, Marshall Islands. Independent from UN Trusteeship (New Zealand): Western Samoa. Independent from UN Trusteeship (Australia, New Zealand and the UK): Nauru. Never colonized: Tonga.

C. *Federalism, Bicameralism.* Belau, Comoros, Federated States of Micronesia and St Kitts and Nevis are federal states, the other are unitary states. Belau and Comoros (since 1992) are bicameral as well. The common assertion that all federal states in the world are bicameral (e.g. Heywood 1997, 301–2) is not correct, as Micronesia and St Kitts and Nevis are unicameral (concerning the quite unique composition of the Micronesian legislature, see, however, Burdick 1988). Like Belau and Comoros, Bahamas, Barbados, Fiji, Grenada, St Lucia and Trinidad and Tobago have bicameral legislatures. There are no parliaments in Bahrain and Brunei.

D. *Parliamentarism, Presidentialism.* The following countries have parliamentary executives: Antigua and Barbuda, Bahamas, Barbados, Dominica, Grenada, Malta, Marshall Islands, Mauritius, Nauru, St Kitts–Nevis, St Lucia, St Vincent and the Grenadines, Singapore, Solomon Islands, Trinidad and Tobago, Tuvalu, Vanuatu and Western Samoa. Presidential systems: Belau, Comoros, Cyprus, Federated States of Micronesia (although the President is elected from the four Senators who represent the federal states), Maldives, Seychelles, Sao Tome and Principe. Cape Verde, Fiji and Iceland are semipresidential systems; the President is elected in Fiji by *Bose Levu Vakaturaga* (Great Council of Chiefs). The system in Kiribati is mixed, likewise the system in Sao Tome and Principe, where executive power is vested in the President, who is accountable to the Assembléia National. Tonga is an authoritarian kingdom, "ruled by the chiefs for the King" (Niu 1988, 307). The regimes in Bahrain and Brunei are authoritarian.

E. *Electoral Systems.* There are no elections in Bahrain and Brunei. Proportional systems: Cape Verde, Cyprus and Iceland operate Party List Systems. Malta uses the Single Transferable Vote (Hirczy 1995) and Vanuatu uses the Single Non-Transferable Vote (van Trease 1995b). Majority systems: Nauru uses The Alternative Vote (the statement in Derbyshire and Derbyshire 1993, 113, that only Australia employs this voting system is therefore incorrect); voting is compulsory in Nauru. All other countries use the single plurality vote; some countries, like Kiribati, Maldives and Tuvalu require or permit multiple member constituencies. Note: Appointment methods are used by several countries. For instance, the Constitution of Mauritius prescribes that eight of the members of the Assembly shall be appointed by the Governor-General from among runners-up at the general election in order to ensure a balance in representation between the island's different ethnic groups (e.g. Mannick 1989, 24–6). The Legislative Assembly of the Kingdom of Tonga introduces a separate representation of nobles and commoners.

F. *Party Systems.* Number of political parties (Anckar, D. 1997a; additional information from *Regional Surveys of the World*, various issues). There are no parties in the non-democracies of Bahrain and Brunei and in the Maldives. Democracies without parties (electoral criterion): Belau, Federated States of Micronesia, Kiribati, Marshall Islands, Nauru, Tuvalu. Two-party systems: Bahamas, Cape Verde, Malta, Tonga, Western Samoa. Limited Pluralism systems (3–5 parties): Antigua and Barbuda, Barbados, Dominica, Grenada, St Kitts and Nevis, St Lucia, St Vincent and the Grenadines, Seychelles. Extreme pluralism systems (6–8 parties): Cyprus, Sao Tome and Principe, Solomon Islands, Trinidad and Tobago, Vanuatu. Atomized party systems (more than eight parties): Comoros, Fiji, Iceland, Mauritius, Singapore.

G. *Assembly Size (Lower House Members),* from Anckar, D. 1997d. Antigua and Barbuda: 17; Bahamas: 49; Barbados: 28; Belau (*Olbiil Era Kelulau*): 14; Cape Verde: 72; Comoros: 42; Cyprus: 56; Dominica: 30; Federated States of Micronesia: 14; Fiji: 70; Grenada: 15; Iceland (*Althing*): 63; Kiribati (*Maneaba ni Maungatabu*): 41; Maldives (*Majlis*): 48; Malta: 69; Marshall Islands (*Nitijela*): 33; Mauritius: 71; Nauru: 18; St Kitts and Nevis: 14; St Lucia: 17; St Vincent and the Grenadines: 21; Sao Tome and Principe: 55; Seychelles: 34; Singapore: 81; Solomon Islands: 47; Tonga: 31; Trinidad and Tobago: 36; Tuvalu: 12; Vanuatu: 50; Western Samoa (*Fono*): 49. There are no parliaments in Bahrain and Brunei.

Bibliography

Alasia, S. (1989) "Politics", in H. Laracy (ed.), *Ples Blong Iumi. Solomon Islands, The Past Four Thousand Years,* Suva: Institute of Pacific Studies, University of the South Pacific.

Alcántara, M. and Martínez, A. (1998) *Las elecciones autonómicas en España, 1980–1997.* Madrid: Centro de Investigaciones Sociológicas.

Alford, R. R. (1963) *Party and Society: The Anglo-American Democracies,* Chicago: Rand McNally.

—— (1967) "Class Voting in the Anglo-American Political Systems", in S. M. Lipset and S. Rokkan (eds), *Party Systems and Voter Alignments. Cross-National Perspectives,* New York: The Free Press.

Allardt, E. and Pesonen, P. (1967) "Cleavages in Finnish Politics", in Seymour M. Lipset and Stein Rokkan (eds), *Party Systems and Voter Alignments. Cross-National Perspectives,* New York: The Free Press.

Alt, J. E. (1984) "Dealignment and the Dynamics of Partisanship in Britain", in R.J. Dalton, S. C. Flanagan and P. A. Beck (eds), *Electoral Change in Advanced Industrial Democracies, Realigment or Dealignment,* Princeton, NJ: Princeton University Press.

Alt, J. and Boix, C. (1991) "Partisan Voting in the Spanish NATO Referendum: An Ecological Analysis", *Electoral Studies* 10: 18–32.

Anckar, C. (1995) "Storlek och partisystem i världens demokratier", *Politiikka* 37: 181–91.

—— (1997) "Size and Democracy. Some Empirical Findings", in D. Anckar and L. Nilsson (eds), *Politics and Geography, Contributions to An Interface,* Sundsvall: Mid-Sweden University Press.

Anckar, D. (1993) "Notes on the Party Systems of Small Island States", in T. Bryder (ed.), *Party Systems, Party Behaviour and Democracy,* Copenhagen: University of Copenhagen, Copenhagen Political Studies Press.

—— (1996) "Noncontiguity and Political Architecture: The Parliaments of Small Island States", *Political Geography* 15: 697–713.

—— (1997a) "Dominating Smallness: Big Parties in Lilliput Systems", *Party Politics* 3: 243–63.

—— (1997b) "Federal and Bicameral Microstates: Gigantic Miniatures?", in D. Anckar and L. Nilsson (eds), *Politics and Geography. Contributions to an Interface,* Sundsvall: Mid-Sweden University Press.

—— (1997c) "Montesquieu in the Pacific: Cabinet Recruitment Patterns in Eleven Small Island States", in V. Helander and S. Sandberg (eds), *Festskrift till Krister Ståhlberg. 50 år den 31 maj 1997,* Åbo: Åbo Akademi University Press.

284　Bibliography

—— (1997d) "Parlamentens storlek i världens små östater", in P. Kettunen, and J. Valanta (eds), *Hallinto ja kansanvalta. Esseitä Voitto Helanderin 60– vuotispäivän kunniaksi*, Turku: Annales Universitatis Turkuensis, Ser. C Tom 136.

—— (1997e) "Small Is Homogeneous: Myth or Reality?", paper presented to the 29th Annual Meeting of the Finnish Political Science Association, Helsinki, January 9–10, 1997.

Anckar, D. and Anckar, C. (1995) "Size, Insularity and Democracy", *Scandinavian Political Studies* 18: 211–29.

—— (2000) "Democracies without Parties", *Comparative Political Studies* 33: 225– 47.

Anckar, D., Anckar, C. and Nilsson, L. (1998) "Constitutional and Political Life in the Republic of Belau", *Scandinavian Journal of Development Alternatives and Area Studies* 17: 75–97.

Andeweg, R. (1999) "Parties, Pillars and the Politics of Accommodation: Weak or Weakening Linkages?", in K. R. Luther and K. Deschouwer (eds), *Party Elites in Divided Societies*, London: Routledge.

Andeweg, R. and Irwin, G. (1993) *Dutch Government and Politics*, London: Macmillan.

Andre, I. W. and Christian, G. J. (1992) *In Search of Eden*, Roseau: Pond Casse Press.

Astudillo, J. (1998) *Los recursos del socialismo: las cambiantes relaciones entre el PSOE y la UGT (1982–1993)*, Madrid: Instituto Juan March, PhD Thesis.

Ayearst, M. (1970) *The Republic of Ireland: Its Government and Politics*, New York: New York University Press.

Baker, K. L., Dalton R. J. and Hildebrandt, K. (1975) "Political Affiliations: Transition in the Bases of German of German Partisanship", Essex: European Consortium for Political Research.

Banfield, E. C. (1958) *The Moral Basis of a Backward Society*, Chicago: The Free Press.

Bardi, L. and Mair, P. (1997) "What is a Party System?", paper presented to the Europaeum Workshop on Party System Change, Nuffield College, Oxford, 17–18 October.

Barnes, S. H., MacDonough, P. and López Pina, A. (1986) "Volatile Parties and Stable Voters in Spain", *Government and Opposition* 21: 56–75.

Barry, B. (1975) "Political Accommodation and Consociational Democracy", *British Journal of Political Science* 5: 447–505.

Bartolini, S. and Mair, P. (1990) *Identity. Competition and Electoral Availability: The Stabilisation of European Electorates 1885–1985*, Cambridge: Cambridge University Press.

Bayliss-Smith, T. P., Bedford, R., Brookfield, H. and Latham, M. (1988) *Islands, Islanders and the World*, Cambridge: Cambridge University Press (Cambridge Human Geography).

Bebe, M. and Clement, L. (1995) "Pentecost", in H. van Trease (ed.) *Melanesian Politics. Stael Blong Vanuatu*, Christchurch: Macmillan Brown Centre for Pacific Studies, University of the South Pacific.

Beilharz, P. (1994) *Transforming Labor: Labor Tradition and the Labor Decade in Australia*, Cambridge: Cambridge University Press.

Bell, D. (1960) *The End of Ideology*, New York: The Free Press.

—— (1976) *The Coming of Post-Industrial Society: A Venture in Social Forecasting*, New York: The Free Press.

Berelson, B. R., Lazarsfeld, P. and McPhee, W. N. (1954) *Voting*, Chicago: University of Chicago Press.

Berglund, S. and Aarebrot, F. (1997) *The Political History of Eastern Europe in the 20th Century,* Chattenham: Edward Elgar.

Berntzen, E. and Selle, S. (1990) "Structures and Action in Stein Rokkan's Work", *Journal of Theoretical Politics* 2: 131–49.

Berry, S. and Kiely, R. (1993) "Is There a Future for Korean Democracy?" *Parliamentary Affairs* 46(4): 594–604.

Bienen, H. (1970) "One-Party Systems in Africa" in S. Huntington and C. Moore (eds), *Authoritarian Politics in Modern Society,* New York: Basic Books.

Bienen, H. and Herbst, J. (1996) "The Relationship between Political and Economic Reform in Africa", *Comparative Politics* 29(1): 23–42.

Blais, A. and Massicotte, L. (1996) "Election Systems", in Laurence LeDuc, R. G. Niemi and P. Norris (eds), *Comparing Democracies,* London: Sage.

Booth, T. H. (1990) *Adventure Guide to the South Pacific,* Ashbourne: Moorland Publishing.

Borg, S. (1996) "Nuoret, politiikka ja yhteiskunnallinen syrjäytyminen" (The young, politics, and social alienation), Helsinki: Ministry of Education (mimeo).

Bosco, A. (forthcoming). "Four Actors in Search of a Role: The South European Communist Parties", in N. Diamandouros and R. Gunther (eds), *Parties, Politics and Democracy in the New Southern Europe,* Baltimore: Johns Hopkins University Press.

Brass, P. (1985) "Indian Election Studies" in P. Brass, *Caste Faction and Party in Indian Politics Vol 2. Election Studies,* Delhi: Chanakya Publications.

Brosveet, J., Henrichsen, B. and Svåsand, L. (1981) "Building Infrastructures for the Social Sciences: Stein Rokkan and the Data-Archive Movement", in P. Torsvik (ed.), *Mobilization, Center–Periphery Structures and Nation-Building. A Volume in Commemoration of Stein Rokkan,* Bergen-Oslo-Tromsø: Universitetsforlaget, 39–47.

Budge, I. (1994) "A New Spatial Theory of Party Competition", *British Journal of Political Science* 24(4): 443–67.

Budge, I., Newton, K., McKinley, R. D. and Kirchner, E. (1997) *The Politics of the New Europe,* Harlow: Longman.

Budge, I., Crewe, Y. and Farlie, D. (1976) *Party Identification and Beyond,* London: Wiley.

Burdick, A. (1988) "The Constitution of the Federated States of Micronesia", in Y. Ghai (ed.) *Law, Politics and Government in the Pacific Island States,* Suva: Institute of Pacific Studies, University of the South Pacific.

Butler, D. and Stokes, D. (1970) *Political Change in Britain,* London: Macmillan.

Caciagli, M. (1986) *Elecciones y partidos en la transición española,* Madrid: Centro de Investigaciones Sociológicas/Siglo XXI.

Cairncross, F. (1997) *The Death of Distance,* Boston: Harvard Business School Press.

Calvo Sotelo, L. (1990) *Memoria viva de la transición,* Barcelona. Plaza & Janés/Cambio16.

Cameron, J. (1992) "The Federated States of Micronesia: Is there a Pacific Way to Avoid a *Mirab* Society?", in H. M Hintjens and M. D .D. Newitt (eds), *The Political Economy of Small Tropical Islands,* Exeter: University of Exeter Press.

Cammack, P. (1994) "Democratization and Citizenship in Latin America", in G. Parry and M. Moran (eds), *Democracy and Democratization,* London: Routledge.

Campbell, I. C. (1992) *Island Kingdom. Tonga Ancient & Modern,* Christchurch: Canterbury University Press.

Capdevielle, J. *et al*. (1981) *France de gauche vote à droite Paris*, Fondation Nationale des Sciences Politiques.

Chibber, P. K. and Petrocik, J. R. (1990) "Social Cleavages, Elections and the Indian Party System" in R. Sisson and R. Roy (eds), *Diversity and Dominance in Indian Politics Vol 1. Changing Bases of Congress Support*, New Delhi and London: Sage.

Chodak, S. (1964) "The Societal Function of Party Systems in Sub-Saharan Africa", in E. Allardt and Y. Littunen (eds), *Cleavages, Ideologies and Party Systems*, Helsinki: Academic Bookstore.

Church, C. (1989) "Behind the Consociational Screen: Politics in Contemporary Switzerland", *West European Politics* 12: 35–54.

Clapham, C. (1985) *Third World Politics*, London: Croom-Helm.

Clark, J. and Wildavsky, A. (1990) *The Moral Collapse of Communism*, San Francisco: ICS Press.

Collier, R. B. (1978) "Parties, Coups and Authoritarian Rule: Patterns of Political Change in Tropical Africa", *Comparative Political Studies* 11(1): 62–88.

Colomer, J. M. (1999) "The Spanish 'State of the Autonomies': Non-Institutional Federalism", in P. Heywood (ed.), *Politics and Policy in Democratic Spain: No Longer Different?* London: Frank Cass.

Converse, P. E. (1969) "Of Time and Partisan Stability", *Comparative Political Studies* 2(2): 139–71.

Craig, A. L. and Cornelius, W. A. (1995) "Houses Divided: Parties and Political Reform in Mexico", in S. Mainwaring and T. R. Scully (eds), *Building Democratic Institutions: Party Systems in Latin America*, Stanford, CA: Stanford University Press.

Crewe, I. (1986) "On the Death and Resurrection of Class Voting: Some Comments on How Britain Votes", *Political Studies* 35: 620–38.

Crocombe, R. (1992) "The Future of Democracy in the Pacific Islands", in Crocombe, R. *et al*. (eds), *Culture and Democracy in the South Pacific*, Suva: Institute of Pacific Studies, University of the South Pacific.

Crozier, M., Huntington, S. P. and Watanuki, J. (1975) *The Crisis of Democracy*, New York: New York University Press.

Daalder, H. (1966) "The Netherlands: Opposition in a Segmented Society", in R. Dahl (ed.), *Political Oppositions in Western Democracies*, New Haven: Yale University Press.

—— (1971) "On Building Consociational Nations: the Cases of the Netherlands and Switzerland", *International Social Science Journal* 23: 355–70.

Dahl, R. A. (ed.) (1966) *Political Opposition in Western Democracies*, New Haven: Yale University Press.

Dahl, R. A. and Tufte, E. R. (1973) *Size and Democracy*, Stanford, CA: Stanford University Press.

Dahrendorf, R. (1959) *Class and Class Conflict in Industrial Society*, Stanford: Stanford University Press.

Dalton, R. J. (1984) "The West German Party System Between Two Ages", in R. J. Dalton, S. C Flanagan and P. A. Beck (eds), *Electoral Change in Advanced Industrial Democracies, Realigment or Dealignment*, Princeton, NJ: Princeton University Press.

Dalton, R. J., Flanagan S. C. and Beck, P. A. (eds) (1984) *Electoral Change in Advanced Industrial Democracies, Realigment or Dealignment*, Princeton, NJ: Princeton University Press.

Daniel, J. (1994) "Smallness and Insularity: Dilemmas of Political Life in the Anglophone Eastern Caribbean", paper presented to the XVIth World Congress of the International Political Science Association, Berlin, August 21–25, 1994.

de Backer, R. (1993) "St Kitts and Nevis. A Decade of Quiet Prosperity", *The Courier* 141 (September–October): 6–12.

Dekker, P. (1994) *Intergenerational Ideological Change and Politics in the Netherlands*, World Congress of Political Science, IPSA (unpublished paper).

Deklin, T. (1992) "Culture and Democracy in Papua New Guinea: Marit Tru or Ginman Marit?", in R. Crocombe *et al.* (eds), *Culture and Democracy in the South Pacific*, Suva: Institute of Pacific Studies, University of the South Pacific.

Derbyshire, J. D. and Derbyshire, I. (1993) *World Political Systems*, Edinburgh: Chambers.

Deschouwer, K. (1994) "The Decline of Consociationalism and the Reluctant Modernization of the Belgian Mass Parties", in R. Katz and P. Mair (eds), *How Parties Organize: Adaptation and Change in Party Organizations in Western Democracies*, London: Sage.

—— (1996) "Waiting for the 'Big One': the Uncertain Survival of the Belgian Party System(s)", in K. Deschouwer, L. Dewinter and D. Della Porta (eds), *Partitocracies Between Crises and Reforms: the Cases of Italy and Belgium*, special issue of *Res Publica* 38(2): 295–306.

—— (1997) "Caught in A Trap. Political Parties and Their Reaction to the Erosion of Voter Loyalty in Belgium", paper presented at the Workshop Party responses to voter loyalties, Vienna, January 1997.

De Winter, L. (1998) "Conclusion: A Comparative Analysis of the Electoral, Office and Policy Success of Ethnoregionalist Parties", in L. De Winter and H. Türsan (eds), *Regionalist Parties in Western Europe*, London: Routledge.

Diaz, V. P. (1991) *The Church and Religion in Contemporary Spain*, Madrid: Instituto Juan March.

Di Palma, G. (1980) "¿Derecha, izquierda o centro? Sobre la legitimación de partidos y coaliciones en el sur de Europa", *Revista de Derecho Político* 6: 133–45.

Dix, R. H. (1989) "Cleavage Structures and Party Systems in Latin America", *Comparative Politics* 22: 23–37.

Dogan, M. (1960) "Le vote ouvrier en Europe occidentale", *Revue Française de Sociologie* I(1): 25–44.

—— (1962) "Le donne italiane tra cattolicesimo e il marxismo", in A. Spreafico and J. LaPalombara (eds), *Elezioni e comportamento politico in Italia*, Cremona, 475–94.

—— (1967) "Political Cleavages and Social Stratification in France and Italy", in S. M. Lipset and S. Rokkan (eds) *Party Systems and Voter Alignments: Cross-National Perspectives*, New York: The Free Press.

—— (1993) "De Gaulle et la classe ouvrière", *Espoir*, Revue de l'Institut Charles de Gaulle, no. 91, mars: 53–62.

—— (1995) "The Decline of Religious Beliefs in Western Europe", *International Social Science Journal* 145: 405–18.

Dogan, M. and Rokkan, S. (1967) "Quantitative Ecological Analysis: Contexts, Trends, Tasks", *Social Science Information* VI: 35–47.

Dogan, M. and Rokkan, S. (eds) (1974) *Social Ecology*, Cambridge, MA: M.I.T. Press.

Domínguez, F. (1998) *ETA: estrategia organziativa y actuaciones,1978–1992*, Bilbao: Universidad del País Vasco.

Donovan, M. and Broughton, D. (1999) "Party System Change in Western Europe:

Positively Political", in D. Broughton and M. Donovan (eds), *Changing Party Systems in Western Europe*, London: Pinter.

Douglas, M. (1987) *How Institutions Think*, London: Routledge & Kegan Paul.

Dunleavy, P. (1987) "Class Dealignment in Britain Revisited", *West European Politics* 10: 400–19.

Duverger, M. (1954) *Political Parties*, New York: John Wiley.

Eckstein, H. (1968) "[Parties, Political:] Party Systems", in David L. Sills (ed.), *International Encyclopaedia of the Social Sciences*, New York: Crowell, Collier & Macmillan, vol. 11: 436–53.

Ellemers, J. (1984) "Pillarization as a Process of Modernization", *Acta Politica* 19: 129–44.

Elster, J. (1993) "Some Unresolved Problems in the Theory of Rational Behavior", *Acta Sociologica* 36: 179–90.

Engelmann, F. (1966) "Austria: the Pooling of Opposition", in R. Dahl (ed.), *Political Oppositions in Western Democracies*, New Haven, CT: Yale University Press.

Epstein, L. (1980) *Political Parties in Western Democracies*, New Brunswick, NJ: Transaction Books.

Eriksen, T. H. (1995) *Small Places, Large Issues. An Introduction to Social and Cultural Anthropology*, London: Pluto Press.

Ersson, S. and Lane, J. (1998) "Electoral Instability and Party System Change in Western Europe", in P. Pennings and J.-E. Lane (eds.), *Comparing Party System Change*, London: Routledge.

Ester, P., Halman, L. and de Moor, R. (1993) *The Individualizing Society, Value Change in Europe and North America*, Tilburg: Tilburg University Press.

Eulau, H. (1969) *Micro–Macro Political Analysis*, Chicago: Alding Publishing Company.

European Bank for Reconstruction and Development (1996), *Transition Report*, London: EBRD.

European Journal of Political Research. *Political Data Yearbook*, published annually by the European Consortium of Political Research.

EVA (1997) *Menestyksen eväät* (Provisions for Success), Helsinki: The Centre for Finnish Business and Policy Studies (EVA).

Evans, G. (ed.) (1998) *The End of Class Politics? Class Voting in Comparative Context*, Oxford: Oxford University Press.

Evans, G. and Whitefield, S. (1993) "Identifying the Bases of Party Competition in Eastern Europe" *British Journal of Political Science* 23: 521–48.

—— (1995) "Economic Ideology and Political Success", *Party Politics* 1(4): 565–78.

Facey, E. (1995) "Kastom and Nation-Making: The Politization of Tradition on Nguna, Vanuatu", in R. J. Foster (ed.), *Nation Making. Emergent Identities in Postcolonial Melanesia*, Ann Arbor, MI: The University of Michigan Press.

Ferdinand, P. (1994) "The Party's Over: Market Liberalization and the Challenges for One-Party and One-Party Dominant Regimes: The Cases of Taiwan and Mexico, Italy and Japan", *Democratization* 1(1): 133–50.

Fishman, R. M. (1990) *Working-class Organization and the Return to Democracy in Spain*, Ithaca, NY: Cornell University Press.

Flanagan, S. C. (1987) "Changing Values in Industrial Society Revisited: Towards a Resolution of Value Debate", *American Political Science Review* 81: 1303–19.

Flora, P. (1992) "Stein Rokkans makro-modell for politisk utvikling i Europa", in B, Hagtvetd (ed.), *Politikk mellom ökonomi og kultur. Stein Rokkan som politisk sosiolog og forskningsinspirator*, Oslo: Ad Notam Gyldendal.

Fourastié, J. (1979) *Les Trente Glorieuses ou la Révolution Invisible*, Paris: Fayard.
Fourth Olbiil Era Kelulau 1993–1996 (1995) Koror: Palau National Congress.
Fox, R. (1996) "Bleak Future for Multi-Party Elections in Kenya", *Journal of Modern African Studies* 34(4): 597–607.
Franklin, M. N. (1996) "Electoral Participation", in L. LeDuc, R. G. Niemi and P. Norris (eds), *Comparing Democracies*, London: Sage.
Franklin, M. N., and Mughan A. (1978) "The Decline of Class Voting in Britain", *American Political Science Review* 72: 523–34.
Franklin, M. N., Mackie, Th. T. and Valen, H. (eds) (1992) *Electoral Change: Responses to Evolving Social and Attitudinal Structures in Western Countries*, Cambridge: Cambridge University Press.
Gallagher, M., Laver, M. and Mair, P. (1995) *Representative Government in Modern Europe*, New York: McGraw-Hill.
Garvin, T. (1974) " Political Cleavages, Party Politics and Urbanisation in Ireland: The Case of the Periphery-Dominated Centre", *European Journal of Political Research* 2: 307–27.
Ghai, Y. (1988a) "Constitution Making and Decolonisation", in Y. Ghai (ed.), *Law, Politics and Government in the Pacific Island States*, Suva: Institute of Pacific Studies, University of the South Pacific.
—— (1988b) "The Political Consequences of Constitutions", in Y. Ghai (ed.) *Law, Politics and Government in the Pacific Island States*, Suva: Institute of Pacific Studies, University of the South Pacific.
Giddens, A. (1976) *New Rules of Sociological Method*, London: Hutchinson & Co.
Glassner, M. (1990) *Neptune's Domain. A Political Geography of the Sea*, London: Unwin Hyman.
Goguel, F. (1946) *La politique des partis sous la Troisième République*, Paris: Seuil.
Goldthorpe, J. H. (1996) "Class and Politics in Advanced Industrial Societies", in David J. Lee and Bryan S. Turner (eds), *Conflicts about Class: Debating Inequality in Late Industrialism*, London: Longman.
González, J. J. (1996) "Clases, ciudadanos y clases de ciudadanos. El ciclo electoral del posocialismo (1986–1994)", *Revista Española de Investigaciones Sociológicas* 74: 45–76.
Goutier, H. (1997) "Antigua and Barbuda. Paradise Troubled", *The Courier* 162: 32–4.
Grunberg, G. (1985) "L'instabilité du comportement électoral", Congrès Mondial de Science Politique (unpublished paper).
Gunther, R. (1986a) "El colapso de UCD", in J. J. Linz and J. R. Montero (eds), *Crisis y cambio: electores y partidos en la España de los años ochenta*, Madrid: Centro de Estudios Constitucionales.
—— (1986b) "Los Partidos Comunistas de España", in J. J. Linz and J. R. Montero (eds), *Crisis y cambio: electores y partidos en la España de los años ochenta*, Madrid: Centro de Estudios Constitucionales.
Gunther, R. and Montero, J. R. (1994) "Los anclajes del partidismo: un análisis comparado del comportamiento electoral en cuatro democracias del sur de Europa", in P. del Castillo (ed.), *Comportamiento político y electoral*, Madrid: Centro de Investigaciones Sociológicas.
—— (forthcoming) "The Anchors of Partisanship: A Comparative Analysis of Voting Behavior in Four Southern European Democracies", in N. Diamandouros and R. Gunther (eds), *Parties, Politics and Democracy in the New Southern Europe*, Baltimore: Johns Hopkins University Press.

Gunther, R., Sani, G. and Shabad, G. (1986) *Spain after Franco. The Making of a Competitive Party System*. Berkeley, CA: University of California Press.

Hadenius, A. (1992) *Democracy and Development*, Cambridge: Cambridge University Press.

Hanlon, D. and Eperiam, W. (1988) "The Evolution and Development of the Federated States of Micronesia", in *Micronesian Politics*, Suva: Institute of Pacific Studies, University of the South Pacific.

Hazan, R. Y. (1997) *Centre Parties. Polarization and Competition in European Parliamentary Democracies*, London: Pinter.

Hearl, D. J. and Budge, I. (1996) "Distinctiveness of Regional Voting: A Comparative Analysis Across the European Community (1979–1993)", *Electoral Studies* 15: 167–82.

Heath, A., Jowell, R. and Curtie, J. (1985) *How Britain Votes*, New York: Pergamon.

Heberle, R. (1963) *Landbevölkerung und Nazionalsozialismus*, Stuttgart: Deutsche Verlags-Anstalt.

Hechter, M. and Brustein, W. (1980) "Regional Modes of Production and Patterns of State Formation in Western Europe", *American Journal of Sociology* 85: 1061– 94.

Heelas, P., Lash, S. and Morris, P. (1996) (eds), *Detraditionalization*, Oxford: Blackwell.

Hellemans, S. (1990) *Strijd om de moderniteit: sociale bewegingen en verzuiling in Europa sinds 1800*, Leuven: Universitaire Pers.

Henrichsen, B. (1992) "Stein Rokkan som institusjonsbygger", in B. Hagtvet (ed.), *Politikk mellom økonomi og kultur. Stein Rokkan som politisk sosiolog og forsknings-inspirator*, Oslo: Ad Notam Gyldendal, 431–39.

Hermet, G. (1985) *Los católicos en la España franquista*, Madrid: Centro de Investigaciones Sociológicas.

Heywood, A. (1997) *Politics*, London: Macmillan.

Himmelveit, H., Humphreys, P. and Jaeger, M. (1984) *How Voters Decide*, London: Academic Press.

Hirczy, W. (1995) "Explaining Near-Universal Turnout: The Case of Malta", *European Journal of Political Research* 27: 255–72.

Hoefte, R. and Oostindie, G. (1991) "The Netherlands and the Dutch Caribbean: Dilemmas of Decolonisation", in P. Sutton (ed.), *Europe and the Caribbean*, London: Macmillan Education (Warwick University Caribbean Studies).

Hopkin, J. (1999) *Party Formation and Democratic Transition in Spain. The Creation and Collapse of the Union of the Democratic Centre*, London: Macmillan.

Hughes, C. (1993) "Cantonalism: Federation and Confederacy in the Golden Epoch in Switzerland", in M. Burgess and A. Gagnon (eds), *Comparative Federalism and Federation. Competing Traditions and Future Directions*, New York: Harvester Wheatsheaf.

Huneeus, C. (1985) *La Unión de Centro Democrático y la transición a la democracia en España*, Madrid: Centro de Investigaciones Sociológicas/Siglo XXI.

Huyse, L. (1984) "Pillarization Reconsidered", *Acta Politica* 19: 145.

—— (1987) *De verzuiling voorbij*, Leuven: Kritak.

Inglehart, R. (1971) "The Silent Revolution in Europe: Intergenerational Change in Post-Industrial Societies", *American Political Science Review* 65: 991–1017.

—— (1984) "The Changing Structure of Political Cleavages in Western Society", in R. J. Dalton, S. C. Flanagan and P. A. Beck (eds), *Electoral Change in Advanced Industrial Democracies, Realignment or Dealignment*, Princeton, NJ: Princeton University Press.

—— (1990) *Cultural Shift in Advanced Industrial Society*, Princeton, NJ: Princeton University Press.

Jabardo, R. (1996) "La extrema derecha española, 1976–1996: estrategias de movilización y estructuras de oportunidad política", *Sistema* 135: 105–22.

Jackson, R. J., Jackson, D. and Baxter-Moore, N. (1986) *Politics in Canada: Culture. Institutions, Behaviour and Public Policy*, Scarborough: Prentice-Hall Canada.

Jacobsen, M. (1995) "Vanishing Nations and the Infiltration of Nationalism: The Case of Papua New Guinea", in R. J. Foster (ed.), *Nation Making. Emergent Identities in Postcolonial Melanesia*, Ann Arbor, MI: University of Michigan Press.

Jaensch, D. (1994) *Power Politics: Australia's Party System*, St. Leonards, NSW: Allen & Unwin.

Jaung, H. (1995) "Cleavage Structure and Party System in Korea". paper presented to the Conference on Party Politics in the Year 2001, Manchester 1995.

Jayanntha, D. (1992) *Electoral Allegiances in Sri Lanka*, Cambridge: Cambridge University Press.

Jepperson, R. L. (1991) "Institutions, Institutional Effects, and Institutionalism", in Walter W. Powell and Paul J. DiMaggio (eds), *The New Institutionalism in Organizational Analysis*, London: University of Chicago Press, 143–63.

Jordana, J. (1996) "Reconsidering Union Membership in Spain, 1977–1994: Halting Decline in a Context of Democratic Consolidation", *Industrial Relations Journal* 27: 211–24.

Justel, M. (1995) *La abstención electoral en España, 1977–1993*, Madrid: Centro de Investigaciones Sociológicas.

Kalivas, S. N. (1996) *The Rise of Christian Democracy in Europe*, Ithaca, NY: Cornell University Press.

Källgård, A. (1994) *Öar*, Göteborg: Bokförlaget Korpen.

Kaspin, D. (1995) "The Politics of Ethnicity in Malawi's Democratic Transition", *Journal of Modern African Studies* 33(4): 595–620.

Katz, R. S. (1980) *A Theory of Parties and Electoral Systems*, Baltimore, MD: Johns Hopkins University Press.

Katz, R. S. and Mair, P. (eds) (1994) *How Parties Organize*, London: Sage.

—— (1996) "Cadre, Catch-all or Cartel? A Rejoinder", *Party Politics* 2(4): 525–34.

Kay, R. (1993) *Fiji*, Hawthorn: Lonely Planet Publications.

Key, V.O., Jr. (1949) *Southern Politics*, New York: Vintage Books.

Kimmerling, B. (1996) "Changing Meanings and Boundaries of the 'Political'", in B. Kimmerling (ed.), *Political Sociology at the Crossroads, Current Sociology* 44: 152–76.

King, P. (1991) "Redefining South Pacific Security", in R. Thakur (ed.), *The South Pacific. Problems, Issues and Prospects*, London: Macmillan.

Kirchheimer, O. (1966) "The Transformation of the Western European Party Systems", in LaPalombara, J. and Weiner, M. (eds), *Political Parties and Political Development*, Princeton, NJ: Princeton University Press.

Kitschelt, H. (1995) "Formation of Party Cleavages in Post-Communist Democracies," *Party Politics* 1(4): 447–72.

Kluge, P. F. (1991) *The Edge of Paradise. America in Micronesi*, New York: Random House.

Knutsen, O. and Scarbrough, E. (1995) "Cleavage Politics", in Jan W. van Deth and Elinor Scarbrough (eds), *Beliefs in Government, Vol. 4: The Impact of Values*, Oxford: Oxford University Press, 492–523.

Kornhauser, W. (1959) *The Politics of Mass Society*, London: Routledge & Kegan Paul.

Kriesi, H. (1990) "Federalism and Pillarization: The Netherlands and Switzerland Compared", *Acta Politica* 25: 433–50.

—— (1997) "The Transformation of Cleavage Politics", Stein Rokkan Lecture, ECPR Joint Sessions, Bern.

Laiz, C. (1995) *La lucha final. Los partidos de la izquierda radical durante la transición española*, Madrid: Libros de la Catarata.

Lal, B. V. (1992) "Rhetoric and Reality: The Dilemmas of Contemporary Fijian Politics", in R. Crocombe *et al.* (eds), *Culture and Democracy in the South Pacific*, Suva: Institute of Pacific Studies, University of the South Pacific.

Lane, J.-E. and Ersson, S. (1994a) *Politics and Society in Western Europe*, London: Sage.

—— (1994b) *Comparative Politics. An Introduction and New Approach*, Cambridge: Polity Press.

—— (1996) *European Politics*, London: Sage.

—— (1997) "Parties and Voters: What Creates the Ties?", *Scandinavian Political Studies* 20(2): 179–96.

Laver, M. (1989) "Party Competition and Party System Change", *Journal of Theoretical Politics* 1(3): 301–24.

Lawson, S. (1991) *The Failure of Democratic Politics in Fiji*, Oxford: Clarendon Press.

—— (1996) *Tradition Versus Democracy in the South Pacific: Fiji, Tonga and Western Samoa*, Cambridge: Cambridge University Press.

LeDuc, L., Clarke, H. D., Jenson, J. and Pammett, J. H. (1984) "Partisan Instability in Canada: Evidence from a New Panel Study", *American Political Science Review* 78: 470–84.

LeDuc, L., Niemi, R. G. and Norris, P. (1996) "Introduction. The Present and Future of Democratic Elections", in L. LeDuc, R. G. Niemi and P. Norris (eds), *Comparing Democracies. Elections and Voting in Global Perspective*, London: Sage.

Lehmbruch, G. (1967) *Proporzdemokratie: Politisches System und Politische Kultur in der Schweiz und in Österreich*, Tübingen: Mohr.

Lenski, G. E. (1966) *Power and Privilege. A Theory of Social Stratification*, New York: McGraw-Hill.

—— (1970) *Human Societies: A Macrolevel Introduction to Sociology*, New York: McGraw-Hill.

Lidström, A. (1996) *Kommunsystem i Europa*, Stockholm: Publica.

Lijphart, A. (1968) *The Politics of Accommodation: Pluralism and Democracy in the Netherlands*, Berkeley, CA: University of California Press (second edition 1975).

—— (1969) "Consociational Democracy", *World Politics* 21: 207–25.

—— (1973) *Cleavages in Consociational Democracies: a Four-Country Comparison*, Montréal: Congrès Mondial de Science Politique.

—— (1976) "Religious vs. Linguistic vs. Class Voting: the Crucial Experiment", *American Political Science Review* 73: 442–58.

—— (1977) *Democracy in Plural Societies. A Comparative Exploration*, New Haven, CT: Yale University Press.

—— (1984a) *Democracies. Patterns of Majoritarian and Consensus Government in Twenty-one Countries*, New Haven, CT: Yale University Press.

—— (1984b) "Time Politics of Accommodation: Reflections – Fifteen Years Later", *Acta Politica* 19: 9–18.

—— (1985) *Power Sharing in South Africa*, Berkeley, CA: University of California.

—— (1989) "From the Politics of Accommodation to Adversarial Politics in the Netherlands: A Reassessment", *West European Politics* 12: 139–53.

—— (1997) "Unequal Participation: Democracy's Unresolved Dilemma", *American Political Science Review* 91(1): 1–14.

Linz, J. (1967a) "The Party System of Spain: Past and Future", in S. M. Lipset and S. Rokkan (eds), *Party Systems and Voter Alignments: Cross-National Perspectives*, New York: The Free Press.

—— (1967b) "Cleavage and Consensus in West German Politics", in Seymour M. Lipset and Stein Rokkan (eds), *Party Systems and Voter Alignments: Cross-National Perspectives*, New York: The Free Press.

—— (1973) "Early State-building and Later Peripheral Nationalisms Against the State: The Case of Spain", in S. N. Eisenstadt and S. Rokkan (eds.), *Building States and Nations*, Beverly Hills, CA: Sage.

—— (1978) "From Great Hopes to Civil War: The Breakdown of Democracy in Spain", in J. J. Linz and A. Stepan (eds), *The Breakdown of Democratic Regimes: Europe*, Baltimore, MD: Johns Hopkins University Press.

—— (1980) "The New Spanish Party System", in R. Rose (ed.), *Electoral Participation. A Comparative Analysis*, London: Sage.

—— (1981) "A Sociological Look at Spanish Communism", in G. Scheward (ed.), *Eurocommunism: The Ideological and Theoretical-political Foundations*, Westport, CT: Greenwood Press.

—— (1985a) "From Primordialism to Nationalism", in E.A. Tiryakian and R. Rogowski (eds), *New Nationalisms of the Developed West: Toward Explanation*, Boston: Allen & Unwin.

—— (1985b) "De la crisis de un Estado unitario al Estado de las Autonomías", in F. Fernández (ed.), *La España de las Autonomías (pasado, presente, futuro)*, Madrid: Instituto de Estudios de Administración Local.

—— (1986) "Consideraciones finales", in J. J. Linz and J. R. Montero (eds), *Crisis y cambio: electores y partidos en la España de los años ochenta*, Madrid: Centro de Estudios Constitucionales.

—— (1993a) "Religión y política en España", in R. Díaz-Salazar and S. Giner (eds), *Religión y sociedad en España*, Madrid: Centro de Investigaciones Sociológicas.

—— (1993b) "Innovative Leadership in the Transition to Democracy and a New Democracy: The Case of Spain", in G. Sheffer (ed.), *Innovative Leaders in International Politics*, Albany, NY: State University of New York.

—— (1995) "La sociedad", in J. A. Gallego, J. Velarde, J. J. Linz, N. González and A. Marquina (eds), *Historia de España. España actual. España y el mundo (1939–1975)*, Madrid: Gredos.

—— (1997a) "Democracy, Multinationalism and Federalism", paper presented at the International Political Science Association World Congress, Seoul.

—— (1997b) "Democracy Today: An Agenda for Students of Democracy", *Scandinavian Political Studies* 20(2): 115–34.

Linz, J. and de Miguel, A. (1966) "Within-Nation Differences and Comparisons: The Eight Spains", in R. Merritt and S. Rokkan (eds), *Comparing Nations*, New Haven, CT: Yale University Press.

Linz, J. J. and Montero, J. R. (eds) (1986) *Crisis y cambio: electores y partidos en la España de los años ochenta*. Madrid: Centro de Estudios Constitucionales.

Linz, J. J. and Stepan, A. (1996) *Problems of Democratic Transition and Consolidation*, Baltimore, MD: Johns Hopkins University Press.

Linz, J. J., Gómez-Reino, M., Orizo, F. A. and Vila, D (1981) *Informe sociológico sobre el cambio político en España, 1975/1981*, Madrid: Euramérica.
—— (1986) *Conflicto en Euskadi*, Madrid: Espasa Calpe.
Lipset, S. M. (1960) *Political Man, The Social Bases of Politics*, Garden City, NY: Doubleday.
—— (1964) "Political Cleavages in 'Developed' and 'Emerging' Polities", in E. Allardt and Y. Littunen (eds), *Cleavages, Ideologies and Party Systems*, Helsinki: Academic Bookstore.
—— (1981) "Whatever Happened to the Proletariat", *Encounter* (June): 18–34.
—— (1991) "No Third Way: A Comparative Perspective on the Left", in Daniel Chirot (ed.), *The Crisis of Leninism and the Decline of the Left*, Seattle, WA: University of Washington Press.
—— (1994) "The Social Requisites of Democracy Revisited", *American Sociological Review* 59: 1–22.
—— (1996) "What are Parties for?", *Journal of Democracy* 7: 169–75.
Lipset, S. M. and Rokkan S. (1967a) *Party Systems and Voter Alignments. Cross-National Perspectives*, New York: The Free Press.
—— (1967b) "Cleavage Structures, Party Systems and Voter Alignments: An Introduction", in Seymour M. Lipset and Stein Rokkan (eds), *Party Systems and Voter Alignments. Cross-National Perspectives*, New York: The Free Press.
Lipset, S. M. and Zetterberg, H. L. (1966) "A Theory of Social Mobility", in R. Bendix and S. M. Lipset (eds), *Class Status and Power*, New York: The Free Press.
Lipset, S. M, Seong, K. R. and Torres, J. C. (1993) "A Comparative Analysis of the Social Requisites of Democracy", *International Social Science Journal* 45(2): 155–70.
Llera, F. J. (1994) *Los vascos y la política. El proceso político vasco: elecciones, partidos, opinión pública y legitimación en el País Vasco, 1977–1992*, Bilbao: Universidad del País Vasco.
—— (1998) "Los rendimientos de los sistemas electorales de las Comunidades Autónomas: el predominio del bipartidismo imperfecto", in J. Montabes (ed.), *El sistema electoral a debate. Veinte años de rendimientos del sistema electoral español (1977–1997)*, Madrid: Centro de Investigaciones Sociológicas/Parlamento de Andalucía.
López Nieto, L. (1997) "Il lungo cammino della destra spagnola. L'ascesa elettorale di Alianza Popular/Partido Popular (1976–1996)", *Quaderni dell'Osservatorio Elettorale* 37: 93–132.
Lorwin, V. (1966) "Belgium: Religion, Class and Language in National Politics", in R. Dahl (ed.), *Political Oppositions in Western Democracies*, New Haven, CT: Yale University Press.
—— (1971) "Segmented Pluralism: Ideological Cleavages and Political Cohesion in the Smaller European Democracies", *Comparative Politics* 3: 141–75.
Lowenthal, D. (1992) "Small Tropical Islands: A General Overview", in H. M. Hintjens and M.D.D. Newitt (eds), *The Political Economy of Small Tropical Islands*, Exeter: University of Exeter Press.
Luther, K. R. (1992) "Consociationalism, Parties and the Party System", in K. R. Luther and W. Müller (eds), *Politics in Austria: Still a Case of Consociationalism?*, London: Frank Cass.
Luther, K. R. and Deschouwer, K. (1999) "Introduction", in K. R. Luther and K. Deschouwer (eds), *Party Elites in Divided Societies*, London: Routledge.

Luther, K. R. and Müller, W. (1992) *Politics in Austria: Still a Case of Consociationalism?*, London: Frank Cass.

Lybeck, J. A. (1985) "Is the Lipset–Rokkan Hypothesis Testable?", *Scandinavian Political Studies* 8(1–2):105–13.

Macdonald, B. (1996) *Governance and Political Process in Kiribati*, Canberra: Economics Division, Research School of Pacific and Asian Studies, The Australian National University.

Mackie, T. and Rose, R. (1991) *International Almanac of Electoral History*, Washington: Congressional Quarterly Press.

Magida, A. (1985) "St Kitts–Nevis: An Uneasy Alliance", *Islands International Magazine* (July/August): 66–77.

Maguire, M. (1983) "Is There Still Persistence? Electoral Change in Western Europe, 1948–1979", in Hans Daalder and Peter Mair (eds), *Western European Party Systems: Continuity and Change*, London: Sage, 67–94.

Mainwaring, S. (1995) "Brazil: Weak Parties, Feckless Democracy", in S. Mainwaring and T. R. Scully (eds), *Building Democratic Institutions: Party Systems in Latin America*, Stanford, CA: Stanford University Press.

Mainwaring, S. and Scully, T. R. (1995) "Conclusions: Parties and Democracy in Latin America – Different Patterns, Common Challenges", in S. Mainwaring and T. R. Scully (eds), *Building Democratic Institutions: Party Systems in Latin America*, Stanford CA: Stanford University Press.

Mair, P. (1983) "Adaptation and Control: Towards an Understanding of Party and Party System Change", in Hans Daalder and Peter Mair (eds), *Western European Party Systems: Continuity and Change*, London: Sage, 405–30.

—— (1987) *The Changing Irish Party System*, New York: St. Martin' s Press.

—— (1991) "The Electoral Universe of Small Parties in Postwar Western Europe", in F. Müller-Rommel and G. Pridham (eds), *Small Parties in Western Europe. Comparative and National Perspectives*, London: Sage.

—— (1993) "Myths of Electoral Change and the Survival of Traditional Parties: the 1992 Stein Rokkan Lecture", *European Journal of Political Research* 24(2): 121–33.

—— (1996) "Party Systems and Structures of Competition", in L. LeDuc, R. G. Niemi and P. Norris (eds), *Comparing Democracies: Elections and Voting in Comparative Perspective*, Thousand Oaks, CA: Sage, 83–106.

—— (1997) *Party System Change. Approaches and Interpretations*, Oxford: Clarendon Press.

Mair, P. and Sakano, T. (1998) "Japanese Political Realignment in Perspective: Change or Restoration?", *Party Politics* 4(2): 175–99.

Mannick, A. R. (1989) *Mauritius. The Politics of Change*, East Sussex: Dodo Books.

Manning, M. (1972) *Irish Political Parties: An Introduction*, Dublin: Gill and Macmillan.

Maravall, J. M. (1984) *La política de la transición*, 2nd ed., Madrid: Taurus.

—— (1991) "From Opposition to Government: The Politics and Policies of the PSOE", in J. M. Maravall (ed.) *Socialist Parties in Europe*, Barcelona: Institut de Ciències Polítiques i Socials.

Maravall, J. M. and Santamaría, J. (1986) "Political Change in Spain and the Prospects for Democracy", in G. O'Donnell, Ph.C. Schmitter, and L. Whitehead (eds), *Transitions from Authoritarian Rule. Southern Europe*, Baltimore, MD: Johns Hopkins University Press.

Marcet, J. and Argelaguet. J. (1998) "Nationalist Parties in Catalonia: *Convergència*

Democrática de Catalunya and *Esquerra Republicana*", in L. De Winter and H. Türsan (eds), *Regionalist Parties in Western Europe*, London: Routledge.

Martikainen, T. and Yrjönen, R. (1991) *Voting, Parties and Social Change in Finland*, Helsinki: Statistics Finland.

Marx, G. T. (ed.) (1971) *Racial Conflict: Tension and Change in American Society*, Boston, MD: Little, Brown and Co.

Mata, J. M. (1993) *El nacionalismo vasco radical. Discurso, organización y expresiones*, Bilbao: Universidad del País Vasco.

McDonough, P., Barnes, S. H., López Pina, A. with Doh C. Shin and José A. Moisés (1998) *The Cultural Dynamics of Democratziation in Spain*, Ithaca, NY: Cornell University Press.

McKenzie, R. T. and Silver, A. (1967) "The Delicate Experiment: Industrialism, Conservatism and Working-Class Tories in England", in S. M. Lipset and S. Rokkan (eds), *Party Systems and Voter Alignments. Cross–National Perspectives*, New York: The Free Press.

Meisel, J. (1975) "The Party System and the 1974 Election", in H. R. Penniman (ed.), *Canada At the Polls: The General Election of 1974*, Washington, DC: American Enterprise Institute.

Mendras, H. (1995) *La Seconde Révolution Française*, Paris: Gallimard.

Merrit, R. L. (1969) "Noncontiguity and Political Integration", in J. N. Rosenau (ed.), *Linkage Politics*, New York: The Free Press.

Michels, R. (1962) *Political Parties: a Sociological Study of the Oligarchical Tendencies of Modern Democracy*, New York: The Free Press.

Mitchell, W. E. (1968) "[Systems Analysis:] Political Systems", in David L. Sills (ed.), *International Encyclopaedia of the Social Sciences*, New York: Crowell, Collier & Macmillan, vol 15, 473–79.

Miyake, I. (1986) "Instability of Party Identification in Japan", in Joji Watanuki *et al.* (eds), *Electoral Behavior in the 1983 Japanese Elections*, Tokyo: Institute of International Relations, Sophia University.

Molas, I. (1977) "Los partidos de ámbito no estatal y los sistemas de partidos", in P. De Vega (ed.), *Teoría y práctica de los partidos políticos*, Madrid: Edicusa.

Montero, J. R. (1981) "Partidos y participación política: algunas notas sobre la afiliación política en la etapa inicial de la transición española", *Revista de Estudios Políticos* 23: 33–72.

—— (1986) "El sub-triunfo de la derecha: los apoyos electorales de AP-PDP", in J. J. Linz and J. R. Montero (eds), *Crisis y cambio: electores y partidos en la España de los años ochenta*, Madrid: Centro de Estudios Constitucionales.

—— (1988) "Las derechas en el sistema de partidos del segundo bienio republicano: algunos datos introductorios", in J. L. García-Delgado (ed.), *La II República española. Bienio rectificador y Frente Popular, 1934–1936*, Madrid: Siglo XXI.

—— (1992) "Las elecciones legislativas", in R. Cotarelo (ed.), *Transición política y consolidación democrática en España (1975–1986)*, Madrid: Centro de Investigaciones Sociológicas.

—— (1994) "Sobre las preferencias electorales en España: fragmentación y polarización (1976–1993)", in P. del Castillo (ed.), *Comportamiento político y electoral*, Madrid: Centro de Investigaciones Sociológicas.

Montero, J. R. and Torcal, M. (1990) "Autonomías y comunidades autónomas en España: preferencias, dimensiones y orientaciones políticas", *Revista de Estudios Políticos* 70: 33–91.

Montesquieu, C. L. (1989) *The Spirit of Laws*, Cambridge: Cambridge University Press.

Moore, M. (1995) "Democracy and Development in Cross-National Perspective: A New Look at the Statistics", *Democratization* 2(2): 1–19.

Moral, F. (1998) *Identidad regional y nacionalismo en el Estado de las Autonomías*, Madrid: Centro de Investigaciones Sociológicas, Opiniones y Actitudes 18.

Moreno, L. (1997) "Federalization and Ethnoterritorial Concurrence in Spain", *Publius: The Journal of Federalism* 27: 65–84.

Morlino, L. (1998) *Democracy Between Consolidation and Crisis. Parties, Groups, and Citizens in Southern Europe*, Oxford: Oxford University Press.

Moses, R. S. and Ashby, G. (1992) "Tradition and Democracy on Pohnpei Island", in R. Crocombe, *et al.* (eds), *Culture and Democracy in the South Pacific*, Suva: Institute of Pacific Studies, University of the South Pacific.

Mphaisha, C. J. J. (1996) "Retreat from Democracy in Post One-Party State Zambia", *Journal of Commonwealth and Comparative Politics* 34(2): 65–84.

Mulgan, R. (1994) *Politics in New Zealand*, Auckland: Auckland University Press.

Murray, D. (1996) "The 1995 National Elections in Thailand", *Asian Survey* 36(4): 361–75.

Nataf, D. (1985), *The Electoral Ecology of Portugal 1976–1983* (unpublished).

Nedelmann, B. (1997) "Between National Socialism and Real Socialism: Political Sociology in the Federal Republic of Germany", *Current Sociology* 45: 157–86.

Neemia, U. (1992) "Decolonization and Democracy in the South Pacific", in R. Crocombe, *et al.* (eds), *Culture and Democracy in the South Pacific*, Suva: Institute of Pacific Studies, University of the South Pacific.

Newitt, M. (1992) "Introduction", in H. M. Hintjens and M. D. D. Newitt (eds), *The Political Economy of Small Tropical Islands*, Exeter: University of Exeter Press.

Nieuwbeerta, P. (1995) *The Democratic Class Struggle in Twenty Countries, 1945–1990*, Amsterdam: Thesis Publishers.

Nilsson, L. (1997) "Internal Geographical Distance as a Predicament for Small Archipelago States", in D. Anckar and L. Nilsson (eds), *Politics and Geography. Contributions to an Interface*, Sundsvall: Mid-Sweden University Press.

Niu, L. M. (1988) "The Constitutional and Traditional Political System in Tonga", in Y. Ghai (ed.), *Law, Politics and Government in the Pacific Island States*, Suva: Institute of Pacific Studies, University of the South Pacific.

Noelle-Neumann, E. (1994) "Left and Right as Categories for Determining the Political Position in Germany", Conference on Political Parties, Madrid, Institute Juan March.

Noelle-Neumann, E. and Kocher, R. (1993) *Allensbacher Jahrbuch der Demoscopie*, Munchen: Saur.

Nordlinger, E. A. (1967) *The Working-Class Tories*, London: Macgibbon.

NSD Katalog (1997) Bergen 1996: Norwegian Social Science Data Services.

Nun, J. (1967) "The Middle-Class Military Coup", in C. Veliz (ed.), *The Politics of Nonconformity in Latin America*, Oxford: Oxford University Press.

Nurmi, H. (1987) *Comparing Voting Systems*, Dordrecht: D. Reidel.

Ogashiwa, Y. (1991) *Microstates and Nuclear Issues*, Suva: Institute of Pacific Studies, University of the South Pacific.

Olsen, J. P. (1997) "Civil Service in Transition – Dilemmas and Lessons Learned," ARENA working paper, no. 15.

Oñate, P. and Ocaña, F. (1999) *Desproporcionalidad y sistema de partidos. España*

(1977–1998). Una propuesta informática para su cálculo, Madrid: Centro de Investigaciones Sociológicas.

Orizo, A. (1983) *Espana entre la Apatia y el Cambio Social*, Madrid: Mapfre.

Ozbudun, E. (1987) "Institutionalising Competitive Elections in Developing Societies" in M. Weiner and E. Ozbudun (eds), *Competitive Elections in Developing Societies*, Durham, NC: Duke University Press.

Pallarès, F., Montero, J. R. and Llera, F. J. (1997) "Non State-wide Parties in Spain: An Attitudinal Study of Nationalism and Regionalism", *Publius: The Journal of Federalism* 27: 135–70

Parenti, M. (1967) "Ethnic Politics and the Persistence of Ethnic Identification", *American Political Science Review* 61: 717–26.

Parsons, T. (1971) *The Systems of Modern Societies*, Englewood Cliffs: Prentice Hall.

Payne, A. (1988) "Multi-Party Politics in Jamaica", in V. Randall (ed.), *Political Parties in the Third World*, London: Sage.

Pedersen, M. N. (1979) "The Dynamics of European Party Systems: Changing Patterns of Electoral Volatility", *European Journal of Political Research* 7(1): 1–26.

Pesonen, P. (1973) "Dimensions of Political Cleavages in Multi-Party Systems", *European Journal of Political Research* 1:109–32.

—— (ed.) (1994) *Suomen EU-kansanäänestys 1994* (The 1994 EU Referendum in Finland), Helsinki: Ministry for Foreign Affairs.

Pesonen, P. and Sänkiaho, R. (1979) *Kansalaiset ja kansanvalta* (Citizens and the power of the people), Juva: WSOY.

Pesonen, P., Sänkiaho, R. and Borg, S. (1993) *Vaalikansan äänivalta* (The voter-power of the electorate), Helsinki: Werner Söderström.

Petersen, G. (1989) "Pohnpei Ethnicity and Micronesian Nation-Building", in M. C. Howard (ed.), *Ethnicity and Nation-Building in the Pacific*, Tokyo: The United Nations University.

Petersson, O. (1994) *The Government and Politics of the Nordic Countries*, Stockholm: Fritzes.

Pinkney, R. (1993) *Democracy in the Third World*, Buckingham: Open University Press.

Podolny, J. (1993) "The Role of Juan Carlos I in the Consolidation of the Parliamentary Monarchy", in R. Gunther (ed.), *Essays in Honor of Juan J. Linz. Politics, Society, and Democracy: The Case of Spain*, Boulder, CO: Westview Press.

Pool, D. (1994) "Staying at Home with the Wife: Democratization and its Limits in the Middle East", in G. Parry and M. Moran (eds), *Democracy and Democratization*, London: Routledge.

Powell, C. (1991) *El piloto del cambio. El Rey, la monarquía y la transición a la democracia*, Barcelona: Planeta.

Puhle, H-J. (1986) "El PSOE: un partido predominante y heterogéneo", in J.J. Linz and J.R. Montero (eds), *Crisis y cambio: electores y partidos en la España de los años ochenta*, Madrid: Centro de Estudios Constitucionales.

Pulzer, P. (1975) *Political Representation and Elections in Britain*, 3rd edn, London: Allen & Unwin.

Quigg, P. W. (1969) "Coming of Age in Micronesia", *Foreign Affairs* 47: 493–508.

Quimby, F. (1988) "The Yin and Yang of Belau: A Nuclear Free Movement Struggles with the Quest for Economic Development", in *Micronesian Politics*, Suva: Institute of Pacific Studies, University of the South Pacific.

Randall, V. and Theobald, R. (1985) *Political Change and Underdevelopment*, Basingstoke: Macmillan.

Ranney, A. (1964) "The Utility and Limitations of Aggregate Data in the Study of Electoral Behavior", in A. Ranney (ed.), *Essays on the Behavioral Study of Politics*, Urbana, IL: University of Illinois Press, 91–102.

Rantala, O. (1982) *Suomen puolueiden muuttuminen 1945–1980* (Change of Finnish parties 1945–1980), Helsinki: Gaudeamus.

Regional Surveys of the World. Africa South of the Sahara 1997, 26th edn, London: Europa Publications.

—— *South America, Central America and the Caribbean 1997*, 6th edn, London: Europa Publications.

—— *The Far East and Australasia 1997*, 28th edn., London: Europa Publications.

Reinares, F. (1988) "Nationalism and Violence in Basque Politics", *Conflict* 8: 141–65.

—— (1996) "The Political Conditioning of Political Violence: Regime Change and Insurgent Terrorism in Spain", in F.D. Weil (ed.), *Research on Democracy and Protest, vol. 3, Extremism, Protest, Social Movements, and Democracy*, Greenwich: JAI Press.

Richardson, B. C. (1992) *The Caribbean in the Wider World, 1492–1992*, Cambridge: Cambridge University Press.

Richardson, B. M., *et al.* (1991) "The Japanese Voter: Comparing the Explanatory Variables in Electoral Decisions", in Scott C. Flanagen, Shinsaku Kohei, Bradley M. Richardson and Joji Watanuki (eds), *The Japanese Voter*, New Haven, CT: Yale University Press.

Robinson, A. D. (1967) "Class Voting in New Zealand: A Comment on Alford's Comparison of Class Voting in the Anglo-American Political Systems", in S. M. Lipset and S. Rokkan (eds), *Party Systems and Voter Alignments. Cross-National Perspectives*, New York: The Free Press.

Rodríguez Jiménez, J. L. (1997) *La extrema derecha española en el siglo XX*, Madrid: Alianza.

Rogowski, R. (1981) "Social class and Partisanship in European Electorates: A Re-Assessment", *World Politics* 33: 639–49.

Rokkan, S. (1964a) "International Co-operation in Political Sociology: Current Efforts and Future Possibilities", in E. Allardt and Y. Littunen (eds), *Cleavages, Ideologies and Party Systems. Contributions to Comparative Political Sociology*, Turku: Transactions of the Westermarck Society Vol. X., 5–18.

—— (1964b) "The Comparative Study of Political Participation: Notes Toward A Perspective on Current Research", in A. Ranney (ed.), *Essays on the Behavioral Study of Politics*, Urbana, IL: University of Illinois Press, 47–90.

—— (1966a) "Norway: Numerical Democracy and Corporate Pluralism", in Robert A. Dahl (ed.), *Political Oppositions in Western Democracies*, New Haven, CT: Yale University Press, 70–115.

—— (ed.) (1966b) *Data Archives for the Social Sciences*, Paris: Mouton & Co.

—— (1969) "Nation-Building, Cleavage Formation and the Structuring of Mass Politics", in S. Rokkan, *Citizens, Elections, Parties*, Oslo: Scandinavian University Books.

—— (1970) *Citizens, Elections, Parties*, Oslo: Universitetsforlaget.

—— (1975) "Dimensions of State Formation and Nation-Building: A Possible Paradigm for Research on Variations within Europe" in C. Tilly (ed.), *The Formation of National States in Europe*, Princeton, NJ: Princeton University Press.

—— (1977) "Towards A Generalized Concept of Verzuiling", *Political Studies* 25(4): 563–70.

—— (1981) "The Growth and Structuring of Mass Politics", in E. Allardt *et al.* (eds), *Nordic Democracy*, Copenhagen: Det danske Selskab.

Rokkan, S. and Urwin, D. W. (eds) (1982) *The Politics of Territorial Identity. Studies in European Regionalism*, London: Sage.

—— (1983) *"Economy, Territory, Identity", Politics of West European Peripheries*, London: Sage.

Rose, R. (ed.) (1974) *Electoral Behavior: A Comparative Handbook*, New York: The Free Press.

—— (1980) "Class Does Not Equal Party: The Decline of a Model of British Voting", *Studies in Public Policy 57*, Glasgow: University of Strathclyde.

—— (1982) "From Single Determinism to Interactive Models of Voting: Britain as an Example", *Comparative Political Studies* 15(2): 145–69.

—— (1995) "Mobilizing Demobilized Voters in Post-Communist Societies", *Party Politics* 1(4): 549–63.

Rose, R. and McAllister, I. (1986) *Voters Begin to Choose: From Closed-Class to Open Elections in Britain*, Beverly Hills, CA: Sage.

Rose, R. and Urwin, D. (1969) "Social Cohesion, Political Parties and Strains in Regimes", *Comparative Political Studies* 2: 7–67.

—— (1970) "Persistence and Change in Western Party Systems Since 1945", *Political Studies* 18(3): 287–319.

Roxborough, I. (1988) "Modernization Theory Revisited: A Review Article", *Comparative Studies in Society and History* 30: 753–61.

Rudolph, L. and Rudolph, S. (1967) *The Modernity of Tradition: Political Development in India*, Chicago, IL: Chicago University Press.

Sani, G. and Sartori, G. (1983) "Polarization, Fragmentation and Competition in Western Democracies", in H. Daalder and P. Mair (eds), *Western European Party Systems. Continuity and Change*, London: Sage.

Sänkiaho, R. (1986) "Poliittinen vieraantuminen" (Political alienation) in J. Nousiainen and M. Wiberg (eds), *Kansalaiset ja politiikka 1980-luvun Suomessa* (Citizens and politics in Finland in the 1980s), Turku: Turun yliopisto.

Santamaría, J. (1981) "Transición controlada y dificultades de consolidación: el ejemplo español", in J. Santamaría (ed.), *Transición a la democracia en el sur de Europa y América Latina*, Madrid: Centro de Investigaciones Sociológicas.

Santamaría, J. and Alcover, M. (1987) *Actitudes de los españoles ante la OTAN*, Madrid: Centro de Investigaciones Sociológicas, Estudios y Encuestas 6.

Särlvik, B. (1969) "Socioeconomic Determinants of Voting Behavior in the Swedish Electorate", *Comparative Political Studies* 2: 99–135.

Särlvik, B. and Holmberg, S. (1985) "Social Determinants of Party Choice in Swedish Elections 1956–1982", Paris: Congrès Mondial de Science Politique.

Sartori, G. (1969a) "From the Sociology of Politics to Political Sociology", *Government and Opposition* 4: 195–214.

—— (1969b) "From the Sociology of Politics to Political Sociology", in S.M. Lipset (ed.), *Politics and the Social Sciences*, New York: Oxford University Press, 65–100.

—— (1976) *Parties and Party Systems: A Framework for Analysis*, Cambridge: Cambridge University Press.

—— (1994) *Comparative Constitutional Engineering: An Inquiry into Structures, Incentives and Outcomes*, Basingstoke: Macmillan.

Sassoon, D. (1996) *One Hundred Years of Socialism*, London: I.B. Tauris.

Schattschneider, E. E. (1960) *The Semi-Sovereign People*, New York: Holt, Rinehart and Winston.

Scheuch, E. K. and Brüning, I. (1964) "The Zentralarchiv at the University of Cologne", *International Social Science Journal*, XIV: 77–85.

Schmitt, H. and Holmberg, S. (1995) "Political Parties in Decline?", in H.-D. Klingemann and D. Fuchs (eds), *Citizens and the State*, Oxford: Oxford University Press.

Sciarini, P. and Hug, S. (1999) " The Odd Fellow: Parties and Consociationalism in Switzerland", in K. R. Luther and K. Deschouwer (eds), *Party Elites in Divided Societies: Political Parties in Consociational Democracy*, London: Routledge.

Scully, T. R. (1995) "Reconstituting Party Politics in Chile", in S. Mainwaring and T. R. Scully (eds), *Building Democratic Institutions: Party Systems in Latin America*, Stanford, CA: Stanford University Press.

Searwar, L. (1991) "The Small State in the Caribbean: Policy Options for Survival", in J. R. Beruff, J. P. Figueroa and J. E. Greene (eds), *Conflict, Peace and Development in the Caribbean*, London: Macmillan.

Seidman, S. (1983) *Liberalism and the Origins of European Social Theory*, Berkeley, CA: University of California Press.

Shabad, G. (1986) "Las elecciones de1982 y las autonomías", in J.J. Linz and J.R. Montero (eds), *Crisis y cambio: electores y partidos en la España de los años ochenta*, Madrid: Centro de Estudios Constitucionales.

Shamir, M. (1984) "Are Western European Party Systems 'Frozen'?", *Comparative Political Studies* 17(1): 35–79.

Shin, D. C. (1995) "Political Parties and Democratization in South Korea: The Mass Public and the Democratic Consolidation of Political Parties", *Democratization* 2(2): 20–55.

Siegfried, A. (1913) *L'évolution politique de la France de l'Ouest sous la Troisième République*, Paris: A. Colin.

Sinnott, R. (1984) "Interpretations of the Irish Party System", *European Journal of Political Research* 12: 289–307.

Smith, G. (1966) "What is a Party System?", *Parliamentary Affairs* 19(3): 351–62.

—— (1989) "A System Perspective on Party System Change", *Journal of Theoretical Politics* 1(3): 349–63.

SOFRES (1989) "*L'Etat de l'Opinion*", Paris: Seuil.

Statistical Yearbook of Finland 1997, Helsinki: Statistics Finland.

Statistisches Jahrbuch für die Bundesrepublik Deutschland 1966.

Steinberg, J. (1996) *Why Switzerland?* Cambridge: Cambridge University Press.

Strom, K. (1990) *Minority Government and Majority Rule*, Cambridge: Cambridge University Press.

Stuurman, S. (1983) *Verzuiling, kapitalisme en patriarchaat*, Nijmegen: SUN.

Sundberg, J. (1996) *Partier och partisystem i Finland* (Parties and party systems in Finland), Esbo: Schildts.

Sundberg, J. and Berglund, S. (1984) "Representative Democracy in Crisis? Reflections on Scandinavian Party Systems", World Congress of Political Science (unpublished paper).

Sutton, P. and Payne, A. (1993) "Lilliput under Threat: The Security Problems of Small Island and Enclave Developing States", *Political Studies* XLI: 579–93.

Taagepera, R. and Shugart, M. (1989) *Seats and Votes: The Effects and Determinants of Electoral Systems*, New Haven, CT: Yale University Press.

Tabai, I. (1993) "The First Twelve Years", in H. van Trease (ed.), *Atoll Politics. The Republic of Kiribati*, Christchurch: Macmillan Brown Centre for Pacific Studies, University of Canterbury.

Takougang, J. (1996) "The 1992 Multiparty Elections in Cameroon", *Journal of Asian and African Studies* 31(1–2): 52–65.

Tanenbaum, E. and Mochmann, E. (1994) "Integrating the European Database: Infrastructure Services and the Need for Integration", *International Social Science Journal* 142: 499–511.

Taylor, D. (1992) "Parties, Elections and Democracy in Pakistan", *Journal of Commonwealth and Comparative Politics* 30(1): 96–115.

Teiwaki, R. (1988) "Kiribati: Nation of Water", in *Micronesian Politics*, Suva: Institute of Pacific Studies, University of the South Pacific.

The Times Guide to the Nations of the World (1994), London: Times Books.

Therborn, G. (1996) "Framtida historier 1925–1995 i framtidens ljus", *Sosiologia* 33: 2–11.

Thorndike, T. (1991) "Politics and Society in the South-Eastern Caribbean", in C. Clarke (ed.), *Society and Politics in the Caribbean*, London: Macmillan.

Tilly, C. (1981) "Sinews of War", in P. Torsvik (ed.), *Mobilization, Center–Periphery Structures and Nation-Building, A Volume in Commemoration of Stein Rokkan*, Bergen-Oslo-Tromsö: Universitetsforlaget.

Tocqueville, A. de (1956) *Democracy in America*, volume I, New York: Alfred A. Knopf.

Touraine, A. (1984) *Le retour de l'acteur*, Paris: Fayard.

Turner, F. C. (ed.) (1992) *Social Mobility and Political Attitudes, Comparative Perspectives*, New Brunswick: Transaction Publishers.

Tusell, J. (1977) *La oposición democrática al franquismo*, Barcelona: Planeta.

Vallès, J. M. (1991) "Entre la regularidad y la indeterminación: balance sobre el comportamiento electoral en España (1977–1989)", in J. Vidal-Beneyto (ed.), *España a debate. La política*, Madrid: Tecnos

van Cranenburgh, O. (1996) "Tanzania's 1995 Multi-Party Elections", *Party Politics* 2(4): 535–47.

van Trease, H. (1993) "From Colony to Independence", in H. van Trease (ed.), *Atoll Politics. The Republic of Kiribati*, Christchurch: Macmillan Brown Centre for Pacific Studies, University of Canterbury.

—— (1995a) "The Colonial Origins of Vanuatu Politics", in H. van Trease (ed.), *Melanesian Politics. Stael Blong Vanuatu*, Christchurch: Macmillan Brown Centre for Pacific Studies, University of Canterbury.

—— (1995b) "The Election", in H. van Trease (ed.), *Melanesian Politics. Stael Blong Vanuatu*, Christchurch: Macmillan Brown Centre for Pacific Studies, University of Canterbury.

Vanhanen, T. (1990) *The Process of Democratization*, New York: Taylor & Francis.

Vengroff, R. (1993) "Governance and Transitions to Democracy: Political Parties and the Party System in Mali", *Journal of Modern African Studies* 31: 543–62.

von Beyme, K. (1985) *Political Parties in Western Democracies*, Aldershot: Gower.

Vowles, J. *et al.* (1995) *Towards Consensus? The 1993 Election in New Zealand and the Transition to Proportional Representation*, Auckland: Auckland University Press.

Ware, A. (1996) *Political Parties and Party Systems*, Oxford: Oxford University Press.

Watanuki, J. (1995) "Political Generations in Post World War II Japan", *Research Papers Series A-64*, Tokyo: Institute of International Relations, Sophia University.

Webb, P. (1992) *Trade Unions and the British Electorate*, Aldershot: Dartmouth.

—— (1994) "Party Organizational Change in Britain: The Iron Law of Centralization?", in Katz, R. S. and Mair, P. (eds), *How Parties Organize: Change and Adaptation in Party Organizations in Western Democracies*, London: Sage.

Wert, J. I. (1997) "Espagne: la droite au pouvoir", in SOFRÊS, *L'etat de l'opinion 1997*, Paris: Éditions du Seuil.

Western, B. (1993) "Postwar Unionization in Eighteen Advanced Capitalist Countries", *American Sociological Review* 58: 266–82.

Zilliacus, K.O.K. (1995) *Finländsk kommunism i ljuset av väljar-stöd 1945–1991* (Finnish communism in the light of electoral support 1945–1991), Helsingfors: Finska Vetenskaps-Societen.

Zolberg, A. (1966) *Creating Political Order: The Party States of West Africa*, Chicago, IL: Chicago University Press.

Index